20

Children Growing Up

THE DEVELOPMENT OF CHILDREN'S PERSONALITIES

John Gabriel

Children Growing Up

THE DEVELOPMENT OF CHILDREN'S PERSONALITIES

AMERICAN ELSEVIER PUBLISHING COMPANY, INC.

SBN 444 19713 3
Library of Congress catalog card number 78-97783

First published 1964
Third edition: second impression 1969
Copyright © 1968 John Gabriel

American Elsevier Publishing Company, Inc.
52 Vanderbilt Avenue, New York, New York 10017

Printed in Great Britain

Foreword

THERE are few, if any, introductory studies of the psychology of personality that are really suitable for the teacher student and others interested in children. Those of us responsible for teaching this aspect of psychology in universities and teacher training colleges have long felt the need for a sound and stimulating descriptive text. In his new book, *Children Growing Up*, Dr. John Gabriel has given us just this. Most books in this field tend to be either aridly scientific and impersonal to the point of inhumanity, or too facile and superficial, or too advanced in their treatment to serve as introductions for the general student. With his experience as a teacher of children in schools, and as a teacher of students in a teacher's college and in universities to draw upon, Dr. Gabriel has succeeded in the difficult task of treating this all-important subject in a way which is at once scholarly, lucid, lively and wise.

His own view of education as a 'creative becoming', which underlies this whole work, is one in tune with the best educational thought of our times. He has not only—as is absolutely necessary in this field—drawn on the most relevant research in the area of the human sciences, but he has managed to combine our growing scientific understanding of human development with the wisdom of common experience and with the insight displayed in literature. He has infused this combination with the vitality that comes from intimate experience and observation of children.

This book will be a great boon to many students and their tutors. It deserves to be widely read and discussed.

BEN MORRIS
Professor of Education and Director
of the Institute of Education,
University of Bristol

Preface to the Third Edition

THIS edition constitutes a considerable revision of the Second. In general, changes include a fuller account of children's intellectual development and some comments on the education of children in relation to this, and to their social and emotional growth. More specifically, to the new chapter included in the second edition, Children's Moral Development (Chapter 20), two further new chapters have been added—Early and Middle Adolescence: Physical and mental development; interests (Chapter 15) and Children's Play (Chapter 19). Others have been considerably revised, especially Basic Needs and Basic Goals (Chapter 8), Primary School Children (Chapter 14), Early Adolescence—Pubescence to Puberty (Chapter 16), Middle Adolescence (Chapter 17).

Chapter 8 now becomes more clearly a transitional chapter. It refers back to the more formal study of personality and its organization; it anticipates much that is to come. Consequently, it has been set off from other chapters to become Part 3 of the book.

I have been privileged to receive the generous help of Professor Sir Cyril Burt in the preparation of this edition. His candid criticisms and innumerable wise suggestions have been invaluable. I should also like to thank the library staff of the University of New South Wales.

University of New South Wales
February 1968

Acknowledgments

THE author and publishers would also like to thank the following for permission to reprint copyright matter in this book: Houghton Mifflin Company, Boston, Mass., for material from *Patterns of Culture* by Ruth Benedict; Michael Joseph Ltd and the Executors of the estate of the late Joyce Cary for a passage from *Charlie is My Darling*; Penguin Books Ltd for a passage from Chaucer's *Canterbury Tales*, translated by Nevill Coghill; Harper and Brothers, New York, for material from *Child Development* by A. Gesell and F. L. Ilg, and from *Personality* by G. Murphy; Professor Charles Morris for material from his book *Varieties of Human Value* (University of Chicago Press); Indiana University, Bloomington, Ind. (Institute for Sex Research Inc.), for material from *Sexual Behaviour in the Human Male* by A. C. Kinsey, W. B. Pomeroy and C. E. Martin; Quality Press Ltd for a passage from *Pastures of Heaven* by John Steinbeck; The Journal Press, Provincetown, Mass., for material from R. R. Sears, *et al.*, 'Some child-rearing antecedents of aggression and dependency in young children', from *Genetic Psychology Monographs*, 1953, **47**; University of Minnesota Press for Fig. 11 adapted from *The Measurement of Man* by Harris, Jackson, Patterson and Scammon.

Contents

Figures

PART ONE

The Meaning of Personality

CHAPTER ONE

Personality and Dispositions

EDUCATION is concerned with 'the whole personality of the child'; its aim is to develop 'the child's personality', 'the child's unique potentialities'. Such statements are often repeated by educationists and, because this book purports to study children's personalities with particular reference to the needs and experiences of the classroom teacher, it is as well to explain what is meant by the term 'personality' by indicating what these statements concerning the aims of education imply.

The term 'personality' is often used in everyday speech to describe a person who is able to attract, to have an appeal for other people; we speak of a film, radio, or television 'personality'. In this sense, he who 'has' personality is successful in his social relationships, popular, and able 'to win friends and influence people'. It is generally agreed among most people in our society that to 'have personality' in this sense means to hold the key to many kinds of successes which we value, such as marriage, possessions and social prestige.

The study of personality made in this book does not stress this element of attraction which one person may have for others. Rather, the term is a conceptual one which implies that an individual's potentialities have developed and that they are organized in a unique way for the fulfilment of personal ends. Within this last statement there are three abstract terms, namely, 'potentialities', 'unique' and 'organized'. An attempt will now be made to show in a more concrete way what may be understood by the concept 'personality' by amplifying the meanings of these three terms.

Potentialities: general

In one of Erasmus Darwin's poems there are these lines: 'No acorn develops into an elm tree, Nor beech-nut into an oak.' His statement, some might argue, means little more than that, if an acorn is planted and other necessary conditions are fulfilled, it will develop into an oak tree; and similarly for the elm seed. Others may say that the statement implies far more than this. It implies, they may say, that within the acorn lies a potentiality for growth, for the unfolding of a plan, which is 'given', hereditary in origin, and not imposed from outside; and that if this potential is fulfilled, it will determine the final form of the acorn and its peculiar functions. This implication can be stated more explicitly in genetic terms since genetic studies suggest the idea of a design unfolding.

When an organism—plant, animal, or human—is conceived, the nucleus of every fertilized cell contains a number of minute structures called 'chromosomes' which are readily coloured and under the microscope appear like beaded threads. These are now known to carry the complex molecules, called 'genes', which are the bearers of hereditary tendencies.

Certain physical and biochemical properties of chromosomes and genes—especially their number, size, shape and chemical structure—determine the nature of the physical features they initiate. Ordinarily all members of a species will have the same number of chromosomes, arranged in pairs and of the same general size and shape; and, since chromosomal and genetic similarity leads to similarity of physique (structure) and behaviour (function), all the members of a species will have similar physical characteristics and ways of behaving.

In the process of cell division (called mitosis) the hereditary tendencies are transmitted from cell to cell immediately after conception. For cell division takes place in such a way that the chromosomes in each new cell are exact replicas of those in the parent cell from which they were derived. Each member of a species will therefore develop *in toto* the characteristics of the species to which it belongs. Thus the acorn will have its own genetic potential and will—provided the necessary conditions are fulfilled—develop the characteristic shape, texture and colour of bark, and shape of leaves, which enables us to distinguish the oak from the elm.

The hereditary tendencies are also transmitted from generation to generation by the germ cells. Germ cells are latent until
puberty. Then they begin a process of division (meiosis) in preparation for becoming active sperms or ova. As a result of this
division, when sperm and ovum meet at conception, each brings
to the union one half of the organism's full complement of chromosomes, so that the fertilized ovum contains the full complement.
Thus each species reproduces its own kind—dogs have puppies,
cats have kittens, oaks bear acorns, and elm trees elm seeds.

For human beings, too, similarity of genetic structure leads to
similarity of physical structure and behaviour. On conception, a
human being receives twenty-three pairs of chromosomes, one of
each pair coming from the male parent and the other from the
female. Within these chromosomes lie the genetic potentialities
for the development of the physical (structural) characteristics
peculiar to human beings, such as an erect body, a hand with
flexible fingers and a prehensile thumb, and an intricate nervous
system with a highly developed forebrain. When these general
physical potentialities become manifest, they are expressed in the
random and relatively uncoordinated movements of the very
young baby. But out of those undifferentiated movements, co-
ordinated behaviour gradually emerges—first of the whole limb,
then of hand and foot, then of fingers and toes.

The nervous system, and especially the brain, is usually assumed to constitute the physical basis of all mental functions, of the
ability to perceive, use language, and evaluate. We may suppose that
at first mental activity, like physical, is uncoordinated: perceptions are blurred and, as William James puts it, 'the world is a bloom-
ing buzzing confusion'. As mental potentialities develop, however,
the universe begins to assume some order and predictability.

Potentialities: unique

We have seen that some biological processes lead to similarity between members of a species. Others cause differences. When the
division of a germ cell takes place, and the forty-six chromosomes
pair off, which of the two chromosomes comes from the father's
pair and which from the mother's is a matter of chance. Consequently the laws of inheritance, as Mendel showed, can and
must be expressed statistically in terms of probabilities. The child's
innate tendencies depend on the way chromosomes, and the genes

they carry, recombine. Thus, except in the case of identical twins, the combinations of each child's genes are quite unique. One brother differs from another, and both may differ from their parents. However, unless one (or sometimes both) parents happen to carry a gene for some particular tendency, the child himself cannot exhibit that tendency. Hence children of the same parents show a partial resemblance to each other and to their parents, expressed in each case by a correlation of 0·50[1]; i.e. the resemblance is roughly 50 per cent.

Accordingly, whilst having features similar to all other oak trees, a particular oak tree will have features which make it unique; its bark and leaves will have markings not found on any other oak tree. While having physical characteristics similar to all other human beings, an individual will also have his own unique characteristics. For example, he may have a unique face and his own particular shape—of head, shoulders, trunk and limbs. This uniqueness of physical structure is expressed in his characteristic walk, and in movements of the head and body generally. Finger prints show that, even in its smallest element, the bodily structure of each person is different.

Uniqueness of bodily structure—particularly of brain and nervous tissue—leads to the development of psychological qualities which are not exactly like those of anyone else, and which, in their manifestations, present a unique grouping of intellectual abilities, emotional reactions, strivings and sensitivities.

[1] A correlation is a relation between variables such that changes in the one are accompanied by changes in the other. A coefficient of correlation is an index figure or fraction varying between +1·00 and −1·00, and is denoted by the letter r. A correlation +1·00 means a perfect positive relation between two variables; when one increases, so does the other and by the same proportional amount, e.g. the temperature and volume of a gas. A correlation −1·00 means a perfect negative relation; when one variable increases the other decreases by the same proportional amount, e.g. the volume and pressure of a gas. A correlation ·00 signifies no relation; changes in the value of one variable are accompanied by no predictable changes in the value of the other, e.g. the colours of people's eyes and their scores on an intelligence test. In psychology and education, correlations are rarely perfect; the degree of relation is then indicated by the extent to which r approaches 1·00 (ignoring the + or − sign). The closer r is to 1·00 the greater the relation; that is, the more accurately we can predict one variable when the value of the other is known. Positive and negative correlations of the same size represent equal degrees of relation. The sign merely indicates that both variables increase together (+) or that one increases while the other decreases (−).

Genes, however, are not the whole story. The environment, too, produces both resemblances and differences between individuals. Similar outside influences tend to make groups of individuals alike; but since, in a strict sense, the environment is never precisely the same for any two individuals, the chances of uniqueness are further increased. An oak tree is subject to the influences which affect every other oak tree growing near by. Consequently, an oak tree growing on a hill ressembles the neighbouring oaks more closely than it ressembles the oaks growing in a sheltered, fertile valley. Yet it has its own particular place, which no other tree can possibly have. This place has its special nuances of influence. It is more or less sheltered from sun and wind; it has more or less of the constituents characteristic of the local soil, more or less moisture.

A particular child is subject to the prevailing influences, material and personal, which affect other children in his neighbourhood. He shares with his brothers and sisters a similar but not identical family background, similar though not identical parents. He is the eldest in the family. When he was born, his parents were younger and less experienced in the ways of children than when his brothers and sisters were born. Because he is the eldest, their attitude towards him is a little different from their attitude towards each of their other children. The boy, like his friends, lives in a similar environment (country or town) and is subject to similar social conditions (enough or not enough material comforts, good or not-so-good schools and teachers); but he has his unique place—in the gang as leader or follower, in the thoughts, feelings and judgments of children and adults outside his family. These unique influences of family and neighbourhood interact with the child's special complement of genetic material to make him yet more unique.

Maturation, readiness, learning

Maturation is the term used by psychologists to refer to this ripening of genetic potentialities. Maturation implies that the tendencies to certain modes of behaviour are innate, and develop gradually so that adequate performance is often delayed, presumably because neural pathways have not developed. Though the process of maturation is largely independent of the environment, the environment may stimulate and aid it by providing external requisites such as food, water, oxygen. Through maturation the body is brought to a state of physiological preparedness for learned behaviour. Formally stated, readiness means a state of maturation sufficient to allow the individual to learn, that is, to increase the level of his performance as a result of instruction and practice. For example, reading implies matured perceptual, intellectual and vocal ability—to perceive and discriminate the shapes and sizes of letters and words, and the various sounds and objects they symbolize. Ideally one waits for these abilities to mature sufficiently before beginning any formal teaching of reading. Whether reading skills develop depends on maturation, which is a biological process, and also on the encouragement and training which the social environment provides.

In this process, there are wide differences between individuals in the age at which similar potentialities mature. Some children are ready for reading before others; some mature physically or sexually or socially before others. There are, too, differences in the degree to which differing skills can be developed by the same individual; in other words, for some skills the genetic potentiality is strong, for others weak. That this is so is reflected in everyday conversation. After watching a child perform, someone may comment that she is (or is not) a 'born', a 'natural' dancer, singer, speaker or whatever the activity may be. Psychological tests are devised to predict possible achievement in various intellectual subjects in a more exact and scientific way than these intuitive judgments.

Readiness has just been described as an end result of maturation—a view which is acceptable, particularly when speaking of the biological processes of maturing that are preparatory to, and precede, the baby's standing, crawling, walking. But, from the teacher's point of view, readiness must inevitably include achievements brought about by learning. The child is ready for reading partly because of a general background of experience with words and books and a desire to read which this background may have stimulated, even though he has not been formally taught to read.

The first sentences of this chapter may now be interpreted in the light of the foregoing discussion. They imply that the aim of education is to draw out, to develop the capacities with which the individual is especially endowed, so that he becomes a person having characteristics some of which make him like, and some of which make him different from, others.

As it has been said (3), a man is:

> Like all other men;
> Like some other men;
> Like no other man.

He is like *all* other men because he has the same kind of body and nervous system. He is like *some* other men because he belongs to the same family and the same national, cultural, social, or professional group as they do. He is like *no* other man because his body and life history are unique.

Organized

The third abstract term was 'organized', and in order to amplify its meaning, the implications of the following four statements will in turn be considered.

> Organized behaviour may be defined as behaviour which is directed towards the fulfilment of some goal or goals.
> Much organized behaviour can be described in terms of 'dispositions'.
> A person's 'dispositions' are themselves often organized, and the term 'personality' can be used to indicate this organization.
> An individual's 'personality' is never static, but always in a state of change or becoming.

> *Organized behaviour may be defined as behaviour which is directed towards the fulfilment of some goal or goals.*

The behaviour of individuals is not usually haphazard but is generally aimed towards the fulfilment of some goal, and we are content in our everyday thinking to accept a statement of the goal as sufficient explanation of the behaviour we observe. A mother sees paper, cardboard, plywood, glue and scissors strewn over the floor with Henry in the middle, and she says, 'What are you doing?' The mother asks for an explanation in terms of a goal. Henry replies, 'I am going to make a model aeroplane.' His mother is satisfied with this explanation, for she now sees that the paper, cardboard, and other materials will become the parts of a model aeroplane. Henry is not merely cutting cardboard, he is making a wing; he is not sticking two pieces of wood together, he is making the fuselage. The behaviour and the situation have meaning. Of course, there are immediate goals and distant goals in terms of which behaviour acquires meaning for us. Thus, Henry might have said, 'I am going to be an aeronautical engineer.' This is a more embracing answer in that it is an explanation in terms of a whole way of life and not just in terms of an immediate purpose.

To take another simple example: a College of Education student is writing an English essay. He might say that he is doing this because he wants to complete the assignment which has been set. Or he might explain his behaviour in terms of more distant goals and say that he is doing it because he wishes, as part of the course, to pass in English to obtain a Teacher's Certificate in order that he can become a qualified teacher. We are satisfied with these explanations in terms of immediate or distant goals because thereby we are able to relate many kinds of behaviour. To take our first example: cutting paper, sketching in pencil, going to the shop to buy glue and to the shed to get nails and screws, though in themselves distinct activities, are related and meaningful in terms of Henry's goal. Such related behaviour may be called 'organized'.

Much organized behaviour can be described in terms of 'dispositions'.

Sometimes we wish to speak of the organization of behaviour in more general terms. Instead of speaking of specific goals—'to make a model aeroplane', 'to complete an assignment'—more abstract terms can be used to imply that behaviour of many different kinds is organized. Thus, we speak of interests, values, ideals, beliefs, opinions, attitudes, sentiments, habits, purposes and so on. These words, and many others in our language, are used with nouns to describe a person's behaviour (for example, 'His interests are motor-cars, horse-racing and variety shows') and the dispositions they represent can be looked upon as the 'units of personality'.

Knowledge of these units—that is, of a person's interests, values, needs, beliefs and so on—enables us to predict his behaviour. Thus, my friend A may say of another person B, 'He loves music', or, as McDougall puts it, 'He has a sentiment of love towards music.' Now, my friend is not telling me anything about what B is doing at the time; B may be tranquilly fishing for trout. But A is telling me that B has a 'disposition' and in saying this, he indicates in a shorthand way how B often behaves. We check A's shorthand statement when we investigate and find that B goes to numerous concerts, spends much money on musical recordings and has many friends in musical circles. Similarly, if we say that 'C hates D', again we are not saying what C is experiencing at the moment. But we are saying that C has a disposition which we call 'a sentiment of hate' towards D, so that he will be unhappy at D's presence, happy at D's absence, annoyed at D's successes and pleased with D's failures.

As may be seen from these examples and as will be amplified later, the term 'disposition' indicates *an inner state of readiness* to behave in prescribed ways. The Oxford English Dictionary definition of *disposition* is given as 'that state or quality of being disposed, inclined (*to* something or *to do* something)' and it is in this sense that the term is used throughout this book. Thus, a person can be in a somnolent mood and his behaviour possibilities are *in potentia:* then someone mentions something relating to a disposition he 'has' and he is suddenly alerted. He experiences an emotion of pleasure, pain, grief, or joy; he is ready to discuss the topic enthusiastically.[1]

Dispositions may be classified as follows:

1   Dispositions which arise from changing bodily states, to refer to which we use such terms as needs, drives, appetites.
2   Dispositions which result from attachment to people and to objects, to describe which we use such terms as sentiments, attitudes, interests, needs, purposes, goals.
3   Dispositions evolving from 2 which relate to a person's evaluation of people (including himself) and of objects, to describe which we use the terms values, ideals, beliefs, opinions.
4   Dispositions which emphasize typical modes of behaviour (trait dispositions); for example, sympathetic, sensitive, assertive.

[1] Because the use of the term 'disposition' may lead us to interpret its meaning in a static way and not dynamically as a state of readiness, some psychologists prefer to speak of 'dispositional states' or 'dispositional tendencies'. The three terms are synonymous, and it does not matter which one of these three is used as long as the reader interprets the meaning as a potential state of readiness. 'Disposition' is short and simple and will generally be used in the discussion which follows. But to avoid the danger of a static interpretation either one of the other two terms will occasionally be used, often in brackets after 'disposition', to remind the reader that we are referring to 'an inner state of readiness'.

These trait dispositions may indicate more or less permanent characteristics, as when we say of a person that he is adventurous, autocratic, benevolent, sincere. On the other hand, trait dispositional terms may be used to describe temporary moods or ways of behaving in a particular situation, as when it is said of a person that he is absorbed, angry, ashamed and so on. In considering the term 'personality' we are mainly concerned with trait dispositions of the former kind which imply a more permanent feature of the person who is being studied.

The next two chapters are devoted to a more detailed consideration of the dispositions classified above.

A person's 'dispositions' are themselves often organized, and the term 'personality' can be used to indicate this organization.

As we have seen, what are separate activities in themselves become related activities because they mutually reinforce the fulfilment of a goal; we then speak of organized behaviour. It may also be said that a person's dispositions are organized insofar as his interests, beliefs and trait dispositions reinforce each other in determining a particular way of life.

To illustrate, take occupations such as clergyman, teacher, army officer, journalist. We speak of the 'ideal' clergyman, or teacher, though we may not have analysed precisely what is meant by this. The use of the term 'ideal' implies this relatedness, this mutuality of dispositions, which gives the person the qualities we deem necessary for the task.

'Character sketches' found in literary studies (and which, from our point of view, should be called 'personality sketches') attempt to depict dispositions and their organization within individuals in a descriptive way. The best of these are of great value to the student of personality. In his Prologue to *The Canterbury Tales*, for example, Chaucer provides us with a wealth of contrasting personalities. Here is a modernized version of Chaucer's sketch of the Oxford Cleric (2):[1]

> There was an Oxford Cleric too, a student,
> Long given to Logic, longer than was prudent;
> The horse he had was leaner than a rake,
> And he was not too fat, I undertake,

[1] page 33.

But had a hollow look, a sober stare;
The thread upon his overcoat was bare.
He had found no preferment in the church
And he was too unworldly to make search.
He thought far more of having by his bed
His twenty books all bound in black and red,
Of Aristotle and philosophy
Than of gay music, fiddles or finery.
Though a philosopher, as I have told,
He had not found the stone for making gold.
Whatever money from his friends he took
He spent on learning or another book
And prayed for them most earnestly, returning
Thanks to them thus for paying for his learning.
His only care was study, and indeed
He never spoke a word more than was need,
Formal at that, respectful in the extreme,
Short, to the point, and lofty in his theme.
The thought of moral virtue filled his speech
And he would gladly learn, and gladly teach.

The dispositions which Chaucer describes (unworldly, love of books, of study, of moral virtue) are inferred from and, therefore, consonant with the behaviour and appearance of the Cleric. The dispositions are mutually related (organized) to the fulfilment of the way of life of a mediaeval scholar, and are summed up in the words 'And he would gladly learn, and gladly teach.'

Individuals vary in the degree to which their dispositions (dispositional tendencies) are organized. For some, dispositions are tightly organized towards the fulfilment of limited goals, or towards a way of life that excludes much that the average person experiences. For others, dispositions are loosely organized and the person has no special goals or may quickly move from the pursuit of one goal to the pursuit of another, neither of which he pursues to completion. When this is so, we often speak of random, capricious, erratic behaviour. Still others appear to effect a balance between a very rigid organization and a very loose one. With a person of this type, though his dispositions are definitely organized towards the fulfilment of goals, the organization is flexible enough to enable him to be interested in other things, to appreciate viewpoints other than his own, and even, if the occasion arises, to accept new goals. Everyday words used to describe personality, such as being broad- or narrow-minded, having an open or a closed mind, being rigid, hard, pliable, impulsive and so on, imply these varying degrees of organization.

This book is concerned mainly with the organization of dispositions towards a creative and constructive way of life. But dispositions may be organized towards other than creative and constructive ends. To take two extreme examples: in the true paranoid person dispositions are rigidly organized and, for the most part, consistent one with the other. But the main goal they fulfil is to maintain the paranoid's delusions, namely that he is being persecuted by others in many kinds of ways. His conception of the universe consequently becomes more and more at odds with the facts of the universe, and he himself more and more isolated from it. By contrast, in the schizophrenic person organization is so loose that he is unable to pursue the rudimentary goals required to live in society and, maybe, even the simple goals required to maintain his own biological existence.

To take a less severe and more common kind of circumstance: one group of dispositions may be inconsistent with another group, and the person may try to pursue goals which are physically and/ or dispositionally incompatible—for example, to be both a good boxer and a good violinist. If the conflict that accompanies such incompatibility is such that the individual cannot make a decision one way or the other, he may suffer a neurosis. Such self-destruction and conflict relate, of course, more to the psychology of mental illness and maladjustment which are mentioned only very incidentally in this book.

An individual's 'personality' is never static, but always in a state of change or becoming.[1]

Human development is a process of becoming. For a child it is the gradual process of becoming an adult. 'When I was a child I spake as a child, I understood as a child, I thought as a child; but when I became a man, I put away childish things.' And yet this process of development is never complete; goals that have been

[1] I acknowledge my debt to Allport (1), since the term 'becoming' is used here in the sense in which he uses it. I read his book after writing this chapter and substituted for the term 'change' his term 'becoming' which has a deeper meaning than 'change', for it implies change which is directed towards a goal.

achieved are replaced by goals yet to be achieved. You may recall dreaming as you worked for the school-leaving examination that if you passed you would be happy ever after; you anticipated a sense of completion. When you did pass, this sense of completion lasted only for a few weeks. New goals arose, fresh efforts began, hopes and fears alternated again in expectation of further successes.

There is a sense in which a 'personality structure' may be spoken of and studied as if it were fixed or permanent. But even for an adult with an established position in society, with set loyalties and set antipathies, changes are taking place, if only those that are inevitable in the process of growing older. For children, almost every day brings new interests, new needs. These arise not only because of fresh experiences and newly-acquired knowledge, but also because of the physical and psychological maturation which is taking place. New skills need to be mastered; as the child's senses develop so do corresponding needs—for beautiful things to look at, music to hear.

Study of common language usages often gives insight into the way we judge and understand people. For example, on seeing a small child whom we do not know, we ask, 'Who is he?' However, of an adult we ask not only, 'Who is he?' but also, 'What does he do?' and 'What sort of a fellow is he?' In the case of the child we are quite satisfied with the reply, 'He's Dick, the shepherd's boy.' This is understandable, since the acquired dispositions of a child are mainly those (classified as 2 above) which arise from attachment to his family. His beliefs, opinions, values (classified as 3 above) are those of the members of his family; the status he has in society is dependent on their status. He is a person because he belongs to them and, apart from this, he has little significance. Clinical evidence has repeatedly shown how devastating the disruption of a family, through separation, divorce, or death, can be for a child. This again is understandable, since disintegration of the family touches the very core of a child's growing personality. He has no certain identity, is without status and security.

But in the case of an adult we are not satisfied with just knowing his family name. We ask the second question, 'What does he do?' which, in the terms already used, means, 'What specific potentialities has he developed and to what extent has he developed them?', since an adult is expected to have developed his abilities towards some personal and social ends. A major criterion of judging this (but not, of course, the only one) is the work he does. The third question, 'What sort of a fellow is he?' may relate to his religious or political beliefs, his interests outside his work (classified as 3 above); most probably, however, the question relates to trait dispositions (classified as 4 above) such as modesty/conceit, kindness/cruelty, sociability/unsociability, placidity/aggressiveness. He is a 'nice fellow' or an 'unpleasant character' according as we feel he has developed the first or second quality in each pair. Answers to these three questions complete a superficial description of an individual's personality, and this may be all we require in casual conversation.

Because we do not ask the second and third questions of children does not mean that they have no personality, but rather that a child is, relative to an adult, a personality in the process of rapid development. The purpose of this book is to describe and to explain a little of the movement from 'Who is he?' to 'What does he do?' and 'What sort of a fellow is he?'

Personality and character

To conclude this introductory discussion of the meaning of 'personality', a distinction will be made between the two terms 'personality' and 'character'. Character is more concerned with those aspects of the personality which relate to stability, dependability and sustained effort. McDougall speaks of character as 'that in a man which gives, or rather is the ground of, consistency, firmness, self-control, power of self-direction' (4).[1] Character, too, is a social concept and is related to the demands which society makes upon individuals. Each social group has its specific problems, needs, values and ideals so that when we speak of a 'good character' we refer to the individual's consistency, his power of direction, his self-control in seeking the solution to such problems and the fulfilment of social purposes and social ideals.

Personality, on the other hand, includes the concept of character, but goes beyond it to stress the uniqueness of each individual. Perhaps this can be made clearer by contrasting the phrases 'the moulding of character' and 'the unfolding of personality'. The former phrase presupposes two things: a set of ideals for which an

[1] page 185.

individual 'ought to' strive and a set of social conditions to which the individual 'ought to' adjust. The latter, 'the unfolding of personality', stresses the growth of the creative and constructive possibilities within the individual. Whereas 'the moulding of character' implies that individuals are means towards the maintenance of social forms and social values, 'unfolding of personality' sees the development of the person as the end and the social environment as the means through which growth can take place. Therefore personality includes within it the idea of character, for an individual develops within a society to which he must, to a large extent, adjust. Yet the stress in personality is on the individual's unique contribution to society, an emphasis on what Allport has called 'creative becoming'.

The psychologist as philosopher

To conclude this chapter, here is a very brief statement of the aims of education, upon the basis of which this book is written.

The qualities and skills that human beings can develop are, of course, many and varied; and educational philosophers are concerned to ask which qualities, which skills *ought* to be developed. It is not within the province of this book to present all the philosophical arguments as to the ideal aim of education, nor is the writer qualified to do so. Psychology is a study of the means by which certain ends can be attained. If a mother asks, 'How shall I bring up my child?' no answer can be given until she answers the question, 'What do you want your child to be, and to be like?' The psychologist, in short, says, 'Give me the ends you have in view, and I can suggest means towards these ends.' Therefore, a psychologist is not an ethical philosopher. But if he writes a book on educational psychology, then he ought to state what he considers the aim of education to be.

From the point of view of this book, the purpose of education is the encouragement of the process of 'creative becoming' spoken of above—that is, the development of the unique creative and constructive potentialities of children—and all the psychologizing that follows has this purpose in mind. Such a statement as it stands is abstract, but as this study proceeds it is hoped that, through descriptions of personality, concrete meaning will be given to this abstract statement of aims.

REFERENCES

1   Allport, G. W. *Becoming*. Yale University Press, New Haven, Connecticut, 1960.
2   Chaucer, G. *The Canterbury Tales*. Translated by Neville Coghill. Penguin Books, Harmondsworth, Middlesex, 1951.
3   Kluckhohn, C., Mowrer, O. H. 'Components of personality: a conceptual schema.' *American Anthropologist*, 1944, **46**, pp. 1–29.
4   McDougall, W. *The Energies of Men*. Methuen, London, 4th edition, 1939.

CHAPTER TWO

'Having' a Disposition

So far, personality has been defined as 'an organization of dispositions (dispositional tendencies)', and dispositions have been classified in relation to changing bodily states, attachment to and evaluation of people and objects and also according to typical modes of behaviour.

It is necessary now to go beyond this simple classification and to consider more precisely what is meant by the concept 'disposition'. This will be done by amplifying the following statements:

1　'Having' a disposition (or dispositional tendency) implies a potential state of readiness to perceive, to experience emotions, and to act in a specific way with respect to people, objects and situations.

2　The behaviour from which dispositions (or dispositional tendencies) are inferred suggests: (*a*) the directive nature, and (*b*) the dynamic nature or driving power of dispositions.

3　Behaviour indicating dispositions (or dispositional tendencies) may be studied from: (*a*) the outside—the way a person behaves, and (*b*) the inside—the way a person feels.

4　To say a person 'has' a disposition (or dispositional tendency) is sometimes to imply that he is emotionally involved with people (including himself), with objects, and with situations.

For the remainder of this chapter the implications of the first three statements will be considered. Statement 4 will be discussed later in Chapter 3.

Take the first statement:

'Having' a disposition (or dispositional tendency) implies a potential state of readiness to perceive, to experience emotions, and to act in a specific way with respect to people, objects and situations.

The runner in a race 'gets ready', 'gets set' and then 'goes'. For him, the sound of the starter's gun is the stimulus to move from a state of potential readiness implied in 'getting set' to the active behaviour of running. This is analogous to what is meant by 'having' a disposition, since the individual who 'has' a disposition is also in a state of being set—to perceive, to feel, to act—and the stimuli which will cause him to change from a relaxed state to one of alertness and then of action will depend upon the kinds of dispositions (needs, interests, purposes) he has.

For example, a teacher is reading his newspaper in leisurely fashion, his glance moving cursorily from one item to another. He slowly turns over the pages (relatively relaxed). Then, suddenly, he notices (perceives) the heading, 'The Teaching Profession' which, for him, stands out prominently from other headings even though, in terms of size and thickness of print, it is considerably less prominent. He is alert and he feels a stir of excitement (emotion). His movements become suddenly brusque and he quickly folds back the paper and reads (acts). The rest of the news can wait.

You may have observed that a mother whose child has an illness which is difficult to cure, such as asthma, notices any reference to the illness in conversation or reading, especially any suggestions as to possible cures and any reports of children who have been cured (perceives). On hearing such reports she feels hopeful (emotion) and proceeds to find out more (acts). It is surprising how much knowledge of the causes, the history and the course of the illness such a mother will have acquired over the years.

Often the disposition is more important than the intensity of the stimulus in determining behaviour. McDougall gives an example something like this. A young man is sitting on the grass by the roadside reading a book. He is awaiting his loved one who is to cycle to meet him. A semi-trailer rattles by. He goes on reading and apparently does not hear it. A motor bicycle and a petrol lorry roar by. Again he takes no notice. He is much too interested in his book. Then from a distance there comes the tiny tinkle of a bicycle bell. He is alerted (perceives) and his face lights up with pleasure (emotion). He quickly shuts the book, jumps up, looks far along the road and joyfully waves (acts).

Turn now to statement 2(a), namely,

The behaviour from which dispositions (or dispositional tendencies) are inferred suggests the directive nature of dispositions.

'Having a disposition' implies more than just a readiness for action; it implies a readiness for action of a kind appropriate to the disposition; a tendency, that is, to seek specific situations and people, to strive for particular goals. This has been implied in the foregoing discussion. The teacher seeks to know what the paper has to say about his profession; the mother seeks a cure for asthma; and the young man seeks to be with his beloved.

Two further examples of this directing function of dispositions may be noted. A mother looks at the clock; Freddie is late again. With a determined air, she slips on her coat and says to her husband, 'I know where *he'll* be.' Freddie has become 'crazy' about bulldozers and she finds him as she expected, on a nearby building site. This may be just temporary interest for Freddie, or it may be the beginnings of a career; but, to Freddie's mother, it means that he is never in time for meals; it also means that she knows where to find him when she wants him.

Secondly, legendary stories about, and imaginative illustrations of, the childhood of famous men often include episodes suggesting the directive function which, in our everyday thinking, we implicitly attribute to dispositions. The child is attracted to a place which is propitious for the early development of those dispositions necessary to his future way of life, and often to people who have achieved or are attempting to achieve the same goals. The boy Handel is discovered playing the clavichord at midnight; the boy Raleigh is down on the beach listening to the thrilling yarns of sailors.

Of course, insofar as a disposition implies the selection of certain goals, it implies also the foregoing of others. Extraordinary people, like Leonardo da Vinci, can be painter, sculptor, scientist and engineer; Schweitzer can be a doctor of medicine, music, theology and philosophy. But most of us, with our limited capacities, must choose one major field and specialize within it. Moreover, a tendency to seek some goals implies a correlative tendency deliberately to avoid other goals that are incompatible.

Now consider statement 2(*b*), namely,
The behaviour from which dispositions (or dispositional tendencies)

are inferred suggests the *dynamic* nature or the driving power of dispositions.

There are certain physiological and psychological accompaniments to hunger, such as contraction of the stomach and the experience of hunger pangs (we speak here of ordinary hunger of, say, a day's duration at most, and not of prolonged starvation). Further, when an organism has been without food for some time, it is active and, though not all the physiological causes of this are known precisely, we can speak descriptively and say that, in hunger, the organism becomes physiologically tense, like a taut piece of elastic, and that energy is generated which manifests itself in restless activity. Observations show that, within limits, the longer the organism is without food, the longer it will persist in food-seeking activity and the more determined it will be to resist being diverted to any other activity. In short, it is more sensitized to the sight and smell of food (perceives), more excited at the prospect of getting food (feels), and more likely to go in search of food (acts). In hunger we, as human beings, experience an urge to seek food and the longer we are without it the more desperate this urge becomes. Similar sensitization, excitement and urge to activity accompany deprivation in the case of acquired physiological needs, like those for drugs, tobacco, alcohol.

The dispositions mainly considered so far in this book, such as interests, beliefs, purposes, values and ideals, have no such clear physiological basis as has hunger. But tension can develop and the urge to action which follows can in each case be as insistent as that which accompanies physiological deprivation. A person can feel impelled to pursue an interest, to defend a belief, and the urge to do so can be as strong as the urge to satisfy physiological needs and may, in some instances, supersede them. An artist may have such determination to express, through his paintings, the ideas he believes an artist should express that he would rather go hungry now and again than paint rustic scenes to sell at three guineas a time (which technically he could do quite easily). Freddie's mother may say, 'The boy is so absorbed with tractors that it's a tussle every time I want him to come to a meal and an even greater tussle when I want him to go to bed.' One adult drives himself to obtain yet more possessions, another to obtain yet more power and a third to satisfy his unlimited academic ambitions, even though

basic physiological needs may be satisfied in the case of all
three.

The Oxford English Dictionary definition of *dynamic* is 'per-
taining to power, strength, to force producing motion'; and it is
in this sense that the term is used in saying that dispositions (or
dispositional states) have 'dynamic properties'. The dynamic
nature of dispositions is particularly relevant to the relationship
between dispositions and learning. Thus, a major principle of
teaching is that children learn more easily and more readily
if the teacher creates within them a 'need', an 'interest', a
'purpose'—if, in other words, a favourable disposition is engendered.

Take a simple example. A teacher wishes to teach a boy of ten,
who is virtually a non-reader, to read. Attempts with the Little
Red Hen and other such characters which intrigue an Infant
School child fail to stimulate him. In fact, he is quite disgusted
with himself and a little ashamed in front of his companions
because such childish things are put before him. The teacher then
discovers that the boy has an absorbing interest in roof-tiling (to
take an example from a recent experience of the writer). The
boy's father and uncle are roof-tilers, and the boy spends all the
time he can after school and on Saturday mornings watching
them at work. About one thing he is quite dogmatic—that when
he leaves school, he is going to be a roof-tiler. The teacher
capitalizes on this interest and shows him how to trace and write
words connected with building, and especially with roof-tiling.
In this way, the boy acquires a small reading vocabulary and so
begins a remedial reading project along the lines suggested by
Grace Fernald (1).

Elsewhere (2)[1] I have compared the process of learning with
the process of healing within the body. There are latent healing
forces within the body. The doctor sterilizes a wound and protects
it from outside sources of infection. Thereby he creates an environment in which the natural healing forces can function. We
can say that the doctor does not heal; he prepares the situation in
which healing takes place. Similarly, learning is a natural process
of the living organism and the teacher's job is to prepare situations in which the natural learning processes can operate. We
can continue the analogy and say that just as a hospital can be seen

[1] page 144.

as an institution specially designed for the creation of situations in which healing can take place, so a school can be seen as an institution specially designed for the creation of situations in which learning can take place.

The point of all this is that the creation of learning situations means, among other things, tapping dispositions already acquired —an interest in nature study, in football, roof-tiling, or whatever it may be—or the generation of new dispositions and the exploitation of these for purposes of painless and efficient learning.

The emphasis so far has been on the *seeking* of objects, situations and people, but to have dispositions (dispositional tendencies) means that a person attracts (or repels) people who have similar (or opposing) dispositions. If a person combines an interest with such qualities as friendliness, wide knowledge and the ability to impart this knowledge, then he may obtain a following. As was stated at the very beginning of this book, our everyday notion of personality comprises mainly the ability to attract others. But it can now be seen that this is only one of the possible ways in which personality is manifested. In short, dispositional tendencies mean that a person becomes attracted to people who, as stimuli, cause him to respond in a certain way; it also means that he is, in turn, a stimulus causing people to respond to him in varying ways. The aggressive boy who is also a bully (stimulus) causes the non-aggressive boy to be fearful, timid, submissive (response). This sequence has its correlative: the fearfulness, timidity and submissiveness of the non-aggressive boy (stimulus) in turn incites the bully to further acts of bullying (response).

The third statement reads as follows:

Behaviour indicating dispositions (or dispositional tendencies) may be studied from: (*a*) the outside—the way a person behaves, and (*b*) the inside—the way a person feels.

There is a sense in which 'disposition' may be used merely as a collective term to indicate many instances of behaviour. In just the same way as we have learned to call combinations of qualities 'table', 'chair', 'house', 'car', so we have learned to call combinations of behaviour 'assertiveness', 'creativeness', 'an interest in', 'a love of', 'a hatred of'. From this viewpoint, the use of dispositional terms is a semantic device providing shorthand signs for describing the way a person behaves.[1]

This outside view by itself is not enough, for to say that a person 'has' a disposition implies a wealth of emotional potentialities and the dynamic, directed drive to perceive, to feel and to act, which have been outlined. We can make a person happy or unhappy, friendly or aggressive, by encouraging or inhibiting the expression of an interest, by applauding or by denigrating a belief, a value, he 'has'. Each of us acquires *felt knowledge* of the emotional experience which 'having' a disposition entails, particularly when a belief or value is threatened. When someone attacks a treasured belief, for example, in democracy, in the beauties of our district, or the importance of our home town, we are alerted; we experience anger and become aggressively active in defence of the beliefs and values we hold. Often, when we have inadvertently offended and aroused a person to a state of emotional distress, we say, 'I did not realize that she *felt* so deeply about it. Otherwise I would not have spoken in the way I did.'

This *felt* realization of a disposition (or dispositional tendency) is also experienced acutely when the expression of a particularly strong disposition has to be inhibited. A child, for example, has developed some particular interest, say in bird's-nesting or marbles. He has waited patiently all the afternoon, but (he glances at the clock) soon he will be able to go out and pursue his interest. Then, at the last moment, the class becomes disorderly and the teacher says that they must all stay in after school for half an hour. Disappointment is like a physical pain and the boy utters a groan.

The boy's feelings may be compared with those of an adult who has had to leave a task at a critical and exciting moment to attend a committee meeting, and the meeting drags on and on. There are moments when he is certain that it will end and that he will be able to go quickly to pursue this special interest. Then, once again, the same committee-member whose hair-splitting

[1] Study of people born blind and who have later been given sight shows that these people have to *learn* to recognize and to name even what, for us, are simple everyday objects, and that this learning takes time and requires specific instruction. Children who from birth have normal sight learn to distinguish these objects in the ordinary process of growing up and without systematic tuition. The argument here is that we also learn to associate and name certain groups of behaviour.

has thus lengthened the meeting raises a small objection, some superficial point which has to be argued out. Our adult's irritation mounts until he feels he is going to burst; he releases the tension by shifting his body, passing a hand through his hair, taking a clump of hair and giving it a tug. The emphasis in these two examples is on subjective experience, on how the person feels. As McDougall says (3), 'Emotion is a mode or quality of experience.'[1]

At this point the reader is justified in asking, 'How can we *know* what a person is experiencing? How can we know this inside aspect of dispositions?' In some ways, the problem is the same as that of *knowing* the outside aspects of a disposition, for just as a disposition such as 'love of sport' is inferred from observation of behaviour, so the inference can be made that a child is angry, anxious, happy, or sad, from observing his behaviour. We do not *see* anger or anxiety in another any more than, as stated in the last chapter, we *see* a disposition. In order that inferences may be valid, it is necessary to systematize observations by stating clearly the kinds of behaviour which it is agreed may be called 'anxious behaviour', 'angry behaviour' and so on. This will be attempted at a later stage in this book, using traits such as 'self-confidence', 'concentration', 'emotional stability."

But there are other modes of observation particularly relevant in attempting to understand this 'inside' view of personality. This is the participation, empathy and sympathy with other people (to be discussed more fully later when the formation of children's personalities is considered) which imply the ability to infer the states of mind of other people from our own in similar circumstances. If we have ourselves experienced some happy or sad occasion which another person is now experiencing, we say, 'I know how he feels. It happened to me once.' However, even though we have never actually experienced the particular occasion in question, we can, through use of our imagination, infer the feelings of a person who has experienced a loss of some kind, whether of a loved one, of property, or of his self-esteem. Although such imaginative understanding is not as amenable to scientific control as the knowledge that comes from observation of overt behaviour, it is very necessary for a full realization of the implications of the phrase 'having a disposition'.

[1] page 315.

REFERENCES

1   Fernald, G. R. *Remedial Techniques in the Basic School Subjects*. McGraw-Hill,
     New York, 1943.
2   Gabriel, J. *An Analysis of the Emotional Problems of the Teacher in the Class-
     room*. Cheshire, Melbourne, 1957.
3   McDougall, W. *Outline of Psychology*. Methuen, London, 8th edition, 1940.

CHAPTER THREE

I, Me, My, Mine

THE fourth statement made at the beginning of Chapter 2 reads as follows:

To say that a person 'has' a disposition (or dispositional tendency) is sometimes to imply that he is emotionally involved with people (including himself), with objects, and with situations.

The development of personality may be seen as a progressively increasing realization of the concepts 'my', 'mine', 'I', 'me', 'myself', since in the process of development a person inevitably becomes attached to people and to objects, and also to himself, not only to his body, but also to the personal qualities he thinks he has. If a person has an interest, then he has an interest in something; similarly, his beliefs, values, loves and hates relate to people and objects. 'It is *my* house, *my* work; they are *my* beliefs, *my* attitudes.' Even trait dispositions can become objects and so he may say '*my* assertiveness', '*my* ability to concentrate', '*my* inferiority', '*my* shame', '*my* tolerance'.

There follows a classification of the things to which a person in our culture tends to become attached so that he will refer to them by using the possessive adjectives 'my', 'mine'.

1   *Material objects*[1] : own body, clothes, money, house, car, etc.

We become attached to our body and its appearance, to our possessions; and we fear their injury or their loss.

[1] In this book the word 'objects' will be used in two senses: (*a*) in its ordinary meaning as a material object (clothes, car, house, etc.) and distinct from a person or activity; (*b*) as a generic term to denote the whole class of items to which we can become attached (see 1–6 of the classification which follows). When used in this second sense, the word will be put in italic thus—*objects*.

2   *Places and institutions:* own home, home town, country, school, college, church, club.

We become attached to places and institutions, and they profoundly influence the dispositions we form. The emotional significance of these attachments are especially felt in the home-sickness that an adolescent, for example, will experience on first leaving his home town with all its personal and institutional associations.

3   *People:* own father, mother, husband, wife, child, brother, sister, friend, workmate.

We are concerned about the recognition these people give us, and we like to be noticed, and noticed favourably, by them. We want them, too, to be a credit to us so that we can be proud and boast a little of our association with them.

4   *Abilities and skills:* own physical, intellectual, artistic capacities, knowledge; the profession we follow.

This is broadly the area of pride in personal achievement. We are proud of the skills and knowledge we have acquired and of our membership of a trade or profession.

5   *Beliefs and values:* own political, ethical, religious beliefs and values.

We become attached to these as firmly as we do to the material objects under 1. We develop and take pride in our capacity to defend our own beliefs and values against attack.

This division of the *objects* to which we become attached corresponds roughly to William James's three aspects of individual personality, namely the material self, the social self, the personal self. Broadly speaking, the material self corresponds to 1 above, the social self to 2 and 3, the personal self to 4 and 5.

Described in this way, therefore, the process of development is in part a process of appropriation. The objects we own, the knowledge we acquire, the trade, the profession we follow, the people we love are *ours*. We have, we know, and so we become.

In some ways these attachments widen; in other ways they tend to narrow. They widen in the sense that a person gets to know more people; he acquires more objects, more knowledge;

he moves to new places. They narrow in that a person tends to
specialize and so to intensify his knowledge and skills within a
particular sphere; that is, he becomes a specialist in some manual,
artistic or professional field. The motor-mechanic is not dismayed
at his inability to translate the school motto (in Latin, of course);
the Latin teacher is not dismayed because he has not the skill of the
motor-mechanic to assemble a carburettor. The film actress is
particularly concerned with her bodily appearance and her clothes;
the athlete with his physical fitness and skill; the mayor with the
welfare of his city and the smooth functioning of its institutions;
the professor with his intellectual capacities, his specialized knowledge in his own field of study and the progress of his students.

6   *Self-concept:* the individual's evaluation of himself as a total
person.

The *idea* of a self-concept presupposes self-awareness—a
realization of 'I', 'me', 'myself'. A distinctive feature of man is his
capacity to evaluate his own behaviour, his own achievements,
his own personal qualities. He is capable of self-reflection and of
judging his behaviour, achievements and dispositions as 'good'
or 'bad', and himself as worthy or unworthy in the light of such
judgments.

The *growth* of a self-concept has inherent within it a dichotomy, namely that a child, as he develops, learns to realize his oneness with others while, at the same time, he learns to realize also
that he is a being separate from others. Because he is at one with
others and dependent upon them he wants to think, feel and behave as they do, to be with and be liked by them. Insofar as he
seeks this oneness, his self-concept is dependent upon what others
think of him. On the other hand, he also desires to achieve
individual significance because this makes him 'distinguished',
and thereby he emphasizes his separateness from others. Insofar as
he seeks this separation, his self-concept depends more upon his
own judgments.

By self-judging and self-reflecting each person acquires an
immediate experience (or, as Jung would put it, '*felt* knowledge')
of the concepts 'I', 'me', 'myself'. Because of this human capacity
to reflect upon one's own thoughts, feelings and behaviour, the
'I' becomes an object to be evaluated. A person does a job; he looks
upon it and says, 'I did it; it is mine; it is good.' He values himself

highly and experiences the joy which accompanies this positive evaluation. If he judges, 'It is bad,' he depreciates himself and experiences the dejection which accompanies this negative evaluation.

In the process of growing up, children will experience many such situations in which they value or depreciate their own behaviour and achievements. They will experience, too, many situations in which their behaviour and achievements are valued or depreciated by adults, especially parents and teachers, who are essential to their happiness and security. In this way, children learn to evaluate themselves and each individual child acquires a 'self-concept', a conception of himself as worthy/unworthy. Because of his positive achievements and because of commendable judgments on these, his own as well as those of others, a child learns and retains a conscious concept of himself that is complimentary. Because of blows to his self-esteem suffered because of personal failures and the criticisms of others, this self-concept will have uncomplimentary aspects. However, he becomes especially attached to the complimentary aspect and it is this that he wishes to maintain.

There follows a brief consideration of the self-concept. This will be based first on the work of G. H. Mead (4), who relates the acquisition of a self-concept to an individual's social experiences, and secondly on a study by Staines (6a) of the importance of the teacher in the development of a child's self-concept. Here first is an illustration:

Susanne has long hair; it is thick, wavy and comely to look upon. She is proud of it, though for convenience's sake wears it in long plaits. The other girls in her class, too, have long hair, which they, too, wear in plaits. Susanne's parents, and Susanne with them, move to a place many miles away. Here girls have bobbed hair. Her new friends comment on Susanne's hair, sometimes obliquely, sometimes directly. The girls suggest it is 'old-fashioned'; and the boys, as they dart past her at play, flick the plaits and shout 'cats' tails'. It is the same hair, equally thick, equally wavy, equally comely, but no longer a source of pride to Susanne. She pleads with her mother to allow her to have it cut. Her mother, reluctant, begs, pleads, cajoles, but gives way in the end. Susanne is now delighted and proud of her bobbed hair. And her friends, triumphant in that their comments and teasings have succeeded in making the odd-one-out the similar-one-in, receive her amicably within their fold.

Mead speaks of the 'me' and the 'generalized other'. The 'me' is an attitude derived from social experience, from other people's speech and tones of speech, and from their gestures—a frown, a lift of the eyebrow, a shrug of the shoulders—each of which reflect their attitudes of approval or disapproval, attitudes which a child tends to absorb and make his own. To take some examples: the mother's smile or words of commendation 'good boy' (the acquired attitude, a 'me', one of approval towards the thing done), the mother's frown or words of disapprobation (the acquired attitude, a 'me', one of disapproval towards the thing done), the children's comments and teasings (Susanne's negative and changed attitude, or 'me', towards her long hair).

As Mead puts it, a child acquires lots of 'me's, each of which is a fragment, an aspect of himself derived from others. These 'me's integrate to form the 'generalized other', a child's total conception of himself, what other people expect of him and, therefore, what he expects of himself; what others think of him, and, therefore, what he thinks of himself. The 'I' is that which is aware of a 'me'; it is also an executor, that which responds. The 'I' of the child responds to the frown of the mother and is aware of the 'me' which the frown reflects. Mead says, 'The "I" gives a sense of freedom, of initiative. The situation is there for us to act in a self-conscious fashion' (4).[1]

Sometimes a parent, like Susanne's mother, may try to persuade a child to stand apart from his group. But this is difficult for a child to do, since his feeling of self-esteem or of self-disesteem is so closely related to the esteem or disesteem of his companions. For, using Mead's terminology, a child is more 'me' and 'generalized other' than he is 'I'.

A number of experimental studies have been undertaken on the influence of the teacher on the growth and maintenance of children's self-esteem. Staines classified teachers' comments on children's work, status and competency in this way:

Positive comment: 'Jack, you're good at this. Help me.'
Negative comment: 'You won't do for Queen. You're not tall enough.'
Ambivalent comment; one that has both a positive and negative component, or is positive for some children, and negative for

[1] page 246.

others: 'You're better at sums than spelling'; 'The red team puts the rest of the class to shame'; 'Ian, you are the only one whose writing is not good.'

Staines then observed four teachers—two Infant and two Primary—and found considerable differences between each pair, one of each tending to give more positive comments, the other more negative and ambivalent comments. He interviewed children and gave them a questionnaire to answer. The pupils' replies and comments led Staines to conclude that they took the teacher's ordinary run-of-the-day comments on their success or failure very much to heart, as they also took it to heart when one child was preferred to another, even on a task that may have seemed to the teacher unimportant.

The study also shows that the children of the teacher who, under experimental conditions, gave the greatest number of positive comments and who planned his work in such a way that they were given opportunities to choose, make comments and to feel competent about their work, tended to have a self-picture that was favourable—much more favourable than the self-picture of the pupils whose teacher gave many negative or ambivalent statements, and who did not plan his work so as to give the children a feeling of certainty and competence. Staines concluded that the self can be deliberately improved by suitable teaching methods, just as it can be impaired by unsuitable methods.

Davidson (6b) has experimentally demonstrated that the more positively a child judges his teachers' opinion of him, the more favourable is his perception of himself, the better his academic work, and the more co-operative his behaviour in class. Davidson's findings have been confirmed in separate studies by Brookover (6c).

Here a person's evaluation of himself and his desire to maintain it have been emphasized. But it should be added that a person tends to value very highly the objects and people to which he becomes attached. He will defend his own evaluation of his mother, father, brother, home town, country, profession and so on, against attempts by others to depreciate them. Indeed, these evaluations are closely related to his evaluation of himself. People tend to make *objects* part of their own personalities and this is expressed in the delights we experience when basking in the reflected achievement of others. If a brother does well, his sister experi-

ences an enhancement of her own feelings of worth because, as
she would put it, 'He is *my* brother.' If we know, have met, or are
related to a person of fame, if our town is significant because of
some singular sporting achievement, or because of its historic or
artistic associations, it is very hard in ordinary conversation to
avoid mentioning the fact, for the joys of reflected glory are great
indeed. The main point is that, in our day-to-day existence, our
estimate of ourselves varies not only with our own sense of
achievement but also with the value we place on people and objects
to which we are attached. The success or defeat of our country in
war, of our school or college in sport, of a son in an examination,
all contribute to our enhanced or reduced feelings of esteem.

So far, the dispositions (or dispositional tendencies) described
have been those which are directed towards the increasing welfare
of the object. But there are dispositions, too, which are directed
towards the destruction of objects or the denigration of a person
or a group of persons. Such dispositions may arise because attachment involves opposite reactions of hatred towards people, situations and beliefs which threaten the condition of the *objects* to
which we are positively attached. To love wholeheartedly often
means to hate equally wholeheartedly. These dispositions are
indicated by such terms as 'prejudice', 'antipathy', 'aversion', 'ani-
mosity', hatred'.

All this corresponds very much to McDougall's idea of sentiments. He defines a sentiment as 'an organized system of emotional dispositions centred around the idea of some object' (3),[1] and
as thus defined it implies the emotional involvement already
described. Sentiments, whether of love or hate, are relatively stable
dispositions: for example, attachments to home, family, country,
or the prejudices and antipathies developed in the process of
growing up. It is true that some sentiments are relinquished, such
as the attachment of children to the 'gang' and its favoured activities, to their childhood hobbies and so on. But at the same time
as children are growing up they are forming lasting, positive
sentiments around vocational, religious and national affiliations,
and these have their correlative negative dispositions. Far from
decaying, these dispositions are subject to the process of becoming
and tend with time to increase in strength and depth. Love and
hate are powerful forces in determining human behaviour.

[1] page 137.

The term sentiment is avoided by most present-day psychologists; they prefer the term attitude.[1] However, it is useful to use both terms, and to regard an attitude as a less enduring attachment and one that is more likely to change than is a sentiment.

This distinction is not a simple one, more especially because the word sentiment is now rarely used in everyday speech. When used at all, it usually refers only to positive attachments, or sentiments of love, and not to prejudices and antipathies, or sentiments of hate. Even so, the term has become debased, as when we say of a person that he is sentimental. Consequently, when referring to sentiments of love centring around the family or a person's profession we tend to use more neutral terms like 'attitude' or 'interest'. We say, 'He has a pleasing attitude towards his mother,' or 'He has an absorbing interest in his work as a teacher.' It would be preferable, following the distinctions made here, to say, 'He has a sentiment of love towards his mother/his teaching.' By contrast, 'attitude' implies a less personal, less stable involvement, so that an attitude is more prone to change than is a sentiment—as is the case, for example, with the attitude of the ordinary voter to a political party or a particular candidate in an election. Further, while both 'attitude' and 'interest' indicate involvement, neither term conveys the idea that the involvement is a warm one, as does McDougall's sentiment of love. Further consideration will be given in Chapter 7 to McDougall's use of sentiments, and especially of the 'self-regarding sentiment', to account for the particular form or organization that a personality will take.

The relationship between *objects* and personality is puzzling, because although the *objects* are separate from the person who is attached to them, yet he says they are *his*. In everyday speech, it is common to speak of *assimilating* knowledge, *possessing* objects, *being* a teacher, a shopkeeper, a dentist, implying that any of these may be an intrinsic part of the person. Perhaps it could be said that they are *his* in the sense that he experiences certain emotions, depending upon the 'condition'[2] of the *objects* concerned. He *fears* if his body is injured; he is *angry* if someone underestimates his abilities and skills; he is *sorry* if his friend has failed to obtain a job; he is *anxious* if a son or daughter is taking an important examina-

---

[1] Cattell (1) is a notable exception to this.

[2] By 'condition' is meant 'the well-being or lack of well-being', 'the safety or lack of safety'.

tion. The teacher, for example, is involved with his class. Good
work, good behaviour and he feels *satisfied:* bad work and bad
behaviour, especially during an inspection or before strangers, is
disconcerting. The teacher feels *anxious, angry, depressed.* 'They
have let *me* down.'

If a person becomes too attached, we speak of a 'possessive
attitude'. The following, from a novel by Steinbeck (5),[1] illustrates
the effects of a man's possessive attitude towards his one and only
beautiful young daughter on his behaviour and emotional experience:

'He (Shark) thought he read covetousness in every male face. Often
when he was working in the orchard he tortured himself by imagining
scenes wherein gipsies stole the little girl. A dozen times a day he
cautioned her against dangerous things; the heels of horses, the
highness of fences, the danger that lurked in gullies, and the absolute
suicide of crossing a road without carefully looking for approaching
motor-cars. Every neighbour, every pedlar, and, worst of all, every
stranger he looked upon as a possible kidnapper. When tramps were
reported in the Pastures of Heaven he never let the little girl out of his
sight. Picnickers wondered at Shark's ferocity in ordering them off
his land.'

In that a person strives to achieve goals to which he is attached,
he *hopes*, he feels *elated* at the prospect of success, *anxious* at the
prospect of failure. When he does fail to achieve desired goals,
he experiences *regret, remorse, despondency, despair.* Insofar as he
forms a disposition of love, he experiences feelings of tenderness,
joy or sorrow, pleasure or disappointment regarding the *objects* of
the disposition; insofar as he forms dispositions of hate, he experiences feelings of anger, jealousy, elation, depression.

Thus, personality development implies expansion—possession
of objects, close identification with some people, lack of identification with others, acquisition of many unique personal skills. In
this process, we experience a mixture of emotions, from the tenderness of love to the harshness of hate, from the joy of achievement to the pain of failure, from the warmth of human com-
panionship to the pain of loneliness.

In turning to the way in which all this relates to the child, a
few only of the psychological implications will be mentioned here

[1] page 30.

since more will be discussed later when the social and emotional
development of children is considered.

Obviously, the early attachments of a child to people (mother,
father, brothers, sisters, friends) and to places (home, playing-
field, street) are the very sources of his security. Members of a
family may bicker and fight one with another, but let someone
outside the family attack one of its members and all rally on the
side of the one who is attacked. Also, children early become attached to their possessions; these may be a source of comfort to
them, as, for example, the old rag doll—tattered and worn though
it is, it is treasured. Possessions, too, are a source of pride. Take, for
example, the child who brings a new set of coloured pencils to
school. His face beams with joy when he shows it to the teacher.
He feels a little catch in his throat, a little anxiety when the friend
sitting next to him asks for the loan of one. Hesitatingly he hands
it to him, but he watches with a side-glance as his friend uses it,
and then, to allay his anxieties, says, 'You won't press *too* hard,
will you?' He packs the pencils carefully away, goes out to the
playground, but comes back almost immediately to make sure he
has put them away. After play, he sits down, takes out the box,
smooths it gently, looks around the class with head high, smiles at
the teacher. The joys of ownership are delicious but sometimes
fraught with anxiety and pain; for example, when the little girl's
doll has been broken; when the boy who cherishes his brand new
bicycle watches with anguish as his sister wobbles during the ride
he had reluctantly to give her because their mother said, 'You
must not be selfish.'

When he knows the 'condition' of the *objects* to which the child
is attached, a teacher may be able to understand the child's
emotional reactions. John weeps: his fox terrier has died. Tommy
is angry and has just savagely attacked Jim: Jim called Tommy's
father a 'gaol-bird'. This last example is a simple illustration of the
desire to maintain the evaluation of a person with whom one is
ego-involved. Tommy wishes to maintain his high evaluation of
his father; in order psychologically to hurt him, Jim attempts to
destroy or diminish it. To the degree that he is 'ego-involved',
Tommy angrily resents this. Jim is no longer a friend of his.
Indeed, people generally accept that their friends must love what
they love and hate what they hate. As the saying goes, 'Love me,
love my dog;' to this could be added, 'Hate me, hate my dog.'

Turning to the dichotomy of (a) oneness with and (b) separateness from others spoken of earlier in this chapter: in some spheres of activity children demand to be like others, as when they desire to dress the same as other children, to have the same kind of satchel, the same kind of lunch box. Mothers sometimes become impatient when children are stubborn and awkward because the tie, the cut of coat, the length of dress is not *exactly* the same as those of the other children. At the same time, in some spheres children strive to be distinct and separate, to stand out from the group and to be significant within it. As I have written elsewhere, 'A good deal of children's behaviour can be interpreted as an attempt to gain such significance. Thus, within the classroom, children jostle among each other for positions of significance. This jostling for significance sometimes seems to adults petty and childish. They strive to be first, or last, in the line when they "fall in" from play. In either of these positions they feel significant; they do not scuffle to be in the middle of the line. They like to be singled out to do a job, and the pleased expression on a child's face as he takes a message around the school witnesses to the delight that this activity has for him. As for possession of objects, they seek the "best", the "biggest" pencil or the pencil which is different. If there are thirty-eight red pencils and two green ones, ownership of the latter gives significance, and they are sought after and struggled for. If there are thirty-eight green pencils and two red, ownership of one of the two red pencils gives significance and is, therefore, sought after' (2).[1]

Children's estimates of themselves are usually uncertain and so they seek greater certainty by frequent appeals to adults. Observe a family of children when they are together with their mother and father in a playing area with swings, see-saws, climbing bars and the like. Father is not often with them in this way because he is at his work, and so the children compete with each other to gain his attention and his approval of their daring acrobatic feats. 'Look at *me*, Daddy!' is repeated maybe a dozen times; the children are all in competition with each other. Or, again, watch a family together at the seaside when young children are making their first efforts to swim and note how their cries of, 'Watch me, Daddy, Mummy!' are continued until one parent verbally approves of the daring and progress implied in a kick of the legs and

[1] page 127.

flapping of arms. The dull, continuing ache to catch attention is most insistent.

REFERENCES

1 Cattell, R. B. *Personality*. McGraw-Hill, New York, 1950.
2 Gabriel, J. *An Analysis of the Emotional Problems of the Teacher in the Classroom*. Cheshire, Melbourne, 1957.
3 McDougall, W. *An Introduction to Social Psychology*. Methuen, London, 22nd edition, 1931.
4 Mead, G. H. *In* Strauss, A. (Ed.) *The Social Psychology of George Herbert Mead*. University of Chicago Press, Chicago, 1956.
5 Steinbeck, J. *Pastures of Heaven*. Quality Press, London, 1948.

BIBLIOGRAPHICAL NOTE
6 Hamachek, D. E. *The Self in Growth, Teaching and Learning*. Selected Readings. Prentice-Hall, Englewood Cliffs, 1965.

These readings provide a comprehensive collection of research studies and writings on the self-concept, with particular reference to the school and classroom. The following articles, to which reference has been made in the chapter, are reprinted in the book.
(a) Staines, J. W. 'The self-picture as a factor in the classroom.' pp. 404–23.
(b) Davidson, H., Long, H. 'Children's perception of their teachers' feelings towards them related to self-perception, school achievement and behaviour.' pp. 424–39.
(c) Brookover, W. B. *et al.* 'Self-concept of ability and school achievement.' pp. 477–85.

PART TWO

The Formation of Personality
and its Organization

CHAPTER FOUR

The Social Environment

BECAUSE the formation of personality is an individual process and the determinants best studied as they relate to each particular person, it is not easy to list in detail all the factors within the environment which play a part in its development. It could be argued that every person met, every object seen and every lived experience influence an individual in some small way. There are, of course, *significant* people, *significant* objects and *significant* events in every person's life, but it is difficult, for a number of reasons, to generalize and say that these particular people, objects, or events are decisively influential in all cases and at all times.

First, an event that is significant for one person's development may be relatively insignificant for the development of another. Many children pay school visits to art galleries, shipbuilding yards, law courts, but only one or two may be so influenced by the visit that they determine there and then to become artist, shipwright, or lawyer, and eventually achieve this ambition. Whereas for most people any experience is interesting and contributes a little towards their growth, for the few the same experience may play a significant part in deciding a whole way of life. The troupe of acrobats who pitched tents just outside St. Omer in France in 1829 made for the people of the town a pleasant diversion from the routines of everyday living. However, for six-year-old Jean François Gravelet (later to become Blondin, the famous tight-rope walker) the acrobats were more than entertainment; they were a source of inspiration and first stimulated his determination to become a tight-rope walker.

Second, an unfavourable circumstance or event may have a serious effect on one child's personality but a less serious effect on that of another. For example, we feel quite justified in concluding that a home in which a child is neglected and unloved is unfavourable. Yet, whereas for one child this circumstance is devastating to his happiness and to his feelings of security, another child may escape, to some extent, the unfavourable effects because he has an affectionate aunt and uncle whom he visits, or a sympathetic neighbour who partly compensates for the neglect and lack of affection within the home.

Third, the same person can influence two people in different ways. Two brothers may reflect in quite opposite ways on the influence their father had upon them. The elder son may say:

'My father was a conscientious man of high principles and high ideals. He was held in undoubted esteem in the neighbourhood where we lived, and we children admired him too. I think he was proud of his good name and pleased with the admiration his children showed him. I must have been about ten or so when I first consciously resolved to be like him, to watch him and mould myself according to him, and this resolve I repeated time and time again. I remain even now very aware of his good influence and of the ideals to which he inspired me.'

The younger son may say:

'My father was, I suppose, a good man in many ways. Yet, he was filled with pride and we children had to bolster up this pride by uncritically admiring him and giving him unquestioned obedience at all times. I feel that he loved himself far more than he loved us, for his goodwill towards us depended not only upon our continued admiration of him but also upon our being as perfect in thought, word and deed as his super-human standards dictated. I remember one time (I must have been about twelve or thirteen) playing with a group of boys from the "lower" part of the town who swore a good deal. I listened, fascinated by the ease with which the words came out. Suddenly, something snapped inside me. I was overcome with daring and experienced a dreadful freedom. I began swearing like the rest of them and felt tremendous exhilaration. A neighbour of ours passed, heard me and told my father who beat me severely and, in righteous anger, admonished me. But I felt then, as I do now, that he was angry not only because I had done wrong but also because he had lost prestige in the eyes of his neighbour because of me. From then on I hated him. His pride and the eager attempts of my brothers and sisters to bolster this pride nauseated me so that as I grew older, I moved away from him and from them.'

As Allport (1) has put it, 'The same fire which melts the butter hardens the egg.' This father was probably, like many of us, a mixture of idealism and conceit. The one son saw only the idealism which he accepted; the other son saw only the conceit and so rejected his father completely.

Because individuals do differ in the way they react to similar situations, any prepared list can be but a general guide and each time we study a person we must assess anew the significance of particular situations for him. Nevertheless, the major social factors which influence the formation of personality will be considered in a general way. In doing so, the following will be emphasized:

1   the kind of technology a society has, whether simple or complex;

2   the values, beliefs and purposes that adults within the society hold, illustrated by reference to the work of social anthropologists;

3   the complexity of our own culture in relation to 1 and 2.

An individual comes into a society which is technologically a going concern. It may be that a simple technology causes children less anxiety than a complicated one. Whereas in primitive societies a child can soon acquire skill to handle the simple tools used, and a comparatively young child can make a contribution to a community effort to collect or grow food, to build a house or to fish, in our society the size and complexity of its technological instruments (buses, trains, tractors) must be confusing and rather ominous for a child. It is interesting that our children implicitly determine to master this technological size and complexity. Small boys generally say that they are going to be train, bus, lorry or tractor drivers; their toy trains, buses, lorries and tractors help them in fantasy to manipulate these instruments and much of their play revolves around activities of this kind. But, unlike children in more primitive groups, they are not able to manipulate the real things until they have matured physically and mentally. Because our society is very complicated, a longer period of preparation is necessary, and so the years of compulsory education and the period of children's dependence on adults usually increase with the increasing technological complexity of a society.

An individual comes into a society which is also a going concern socially, consisting of people who have their characteristic ways of thinking, feeling and behaving. As Benedict puts it, 'A society can be seen as a group of people with specific problems, values and purposes, and the traditions, customs, rituals and institutions of a group are designed to fulfil these values and purposes' (4). Older members of a society try to cultivate in young people the interests and the needs which will enable these values to be accepted, these purposes to be fulfilled. It is within this social matrix that the individual's personality is formed.

Benedict goes on to say that the potentialities within human beings are so many and so varied that never can any one individual, or group of individuals, give expression to all possible kinds of behaviour within, as she puts it, 'this huge arc of human potentialities'. Therefore, individuals will tend to specialize and how they will specialize will depend upon the pressure put upon them by the members of the particular group to which they belong. Thus, in some societies people will be co-operative and peaceful, in others aggressive and warlike; in some societies they will be individualistic and expansive, in others conforming and modest. In short, behaviour can be understood in terms of the values and purposes which the people within a society have been taught to accept, and each society will have its ideal person who embodies the qualities valued by most members of the group.

She illustrates her point of view by a description of the contrasting ways of life or, to use her own phrase, the contrasting 'patterns of culture'[1] of the three primitive groups, the Zuni Indians of New Mexico, the Kwakiutl Indians of the north-west coast of America, and the Dobuans of New Guinea.

The Zuni people value sociability and individual modesty. The person they admire is the good mixer, the conversationalist who is dignified, affable and inoffensive. In behaviour he conforms with the group in deportment and dress and carries out his religious rituals in accordance with tribal custom. Individual initiative, attempts on the part of individuals to do better than others or to change the traditional customs and rituals, is punished by ostracism of the offending person for, as one of the chiefs told Benedict,

[1] The term 'culture' is not used to indicate only artistic pursuits, but means here the whole way of life of a given society, and includes the material culture (houses, clothes, manufactured products, etc.), the behaviour of individuals which can be directly observed, and the knowledge, attitudes and values shared by members of a society.

'An individualist may disturb the co-operative pattern and dis-organize the group.' Competition is absent; fields are cultivated co-operatively and the produce pooled in a common storehouse. Little weight is attached to the possession of material goods; if a man does acquire wealth, he gives it away at the festivals held during the winter. For a Zuni, the purpose of living is to cultivate one's field, to share its products with others, to take part in a complicated round of religious and tribal ceremonies. In short, the ideal life is a faithful following of traditional ways of thinking and behaving—no unpleasantness, no disturbing individualists to upset this ritualistic and peaceful way of life.

The Kwakiutl, on the other hand, extol the gaining of pres-tige, and the expansion of self that comes through acquiring prop-erty or titles of nobility. The tribe is divided into two classes, noblemen and commoners; the former regard the latter with contempt, encouraging their children to do likewise. However, it is not how much property you possess that gives prestige but how much property you give away. Thus, there is the custom of giving a feast (called a potlatch) at which a nobleman will show his superiority by distributing gifts. Those who receive gifts must, for their part, in return give potlatchs—and at them give away more than they received, or they will lose status and so suffer a severe blow to their self-esteem. Another way of beating a rival is to challenge him to a feast at which property is burned, the victor being he who puts the last piece of property on the fire.

Because they have very little property, commoners indulge in these customs in less spectacular form, but the accepted way of silencing an individual in an argument by giving away property is maintained. Benedict tells of two women having an argument on the street; a crowd gathers, and one woman goes into her house and brings out several pieces of silver which she throws to the crowd. The second woman is effectively silenced; she has lost the argument for she is quite unable to distribute a gift of equal value. As can be imagined, such a competitive culture imposes great strain on individuals within it. Murder is fairly common, as is suicide, and we can contrast this with the Zuni where murder is rare and suicide is unknown.

The Dobuan society tends to draw out man's potentialities for assertion and aggression, his tendency to be suspicious and malignant. The main institution by which the tribe is sub-divided is the *susu*, a word which literally means 'mother's milk' and which, when used for a group, means people who are of the same matrilineal descent. All people outside this group are regarded with suspicion and hostility. The aim of life is to steal, to cheat in a commercial transaction or, by magical means, to destroy the crops of anyone who is not within one's own *susu*. As Benedict puts it, 'The Dobuans put a premium upon ill will and treachery and make of them the recognized virtues of their society'(4).[1] Much anxiety is naturally generated in such an atmosphere of suspicion and hostility. Consequently, there is much competition in the use of magical formulas: malevolent formulas to injure another, benevolent formulas to prevent or neutralize the malevolence of others.

In summarizing these brief descriptions, we may say that the Zuni draw out from their people man's capacity to be peaceful and co-operative, the Kwakiutl man's capacity to be conceited and boastful, and the Dobuan man's capacity to be aggressive, suspicious and malignant.

By means of these contrasting illustrations Benedict makes her point well, namely that an individual's personality is the product of his culture.

Social anthropologists have been concerned to consider how this comes about. Their studies have shown that the personalities of adults tend to be reflected in the way they bring up their children. Take, for example, the routines of feeding and weaning a baby as carried out respectively by the Arapesh and the Mundugumor, two New Guinea groups studied by Mead (8). The Arapesh are, like the Zuni, a gentle, co-operative and peaceful people. During feeding, an Arapesh mother handles her baby gently, massaging her own breasts to make the flow of milk easier. It is a slow, leisurely process during which the mother laughs and plays with the baby. Provided the mother does not become pregnant, a child is allowed to suckle at the breast whenever he wishes and may not be weaned until he is three or four.

By contrast, the Mundugumor, a head-hunting tribe also of New Guinea, are an aggressive, warlike people like the Dobuans. The Mundugumor mother suckles her baby standing up so that the infant is tightly pinioned in her grasp. If the baby stops sucking, he is immediately placed back in his basket. Consequently, a baby adopts a 'definite purposive fighting attitude' holding on

[1] page 131.

tightly to the nipple and sucking vigorously, often choking in the process, to the extreme annoyance of the mother. As Mead puts it, 'There is none of the mother's dallying sensuous pleasure in feeding her child that occurs among the Arapesh'(8).[1] The baby is weaned within six months. To do this the mother pushes the child roughly away from her breasts, or she may smear them with a bitter sap.

The general attitude towards babies also differs within the two cultures. The Arapesh people value children. When they speak of rearing children they use the same word as they use for growing and tending yams, their staple diet. Bringing children up is an essential part of living and life would lose its significance for them were there no children to 'grow'. The Arapesh are easy and permissive; childhood is regarded as a time of carefree enjoyment. A child is not expected to be precocious and in advance of his years. Indeed, he is discouraged from being so. Amongst the Mundugumor, on the other hand, children are not welcomed and rearing them is not seen as an enjoyable activity or as one which gives pleasurable purpose to life. A mother tends to be resentful and irritable—particularly when a child is ill. For her, illness means that the child is making yet more trouble for her. Naturally enough, infant mortality is high because only the strongest can survive the rough treatment babies receive.

Each mother, Arapesh and Mundugumor, in bringing up her children reflects her own personality as shaped by the traditions and ways of behaving of the group to which she belongs.

It is too simple to suggest that ways of feeding or weaning are *the* causes of later adult manifestations of personality. The final shape that a personality will take will partly depend on whether the same pattern of tenderness or aggression, permissiveness or severity is continued as the child grows up. If it is continued, then the pattern will be reinforced in the child himself. In short, children go through common experiences to develop personalities which are similar to those of the adults who are important to them. In this way, the cultural pattern is perpetuated.[2]

According to the group to which they belong, so individuals will acquire specific ways of satisfying needs: a liking for certain

[1] page 195.
[2] The more precise mechanisms by which this comes about will be considered later (see Chapter 18) with special reference to our own culture.

kinds of food and certain ways of eating them, for certain ways of reacting to other people—to share the products of their fields (Zuni), to outdo a rival in a potlatch (Kwakiutl), to destroy another by magical incantation (Dobuan). In our own society individuals acquire general life purposes ('to get on', 'to acquire possessions', 'to acquire prestige', 'to serve others') and also more specific life purposes (to become carpenter, doctor, nurse, scientist, shop-keeper, soldier, teacher) by means of which they are able to fulfil one or more of these general purposes in their everyday life. But in order that the needs and purposes accepted by most members of a group can be carried out, the individuals in it must develop the personality traits[1] appropriate to this end. A group devoted to war-like pursuits seeks to develop aggressive, ascendant, belliger-ent individuals; one devoted to co-operative and peaceful pursuits seeks to develop affectionate, amiable, gentle individuals. A society placing great value on individual possession of property will seek to develop people who are acquisitive, thrifty, possessive.

Out of needs, purposes and traits will arise beliefs concerning the relationships between events. For example, around food will develop beliefs, magical or scientific, according to the group to which one belongs—that to eat a lion is to partake of its strength, to eat fish is to nourish one's brain, to eat vitamins is to guard one's general health. Beliefs arise also around general purposes—to obtain property or prestige or power will lead to personal happiness, to go to war is to appease the anger of the gods, to be gentle and unaggressive is to preserve the equilibrium, the balance of the universe (a belief of the Hopi Indians described below).

Further, out of needs, purposes and beliefs arise sentiments—of love for some things, of hatred of others. Certain kinds of food are preferred; others are disliked. We often associate a particular food with a particular national group, as, for example, German

[1] A trait is a disposition (dispositional tendency). Unlike a sentiment or an attitude it is not related to a specific *object* but denotes a prevalent tendency on the part of an individual to behave in a certain way. If we speak of an individual as affectionate we imply that he shows affection towards most things. In everyday speech we often use the term 'nature' to indicate the generality of a trait (he has a generous nature). Yet a trait, like a sentiment and attitude, is a dynamic and directive inner state of potential readiness to act in a particular way. This is implied when we say of the egotistical person that he seizes every opportunity to talk about himself, or of the aggressive child that he seems always to be looking for a fight.

sausages and lager beer, Italian spaghetti, Scots porridge. Often sub-groups have their distinctive dishes, as, for example, York-shire pudding, Banbury cake. Such foods do more than nourish the body; they represent close kinship with one's own people. In eating them, this close kinship is renewed, as when a group of expatriates meet to partake of their national dish. By the same token, individuals develop sentiments towards family and national groups and towards the purpose they fulfil. Those who fulfil the more important purposes of the group receive special esteem—the warrior or the scientist, the artist or the wise man.

As Lee has stressed (7), it may not be enough to explain human behaviour only in terms of satisfaction of needs, physical and psychological. For even the means by which these needs are satis-fied often acquire a significance all of their own. She illustrates this point of view with reference to the Hopi Indians living in north-east Arizona. Once a year the whole tribe sets out to gather salt. It is a long and somewhat arduous journey. But when a trader once offered to sell them salt at a reasonable price, they refused. Arduous as it is, the journey is part of their way of life and not to take it would upset for them the patterned cycle of the year's activity.

We often find similar resistance to change in our own society when, for example, a suggested change is the result of some new technological invention. A housewife may resist the idea of a washing machine. She has become accustomed to the rituals of the Monday wash-day. These rituals serve more than a practical pur-pose; they are part of her way of life and to upset them is to upset her. She will rationalize in all sorts of ways to avoid having a machine—machines do not clean thoroughly, they tear the clothes, they are dangerous.

Some psychologists would explain this in terms of habit. The Hopi and the housewife have acquired respectively the habit of journeying for salt, of washing with tub and board. But this is hardly enough. The activities have a dispositional source and are better called sentiments, or perhaps values.

To define a 'value' is difficult, but perhaps the following account may be acceptable. Values are means, among others, by which behaviour is regulated when several choices or courses of action are available to a person. Biological or psychological needs, even sentiments, leave a wide range within which to choose. But value implies more than just choice; it implies that certain standards have been accepted by an individual—'To do this is good, to do that is bad.' If a person does what he thinks he 'ought', he experiences a feeling of warm self-regard; if he does not, he will feel guilty, or 'uncomfortable' as we say in everyday conversation. For example, we speak of the '*code* of the thief', meaning that though his attitude towards stealing leaves him a wide choice of persons from whom to steal, he does not steal from his friends or from a person who has been very kind to him. McDougall implies much the same when he says that a value is an integral part of the self-regarding sentiment. To this we will return in a later chapter.

Values vary in the degree to which they are all-embracing. Religious, philosophic values or activities relating to a whole way of life are obviously more significant than the washing day or an annual expedition. This may be illustrated again with reference to the Hopi people. They depend on corn for food, but the planting, tending and harvesting of corn provide more than just nutrient satisfaction. They provide a way of life because it is around these activities that their daily and seasonal routine revolve. To become industrialized and buy corn would enable them to acquire more goods and more possessions, but it would destroy the pattern of living for them. The Hopi have, therefore, resisted the temptation to become absorbed into the more industrialized society of America. They value their own way of life too highly.

The values they hold are also reflected in their views on the nature of the universe. They believe that, within it, there is potentially a balance or equilibrium towards which all things contribute—men, animals, plants, the sun, moon and stars. All things are, therefore, interdependent and the equilibrium is attained when they work together for the mutual benefit. How do men help to achieve this balance? The answer for the Hopi is, 'By following the Hopi way.' This means being peaceful, co-operative, modest, protective of all life. Before they hunt (and they hunt only for food, never for the pleasure or joy of killing) and before they gather crops, they follow certain rites in order to propitiate the animal or plant people and to ask forgiveness, explaining that they kill only because of their great need (2). Such a total way of life, or such a total philosophy illustrates the all-embracing nature values can take.

Man is, too, a creature with imagination. He can conceive what might be, as well as perceive what is. This imaginative apperception of what might be is the source, among other things, of man's ideals. There is the *ideal* way of bringing up children, ploughing the fields, or making a boat, and, although human abilities are too defective to attain it, the imaginative ideal becomes a yardstick (somewhat imprecise it is true) by which to judge personalities and performances. This is what Jung meant when he said that ideals are signposts, never goals. Further, although all but a very few individuals are too frail and too imperfect to attain this ideal, we speak of the ideal person for a particular job, or of the ideal person in a more comprehensive sense as one who combines the ability, the traits, the sentiments and purposes which are important to the group.

So far the case for social determination of personality has been stated and illustrated. But to see individuals as merely passive products of their culture is to overstate the case. Each person has his idiosyncratic features and no two individuals respond to their culture in precisely the same way. How any one individual responds will depend on his intelligence, his imaginative capacity, and his inherited temperament (to be discussed in Chapter 6). Even in small tribal groups variations are seen and there will be individuals who deviate markedly from accepted tribal custom. Mead speaks of the difficulties which beset an aggressive Arapesh man in a society in which there is no place for the individualist, the innovator, or the strong leader, and no opportunity for initiative, or for the display of individual strength. If a man does express his aggression by attacking or killing another, he is not himself killed but subjected to a 'mute ostracism'. Violence is looked upon by others with shocked and amazed horror. Most of the Arapesh refuse to recognize the right to be violent and the aggressive individual usually ends up by living in isolation on the outskirts of his village.

Mead speaks, too, of non-aggressive men amongst the Mundugumor who form a deviant group and live peaceably by themselves fishing and cultivating the soil. They are subjected to the jeers and taunts of others because they have no skulls to prove their skill as head-hunters, and because fishing and cultivation are the work of women.

While the best way to show how group determination works

is by reference to small groups such as the Zuni, the Mundugumor or the Kwakiutl, it is well to remember that these groups are relatively homogeneous, with no sharp separation of people into sub-groups having differing purposes and values. Ours is a more complicated society, one divided into social classes whose values and purposes vary, and one in which ethical codes and religious beliefs vary even from individual to individual within the same group. There is a sense, too, in which it encourages all three of the modes of thinking, feeling and behaving which Benedict depicts. Our Christian heritage stresses the humility and affection of the Zuni people, while the competitive worlds of business and professional advancement, with their strivings for possessions, prestige and power, stress the ego-expansiveness of the Kwakiutl and the assertiveness of the Dobuans. This gives rise to basic contradictions within our culture which, Horney (6) suggests, are a significant source of neurotic conflict in many people.

Because of the diversity in ways of thinking, feeling and behaving, it is difficult to speak of a 'cultural pattern' applicable to the whole of our society. One could not as easily speak, for instance, of one pattern of child rearing as was done in the case of the Arapesh and Mundugumor. The complexity in our society is such that there are differences at any one period of time and, further, the ways of child rearing change from decade to decade.

At an international seminar on child care, three of the countries represented, France, the United Kingdom, and the United States, agreed on the impossibility of speaking of a typical pattern or of a typical French, English or American child. Besides differences within individual families, there are regional and social class differences. For example, Miss Fauvez-Boutonier of France stated that for the French child, a rural environment means more freedom and fewer prohibitions, and that toilet training is begun later and is less exacting. 'In the living-rooms of French farms, where from time to time the chickens deposit their little offerings, never mind where, the fact that the child does the same is not likely to bother anyone' (10).[1]

In deciding how to bring up their children, poorer French parents follow traditional routines and do as their mothers did; educated parents read the literature and attempt to follow the latest trends; others rely on personal advice given by authorities—

[1] page 19.

doctor, nurse, teacher. A similar pattern is followed in England and America.

Secondly, even apart from differences in child rearing arising from idiosyncratic differences between mothers at any given moment, there would appear to be fashions in child rearing which change from time to time. For instance, during the 1930's mothers in America were advised to follow a strict schedule, to wean 'with firmness' and to begin bowel training early 'and with great determination'. Between 1939 and 1945 there was a change, and mothers were advised to be more permissive, to breastfeed their babies and not to wean too early. Then, in the early 1950's, the advice given suggested a mean between the strict schedules of the first and the permissiveness of the second period (11).

Yet, despite diversity between sub-groups and basic conflicts within our culture, there may be agreement amongst most people in our society regarding specific purposes and values and in their conception of what constitutes the ideal person.

An attempt will be made to illustrate this by a brief reference to interesting work done by Charles Morris. He has formulated thirteen 'Paths of Life' which describe certain patterns of thoughts, purposes, values and ways of behaving, each path being distinct in its own specific way (9).[1] Certain of the paths are obviously based on one or other of three major modes of response, namely affection towards, assertion against, and withdrawal from people. Thus, one path stresses affection and sympathetic concern for others ('affection should be the main thing of life, affection that is free from all traces of the imposition of oneself upon others or of using others for one's own purpose'). Another stresses the manipulation of objects, outward energetic action and the excitement of control and of power ('a person must stress the need of constant activity—physical action, adventure, the realistic solution of specific problems as they appear, the improvement of techniques for controlling the world and society'). A third path stresses the contemplative life ('the rich internal world of ideals, of sensitive feelings, of reverie, of self-knowledge, is man's true home'); and a fourth, enjoyment ('the aim of life should not be to control the course of the world or society or the lives of others but to be open and receptive to things and persons, and to delight in them').

[1] pages 15–18.

One path combines all modes and is expressed much as follows: 'We should at various times and in various ways accept something from all other paths of life, but give to no one our exclusive allegiance. At one moment one of them is the more appropriate; at another moment another is the more appropriate. Life should contain affection, enjoyment, action and contemplation in about equal amounts. When any one is carried to extreme we lose something important for our life. So we must cultivate flexibility, admit diversity in ourselves, accept the tension which this diversity produces, find a place for detachment in the midst of affection, enjoyment and activity. The goal of life is found in the dynamic integration of affection, enjoyment, action and contemplation, and so in the dynamic interaction of the various paths of life. One should use all of them in building a life, and not one alone.'

Investigations carried out in America (9), New Zealand (3) and Australia (5), using Morris's original texts, indicate that this composite path is the most preferred in all three countries. Insofar as such a composite path is preferred, people will seek to develop in their children this balancing of numerous tendencies which is personified in the 'all-round' adaptable man, able to enjoy life and, as the occasion demands, to be sociable, or active, or contemplative.

REFERENCES

1   Allport, G. W. *Personality*. Constable, London, 1937.
2   Beaglehole, E. *The Hopi Indians*. Paper read to British Psychological Society, London, 1949. Unpublished.
3   Beaglehole, E. *Paths of Life* (survey study). Victoria University College, Wellington, 1951. Unpublished.
4   Benedict, R. *Patterns of Culture*. Routledge & Kegan Paul, London, 1934.
5   Gabriel, J. *Paths of Life* (survey study). University of New England, Armidale, 1957. Unpublished.
6   Horney, K. *The Neurotic Personality of Our Time*. Norton, New York, 1937.
7   Lee, D. 'Are basic needs ultimate?' *In* Kluckhohn, C., Murray, H. A. *Personality in Nature, Society and Culture*. Knopf, New York, 1959.
8   Mead, M. 'Sex and temperament in three savage societies.' *In From th South Seas*. Morrow, New York, 1939.
9   Morris, C. *Varieties of Human Value*. University of Chicago Press, Chicagc 1956.
10 Soddy, K. *Mental Health and Infant Development*. Routledge & Kegan Pat London, 1955.
11 Wolfenstein, M. 'Trends in infant care.' *American Journal of Orthopsychiat* 1953, **23**, pp. 120–30.

CHAPTER FIVE

Parents and Teachers

PARENTS AND THEIR CHILDREN

To be a parent is to experience all the feelings, the ambivalences, of 'my' and 'mine' described in Chapter 3. As parents, we are attached to our children; they are ours. We become anxious about their physical safety, the way they behave and their achievements. We love them for their own sakes, yet we want them to be a credit to us. When her child is criticized by a neighbour or teacher, a mother is perturbed. If she feels the criticism is unjust, she becomes indignant and rushes to her child's defence. If she feels it may be just, she puts pressure on the child to change his behaviour, or to work harder to achieve better results.

Sometimes a mother may notice that the children's grandparents are more relaxed, affectionate and indulgent than she is herself. She may comment, 'Mother and Father spoil them.' Such a comment contains a note both of envy and fear; envy because of the continuing sense of responsibility she feels for the children and for their good behaviour (a responsibility the grandparents do not feel to nearly the same extent) which prevents her from relaxing control and from being indulgent and affectionate; fear because she feels that the grandparents' 'spoiling' may upset the control she imposes.

The main responsibilities of parents to their children may be summarized as follows, and the way parents fulfil these responsibilities may be expressed at one of the extremes or somewhere between the extremes suggested by the terms in the brackets:

to provide food, clothes, shelter, toys (over-indulgent/ neglectful);
to give affection (over-affectionate/rejecting);
to protect—from physical and psychological harm (over-protective/indifferent);

to encourage the development of skills (over-demanding/
unconcerned);
to control (authoritarian/over-permissive).

It is proposed now to show the varying ways in which parents
carry out these responsibilities and what, according to the research findings, their differing effects on children's personalities
are. Many sources will be drawn upon, but more especially the
work of Baldwin (4, 5) and of Schaefer (15, 16), both of whom
have rated parents on or between such extremes as those given
above.

Over-possessive parents

Possessive parents combine over-affection with the tendency to
over-protect and, maybe, to over-indulge their children. They
become *too* involved and there is a suggestion that one parent, if
not both, is using the children to compensate for some deficiency,
for some felt deprivation, or for a past loss, as may be the case with
a widow and her son, for example. Studies have shown that
possessive parents, more often than chance would allow, have
had some such experience as the following: the baby came after
many years during which time it seemed that they would never
have one; as a baby the child suffered an illness or defect and for
some time there were doubts whether or not it would survive;
often they have only one child. Such circumstances as these make
a child more precious and parents so anxious for his welfare and
his safety that they *over*-protect him. Many of these parents had
an unhappy childhood and, in reflecting upon this, say that they
had been deprived of parental affection or not been given the
opportunity to develop because of household and family responsibilities imposed upon them too early. In their determination that
the same would not happen to their own children, they become
over-affectionate or over-indulgent (10).

Steinbeck's Shark (see page 49) illustrates a typically possessive
parent. His daughter's beauty and her femininity contrast with the
drab toughness of his own life. She affords him an opportunity to
cherish, to express tenderness, to be gentle—to demonstrate
qualities which at other times he has severely suppressed. Besides,
she is a source of great pride to him.

Parents may not be consciously aware of this fierce involvement, but they do reveal it by excessive fondling and a general
anxiety about the child's safety that prevents them from allowing
him to be independent, to explore alone, to adventure with other
children. Often the parent will seek confirmation, 'Do you still
love Mummy?', or imply a reproach, 'I don't think you love
Mummy as much as you used to.' The demand for more affection
than he is able to give confuses a child and the reproach may
cause a depressive feeling of guilt.

Children of possessive parents are generally apprehensive, as if
the world were a dangerous place. In the Nursery School they
are afraid to abandon themselves to free and expansive bodily
activity which involves the use of large muscles, as in swinging
and in climbing ropes and frames. On the average they show less
originality and less desire to explore new situations and new
places (2, 3). This is understandable, for to be original and to explore means to move into the unknown; to be freely active
physically means taking risks. The anxiety which these children
have acquired from their parents and the confusion they feel make
them unable to do this.

In Primary School, children of over-protective parents tend to
be well-behaved and to be prodigious readers, but they find
difficulty in making friends and in participating in regular social
activities with other children. This behaviour at school often contrasts with behaviour at home, where the child may have tantrums and be disobedient, impudent and demanding (10). Because he is so good at school, his teacher, if she hears about this,
is surprised and puzzled by the inconsistency which the child
shows. The misbehaviour at home may perhaps be explained as
an attempt on the child's part to free himself from the subtly
confining effect of his parents' over-protection. On the other
hand, the school provides contact with adults which does not
constrict him in this way and so he feels less anxious, and is therefore happy to conform.

Rejecting parents

Not only do these parents reject their children, but they show, too,
a general indifference to their children's safety, and a lack of real
concern for their personal and social development. In this sense,

they are quite the reverse of over-possessive parents. They may also neglect their children physically. But the extent to which they do so will vary, according to the particular economic and social circumstances of the parent.

A wealthy mother may employ a nurse and dutifully visit the nursery at breakfast and at bed-time. When the child asks for a kiss the mother says, pointing to her cheek, 'Just a peck there, or you will smudge Mummy's lipstick.' A working mother, with academic or vocational aspirations, may do much the same.

Sometimes a baby may arrive at an inopportune time, causing a conflict between a mother's desires both to look after her child and to fulfil other duties. For example, a couple take on a 'one-man' general store with house at the back. They are ambitious to develop the business, and then along comes a baby. He is accepted as inevitable, but a strict routine is established whereby his coming does not interfere with the business of the store. The mother is thus able to continue to serve customers and to supervise the store when her husband is out delivering orders or collecting fresh stocks. The child is cared for in an efficient though distant way. Because the mother has only limited time to devote to him, he lacks warm contact and the personal encouragement to develop his maturing skills, such as walking, talking, the manipulation of toys.

Much the same may happen in a very poor home; here, a parent may not establish any routine of child care, and the child may be physically as well as emotionally neglected.

Children of rejecting parents show characteristics similar to those who are brought up in an institution where the staff is too small to give individual and personal care and encouragement (4). Thus, the children tend to be retarded in the development of their bodily, language and social skills, and often show an inordinate desire for affection and approval. In the Nursery School they are less physically active, sometimes clinging to the teacher and refusing to leave her. They often sit and do nothing, and are less curious about the many activities going on around them. When they do start an activity of their own, they lack the tenacity to continue at the task for any appreciable length of time (3). These findings are understandable. Because these children receive little affection, they are hungry for it. Further, as children mature and begin to acquire the rudiments of many simple skills, they need the individual encouragement which a mother can give. Without this, progress is slow and there is no stimulus to persist.

In school, the lack of persistence may continue and the teacher may speak of 'poor work habits'. On the other hand, a child may be so eager to gain the teacher's affection and so sensitive to any loss of the teacher's good-will that he is a well-behaved pupil who works well. But he is somewhat insecure which makes him timid when at play with his companions.

Authoritarian parents

Parents who are authoritarian combine over-control with lack of warm affection. The control may be obtained through moral precepts with little or no physical punishment. An extreme approach of this sort may be based upon religious convictions of a fundamentalist kind—that a child is born depraved and that complete obedience and submission is necessary if the child is to be kept from sin and evil. Such attitudes are relatively rare in modern times. They were, however, prevalent during the eighteenth and nineteenth centuries, as Sundley (18) has illustrated by drawing upon original early nineteenth-century sources, including writings on child-rearing practices in parent and family magazines, and medical and religious books.

The moral precepts may not necessarily be so based, and other authoritarian parents, themselves convinced of the value of obedience, orderliness and control, seek to imbue their children with similar virtues. They adopt a philosophy of strict upbringing involving mandatory routines and unquestioning obedience which they may justify as a determination not to spoil their children. Often they are themselves over-controlled and their control of their children is a reflection of this. A mother, for example, has deeply repressed her emotions—feelings of affection, tenderness, joy, sorrow—and, having done so, interprets display of such emotions (or indeed, any impulsive, spontaneous expression) as weakness. She appears a little hard, tight-lipped, rigid. Not to control oneself is a weakness. Not to control one's children is also a weakness. She may register a certain scorn for the over-permissive mother across the street who looks somewhat pathetic and bewildered as her children 'run rings' around her.

Sears found that such a mother imposes high standards in table manners, care of household furniture, neatness (not getting dirty), tidiness (not leaving clothes or books lying around), orderly and quiet behaviour, and that she expresses little warmth towards the children, her husband or towards herself. The standards she imposes on them she also imposes on herself. She is particularly intolerant of any sex play or of any display of aggression by her children (17). She may sometimes use physical punishment but, with her kind of personality, this is rarely necessary. She looks and that is all.

There are other forms of control, such as by excessive physical punishment. In this case, parents are cold, hostile and punitive, and they make no attempt to invoke moral judgments. Again, authoritarian parents may not be as consistent, either in a moral or punitive way, as is implied in the foregoing descriptions. The authoritarianism may then be expressed as continuous nagging with an occasional resort to physical punishment.

There are two main effects on children of authoritarian parents: where control is predominantly by moral precept, the child becomes socially timid and non-assertive; when it is imposed by means of severe physical punishment, the child is the opposite— socially outgoing and aggressive.

In the Nursery School, children of parents whose chief mode of control is through moral precepts are less curious, explore and play less and are less sociable than the average child (2). The overcontrol and the demands for absolute obedience seem to suppress children's spontaneity, originality, creativity, and the growth of social skills. The parents are so concerned with conformity that all else is sacrificed to this end. At school, these children are generally obedient and submissive, polite and dependable, but somewhat inhibited and unable, for example, to be expansive in their play, to answer up in class. They tend to be somewhat withdrawn from other children (10, 19).

Such behaviour may arise because the predominance of moral precepts, understandable only to an adult, creates a universe which a child cannot comprehend, and he is confused and anxious because of this. This over-control and the resulting anxious confusion seem to impair the development of initiative, independence and the ability to hold his own with his companions.

When the environment is unequivocally cold, hostile and punitive, a child tends to be other than obedient, submissive, polite and so on; at Nursery School he tends to be aggressive, to have frequent temper tantrums, and to be a little rebel, refusing to accept the restrictions necessary in such a social environment (4). At school age he is disobedient, unruly, coldly aggressive and sadistic towards his companions. He may use dictatorial methods to control and dominate other children (7). This contrasts with his behaviour at home where he is generally submissive and subdued. Perhaps this inconsistency in his behaviour can be understood in terms of the following comparison: it is well known that a class of children who have had a very strict authoritarian teacher for a long time become quite out of hand immediately they have a new and permissive teacher. Similarly, a child of punitive authoritarian parents is unable to adapt to the atmosphere at school which, relative to that at home, is benign and permissive.

In that he is without warm affection, the authoritarian parent is like the rejecting parent. One could, therefore, following Baldwin, describe both as 'rejecting' parents, the one, as he says, 'passively rejecting' and the other 'actively rejecting' (4, 5). For both, a child interferes with an established way of life: in the examples given, a mother's social or professional aspirations, work in the store, a noiselessly quiet existence, a rigid set of principles. In a very poor home a child may be resented because he increases a poverty that is already crippling.

Over-permissive parents

These parents allow a child to do more or less exactly as he wishes. Usually, they are over-indulgent so that the child is given far more possessions than he reasonably needs. The mother may appear indifferent about the child's safety because she does not stop him from behaving in an uncontrolled way—throwing stones, swinging a bat, speeding on a tricycle, with possible danger to himself and others. But the child is allowed to do these things not because the mother is unconcerned (such a mother may be very anxious about his safety) but because she is unable to assert herself, to make a stand and say, 'No!' Occasionally, a mother may for a moment realize, and then over-compensate for, this inability. To the surprise, consternation and confusion of the child, she suddenly gives vent to an outburst of scolding and screaming because of his continued rowdy and uncontrolled behaviour.

It is sometimes difficult to distinguish between the over-permissive and the over-possessive parent. Both tend to be indulgent and unassertive. But there is a difference. The over-possessive parent is anxious and her anxiety causes her to be hyper-sensitive about, and to fear, overt assertion: that is, physically punishing or admonishing her child (though such a mother may use more subtle forms of control, by demanding affection, by a pained and silent admonishment, or by saying, 'How could you do this and hurt Mummy so?'). The main problem which the over-permissive parent experiences in bringing up her children is this inability to assert herself. It causes her to feel personally inadequate in coping with the many difficult situations which inevitably arise with children; and the uncertainty she feels may cause her many moments of anxiety.

This uncertainty is reflected in the children. They tend, for example, to be unstable and to show swings of mood and of behaviour—from confidence to lack of confidence, from independence to dependence, from control to lack of control, from friendliness and sociability to hostility and aggression (10). In short, children of over-permissive parents present the picture of the typically 'spoilt' child—disobedient, rebellious, given to frequent temper tantrums, excessive in their demands on other people, domineering over other children (19). They misbehave in these ways partly because they have no external control to protect them from their own impulsiveness. Such behaviour may also be an implicit plea to their parents to make a stand, not to give way to their every whim, and so to set limits to what they, the children, are allowed to do.

These children may show the same kind of inconsistency as do the children of possessive parents, being model children at school and terrors at home. The reason for this could be that the school, in contrast to the home, provides an ordered and controlled environment which makes such children feel less anxious. This is then reflected in more stable behaviour.

Democratic parents

The nearer parents approach to a mean between the extremes of which we have spoken, the nearer they approach to the democratic parent. Baldwin (4, 5) makes a distinction between the cold democratic and the warm democratic parent. Cold democratic parents approach a mean between all extremes except that they do not express warm affection; they are direct, rational, un-emotional. The child is given reasons why he should do this and should not do that; if he is in the way, he is told quite dispassion-ately that this concerns adults only and is of no interest or impor-tance to him. He is given freedom to express his own ideas; he is given materials and is encouraged to develop his maturing skills. But about it all there is a lack of warmth, a scientific detachment from the child. He is not cuddled when he comes crying to his mother because he has been hurt. Instead, the wound is attended to in a precise, medically prescribed way and that's the end of the matter. And there is no 'nonsense' about Santa Claus. Such parents suppress expression of spontaneous affection. Behaviour is controlled and rational. There is a 'taboo on tenderness'.[1]

Such parents may show over-concern with the child's progress and attempt to accelerate this. In the pre-school years the child may be given special puzzle-type toys, or problem situations may be devised, such as placing a treasured object in an unusual place and getting him to find it. He is encouraged to do things not usual for a very young child, such as a little shopping in the local store, answering the telephone, receiving and taking mes-sages (4). This persistent encouragement of his independence and mastery usually continues during the school years and parents may have high aspirations for their child and will watch his progress with concern and interest, assessing this progress relative to the rest of his classmates. In this way, they imbue the child with a sense of the importance of scholastic achievement (14, 20).

The warm democratic parent has many of the characteristics of the cold democratic parent—giving the child freedom to express his own ideas; materials, opportunities and encourage-ment to develop skills. But these parents are warm. They are able to be tender or sympathetic as occasion demands, and to be affectionate without that excess of fondling which confuses and embarrasses a child. They are able to view their children object-ively, to assess their good and not-so-good qualities. With an admonition or humorous reminder a mother will convey to one of her children that she knows he's up to some tricks to score one over his brother. There is a balancing of extremes—for the

[1] To be referred to later: see Chapter 10, page 187–8.

very young child, chances to explore, yet the realization that an eye must be kept on possible hazards; for older children, freedom of choice wherever possible, yet the realization that they need help, support and advice on many issues that are important to them. Such parents are not obsessed with their children's progress, although they are happy to have them succeed and encourage them to do so.

It is difficult to review the results of investigations of warm and cold democratic parents because most investigators speak of the democratic home without making the distinction made by Baldwin. However, from the descriptions they give and the assessments they make, it would seem that when these writers speak of the democratic home they are including the idea of warmth. It is the effect of such a home that will be considered in what immediately follows.

Radke (12) presents a rather idealized picture of the behaviour of children of democratic parents in the nursery and kindergarten. She speaks of them as being emotionally stable, popular, sensitive to the opinions of others and less quarrelsome than other children. Baldwin (4) does not report such ideal social relations and finds that these children are not particularly sociable although he does find them to be intellectually curious, original, constructive and able to plan their own activities. In other words, he finds that their social development is not so advanced as their intellectual development. This is understandable. At home they have been encouraged to develop maturing skills, but, because the home is 'warm and cosy', the child finds the many children, the bustle and noise of the Nursery School, hard to take. He is content, therefore, to make use of the toys and apparatus available and to explore and to play alone. Such behaviour should not be interpreted as neurotic withdrawal; the child is happy and actively busy.

At school, children of democratic parents are independent, responsible and co-operative (1). Baldwin himself says that the picture presented above is now different. The democratic group are sociable, not in a dominant, but in a good-natured way. They are often precocious and able to converse with grown-ups on a surprisingly adult level.

Children of cold democratic parents show many similar characteristics. In the Nursery School they are active, curious, original, but socially uninhibited and aggressive, exuberant in an extraverted kind of way, always ready to join in a social activity and more than able to look after themselves in competition for toys and for the notice of the teacher (4). At school they are also socially active, prepared to take part in competitive games and in competitive strivings within the classroom. They show the same precociousness when conversing with adults as do the children of warm democratic parents. Because of the continued pressure put on them for high achievement and independence, these children 'excel in planning ability and performance' (6).[1] This planning ability may be seen in their play, for here we may have the 'bossy' child who tells all the others what to do.

Their determination to excel may become a compulsive 'search for glory', such as Horney describes (9)[2], and be accompanied by a vindictive drive to triumph over other children.

So far it has been assumed that both parents are, or at least the parent who plays the dominant part in bringing up the child, is possessive or authoritarian and so on. But it is important to look for a moment at the effect on boys and girls of the respective disciplinary roles of mother and father. It would appear that a mother who is extremely dominating—strict, cold, punitive— has a detrimental influence on a boy. To be dominated and controlled by a woman, even his mother, is such an indignity for him that he develops feelings of dejection and inferiority, and in the presence of his companions, he feels ashamed. Further, physical punishment by the mother paralyses a boy's powers of assertion. He 'swallows' ('introjects', as Freud would say) the aggression he feels towards her and is unable to displace it on to others (7, 8). Consequently, he is unable to assert himself even in a legitimate way, as in standing up for himself while at play with his companions.

Similarly treated, a daughter tends to become like her mother, somewhat hard and lacking tenderness, suggesting that such a mother is not an appropriate model for the development of feminine behaviour in a daughter (13).

When it is the father who is very strict, cold and punitive, the son does not introject the aggression he feels but gets rid of it on others ('displaces' it, as Freud would say). He behaves in a manner generally characteristic of children of cold, authoritarian parents

[1] page 82.   [2] Chapter 1.

which has already been described, being aggressive and using physical force in getting his own way with his companions. He may become the dominating leader of a 'gang', but, if he has not the qualities of leadership necessary for this, he becomes instead a typical bully and takes it out on younger children. His aggressive behaviour, especially if he is the leader of a 'gang', may become delinquent.

The effect is somewhat the same on a daughter, who also tends to become hard and aggressive. She may, for example, become the leader of a group of children who make scapegoats of weaker children (7, 8).

By contrast, a father who is warm and companionable yet firm, and who imposes discipline only if necessary, is likely to have sons who are self-confident, positively assertive, use little physical force, and are able to make friends and to accept such frustrating situations as inevitably occur. Hoffman (8) sums up the research findings in this way: 'It would appear that a mother's love makes a boy feel warm and cosy, but a father's love equips him to face the world.'[1] The daughters of such fathers are also confident, sociable, able to assert themselves in a positive way.

All this suggests that while each parent needs to combine both warmth and control, it is more appropriate in our own culture for the mother to be the main source of warmth and affection, and for the father to be the main source of control. Thereby each parent provides an appropriate model which accords with the accepted views of most members of our society on what is a predominantly feminine and what is a predominantly masculine role.

In concluding this study of parents and their children, it will be useful to look for a moment at control through the consistent use of physical punishment, since effects here are somewhat complex and confusing (one is not thinking of the occasional slap). As has been seen, physical punishment can increase a child's aggressiveness: the more severe it is, the more aggressive he becomes, and when it is coldly punitive, the child will tend to become viciously aggressive and sadistic. On the other hand, overpermissiveness may also lead to aggressive behaviour—that of the spoilt child—although here the aggression is more impulsive,

[1] page 103.

as in a temper tantrum. The answer to this apparent paradox probably lies in the fact that neither environment allows inner controls to develop as they do in an environment combining reasonable restraints with warm affection.

When outer control is itself aggressive, an eye is taken for an eye, a tooth for a tooth, and parents provide a cold, aggressive model for the child to follow. He does not then generate feelings of guilt and therefore inner controls are not developed. In short, severe physical punishment leaves him free to be aggressive, his only fear being of the outer control, of being caught and punished.

On the other hand, the over-permissive parent provides no external control over aggressive tendencies, despite the fact that anger is a powerful emotion and the urge to be aggressive hard for a child to restrain. Further, there are no inner controls because, to develop, these must be preceded by reasonable external controls. Consequently, over-permissiveness again leaves a child free to be aggressive. In short, in the over-permissive environment the absence of external controls hinders the development of inner ones; in the punitive environment it is the lack of warmth and the severity and quality of the restraint that hinders their development.

It may be well at this stage to pause and utter a word of caution. Parent-child relationships are complex and it has not yet been found possible experimentally to isolate all the nuances within the kinds and degrees of affection shown, control exercised, demands made, and so on. It is only the broad categories that have been described. The danger is that, in doing this, an impression may be given that the complex is, after all, simple. This would be erroneous. The complexity remains. Thus, not all parents by any means 'fit' into the categories described above. Although differing from the more detailed combinations suggested by Baldwin (4, 5), these categories are partly based on his findings. And even using his more detailed combinations, he was unable to classify 25 per cent of the parents whom he studied.

Following an earlier inquiry (11a), the Newsons made a detailed study (11b) of what actually happens between four-year-old children and their mothers. The Newsons studied seven hundred mothers and children who lived in an English urban

environment, and their results demonstrate most clearly the
complexity of mother-child relationships and the difficulty of
classifying parents. The actual number of occasions which led the
mothers to take issue with their children were numerous: meal-
times and eating, sex play and physical modesty, jumping on beds
or disarranging furniture, uncleanliness, untidiness, and so on.
But the importance the mothers attached to these issues varied
considerably.

Most parents demanded obedience, but in differing ways.
For example, one mother, corresponding more nearly to our
cold democratic parent, demanded the independence of her
child; she expected him to dress himself, to run errands, to keep
himself occupied independently of her, and to stand up for
himself. Another mother, corresponding more to our morally
authoritarian parent, demanded controlled behaviour; she expected her child to stand or sit perfectly still while she washed
or dressed him, to play in a quiet orderly way, stay in the
garden, and come indoors when neighbouring children began
quarrelling.

Some mothers were both permissive and authoritarian,
according to the issue involved. To take two examples: one of the
mothers of the study allowed her children to play messily with
paint, earth or water, and to make a noise; she ignored genital
play, and satisfied her children's curiosity about where babies
come from. Yet this same mother said, 'We do not have many
rules, but one is that you do *as* you're told, *when* you're told and
how you're told.' Another parent allowed her child a dummy and
showed considerable tenderness, cuddling the child to sleep each
night; yet she would not allow him to jump on the bed, smacked
him for touching his genitals, and insisted that 'babies come from
the sweet shop'.

Further, while the effects of the behaviour and attitudes of
parents on their children are, in general, much as has been
indicated in the course of this chapter, the investigations also
show that there are exceptions. A particular child may or may not
respond in one of the various ways described and summarized
immediately below, depending upon other social circumstances[1]
and upon his particular temperament.[2] It would be unfortunate
if a teacher over-simplified the position and interpreted the

[1] See Chapter 4.   [2] See Chapter 6.

results in an absolute sense—for example, in thinking about a particular child, reasoned as follows: 'He's nasty, aggressive and a bully in school, and must have authoritarian parents.' In many cases such a judgment will be found to be true. But human beings are generally far too complex to fit within the simple formula 'one cause, one effect' and it is necessary to beware of making snap judgments.

Despite this, certain broad principles are suggested, namely:

Extreme attitudes on the part of parents tend to result in extreme behaviour of some kind in their children.

A balancing of extremes tends to produce a balanced child.

In some respects children's personalities are a reflection of the personalities of their parents. The following summary of what has already been said illustrates this:

Anxious and apprehensive	— over-possessive parents and their children.
Unstable	— over-permissive parents and their children.
Over-controlled	— morally authoritarian parents and their children.
Aggressively cruel	— punitive authoritarian parents and their children.
Drivingly ambitious	— cold democratic parents and their children.
Stable, balanced	— warm democratic parents and their children.

From the point of view of a child's 'creative becoming', the most beneficial ingredients of child care are freedom (to enable him happily to explore or to adventure); warmth, shared relationships with, and genuine affection of, a trusted adult (to give security); encouragement (to stimulate the development of maturing skills). These broad principles are very much in accord with the commonsense judgments we make from our everyday observations of children and their parents.

TEACHERS AND THE CHILDREN THEY TEACH

Because teachers vary considerably both in their attitudes towards children and in the ways they teach, it is not possible to speak in blanket fashion about 'the influence of the teacher'. In order to comprehend the complexity of the situation, it is valuable to study, as has been done in the case of parents, some prevalent attitudes and ways of teaching and how children respond to them.

The term 'classroom climate' has often been used to describe classes at work. It means much the same as do the terms 'atmosphere', 'morale', 'emotional tone', and refers to the complex pupil-teacher pupil-pupil relationships, classroom activities and the ways they are carried out, and the attitudes of teacher and pupils towards these. It is the teacher who is most crucial in determining the 'climate' of the classroom. Not only does the 'climate' a particular teacher engenders remain much the same during any one school year or from year to year, so that a change of class within the same school does not radically change his mode of approach, but also a change of teacher will change the behaviour of children very considerably, especially when they move from a very dominant to a very permissive teacher or vice versa (23).

Three main 'classroom climates' will now be described and, following Lewin (28), will be called respectively authoritarian, laissez-faire, democratic.[1]

An authoritarian climate

The teacher is a strict disciplinarian. He gives orders and instructions in a decisive manner, implying that they must be obeyed or followed without question. When it is necessary to do so, he reprimands so sharply that the offending pupil literally jumps to order. Lesson procedures and classroom organization are carefully planned, ordered routines. In learning a new skill, all pupils proceed step by step according to the preconceived plans of the teacher. The children sit behind one another in very definite rows and there is only the minimum of movement. Exercise books are neat; rulers have been used to draw margins exactly one inch wide and to underline the dates and headings. The work in the books is formal; there are numerous English exercises; compositions are short and neatly written, but their contents tend to be somewhat stereotyped and unoriginal. Neatly arranged

[1] I would like to thank Professor W. F. Connell, Editor, for permission to reproduce in this chapter some material contained in an article published in the *Australian Journal of Education* (27).

on the wall are pictures, some specimens of the children's written work and some of the children's drawings. In these drawings, much detail has been accurately reproduced. There is a hushed silence that strikes one as being a little unnatural (21, 30, 31, 33).

A laissez-faire climate

In this climate there are no ordered routines; children are working from different parts of the same book, some at the beginning and some at the end of the progressive steps in a learning skill. The exercise books are untidy, lines are not drawn or are drawn free-hand, the dates may or may not have been inserted and there are margins on some pages but not on others. The compositions are long and formless, full stops and commas are rare. When we read them, we find many fantastic stories about voyages into space, chasing thieves, catching spies and going on commando raids. Sometimes, amidst all this and the untidy writing and the blots, we read an imaginative tale, an insightful comment, a sensitive description that intrigues us because of its originality. The drawings on the wall hang untidily, some by just one corner; there are numerous aeroplanes, space ships, battleships, bombers and the like, but there are one or two less prosaic drawings—of people at work, of a child at play. These please us because they appear to be spontaneous and to relate to some emotional experience in the young artists' lives. The classroom is noisy; children are walking around, some aimlessly. Each child has been allocated his place in a group and each group has been assigned a particular space within the classroom which they refer to as 'home'. But like most children, they do not seem to relish being at home very often. Some children are fooling around a bit. When we first enter the classroom, we cannot see the young teacher. Then he greets us on tiptoe from the midst of a group of boys to whom he is explaining something.

A democratic climate

It is not easy to describe a democratic climate; how the classroom will appear depends upon the particular activity going on at the time. Sometimes the room is very silent and very tidy, as when children are sitting in rows doing an English exercise or listening to a story being read. Sometimes it is very noisy, as when children are doing group work in reading, in arithmetic, or when they are doing a social studies project; but there appears to be purposive activity going on within the noise. Sometimes the room is quite untidy, as during a drawing lesson when each child appears to be doing something different from any other. It may strike you as a little chaotic until you talk to individual children and realize that each has a very definite task to do.

The children have two English exercise books each. One is very neat with lines drawn straight with rulers; work in it consists mainly of exercises in formal English. These have been carefully marked. The other exercise book is one reserved for the child's own creative efforts. The writing is not neat, as in the other book, but there is a good deal of it. The only sign that these books have been marked is a note at the end of a piece of work about its being interesting or original, or a criticism of style and theme with a request to see the teacher to chat about these. No notice has been taken of spelling mistakes or of the missing full stops and commas, for the teacher believes these will correct themselves later when the children's formal English has caught up with their creative capacity and that meanwhile there is no need to impede their creative expression because they are unequal to formal skills.

When he introduces a new topic, as in social studies, or when he begins to teach a new skill, as in arithmetic, he allows a wide range of questions and is not concerned to prescribe definite limits to what may be discussed. In this way, he hopes that the pupils will get the 'feel' of a new topic or skill and its relationship to what has already been learned. By thus freeing the topic from its more specific and narrow implications he widens the scope of his teaching and gives his pupils greater opportunity to participate, thereby increasing their understanding. Yet, when he wishes to teach definite facts or to demonstrate a definite skill, he moves from this indirect approach and becomes direct and explicit. What strikes us most about the teacher is his flexibility, which enables him to move from one method of teaching to another according to the aim of the moment. This flexibility is seen, too, in the way he organizes the classroom and in the varying relationships between him and the children. Sometimes, when the lesson is formal, classroom organization and teacher-pupil relationships are formal. At other times, say during a creative English or painting lesson, organization is on an informal group or individual basis (21, 24, 30, 31, 33).

This completes the simple descriptions of teachers at work. In studies of the effects of differing climates on the behaviour and productivity of children, it is the authoritarian and the democratic climates that have been compared. This is because few teachers deliberately develop a laissez-faire climate. Its incidence is very rare and probably accidental. It may occasionally be found in the classroom of a young teacher, who is full of enthusiasm, but who as yet lacks the experience and the ability to organize activities and to control children's behaviour. From an educational point of view, it may be suggested that while lack of control may permit an expansive freedom, it may also mean that children are anxious and frustrated within it, anxious because their own hates and impulses are uncontrolled, frustrated because they are given no direction and amble along aimlessly and without purpose from one day to another. It is an amorphous climate in which the originality of which we spoke is vague, accidental, occasional.

An authoritarian climate has advantages. Organization and procedures are prescribed, the amount of movement and talking is clearly laid down so that children know where they are. In contrast to a laissez-faire climate, it is consistent and predictable. Children do not experience the anxieties which result from lack of control or the boredom that may come from lack of purposive activity. For the teacher, too, the controlled environment provides predictability and security. Pupil-teacher relationships are relatively impersonal. Because the teacher is at a distance from his pupils he does not know much about their personal lives. Despite the educational disadvantages of this, it could be said that he does not become emotionally involved and that this impersonal relationship is at least precise, clear, business-like.

There are disadvantages, however. The strict, prescribed environment inhibits children's natural inquisitiveness and individuality of thought and expression; it impedes exploration, experiment and initiative. The children, therefore, tend not to be willing, for example, to volunteer suggestions or talk of relevant out-of-school experiences. The effect of the authoritarian teacher is much the same as that of the very strict parent. Children conform and are obedient, but to the detriment of their spontaneity, originality and creativity. Social interaction between pupils is limited, and consequently they lose the educative value of discussion and exchange of ideas amongst themselves by which to clarify their thought, in pairs or in groups. They are deprived, too, of the help they can give each other in mastering specific skills (31).

Because procedures are so ordered and directed, children tend to be very dependent on the teacher and unable to proceed except under his close supervision (24). They may stop work when he leaves the classroom for any considerable length of time. If the climate is very severe the pupils become more concerned to adjust to the teacher, to know just enough facts to avoid humiliation, than they are to understand (24). They become guarded in what they say and inhibited about asking questions. Then the teacher is himself hampered in his work in that he is not sure what exactly the children know and what their difficulties are (25).

By contrast, children in a democratic climate behave more spontaneously, volunteering suggestions and asking questions (22, 23, 31). The freedom which such a climate provides for children to experiment without fear of making mistakes means that children are more ready to attempt a new skill, or have a go at answering a question, and so are more spontaneous, original and creative. The children are relatively independent (24); this is partly because the climate aims at making them so. Besides, the teaching is open-ended, meaning that many gaps (diagrams, charts, illustrations) are left for children to complete during their spare time. They are consequently less easily distracted and are able to carry on working during the teacher's temporary absence. Being reasonably free to exchange ideas one with the other and sometimes to co-operate in a group pursuit, they are more ready to give help to, and to solicit help from, other children (30).

It would appear that the amount of knowledge and skill acquired in the formal subjects, such as in the three R's and in social studies, is not significantly different when children in authoritarian classes are compared with those in democratic classes. But children taught democratically have broader interests, a wider knowledge of current affairs, greater ability to express themselves creatively in art and free writing, and to co-operate with others in a joint project so as to carry it to a successful conclusion (29, 32, 34).

The foregoing classification suggests a division into absolutes —absolute authoritarians and absolute democrats. But such absolutes are rarely found. In the researches referred to, teachers are assessed and those *predominantly* authoritarian are compared with those *predominantly* democratic. What has been said about child-parent relationships applies to pupil-teacher relationships: they are complex.

The most important factor in teaching is probably the flexibility spoken of earlier. This implies a certain resilience which enables the teacher to cope with the unexpected (and the unexpected can often arise in the classroom), the ability to be both discursive and direct—discursive when introducing a new topic, yet clear and direct when clarifying a specific idea or teaching a specific skill. It implies, too, the ability to be either formal or informal in classroom organization according to the type of learning that is taking place. What distinguishes the predominantly democratic teacher is not only this greater flexibility but also his skill in seizing upon children's own ideas and experiences, using these to illustrate and to clarify the subject-matter which he is teaching (24, 30, 32, 33).

Probably the democratic climate is the most difficult to sustain both by parents within the family and by teachers in the classroom. This is understandable enough. During pre-school years, children at home face fewer physical and social hazards within the protective environment of the home. The child is relatively easy to manage and not able to argue his own viewpoint on critical issues. In later years, possible dangers increase: getting into trouble with outside authorities because of 'gang' activities, reckless riding on a bicycle and, in later adolescence, 'Can I have a motor-cycle?' or 'Can I take the car?'

In the school, there may be impediments to a democratic climate which are outside the teacher's ability to control—a very large class; a class which has been subject for a long time to a climate of one or other extreme (authoritarian or laissez-faire); a class of underprivileged children in the poorest part of a city; inappropriate physical features such as small classrooms, heavy old-fashioned desks, inadequate lighting; the pressures of an external examination (26). There are also psychological difficulties, such as avoiding the swings towards over-control and under-control. Sometimes, a teacher may envy the definiteness, the firm control always exercised by the authoritarian teacher. The democratic climate is less definite. It attempts to unify the opposites of the authoritarian and of the laissez-faire into a middle way, to retain freedom of expression and of movement without loss of control. The teacher within a democratic climate tolerates a little untidiness, occasional anxiety, some uncertainty and some unpredictability. This is not easy. Yet these are ingredients necessary in a climate which would stimulate creative and original work. It has been suggested that the democratic climate is particularly difficult for the young teacher and that 'most young teachers will find directive teaching easier and more successful' (33).[1]

Because the flexibility of a democratic climate demands a sureness and a skill which come only with some years of experience, young teachers may be well advised to begin teaching in a direct and definite way and, then, as they develop in confidence and skill, change to a more democratic one.

The implication of all that has been so far discussed may perhaps be summed up as follows. Education is not only a process by which children learn facts; it is also one of the means through which they become unique persons. Teaching, then, is a human process. It is a social process. Consequently, teaching children is not only a matter of lesson techniques, classroom organization and administration. If this were all it would be a relatively easy job. It is also one in which the teacher needs to understand himself and his pupils and how the relationships between them help or hinder the processes of learning. Far from being easy, it probably is among the most difficult of occupations, calling for understanding and acceptance of children as children, an ability to see and acknowledge one's mistakes (and what teacher does not make them?), to rejoice in one's successes and to benefit from both. It is these things that make the teacher's job always exacting and sometimes frustrating; yet these very same things make the teacher's job exciting and rewarding (27).[2]

REFERENCES

Children and their parents

1   Anderson, J. P. 'The relationship between certain aspects of parental behaviour and attitudes and the behaviour of junior high school pupils.'

1 page 184.   2 page 104.

Teachers' College Contributions to Education, No. 809. Columbia University Press, New York, 1940.

2   Baldwin, A. L. 'Socialization and parent-child relationships.' *Child Development*, 1948, **19**, pp. 127–36.

3   Baldwin, A. L. 'The effect of home environment on nursery school behaviour.' *Child Development*, 1949, **20**, pp. 49–62.

4   Baldwin, A. L., Kalhorn, J., Breese, F. H. 'Patterns of parent behaviour.' *Psychological Monographs*, 1945, **58**, No. 268.

5   Baldwin, A. L., Kalhorn, J., Breese, F. H. 'Appraisal of parent behaviour.' *Psychological Monographs*, 1949, **63**, No. 299.

6   Bronfenbrenner, U. 'The changing American child.' *In* 'Childhood and mental health: the influence of the father in the family setting.' Reprinted from *Merrill-Palmer Quarterly of Behaviour and Development*, 1961, **7**, pp. 73–84.

7   Henry, A. F. 'Sibling structure and perception of the disciplinary roles of parents.' *Sociometry*, 1957, **20**, pp. 67–74.

8   Hoffman, L. W. 'The father's role in the family and the child's peer-group adjustment.' *In* 'Childhood and mental health: the influence of the father in the family setting.' Reprinted from *Merrill-Palmer Quarterly of Behaviour and Development*, 1961, **7**, pp. 97–106.

9   Horney, K. *Neurosis and Human Growth*. Routledge & Kegan Paul, London, 1951.

10 Levy, D. M. *Maternal Overprotection*. Columbia University Press, New York, 1943.

11 (a) Newson, J. and E. *Infant Care in an Urban Community*. Allen and Unwin, London, 1963.
    (b) 'Patterns of discipline. The four-year-old and his mother.' Mimeographed, 1964. (In personal correspondence).

12 Radke, M. J. *The Relation of Parental Authority to Children's Behaviour and Attitudes*. University of Minnesota Press, Minneapolis, 1946.

13 Rau, L. *Identification and the Mother-child Relationship*. Stanford University, Palo Alto, California, 1959. Mimeographed report.

14 Rosen, C. B., D'Andrade, R. 'The psychosocial origins of achievement motivation.' *Sociometry*, 1959, **22**, pp. 185–217.

15 Schaefer, E. S. 'Converging conceptual models for maternal and child behaviour.' *In* Glidewell, J. C. *Parental Attitudes and Child Behaviour*. Thomas, New York, 1961.

16 Schaefer, E. S., Bayley, N. 'Maternal behaviour, child behaviour and their intercorrelations from infancy through adolescence.' *Monographs Society Research in Child Development*, 1963, **28**, (Serial No. 87).

17 Sears, R. R., Maccoby, E. E., Levin, H. *Patterns of Child Rearing*. Row, Peterson, Evanston, Ill., 1957.

18   Sundley, R. 'Early nineteenth-century American literature on child rear-
     ing.' *In* Mead, M., Wolfenstein, M. *Childhood in Contemporary Cultures.*
     University of Chicago Press, Chicago, 1955.

19   Symonds, P. M. *The Psychology of Parent-child Relationship.* Appleton-
     Century-Crofts, New York, 1939.

20   Winterbottom, M. R. 'The relation of need achievement to learning ex-
     periences in independence and mastery.' *In* Atkinson, J. W. (Ed.), *Motives
     in Fantasy, Action and Society.* Van Nostrand, Princeton, 1958.

Children and their teachers

21   Anderson, H. H., Brewer, J. E. 'Studies of teachers' classroom personal-
     ities. I: Dominative and socially integrative behaviour of kindergarten
     teachers.' *Applied Psychological Monographs*, 1945, **6.**

22   Anderson, H. H., Brewer, J. E. 'Studies of teachers' classroom personal-
     ities. II: Effects of teachers' dominative and integrative contacts on
     children's classroom behaviour.' *Applied Psychological Monographs*, 1946,
     8.

23   Anderson, H. H., Brewer, J. E., Reed, M. F. 'Studies of teachers' class-
     room personalities. III: Follow-up studies of the effects of dominative and
     integrative contacts on children's behaviour.' *Applied Psychological Mono-
     graphs*, 1946, **11.**

24   Flanders, N. A. *Teacher Influence, Pupil Attitudes, and Achievement.* Univer-
     sity of Minnesota, Minneapolis, 1960. Mimeographed report.

25   Flanders, N. A. 'Personal-social anxiety as a factor in experimental learn-
     ing situations.' *Journal of Educational Research*, 1951, **45,** pp. 100–10.

26   Gabriel, J. *An Analysis of the Emotional Problems of the Teacher in the Class-
     room.* Cheshire, Melbourne, 1957.

27   Gabriel, J. 'Resolution of opposites and the teaching of children.' *Australian
     Journal of Education*, 1960, **5,** pp. 91–105.

28   Lewin, K., Lippitt, R., White, R. K. 'Patterns of aggressive behaviour in
     experimentally created "climates".' *Journal of Social Psychology*, 1939, **10,**
     pp. 271–99.

29   Rehage, K. J. 'A comparison of pupil-teacher planning and teacher directed
     procedures in eighth grade social studies classes.' *Journal of Educational
     Research*, 1951, **45,** pp. 111–14.

30   Thelen, H. A., Withall, J. 'Three frames of reference: the description of
     climate.' *Human Relations*, 1949, **2,** pp. 159–76.

31   Thorndike, R. L., Loftus, J. J., Goldman, B. 'Observations of excursions
     in activity and control schools.' *Journal of Experimental Education*, 1941,
     10, pp. 146–9.

32   Trow, W. C. 'Group processes.' *In* Harris, C. W. (Ed.) *Encyclopaedia of
     Educational Research.* Macmillan, New York, 3rd edition, 1960.

33   Withall, J. 'The development of a technique for the measurement of

social-emotional climate in the classroom.' *Journal of Experimental Psychology*, 1949, **17**, pp. 347–61.

34   Wrightstone, J. W. 'Evaluation of the experiment with the activity programme in the New York City Elementary Schools.' *Journal of Educational Research*, 1944, **38**, pp. 252–7.

BIBLIOGRAPHICAL NOTE

Gage, N. L. (Ed.) *Handbook of Research on Teaching*. Rand McNally, Chicago, 1963.

This book is a most comprehensive study (1218 pages) of teaching in all its aspects, and very technical in many of its parts. Yet for the non-technical reader there are short descriptive accounts of most of the investigations mentioned above. Readers who wish to search into the complexities behind the relatively simple descriptions given here are referred especially to the following contributions:

Medley, D. M., Mitzel, H. E. 'Measuring classroom behaviour by systematic observation' (Chapter 6).

Getzels, J. W., Jackson, P. W. 'The teacher's personality and characteristics' (Chapter 11).

Withall, J., Lewis, W. W. 'Social interaction in the classroom' (Chapter 13).

CHAPTER SIX

Personality and Temperament

A mother says of her child of four, 'John's insatiably curious.'
This she does because he is 'into everything', incessantly exploring
here, there and everywhere. She then adds, 'He's so much more
curious than Alan was at his age', Alan being John's elder brother.
There are other differences that she notices between the two boys.
John seems livelier, more alert, more 'highly strung'; he laughs
more than Alan did. She then adds, 'He's *made* differently from
Alan'; and she shakes her head as if puzzled by the mystery of it.
Both are her own children, but they are so unlike one another.

The discerning parent and teacher realize that there are such
differences between children which seem to be innate. These
differences, they notice, occur between children who are subject
to similar environments, children of the same neighbourhood
groups and even of the same family. Thus, for example, to use
the phrases of Murphy (14), some revel in sound and they
'hear richly', some revel in sight and they 'see richly', some in
touch and they 'touch richly'. There are differences in physical
energy; some children are constantly active and others are slower,
quieter and more restrained in movement. There are differences,
too, of emotional reaction. A teacher knows that if he speaks
sharply to Henry, Jim and George, Henry will become pathetically
penitent and burst into tears; but Jim will become aggressive, and
he may answer back; George will become depressed and withdraw
into himself.

Such fundamental differences which parents and teachers
observe may stem, in part, from the fact that each child, including
brother or sister, has his own unique patterns of genes. Indeed,
there is evidence to indicate that the differences of the kind mentioned have a genetic or heredity basis as well as an environmental

one (6); this is so of children's vulnerability to stress (11) and even of the amount of curiosity a child may show (4).

We assume that there are constitutional differences between people even from our everyday observations of the obvious differences in their bodily structures, as when we contrast the soft, round fat man with the sturdy, muscular man or with the thin, linear man. Researchers point to more basic constitutional differences between people, for example, in their nervous and sensory systems, tending to make them more or less receptive to outside stimuli, such as loud noises, bright lights and so on; in their muscular and motor systems, tending to make them more or less physically active; in their autonomic systems[1] tending to make them more or less agitated in times of stress. Further, just as individuals differ in minute physical details such as the patterning of their finger prints, so, too, there are many subtle physiological and chemical differences between them. These differences are now beginning to be revealed by research studies.

The differences in personality and behaviour which result from such hereditary and constitutional differences are called *temperamental* differences. In everyday speech, the adjective 'temperamental' is used to describe a person who gives way to extreme, uncontrolled emotional outbursts; it implies emotional instability and so we speak of the 'temperamental actress'. But the term, as used here, has not this specific meaning, for although it is concerned with emotional experiences and their expression, it is not concerned solely with stability or instability of emotional expression. Furthermore, as used here, the meaning of the term extends beyond purely emotional experiences to include states of feeling— the sensory characteristics spoken of above—and also the typical responses of an individual to other people.

In the course of this chapter this initial statement on the meaning of the term 'temperament' will be descriptively expanded by considering in more detail some of the hereditary and constitutional determinants of personality.

The obvious way to discover the effects of heredity on behaviour is to study babies as soon as possible after birth, before the post-natal environment has had much of a chance to make its influence felt. The results of such studies confirm the impression a

---

[1] The autonomic system is the main physiological centre for initiating the bodily changes which accompany feelings and emotions.

mother often forms—that some of the differences between her children which she sees so clearly now they are older were also evident during babyhood.

For example, the results show that babies differ from each other in their readiness to smile (23), to laugh (2), to cry (1), and in their mode of sleeping (7). The sleep of some is shallow and fitful, and they are more easily aroused; others sleep soundly and continue to sleep even if the household is in chaos. Some babies are very active, and this is seen in vigorous kicking of arms and legs and in restlessness during sleep; some babies are only 'moderately active', some quiet; and baby boys tend to be more active than baby girls (5).

A baby, too, tends to have its characteristic way of reacting to tension, when he is tired, hungry, or subjected to a sudden change of environment. One baby may have a gastro-intestinal disturbance, and will vomit or have diarrhoea; another may have difficulty in breathing and will gasp or pant; yet another may show increased flushing of the face and another may develop a skin rash (9).

But accurate observation of babies in the first few weeks or months after birth is very difficult; and tests suitable for very young babies are not easy to devise, and even when devised, they require great skill to administer. It is generally the case, therefore, that by the time a child has reached the age when his varying abilities can be estimated or measured with a satisfactory degree of accuracy, environmental influences have become inextricably conjoined with the influences of heredity in determining the degree of skill the child has achieved.

For example, it would be very difficult to decide the extent to which John's greater curiosity is determined by hereditary differences between himself and his brother. It could be, for instance, that his mother was less anxious and more relaxed in bringing him up than she had been in bringing up her first child, Alan. Because of this, she might have been able to allow John much greater freedom to explore than she had been able to allow Alan, and that this environmental difference is the more important one.

Because hereditary and environmental influences work together and because one influence cannot be separated from the other, it is very difficult to study the exact part which heredity (the main concern of this chapter) plays in the acquisition of a skill or of a personality characteristic. But scientists have devised various techniques by which to do this. One of them is to breed animals selectively, that is, to mate animals which show a required psychological trait very clearly, and then to test if continued selective breeding over a number of generations leads to a strain demonstrating the characteristic to an even greater degree.[1] In this way, rats have been bred to obtain a strain (a high fear strain) which shows much fear and anxiety in new situations, and another (the low fear strain) which shows significantly less fear and anxiety in new situations. In the same way, active as contrasted with quiescent, aggressive as contrasted with non-aggressive strains of rats have been reared (10). Such experiments indicate that these characteristics have some basis in heredity.

The method usually used with human beings is to compare identical twins one with the other on a trait or task such as intelligence; then to compare non-identical twins one with the other on the same task. If the scores of identical twins are significantly closer than are the scores of non-identical twins, then the difference is attributed to heredity, since identical twins share virtually the same heredity, non-identical twins do not. Here it is assumed that for each pair, taken separately, the influence of the environment is the same.

But, of course, the environment is never absolutely the same for any two children and, like similarity of heredity, similarity of environment is likely to be greater for identical than for non-identical twins. Sometimes, therefore, identical twins living apart are compared with non-identical twins living together. In such cases it is justifiable to assume that the differences in the environment are greater for the identical than the non-identical twins, and that if the scores for the identical twins are significantly closer together than are those for the non-identical twins, this greater closeness of scores for the identical twins will be due to heredity. A brief statement on the results of three investigations using this co-twin method will now be given.

First, in a comparative study (16) of fifty pairs of identical and fifty pairs of non-identical twins, and of nineteen identical twins separated in infancy, three research workers found that the contrast between identical and non-identical twins is greatest for

[1] The same process of selection is used, of course, to breed animals with salient physical characteristics—'pure breeds' as they are called.

physical traits, next for intelligence, rather less for tests of school achievement and least of all for tests of personality. Their results indicate that inheritance is a greater factor in producing likeness and differences between people in some attributes (physical traits, intelligence) than it is in producing likenesses and differences in other attributes (school achievement, personality traits).

However, despite this finding that personality traits are least determined by heredity, Gottesman (8) concluded, after a study of thirty-four pairs of identical twins and thirty-four pairs of non-identical twins, all adolescents, that genetic factors, in part, determined whether his subjects tended to be:

either sober and serious or enthusiastic, happy-go-lucky;
either liking group activity or fastidiously individualistic;
either submissive or domineering;
either shy, sensitive or brashly adventurous.

Gottesman added that the tendency towards extraversion was most influenced by genetic factors.

Thirdly, by using pairs of twins as subjects, Jost and Sontag (12) have shown that there are individual differences in the way the autonomic system functions from one individual child to another. Over a period of three years measures were taken of the heart beat, blood pressure and the pulse and respiration rates of a group of children, aged between six and twelve. It was found that similarity of measurements was greater between identical than non-identical twins, greater between non-identical twins than between siblings, and greater between siblings than between children who were not related. The two scientists spoke of an 'autonomic constitution' which may at least be partially inherited.[1]

Many personality characteristics tend to persist. Observers who saw films of babies in their first year and then films of the same children at five were able to match baby with child on fifteen traits with a degree of accuracy that could not be attributed to chance. These traits included social responsiveness, emotional expressiveness, and self-dependence. The interval here was only five years; yet judges reached an accuracy that was well beyond

[1] The similarity between identical twins was not by any means an exact one (the correlations ranged between ·43 and ·49) suggesting that heredity contributes to, but does not wholly determine, these responses.

one attributable to chance even with a fifteen-year interval, when they matched the personality profiles of babies made during their first two years with personality profiles made when the same individuals were sixteen years old (15).

A very comprehensive, continuous study of children from birth to about twenty-four years by Kagan and Moss (13) shows that subjects who, as children, were predominantly dependent (moving towards people) or assertive and aggressive (moving against people) or passive and withdrawn (moving away from people), tended to show a predominance of the same one of these three characteristics during adolescence and early adulthood.

It may be argued that the continuation of personality traits, which these three studies suggest, are due mainly to the environment; that, for example, parental attitudes, such as those described in the last chapter, begin early and continue to exert their influence. This is undoubtedly so. However, there are a number of pointers which suggest the significant part heredity also plays. Thus, when they were first studied, the subjects were very young. Secondly, in speaking of the many studies he and his collaborators have done with the same children over a span of many years, Gesell (7) says that the persistence of traits within individuals suggests a unique patterning of dispositions that require more than the influence of the environment to explain. Thirdly, Kagan and Moss (13) have shown that the tendency towards continuity of particular traits is related to physical characteristics. This suggests that hereditary as well as environmental influences are important. For example, they have shown that children who are assertive and aggressive tend to have large muscles, while children who are passive and dependent tend to have small muscles.

This tendency towards a relationship between certain kinds of bodily structure and certain kinds of traits is another way by which the influence of heredity has been studied. We will return to this later in the chapter.

Because so few studies have been carried out on temperamental differences between children, an attempt will be made to describe these differences as they apply to adults and then to consider the value and limitations which these studies may have for our understanding of children's behaviour.

The division of people into either extraverts or introverts is probably the best known of the ways by means of which people are classified into temperamental types. The two terms are commonly used in everyday speech, and the generally accepted meaning is that an extravert is a person who is more orientated towards the outside world, while an introvert is one who is more orientated towards his own mental experiences.

Thus, when the term 'extravert' is used, we usually mean a person who is 'at home' in the company of others, who can speak unselfconsciously, smile and laugh with others and be spontaneously demonstrative in expressing affection, praise, sympathy and so on. He is a person who freely expresses his own feelings, attitudes and opinions, although sometimes we may think that he speaks too impulsively and expresses opinions without adequate knowledge of the subject and without having deliberated deeply about it. In conversation he tends, rather like housewives as they gossip together, to flit from one topic to another. (This does not, of course, preclude the fact than an extravert can become an expert in some field of study. If this is so, then on this subject he speaks after deliberation and he keeps to the subject; but even he, in general conversation, tends to 'flit'.) The extravert likes to receive attention and approval, and will become disturbed and anxious if he loses the goodwill and affection of others.

The introvert, on the other hand, often finds it difficult to be sociable. It is an effort to face a company of people and, when he has to do it, he is nervous and self-conscious. He is not able easily to express to others the emotions he experiences and so he tends to keep things in his heart. Although he feels affection, joy, sympathy, he may find it difficult to express these, and because of this inability to be demonstrative, we may think quite wrongly that he is without emotion. The introvert has capacity for deep feelings and for close attachments to a few selected friends, but he is not demonstrative in expressing these. When he speaks he is hesitant and will express opinions only after deliberation and reflection, for he tends to *assimilate* knowledge and experiences— that is, to brood deeply about them. He values his independence of people rather than their attention and approval.

Incidentally, it is important to avoid the error of thinking that the introvert is unhealthy and morbidly introspective, an error very possible in our society which places more value on extraversion, on the ability to deal with practical situations and to be pleasantly sociable. Because of this, we tend to value the extravert and he is looked upon as 'healthy'. The introvert can also be healthy; we may call him 'introspective' and he may be 'different', but both the extravert and the introvert can be mentally well or mentally sick.

Such a division of people into two extreme types is very naturally open to criticism. Only rarely is a person a pure extravert or a pure introvert. Most of us are mixtures, and the term 'ambivert' (turning both ways) has been used for people who are not definitely one or the other. Again, even though a person may be predominantly extraverted or predominantly introverted, in certain situations an extravert may behave in a manner more appropriate to an introvert and an introvert may behave in a manner more appropriate to an extravert. Thus Jung, who first drew the extravert-introvert distinction, tells a story of this sort (here it is modified somewhat). Two friends, one an extravert, the other an introvert, are out walking on a country road which is strange to them both. Suddenly, they come to some wrought-iron gates inside which a long drive leads to a large country house, the tower of which can be seen behind the trees in the distance. The extravert is keen to explore the situation, urging that they go through the gates and walk up the drive to the house. The introvert is puzzled by the confidence which the extravert displays in this unknown situation. He follows the lead given by the extravert, but he does so reluctantly and with misgivings. They arrive at the house to find that it is an art gallery devoted to modern art, including works of Picasso and of the 'non-objective' school of art led by Kandinsky. Our extravert is disappointed and wants to withdraw from the situation. He becomes silent. But our introvert's face lights up. He goes from one picture to another, seeks where he can get a catalogue, requests of the attendant an interview with the curator. The curator is delighted with the enthusiasm which the introvert expresses and personally escorts him around the gallery, discussing with him the pictures and their esoteric meanings. It is now our extravert's turn to be puzzled. He follows behind, morose, silent, withdrawn. The typical roles of the two have been reversed.

Although there are obvious difficulties in this twofold classification, the following suggested modification may prove of value in understanding the behaviour of people. It is that there are two kinds of extraverts, and these may be called the social extravert and the manipulative extravert. The social extravert, as the name implies, is sociable; he loves people and he loves being with people. Here is the extraversion of the person who is always seeking the company of others, the good mixer—the benign clergyman who meanders smiling, affable, considerate and polite among a roomful of his parishioners. The manipulative extravert, however, sees the world of people and objects as material over which he can exercise power. Here we have the extraversion of the engineer who shapes a mountain, bends a river as he wills; the extraversion of the business executive, of the army officer, of the dictatorial father, teacher, or politician. Whereas the first is the extraversion of affection and conservation, the second is the extraversion of assertion and change.

This gives a threefold classification into: (1) the social extravert who turns towards people; (2) the manipulative extravert who asserts himself against pe.ple; (3) the introvert who moves away from people. Again, in relation to these three components, we are all in varying degrees 'mixtures'. This is understandable enough, for sometimes, as occasion demands, we want to love, to assert ourselves, or to be alone. Thus, we need at times to love the universe and the people in it in order to experience the delicious sense of community and the freedom from anxiety which comes with such rapport. At other times, we need to strive against the universe and the people in it in order to manipulate or overcome the dangers of the physical world and to withstand the threat of domination by other people. Such assertion is also needed to acquire skills and to co-ordinate those skills towards the fulfilment of immediate or distant goals. Thirdly, we need at times to withdraw from social activity, not only to complete a piece of individual creative work or to do some individual thinking, but also to recover from the draining of energy which extraversion of both kinds can entail unless such extraverted activities alternate with periods of withdrawal. Analogously, such a process compares with the recharging of a battery; its physiological expression is in sleep.

Yet there are individual differences in the absolute and relative strengths of each component, and sometimes we can point to people in whom one of the components is very strong and the other two relatively weak—that is, to people who tend to be predominantly affectionate, or assertive, or withdrawn.

So much for the description of temperamental components in adults; to what extent can this kind of descriptive classification be used to help us in understanding children? There are difficulties and there are scientific objections. Investigations in this field, to which reference will be made later in this chapter, have mainly been done with adults as subjects and we cannot apply these results directly to children. Further, children's minds and bodies are not fully developed and we rarely meet the extreme, or the 'pure', cases which we sometimes meet in adults. There is also a sense in which all children are extraverted; this will be seen more clearly later in the study of children's emotional and social growth. Thus, children are eager to get to know about the world in which they live; this they do by handling and experimenting with objects, and by exploring their environment.

However, despite difficulties and possible objections, this classification may help in the observation and understanding of children. The following imaginary descriptions of three boys, aged, say, about eleven and of good average intelligence, illustrate this. William is a social extravert, Peter a manipulative extravert, and Paul is an introvert.

WILLIAM

In physical appearance William is round; his legs and arms are short and his movements are slow; he seems to amble rather than walk and often you will hear his teacher say, 'Hurry up, William, and *do* pick up your feet.' His eyes seem a little small within his round face and he can sometimes be seen blinking sleepily and slowly at his desk, his body completely relaxed. Emotionally he is even and not often given to outbursts of temper or tears.

Outside the classroom he plays amongst other children; 'amongst' because he seems at home, happy and delighted to be surrounded by his companions. He takes part in their activities as a follower rather than as a leader; he rarely initiates an activity, but when it has been organized and the decision made that 'Fatty will do so-and-so', he generally accepts the role he is called upon to play. When children call him 'Fatty' they do so without malice; indeed, it is a term of endearment. This is seen especially when he does something of which the group approves and the cry goes up, 'Good old Fatty.'

As far as is possible he avoids quarrelling and will rarely, if ever, begin a fight. If an aggressive boy attacks him with fists, he attempts to defend himself by extending his short arms, but rarely will he actively retaliate. In such a situation the crowd is always in sympathy with 'Fatty'—in secret sympathy, maybe, because of the power which the attacker may have in the group. Tears fill and overflow William's eyes. He is deeply hurt that the friendship which he always proffers has been disrupted by this fierce attack, especially as he has offended unwittingly.

In the classroom, he is very little trouble; inclined to be an incorrigible chatterbox, maybe, but if the teacher speaks to him (and not too sharply) he smiles benignly and the teacher is appeased, for William's smile radiates good-will, and is, in part, his charm and, in part, his defence against attack.

William's work is usually satisfactory, but he likes to take his time. He cannot be bustled into rapid bodily movements or rapid mental effort. He is at a disadvantage when it comes to work for which such rapid movement and thinking are important. The order to do twenty quick mental sums demands a quickness of thought which is difficult for him to achieve. There are occasions when, in exasperation at his lack of urgency, you may call William 'lazy' or think him 'complacent'. It is difficult to get him to 'spark' and his very virtue of tolerant placidity may sometimes appear a fault, especially when you want to speed things up.

PETER

Peter, who is the leader of his group, has a firm, strong, upright body. His shoulders are held square, not from any conscious effort or because of constant correction; they seem naturally so. In his movements there is a trace of that swing of the arms, that click of the heels so typical of the army guardsman. He has a certain maturity of appearance, and seems a year or two older than his contemporaries. He revels in sport.

Peter is not particularly democratic as a leader; he likes to initiate activity and he likes his gang to follow. The activities are usually adventurous, generally physically strenuous and often a little dangerous. (There is always the possibility that they will overflow into delinquency, not always at Peter's initiation, but because one of the group has 'dared' him, and he cannot 'lose face' by refusing a 'dare'.) When he is older these activities will be sublimated into prefectorial duties, organized sport and leadership in the cadet corps. Peter is a 'daredevil'; his followers admire rather than love him, and are proud to belong to his gang. There is always the danger that he will become too dictatorial, driving them too much and demanding too great an obedience.

In school the adventurous tales of Drake may inspire him, but the nuances of poetry elude him. However, he is able easily to dispel this personal deficiency by calling poetry and music 'cissy stuff'. During such lessons he may sometimes be seen surreptitiously reading a copy of *Superman* underneath his desk.

He has a good deal of executive ability; he can organize and get things done. Perhaps one of the best ways of getting him to identify himself with classroom activities is to capitalize on this executive ability. He can organize the gymnastic and sporting equipment, or act as a marshal when children are being escorted to swimming, to dinner, to the concert at the Town Hall, but one has again to watch that he does not become too dictatorial.

It is well to see that his monitorial activities are done chiefly outside the classroom, for in the classroom his movements may be noisy. If he gets up from his desk he disturbs all around him, his feet clatter noisily and he may knock into a piece of furniture. If he goes out, the door may shut with a bang. This is not necessarily deliberate but is part of his general vigour. In exasperated moments you might call Peter 'conceited', 'cocky', 'a nasty little exhibitionist' and during such moments might decide to put him in his place. But he is sensitive to slights, more so because they are detrimental to his standing with his 'gang'. Even though you squash him, you may leave a residue of antagonism which is more difficult to heal than the 'cockiness'.

PAUL

Whereas, physically, William tends to be rotund and Peter muscular, Paul tends to be linear. He is thin; there is a tendency towards a stoop of the shoulders and the head inclines forward a little. He walks softly, quickly, with a somewhat jerky and rapid movement of the legs. His reactions generally are fast. If you say, 'Paul, bring me your English book,' he jumps up quickly, searches the surface of his desk rapidly, picks up the book and walks quickly to your desk. (To William you would have to say, 'Come on, William, I haven't all day.') Paul is inclined to be 'jumpy' and to react to stimuli, such as a sudden sound, with a quick movement of the body or head.

He does not seem to belong to a gang. He may have a few friends with whom he talks, laughs and plays, but often he is engaged in activities that are essentially his own. His magnifying glass is a source of great pleasure to him. Specially bought to study leaves, flowers and pond-life, he often takes it out of his pocket to look at a piece of wood or brick or cloth as if to satisfy a need for depth of knowledge—'What ultimately does this consist of?'

In the classroom Paul is no trouble from the disciplinary point of view; his fault may be that of being too inconspicuous. He seems to cherish a delicious private life and he may not often contribute to class discussion. Then some subject arises in which he is interested. His eyes sparkle, he shows an immediate enthusiasm and becomes talkative, demonstrating one of his experiments and outlining his knowledge of a topic. He might talk too fast with consequent stumblings (a contrast to William's slow measured speech) and his teacher may justifiably restrain him so that he can gather his thoughts, control his enthusiasm and speak clearly. For a while he loses his self-consciousness, his apparent shyness. His teacher is pleased, and perhaps a little surprised. She may say to herself, 'I must get him to contribute more often.' But, rather than force frequent contributions, the teacher is probably best guided by the boy's spontaneously-aroused enthusiasms.

Paul's mother may say that at home he becomes over-excited, especially at the prospect of a treat or an outing. She is probably right, for Paul is the kind who might literally 'become sick with excitement'.

He is never noisy and his voice is restrained; in the playground it does not carry as does Peter's loud boom which can be heard above the noise of a hundred chattering children. In the classroom the teacher has constantly to say 'Speak up!' for here his voice ordinarily carries little beyond the children in the desk in front of him.

To conclude this chapter some theoretical issues arising from these sketches will now be considered. Ths issues relate to the inheritance of physical and psychological characteristics, since, if temperamental qualities are constitutionally based, heredity must play a part in determining their expression.

As we have seen (Chapter 1), a human being inherits 46 chromosomes, 23 from each parent, and replicas of these 46 chromosomes are present within each of the millions of cells within a living organism. Each chromosome contains chemical activators (the genes), the nature of which partly determines the physical and psychological characteristics of the individual.

Heredity probably plays an important part in determining:

1   simple physical characteristics such as eye colour, hair colour, blood group, and numerous physical defects (e.g. haemophilia) —all due to unifactorial inheritance (single genes);

2   more complex physical characteristics such as body build, shape of head, facial structure—all due to multifactorial inheritance (many genes);

3 physical movements, walking, moving the head, smiling;
4 sensory sensitivities, such as sensitivity to touch, light and
   sound, spoken of at the beginning of this chapter;
5 general emotionality and specific emotional reactions (sex,
   anger, fear and probably others).

It is understandable that heredity should be important here, since the characteristics listed have a physical basis. But inheritance can never be the sole determinant; a person may inherit a tendency to tallness, to sensitivity, to a high degree of emotionality, but whether these predispositions are expressed will depend upon environmental conditions, such as nutritional standards, social pressures to behave in certain ways and so on. Even though we speak of an inherited tendency, the manner in which it is expressed will partly depend on learning and imitation, as when, for example, a son walks or talks like his father. Social influences would seem particularly important when psychological characteristics, such as affection (turning towards people), assertion (turning against people) and withdrawal (turning away from people) are considered.

Yet certain studies, based on the morphology[1] of the body, suggest that heredity may play a part in determining the respective ways of behaving and feeling of the three boys described. Thus Sheldon (19, 20), who has done important work in this field, has described the three basic temperamental components of 'towards' (William), 'against' (Peter) and 'away from' (Paul). Further, he has indicated that there is a relationship between a person's temperament and his bodily structure. According to Sheldon, the social extravert will tend to have a round body, the manipulative extravert a muscular body and the introvert a linear body in which the chest is flat and the viscera and muscles are relatively undeveloped. The descriptions drawn of the three boys owe much to the work of Sheldon.[2]

Sheldon's original work was done with subjects aged 18–30, but there are researches going on with children which tend to support the relevance of these three temperamental components to the study of children. There is the work of Parnell (17) in

[1] From Greek *morphe* meaning shape.
[2] A description of, and a theoretical comment upon, Sheldon's work is given in the next chapter.

England; of Walker (21, 22), and Sheldon himself, who is now supervising a longitudinal research study, with American children.

At this point a word of caution is needed. I do not wish to give the impression that every child's personality is wholly determined by the kind of body he has. Rather, the position is this: two views have been presented—in the last two chapters the emphasis has been upon environmental influences; in the present chapter the emphasis has been upon possible hereditary influences. Because these two influences have been studied separately, we may fail to see that they can never in fact be separated and that personality results from their interplay.

On the one hand, as stressed in this chapter, an individual may be temperamentally prone to certain modes of behaviour: to be affectionate, or to be assertive, or to be withdrawn. On the other hand, as stressed in Chapter 4, most members of the society or group to which he belongs may encourage some and discourage other modes of behaviour according to the needs, purposes and ideals they have accepted. The Zuni people would encourage William, in his affectionate moving towards people and he would adjust easily to their way of living; but they would ostracize Peter because of his assertiveness, and it would be hard for him to adjust to the pressure exerted upon him to be gentle and non-assertive. Not so the Dobuans. Here Peter's assertiveness would be encouraged and William would be handicapped.

To take a further illustration, one more applicable to our own society: if a school places very great emphasis on sport, which demands vigorous activity, assertion and a hard, tough body, then Peter will thrive. But it is an environment to which neither William nor Paul will adapt naturally and spontaneously, although they may try hard to do so. The point of these illustrations is to show that a person's temperament will influence his capacity to acquire the dispositions and to follow the ways of behaving approved by most members of the society or group to which he belongs.

It follows that people's differing temperaments affect the ways in which they will react to similar social situations. For example, close study of the results of parental control and children's behaviour shows that there are exceptions to the general trends indicated in the last chapter. It would seem that not all children react equally severely to the extreme parental attitudes described, and that some appear to be more resilient to a particular kind of family climate than others.

These differences may have a temperamental basis. One child, like William for example, may be able to withstand more of the over-affection of the possessive parent; another, like Peter, more discipline; yet another, like Paul, more parental indifference (because Paul is more self-sufficient than most children). However, the imaginary descriptions of William, Peter, and Paul are purposely made extreme in order to provide 'pure' cases; and most children are not like any one of the three boys. Most children are mixtures; they turn towards, against, or away from as different occasions demand. In these cases, it is more likely that the pressure of the environment will be important in determining the particular way of reacting, so that most children assimilate the anxiety, ambition, aggression, stability and so on of their parents, as described in the preceding chapter.

It is not, therefore, a case of *either* heredity *or* environment, but of *both*. Each sets limits to the influence of the other. Applying this to a specific ability: a person may have great musical potentialities but there are no social forces to encourage their development; alternatively, a social environment may be such that it encourages the development of musical potential in every possible way but the person concerned has little to develop.

In this and the two previous chapters, only the surface of the problem of individual differences has been touched on in a suggestive and descriptive way. Nevertheless, even though we do not have in our family or class a child who is exactly a William, a Peter, or a Paul, the three sketches and the three responses ('towards', 'against' and 'away from') may provide valuable indicators for our observation of individual differences between children.

REFERENCES

1   Bayley, N. 'A study of the crying of infants during mental and physical tests.' *Journal of Genetic Psychology*, 1932, **40**, pp. 306–29.
2   Brackett, C. W. 'Laughing and crying of pre-school children.' *Journal of Experimental Education*, 1933, **2**, pp. 119–26.
3   Campbell, R. V. D., Welch, A. A. 'Measures which characterize the individual during the development of behaviour in early life.' *Child Development*, 1941, **12**, pp. 217–40.

4   Escalona, S., Heider, G. M. *Prediction and Outcome: A Study in Child Development.* Basic Books, New York, 1959.

5   Fries, M. E. 'Factors in character development, neuroses, psychoses and delinquency.' *American Journal of Orthopsychiatry*, 1937, **7**, pp. 142–81.

6   Gesell, A., Ames, L. B. 'Early evidences of individuality in the human infant.' *Journal of Genetic Psychology*, 1937, **47**, pp. 339–61.

7   Gesell, A. 'The ontogenesis of infant behaviour.' *In* Carmichael, L. (Ed.) *Manual of Child Psychology.* Wiley, New York, 1954, pp. 358–64.

8   Gottesman, I. I. 'Heritability of personality.' *Psychological Monographs*, 1963, **77**, No. 9.

9   Grossman, H. J., Greenberg, N. H. 'Psychosomatic differentiation in infancy.' *Psychosomatic Medicine*, 1957, **19**, pp. 293–306.

10 Hall, C. S. 'The genetics of behaviour.' *In* Stevens, S. S. *Handbook of Experimental Psychology.* Wiley, New York, 1951, pp. 304–29.

11 Heider, G. M. 'Vulnerability in infants and young children.' *Genetic Psychology Monographs*, 1966, **73**, pp. 1–126.

12 Jost, H., Sontag, L. W. 'The genetic factors in autonomic nervous system function.' *Psychosomatic Medicine*, 1944, **6**, pp. 308–10.

13 Kagan, J., Moss, H. A. *Birth to Maturity.* Wiley, New York, 1962.

14 Murphy, G. *Personality.* Harper, New York, 1947.

15 Neilson, P. 'Shirley's babies after fifteen years.' *In* Dennis, W. (Ed.) *Readings in Child Psychology.* Prentice-Hall, New York, 1951, pp. 461–72.

16 Newman, H. H., Freeman, F. N., Holzinger, K. J. *Twins: A Study of Heredity and Environment.* University of Chicago Press, Chicago, 1938.

17 Parnell, R. W. *Behaviour and Physique.* Arnold, London, 1958.

18 Scheinfeld, A. *The New You and Heredity.* Chatto and Windus, London, 1952.

19 Sheldon, W. H., Stevens, S. S. Tucker, W. B. *The Varieties of Human Physique.* Harper, New York, 1940.

20 Sheldon, W. H., Stevens, S. S. *The Varieties of Temperament.* Harper, New York, 1942.

21 Walker, R. N. 'Body build and parents' ratings.' *Child Development*, 1963, **34**, pp. 1–23.

22 Walker, R. N. 'Body build and nursery school teachers' ratings.' *Monograph of the Society for Research in Child Development*, 1964, **27**, No. 3 (Serial No. 84).

23 Washburn, R. W. 'A study of the smiling and laughing of infants in the first year of life.' *Genetic Psychology Monographs*, 1929, **6**, pp. 403–537.

The Organization of Personality

MOST of what has been said so far is contained within the following schema (Fig. 1):

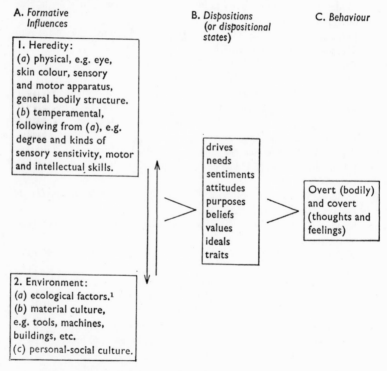

FIG. 1 Schematic representation of the formation of personality

¹ Ecological factors refers here to external factors which are not man–made, e.g. climate, soil, topography, endemic diseases, animals.

This schema has been adapted from one presented by New-comb (14)[1] and may be worded as follows: owing to the interplay (↑↓) of hereditary and environmental influences (A) an individual develops (⟩) certain dispositional tendencies or states of readiness (B) which determine (⟩) his overt bodily behaviour and his covert thoughts and feelings (C).

The movement need not necessarily be in the sequence A to B to C. For example, a boy may have no interest in stamp collecting at the time he is persuaded by a friend to go reluctantly to a meeting of the stamp club. But he is so stimulated that an interest is developed and of his own accord he studies stamp catalogues, borrows books on stamps from the library and haunts shops which sell stamps. The movement here is from C to B to A_2.

Such a schematic representation, while useful for descriptive purposes, can be misleading: (*a*) because it tends to give the impression that personality is static and unchanging; (*b*) because it fails to show, in clear perspective, the place of the individual within his total environment. The problem of (*a*) has already been emphasized in Chapter 1, when it was said that an individual's personality is always in a state of change or becoming. For (*b*), a diagram such as Fig. 2 (below) adapted from Murphy (13)[2]

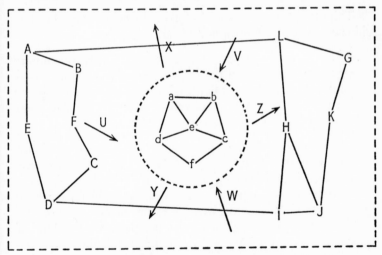

FIG. 2 Schematic representation of the organization of personality

[1] page 131.   [2] page 8.

complements the schema and corrects this lack of perspective. Fig. 2 may be explained as follows:

1   The rectangle represents the environment: material, social, cultural. The lines are broken to indicate that for any individual the environment is never absolute but always capable of expansion.

2   The circle represents the individual, and it is broken to indicate that the individual is 'open' to his environment.
    a) A, B, C, . . . , L represent all the factors in the environment which influence the individual. They are connected by lines showing that they are related. The three arrows, U, V, W represent all these 'inflowing' influences.
    b) a, b, c, . . . , f, within the circle, represent dispositions. These are connected by lines to indicate that dispositions tend to be organized. The three lines X, Y, Z represent the 'outflowing' influences for, while it is true that the environment influences the individual (arrows U, V, W), once the dispositions are formed and organized the individual makes his impression upon the environment and he may change it quite markedly, as do outstanding artists, musicians, scientists.

This discussion may be taken further by considering this five-fold classification of human behaviour.

1   *Behaviour involving simple reflex movements*, that is, involuntary segmental responses of the body to stimulation, such as eye-blink response to bright light, withdrawal of hand or foot on pin-prick, plantar reflex, movement of the eyes in response to movement of the head.

2   *Behaviour involving the organization of simple reflex movements.* This is more complex and includes the reflex movements involved in: (*a*) walking, movements of the head and eyes, righting reflexes which come into play particularly when the body is off balance or when we change our position (for example, from lying down to standing); (*b*) building up states of physiological need within the body and the mechanical processes of their satisfaction, that is, the purely reflex processes involved in eating (salivary secretion, swallowing and so on), digestion of food, drinking, or sexual behaviour.

3 *Behaviour in which automatic actions are organized into habits.* As a result of learning, the form of behaviour under 1 and 2 becomes organized into simple skills which individuals learn to carry out in a routine way: (*a*) the reflexes involved in motor movements are organized into the routines of getting up, washing, shaving, dressing, catching train or bus, and the routines which are part of every job; (*b*) the reflexes involved in physiological processes become organized within the context of social rituals, customs and institutions—set meals appropriately eaten, sexual activity according to the norms set by society.

Such habitual behaviour is on an 'in-between' level as it were. It obviously presupposes levels 1 and 2, but it is also connected with the dispositional level (level 4) mentioned below, for we develop attitudes towards food, drink and sexuality. There are the 'right' foods and drinks, and 'right' sexual behaviour. We learn to approve the socially 'right' ways of walking, gesturing, holding the head.

4 *Behaviour from which a disposition (or dispositional tendency) is inferred.* 'Disposition' has a more dynamic meaning than 'habit', and implies such forms of behaviour as goal-seeking behaviour (from which we infer a need, a drive, a purpose), loving, hating, evaluating, imagining (from which we infer sentiments, attitudes, values, ideals); also behaviour, such as has been illustrated in Chapter 2, which involves perceiving, feeling, acting.

5 *Behaviour from which it may be inferred that dispositions are organized.* This is more clearly the level of behaviour from which 'personality' is inferred, for personality has been defined as 'an organization of dispositions'. To this definition may be added the phrase 'towards a particular way of life'.

It may be argued that the term 'personality' should embrace all five classes of behaviour, for the reflective, automatic and routine forms of behaviour are necessary conditions for 'dispositional' behaviour. The first three levels are concerned with man as a physiological and physical being; the second two levels with man as a psychological being. If these varying levels of organization are called 'systems', then we have (*a*) neuro-physio-physical systems and (*b*) psychological systems. Further, if the meaning of personality is extended to include all five levels, our definition can be stated as 'the organization within the individual of those psycho-neuro-physio-physical systems which determine his unique way of life'. This definition becomes, in essence, the same as that given by Allport (1).[1]

Of course, everything there is to know about a person, including intellectual abilities, aptitudes and skills of all kinds, could be included within the concept 'personality'. But usually personality study is not specifically concerned, for example, with the nature and measurement of intelligence and aptitudes, but rather with dispositions as we have described them and with states of readiness to perceive, to experience emotions and to act, which the concept 'disposition' implies.

So far the exposition has been simple; it is mainly the 'ingredients' of personality that have been described, with the simple statement that these ingredients cohere to form a unit called personality which is organized towards a particular style of life. But in their explanation of how these ingredients cohere, psychologists divide themselves sharply into differing schools of thought, the more important of which will now be broadly outlined.

Personality has its history in the past; it operates in the present towards the future. Individual psychologists often stress one of these three components—past, present or future—to the relative neglect of the other two. Thus, some psychologists stress that man has his history in the past; some that he functions in the present; some that he operates towards the future. Each of these points of view will be taken in turn.

Emphasis on the past

There are two fairly distinct groups amongst those psychologists who emphasize past history: (*a*) those who take a mechanistic and (*b*) those who take a predominantly personalistic view of man. Each will be studied in turn.

The mechanistic psychologist is usually a behaviourist—that is, he studies outward behaviour and does not concern himself with man's inner mental experiences. He would argue thus: the physical

[1] page 48.

scientist observes, experiments, makes laws. This enables him to predict the positions, speeds, and directions of bodies and so to understand and control the physical world. If psychologists are to understand, predict and control human behaviour, then they must proceed along mechanistic lines, studying only overt behaviour and, as far as possible, following the methods of the physical scientists.

Accordingly, the mechanists take the simply reflex response (form of behaviour 1) as the basic unit of behaviour. For them, more complex behaviour, as in walking, running and so on, consists of a number of such simple reflex responses. One simple reflex response becomes the stimulus for another simple reflex response and in this way a long chain of successive stimulations and responses accounts for more complicated behaviour (form of behaviour 2).

But these simple formulas, reflexes and chains of reflexes are not on their own adequate to explain the complicated behaviour of animals and, more especially, the behaviour of man in society. It was Pavlov who provided the mechanists with a solution to this difficulty as the result of his series of experiments which led to his idea of the conditioned reflex.

Pavlov's classic experiment may be summarized as follows:

1 He presented a natural or unconditioned stimulus (food) to a starving dog who responded with a natural or unconditioned response (the dog salivated).

2 He presented an unnatural stimulus (the sound of a bell) to the starving dog and the dog made no response. A few seconds afterwards he gave the dog food.

3 He repeated the procedure many times with the result that at the sound of the bell (now the conditioned stimulus) the dog salivated (now the conditioned response).

Through a process of training he thus established a connection between a stimulus (sound of a bell) and a response (salivation) which were unrelated before the training began. Pavlov proceeded further with his experiments. For example, he varied the sound of the bell to see if the dog would respond to tones varying from that of the original. He discovered that, within limits, a dog could distinguish one sound from another. He stopped rewarding the dog and found that after a time the dog ceased to salivate. The conditioned reflex was 'extinguished'. He punished the dog with electric shocks; he randomly alternated reward and punishment. Dogs so treated became nervous, fearful, irritable and aggressive. This behaviour has been compared with neurotic behaviour in human beings.

Figuratively speaking, the bell which Pavlov's dog heard reverberated throughout the psychological world: although he was himself a physiologist, Pavlov had provided the psychologist with a new unit of behaviour, the conditioned reflex. In the same way as complicated behaviour, such as walking, running, is seen to be made up of a series of simple reflex responses, so the organized and routine behaviour which we call habits (form of behaviour 3) is seen to be derived from more simple conditioned reflexes. In short, as a result of conditioning men learn habits.

By thus using the first three forms of behaviour (reflexes, chains of reflexes, habits) together with Pavlov's idea of the conditioned reflex, the responses of the trained or domesticated animal, the behaviour of man in society and even neurotic breakdown are explained in mechanistic terms.

Many theories of behaviour have arisen, differing from one another in some of their details, but essentially based on these principles. The work of Hull (9) is probably the most systematic attempt to work out a theory on these lines. His theory is based upon the biological adaptations to the environment that living creatures make. When there is some deviation from optimal biological conditions, a creature is said to be in a state of need, and this is accompanied by noxious stimuli, such as those connected with the contraction of the stomach in hunger, dryness of the mouth in thirst, hot or cold stimuli following deviation from optimal bodily temperature. The connection between a stimulus and a response is reinforced or strengthened when the response is followed by 'need reduction', as Hull puts it—that is, by a reduction in the state of deviation from optimal biological conditions prevailing before the response was made. This way of explaining the connection between a stimulus and a response applies to an unconditioned response: for example, a bird ruffling up its feathers during very cold weather. The connection between extreme cold (stimulus) and ruffling of feathers (response) is strengthened because ruffling has in the past been followed by 'need reduction', that is, cessation of cold stimuli. This way of explaining a connection applies also to conditioned responses. Hull would say, for example, that the connection between hearing the bell and salivation has been strengthened in Pavlov's dog because salivation has been followed many times previously by 'need reduction'— that is, by the cessation of hunger. For Hull, habits are stimulus-response connections that have been established in this way.

It would go beyond the purpose of this book to consider such theories in any detail. The main point is that they illustrate the view that the behaviour of man is determined by past training. Connections or bonds are established between events (stimuli) and behaviour (responses). The theorists agree in that they take a mechanistic point of view, seeing man as a relatively passive creature who, as a result of conditioning, acquires habits.

They differ, however, on the crucial question as to how these connections are established. Some say that such connections are established because of the rewards received on the completion of a stimulus-response sequence, as when a pony is given a lump of sugar on successfully taking his first jump (called the Law of Effect). As Thorndike, one of the early workers in this field, has put it, 'pleasure stamps in'. Actually, Hull's need-reduction is a form of the Law of Effect, but Hull would not use a word such as 'pleasure' because he was a thoroughgoing mechanist who avoided any reference to consciousness.

Other theorists, for example Guthrie (7), lay more stress on the way a particular stimulus-response sequence is related to the reward that follows it. They would say that the closer a stimulus-response sequence and the reward are together in time and space, the more probable it is that later presentation of the same stimulus will lead to the same response (called the Principles of Temporal and Spatial Contiguity). According to these principles, the pleasure the pony experiences from the lump of sugar is not as important as the fact that the sugar is given to the pony immediately he has made the jump (contiguity in time), or as near to the jumping stand as possible (contiguity in space). Many experiments have been and are being done, chiefly with albino rats, to investigate the relative effects of rewards and punishments in strengthening ('reinforcing') or breaking ('extinguishing') such connections (7, Chapter 4).

These experiments and the theories derived from them come under the area of study known in psychology as 'learning theory'.

Learning is seen as the establishment of connections, or the strengthening of connections already established. It takes place under the impetus of a need or drive, and may be reinforced or extinguished by means of reward, punishment, repetition of established connections and so on.[1]

Mechanistic theories of learning have not, as yet, exerted a significant influence on everyday classroom procedure. This may be because the concepts used, though providing a relatively simple explanation of learning, do not adequately encompass the complexities and nuances of teacher-pupil relationships (as described briefly in Chapter 5) and the varying effect of these on children's learning. It should be added, however, that this approach to learning has provided the theoretical inspiration behind the idea of teaching machines and, in that this is so, its influence in education is beginning to be felt.

This brief account of mechanistic theories of learning is given here because attempts have been made to explain the organization of personality in these terms. Eysenck (6b), for example, bases his theory of personality mainly upon the work of Pavlov and Hull.

Another group of psychologists who emphasize man's determination by his past are concerned more with dispositions and with organized dispositions (forms of behaviour 4 and 5). For them, outside events lead to the formation of dispositions having the dynamic and directive properties indicated earlier. They are important antecedents of man's behaviour, and mediate between outside events on the one hand and a person's response to them on the other. Dispositions are emphasized throughout this book (although not their determination wholly by the past), and this emphasis is implied in the schema and the figure (Figs. 1 and 2) presented earlier in this chapter.

The difference between the mechanistic and personalistic viewpoints may be illustrated in this way. A mother notices that her fifteen-year-old son has suddenly taken to cleaning his teeth and that she has no longer to cajole and nag to persuade him to do so.

---

[1] It should be added that theories which take an essentially mechanistic approach do not exhaust the area of study known as 'learning theory'. Other theorists stress the role of purpose in learning, and define learning in terms of 'insight' or of changes in 'cognitive structure', that is, changes in an organism's knowledge and understanding of a situation (see (7), Chapters 7, 8).

The mechanist would say that the behaviour reinforced by past training has at last been 'stamped in' and a habit thoroughly established. By contrast, those who stress dispositions would say that the child has developed new values, purposes, attitudes. Whereas, as a grubby youngster of ten, he did not care about his appearance and whether or not his teeth decayed, he is now very much concerned with these things. It is this dispositional change that accounts for the change in behaviour. According to this view, a mother may be unwise to congratulate herself too heartily on what she believes is the delayed though successful outcome of her past training, because past training in itself is not enough to establish the behaviour. It served a useful purpose in preserving his teeth only until he acquired his present values, purposes, attitudes.

The emphasis on dispositions is also illustrated in the work of Freud and his followers who see the personality of man as determined by events occurring during the very early years of childhood. For example, there is Freud's classical conception of the 'oral' and 'anal' characters. He traces the oral character back to the satisfaction or lack of satisfaction of the need to feed and to suck during the first year of life, satisfaction at this early stage leading to adult traits of self-assurance, generosity, optimism, and lack of satisfaction to loss of confidence in one's own abilities and uncertainty about one's capacity to maintain the affection of others. He traces the anal character back to the effects of a toilet training which was so severe that the child, in his determination to conform, over-conformed. The adult is an adult who is also conforming, extremely neat and tidy in his person, punctual, and orderly in arranging and classifying his thoughts and experiences. For the Freudians, a major process in therapy is to trace the history of the early years so that an individual understands how such events as these are related to his present dispositional tendencies.

An experimental study supporting this emphasis on the past is given by Bowlby (3a). He seeks to prove that children who experience no affection in early childhood and who suffer from what he calls 'affect hunger' become psychologically crippled and unable to accept or to give affection in later life. Bowlby states further that the younger the child is when he suffers from 'affect hunger', the more crippling the effect in adult life.

Emphasis on the present

Some psychologists protested against this extreme determinism by past events. The behaviour of man obviously has its historical antecedents, but a man's personality can be relatively independent of past events. Allport (1) gives this illustration. A boy of fifteen does not get on with his father. The father and son have a violent quarrel and the son runs away to sea as a cabin boy. Forty years pass and the boy is now captain of a large trading vessel. He has done well in his chosen career, is a skilled seaman and genuinely enjoys the life of a sailor. Allport argues that we cannot say that the sailor's hatred of his father and their final quarrel are *the* cause of the sailor's present personality. It is more appropriate to explain it in terms of the beneficial events of the present and the favourable attitudes of the sailor to his job. Allport generalizes this viewpoint with his Principle of Functional Autonomy: 'Adult motives are infinitely varied, self-sustaining, *contemporary* systems growing out of antecedent systems but functionally independent of them' (1).[1]

Allport adds that it may be unwise to do as Freud does and base a general theory of personality on the experiences of people who break down and become neurotic or psychotic. For these people, events in early childhood may have a potency that does crucially affect their contemporary behaviour. But this may not be so for the majority of people who function pretty effectively at the present. Allport's point seems to be a very relevant one. For example, suppose our young man, instead of running away to sea, had gone to a large city and taken a menial job in the dingiest part of the city and that he had stayed there for years hating the job and hating the place. This hatred would perpetuate his earlier hatred of his father and keep alive the bitter memory of the final quarrel. He would probably say, as he reflected upon his miserable existence, 'My father was the *cause* of all this.' In short, whereas happiness in the present may well dissipate the effects of painful experiences of the past, unhappiness in the present not only perpetuates the painful experiences and associations of the past but may also cause a person to exaggerate them.

This point of view receives support from the later work of Bowlby (3b), as a result of which he revised his earlier conclusion mentioned above, namely, that deprivation of affection in the

[1] page 194.

early days inevitably leads to an inability to give and to receive affection in later life. In this subsequent study, Bowlby observed children, aged between six and thirteen, who had been patients in a T.B. sanatorium for period of months or years before their fourth birthday and who, at the time of the investigation, were at home and attending school. Only thirteen of the sixty children studied showed the inability to give and to receive affection which Bowlby had emphasized in his earlier work. He concludes that experiences after as well as before the sanatorium experience were also important in deciding the children's later behaviour, a conclusion supported by two further studies (5, 16).

Emphasis on the future

A man behaves as he does partly because he believes there is a future and that he will be a part of it. He hopes, aspires, dreams; he has visions; he plans, he makes decisions in terms of the future. It is true that man does reflect on the past and plan in the present, but his hopes, his aspirations, his dreams and his visions, are projected into the future. If he knew there were no future for him and that soon he would die, he would behave differently.

Man is therefore a creature of purpose, a viewpoint that has been implied throughout the preceding chapters. Behaviour and dispositions have been described as organized towards the completion of a specific task or a particular way of life (Chapter 1). Biologists (e.g. 17, 18, 22) have given many examples of the way in which insects and animals are active in the pursuit of ends which serve some biological purpose—growth, self-maintenance, reproduction. They have put impediments in the way of these animals and insects as they pursue these ends. They find that these creatures will persist and continue to persist if their goal is not reached, that they will vary the means towards the goal because of the impediments and will actively push, pull and strive, ceasing such activity only when the goal is reached. In this way, they show all the marks of purposive behaviour as described by McDougall (12).[1]

But it is safe to assume that insects and animals are not consciously aware of their goals and of the biological purposes they serve. Because this is so, Russell (18) speaks of such behaviour in insects and animals as *directive*. By contrast, *purposive* behaviour

[1] page 43.

implies that an individual is consciously aware of the goals he is pursuing.

This distinction which Russell makes between directive and purposive behaviour is an interesting one. Some human behaviour, especially that of children, may be interpreted as directive rather than purposive. For example, we are sometimes puzzled by the 'knowing' behaviour of a very young child when he appears not to want to go to bed or to have his bath. In all sorts of ways he may divert his mother's attention away from the preparation of either. On observing such behaviour, we say the child is 'cunning', 'a knowing little boy', as if he is consciously aware of what he is doing. But it may be more apt, following Russell's distinction, to call his behaviour directive rather than purposive.

This probably applies to much of the behaviour of even older children. As I shall explain in the next chapter, children want 'to love', 'to have', 'to learn'; they 'seek adventure'. Throughout the study of children's emotional and social growth which follows, such phrases as these will often be repeated: children *want* 'to grow up', 'to be independent', 'to be a boy', 'to be a girl'. But children may well be unaware of purposes in this explicit way. They are aware only of a spontaneous desire to do this, that or the other, of a painful feeling of frustration or a compulsive urge to persist if they are thwarted. Adults, with their wider perspectives on human growth, are able to look at behaviour in the present and see its relevance for, and relation to the future, just as does the biologist in his study of insects and animals.

But, of course, the distinctive feature of man is that his behaviour is purposive as well as directive; he pursues vocational and life goals and is consciously aware of the end he has in view. There is a sense in which it may be said that the process of healthy growth is one in which there is a gradual progression from directive to purposive behaviour. As children approach middle and late adolescence, they decide on the career they wish to follow and will work consciously towards this end. Allport puts it as follows: 'The possession of long range goals, regarded as central to one's personal existence, distinguishes the human being from the animal, the adult from the child and in many cases the healthy personality from the sick' (2).[1]

In summary, the theories presented have their individual

[1] page 51.

emphases. Man's personality is explained as the result of previous training or of the past influence of events and people; in terms of present needs, desires, purposes, or in terms of hopes and aspirations for the future.

All four points of view have a place in helping us to understand children's developments and no one theory is sufficient in itself. Thus, the mechanistic approach helps us to understand the acquisition by children of the many routines of everyday living, such as those involved in biological care—meals, excretion, sleep, bathing, cleaning of teeth, dressing—and the relative value of rewards and punishments in acquiring these routines. Secondly, when a child is neurotic and unable to function happily in the present, clinical emphasis on the past is appropriate in order to diagnose the trouble and to suggest a possible solution. Thirdly, when we are concerned with healthy children who are developing their mental, physical and social resources in a satisfactory way and when we are concerned (as we shall be later) with the typical behaviour of such children at varying stages of their development, the emphasis is necessarily on the needs, values, attitudes of the present and with immediate rather than long-term purposes. Finally, children are creatures of the future and we are justified, therefore, in seeing their behaviour as related to the future, and in trying to comprehend some of its complexities in terms of the future. But the specific purposes a child acquires, and the means he will use to achieve them, have been learned in the past and are partly understood by reference to the past. Thus, all three emphases—past, present and future—are necessary to a total study of the personality of man.

This does not by any means exhaust all the many theoretical approaches to the study of personality, and two more will now be considered.

Constitutional psychology

Since Sheldon presents yet another way of explaining how dispositions cohere, and since the personality sketches given in the last chapter were based on his findings, his work will now be described in greater detail and its theoretical implications further discussed.

Sheldon is a constitutional psychologist who has investigated the relationship between the bodily structure of individuals and the way they behave. The work upon which his main findings are based has three main phases.

The first aimed to discover and to measure basic components of physique. Four thousand students were photographed in three positions, frontal, dorsal, lateral. After inspecting the films and making diameter measurements of various parts of the body from the films themselves and expressing these measurements as an index of height, Sheldon arrived at three components of bodily structure which he called endomorphy, mesomorphy and ectomorphy.[1] The process of measuring the components he called somatotyping (20). An endomorphic body is round and soft; the digestive viscera are large and highly developed. The arms and legs are relatively short. A mesomorphic body is hard, firm, upright: muscle, bone and connective tissue are highly developed. An ectomorphic body is linear, the chest flat and both viscera and muscles are but slightly developed. The arms and legs are like pipe stems with no protruberances caused by bulging muscles or fat.

All people have some at least of each component. Sheldon used a seven-point scale to indicate the relative strength of each component with 7 as the maximum and 1 as the minimum strength of any component. Thus, 7-1-1 represents an extreme endomorph; 1-7-1, an extreme mesomorph; 1-1-7, an extreme ectomorph; a somatotype such as 2-4-5 represents a greater mixture of components, with ectomorphy the most predominant.

The second phase aimed to discover and to measure some basic components of temperament. To do so, Sheldon made a detailed study of two hundred students by means of interviews, questionnaires and observation of their day-to-day behaviour. As a result, he proposed three main components of temperament which he called viscerotonia, somatotonia and cerebrotonia (21). The viscerotonic person is generally relaxed, loves ease and comfort and is sociable. He moves towards people. The somatotonic person is vigorous and assertive. He wants to control situations and people. In that he is often aggressive, he moves against

[1] The terms are derived from the names of the three kinds of cells from which different parts of the body are embryologically derived—that is, endoderm cells (digestive system), mesoderm cells (muscular system), ectoderm cells (sensory system). See pages 172-3.

people. The cerebrotonic person is restrained, inhibited, hyper-sensitive. In that he keeps himself emotionally and socially at a distance, he moves away from people.[1] These three temperamental components correspond to what has earlier been called social extraversion (viscerotonia), manipulative extraversion (somatotonia) and introversion (cerebrotonia). Sheldon again uses a seven-point scale to indicate the degree of each component a person possesses, 7-1-1 representing extreme viscerotonia, 1-7-1 extreme somatotonia, 1-1-7 extreme cerebrotonia; a temperamental rating such as 4-5-3 represents a greater mixture of components, with somatotonia predominant.

During the third phase Sheldon studied another two hundred students in order to assess the relationship between bodily structure and behaviour. His results suggest that there is a relationship between:

1 having an endomorphic body and behaving like a viscerotonic;
2 having a mesomorphic body and behaving like a somatotonic;
3 having an ectomorphic body and behaving like a cerebrotonic.

The reader will now see how the imaginary studies of William, Peter and Paul, given in the last chapter, have been built up on the basis of Sheldon's findings. William is predominantly an endomorph and his behaviour is viscerotonic, Peter predominantly a mesomorph and his behaviour somatotonic, Paul predominantly an ectomorph and his behaviour cerebrotonic. For Sheldon, therefore, the way dispositions cohere depends upon the individual's bodily structure (see Fig. 3, page 126).

Other psychologists have classified people in a similar way; Kretschmer (10), for example, the most outstanding of these psychologists, preceded Sheldon in presenting a classification similar to, but by no means identical with, his. The sketches presented in the last chapter have been based on Sheldon's findings because he gives the most significant pointers to date regarding the possible relationship between certain ways of behaving and certain bodily characteristics, and, as these latter are inherited, to

[1] These three forms of behaving, namely, moving towards, against and away from people, are also described by Horney (8).

the possible place of heredity in determining the way personality functions.

In summing up Sheldon's work, this may be said: like the psychologists mentioned earlier, who specialize within their own

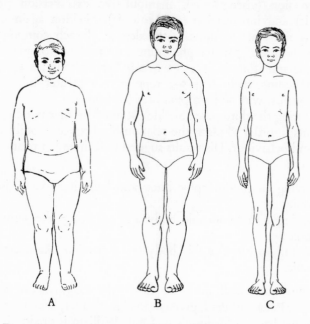

FIG. 3 Contrasting somatotypes in three boys: A. endomorphic;
B. mesomorphic; C. ectomorphic

fields and emphasize past or present or future, Sheldon gives us one among many other possible cues to the many influences which determine the shape a personality will take. In the case of people who are heavily endowed with one of the bodily components and with the corresponding temperamental component, the cue may be an important and significant one. Even here, however, the individual is likely to modulate the amount of affection or assertion or withdrawal he expresses according to the needs and the demands of the group to which he belongs. Moreover, as most people are mixtures, it is more likely that the pressures of the environment will tip the balance towards one way of behaving rather than another.

The 'self' and the 'self-concept'

Some psychologists feel that all five approaches so far described are together not enough to explain the unity of personality. They would say that, over and beyond these determinations by bodily structure, or by past, present or future events, each individual develops a sense of self or 'I-ness' which is the main source for the organization of his personality.

The term 'self' is a precarious one for a scientifically-minded psychologist to use. The mechanists see it as a question-begging, mystical concept, evoked, like the rabbit out of the magician's hat, to explain a unity that is best studied on the scientific level of the organization of reflexes, unconditioned and conditioned, and of habits. But whatever the behaviourists say, there are regions of a person's life that he regards as essentially *his* and, because this is so, he experiences in his private world a sense of unity, of coherence which we may call an experience of self or 'I-ness'.

Allport (2) has used the word 'proprium' as a collective word to refer to these regions of the self that appear to be closest to the individual. Consideration of this 'proprium' has partly been anticipated by study of *I, me, my* and *mine* (Chapter 3) and what follows is in essence an amplification of this.

I have a body and the sensations which occur in this body are experienced as an essential part of me. Despite the fact that cells are continually dying off and being replaced by new ones, I feel I have the same body now as I had a year or so ago. I can also remember past events and I experience these as having happened to me. If I have done something mean in the past, I still feel it is 'I' who did it, and, when I recall the event, I still feel a sense of shame because of it. The law also acknowledges a continuing identity. If a man commits a crime, he may be tried many years later just as if he had been arraigned immediately after he had committed the crime. The law does not question the justice of this. He is the same man.

The sense of 'I-ness' is particularly affected by the way we view ourselves—the self-concept spoken of in Chapter 4. Praise is a means of encouraging a positive self-concept. A child does a piece of work and he is not satisfied with it. Then a favourite adult points out its good qualities and the changed self-concept, the enhanced self-feeling, is expressed in a change of countenance, a

smile, a little shuffle of the body. Blame is a means by which a
negative self-concept is engendered and the private feeling may
be one of dejection. We are aware that these changes of feeling
do take place and we may use this knowledge to reward (praise)
or punish (blame), to gain favour with or to offend another person.

The sense of 'I-ness' is also experienced in purposive activity—
passing an examination, becoming a teacher, writing a book. The
very continuity of such long-term projects gives us a private experience of unity. This sense of unity is also engendered by an
extension of the proprium to *objects*—*my* house, *my* home town;
my wife, *my* daughter. The continuity of these is felt as part of my
own continuity. As Sartre (19) has said, it is interesting to observe
that in primitive groups a man's private possessions are buried
with him—the utensils, the spears, the clothes he used. They are
regarded as so much an essential part of a person that the burial of
a man would not seem complete unless they were buried with
him.

These private experiences—the sense of identity in the present,
of continuity of this identity through time, of being active and
striving, are as real a part of a person's life and are as much facts of
his experience as is his outward behaviour.

To describe these experiences, it may be well to avoid the use
of 'self' as a noun and to use verbal compounds such as *self-
reflecting, self-evaluating, self-enhancing, self-depreciating*. In this way,
it is clear that we are referring to a person's behaviour. Often such
behaviour is covert, consisting of events happening in a person's
private world which he may or may not communicate to others.
By thus stressing behaviour, a psychologist *qua* psychologist is
not bound to get involved in metaphysical problems about the
nature of the self.

The hierarchical organization of personality

Some psychologists, including McDougall, have conceived the
organization of personality as a hierarchy of motivational tendencies. The word 'hierarchy' implies a succession of levels, the units
on the lower level being simpler and more numerous than those
on the higher; those on the higher levels diminish in number, but
increase in complexity and comprehensiveness, and in the extent
of the control they exercise over the lower.

McDougall did not believe that mind or consciousness is in itself a physiological entity; nevertheless, his aim was to use physiological knowledge—so far as it would go—to explain the facts of mental life. He accepted the results of evolutionary and experimental physiology as expounded by Sherrington during the early years of this century. These results indicated that the central nervous system was organized in a hierarchy made up of systems and sub-systems of sensori-motor circuits, the higher system controlling the lower (*Physiological Psychology*, 1905, p. 25). Accordingly, McDougall fitted his description of mental life into this scheme. He conceived the organization of personality as consisting of four main levels or 'strata', roughly corresponding to the four main periods or stages in the development of character.

The innumerable sensori-motor reflexes of the first level are organized into a much smaller number of instincts (second level). An instinct McDougall defines as 'an innate disposition which determines an organism to perceive (pay attention to) an object of a certain class and to experience in its presence a certain emotional excitement and impulse to action which find expression in a specific mode of behaviour in relation to that object' (12).[1]

He lists fourteen instincts, which include food-seeking, mating, parental instincts, the instincts of combat, escape, self-assertion, self-submission, acquisition, curiosity, construction, and gregariousness. We are all familiar with the distinctive emotional excitement which accompany most of these instincts—love (in the sense of tenderness) accompanying the parental instinct, anger the combative instinct, fear the instinct to escape, pride that of self-assertion, and so on.

A number of instincts are organized into a single sentiment. Sentiments form the third level. McDougall classified them into (a) concrete particular sentiments, such as love of one's own child, one's own church, and one's own family, (b) concrete general sentiments, such as love of children, of 'the church', of 'the family', as institutions, (c) abstract sentiments, such as love of justice, freedom and democracy.

Instincts are satisfied within the context of family, school and neighbourhood. Therefore, concrete sentiments regulate and control behaviour because a person wishes to satisfy these instinctive needs to conform with social custom. He does not

[1] page 110.

want to offend, but to share the loves and hatreds of the people closely associated with him, to preserve the things to which he is attached and to hate the things which threaten them. This kind of control has an element of expediency—to maintain the good-will of one's fellows and the security which comes from living within social institutions around which the concrete sentiments have been formed. As McDougall says, 'A man's concrete sentiments are apt to lead him to judgments that are valid only for himself' (11).[1]

McDougall regards the abstract sentiments as a more powerful source of organization. For, whereas the concrete sentiments are the product of social habit and memory, the abstract sentiments are the product of reason and reflection. Although they are acquired as a result of social learning, such sentiments as love of justice, truth, honesty, courage and freedom have a universal application. They correspond to our everyday notion of values, and McDougall has called them the 'moral sentiments'.

In a fully integrated personality, all the sentiments are organized under the control of the self-regarding sentiment, which is at the apex of the hierarchy (fourth level). The self-regarding sentiment is a product not only of reason and reflection, but also of morality and is therefore to be equated with the everyday notion of conscience. It implies a person's full acceptance of the values he has been taught. Even apart from what people think, he wishes to become and to remain a good workman, a good husband, a good neighbour. For McDougall, the organization of personality derives from the development of sentiments that are harmonious, with the self-regarding sentiment as the dominant one.

Sir Percy Nunn (15)[2] has traced the growth of personality. He uses McDougall's scheme and Shand's theory of sentiment, upon which McDougall's own was based. An outline of what Nunn has said follows.[3]

Jack, a six-year-old, is taken to the city and has his first ride in a train. For days afterwards he does little else except play trains. He is driver, guard and passenger in turn; and as he takes each role, he talks, walks and dresses the part. The whole of his instinctive

[1] page 188.
[2] Chapter 13, 'The growth of self'.
[3] The account does not cover in all its detail what Nunn has to say about the growth of self; it includes some additions and an emendation or two of my own.

life revolves round this activity. He makes a train out of whatever materials are to hand (construction); he hoards old tickets (acquisition); he seeks out friends to play with him, more especially to take the role of passengers (gregarious); as guard, he tells the driver to go faster (assertive); he shows his uniform to everyone (display). His whole emotional life, and his feelings of well-being depend upon this activity: joy, pleasure, excitement when he is able to pursue it, pain, sorrow, anger when he cannot. Towards trains he has developed a sentiment which Nunn describes as 'a system of feelings, emotions, desires, appetites centred around a particular object'.

When Jack is in his late adolescence he decides to become an electrical engineer and begins to work accordingly. The principles guiding our understanding of his behaviour now are similar to those which guided our understanding of Jack when he was six years old. He has again formed a sentiment (disposition), this time more enduring, with all the behaviour potentialities implied by dispositions and described in earlier chapters. Instinctual drives are directed towards the end of becoming an electrical engineer; feelings of well-being depend upon the success or failure of each step on his way towards professional status.

When he was very young, Jack had many sentiments—as many as the *objects* to which he was attached (see Chapter 3); but they were shifting and relatively outside him. The exclusiveness of the train play was short-lived. Jack at six moves on to other things—to become milkman, postman, doctor, shopkeeper. The self-regarding sentiment is but poorly formed.

For Jack at adolescence, becoming an engineer is inseparably linked with himself as a feeling, acting being. In other words, his self-regarding sentiment has firmly attached itself to the prospect 'myself-as-an-electrical-engineer'. This master sentiment controls his behaviour, so that, for example, he chooses to work at his books rather than go out in the evening.

A vocational sentiment would be among the dominant ones at this time in a young man's life. But there would be others, again as many as there are *objects* to which he is attached—his old school, his home town, sport and sports friends, his girl-friend, for example; and all are inseparably linked with his self-regarding sentiment. So are the major moral sentiments. Jack now recognizes a personal as well as a social mode of control. If he does not follow the moral judgments of the self-regarding sentiment, he will feel guilt and self-hatred.

At forty, Jack is still an enthusiastic electrical engineer. He is also a husband and father, identified with his wife's social aspirations, concerned with his children's progress at school, a church-warden who wants to be well thought of by the other members of his church as well as by the townspeople in general. He is a bowler of some note in the district, and pleased with his skill at the game; he hopes to win the next club tournament. The diversity of these many selves is more apparent than real. In that Jack is identified with all these roles, and in that his feelings of well-being depend upon their continuance, they are an organized part of his self-regarding sentiment. But, as Nunn puts it, 'He will be singularly fortunate if his organism can carry these diverse selves without occasional distraction and conflict' (15).[1]

To summarize this study of the organization of personality: man has been shown as a constellation of needs, purposes, sentiments and attitudes, which have collectively been called dispositions. For each individual there develops a pattern of dispositions, which, once formed, determines the way he will *respond* to situations and people, and the way he *judges* or *evaluates* his own and other people's ways of thinking, feeling and behaving. It determines what he *seeks* (his purpose and goals), and the way he *influences* other people by attracting, repelling, irritating or frightening them. In short, because a man 'has' a personality he is not inert and at rest until he is stimulated from outside. Rather he is continuously in a state of dispositional readiness—to receive and to react to events, ideas, opinions, and values.

In that these dispositions enable an individual to pursue a particular way of life, we may speak of them as cohering in a comprehensive organized system. To attempt an analogy: just as a building is built to function as a school rather than a hospital or a church, so the dispositions of an individual are patterned in such a way that he is able to function in one way rather than another. Just as we say of a building, 'It is well or badly designed for this particular purpose', so we say of a person, 'He has or he has not the personality (or pattern of dispositions) for the job.'

Finally, it must be emphasized yet again that this is merely an introductory study. Within it lie many difficulties. To mention just

[1] page 202.

one: the term 'disposition' has been used in different ways by different writers, and only a superficial attempt has been made to indicate its ambiguity.

The modern approach to the study of personality is highly scientific, necessitating the use of statistical and scientific procedures to study differing forms of behaviour, to measure the varying strengths of dispositions and to find out how they cluster together (e.g. 4, 6a).

REFERENCES

1   Allport, G. W. *Personality*. Constable, London, 1937.
2   Allport, G. W. *Becoming*. Yale University Press, New Haven, Connecticut, 1960.
3a Bowlby, J. *Maternal Care and Mental Health*. World Health Organization, Geneva, 1951.
3b Bowlby, J., Ainsworth, M. B., Rosenbluth, D. 'The effect of mother-child separation: a follow-up study.' *British Journal of Medical Psychology*, 1956, **29**, pp. 211–47.
4   Cattell, R. B. *Personality and Motivation Structure and Measurement*. World Book Co., New York, 1957.
5   Clarke, A. D. B., Clarke, A. M. 'Some recent advances in the study of early deprivation.' *Journal of Child Psychology and Psychiatry*, 1960, **1**, pp. 26–36.
6a Eysenck, H. J. *The Structure of Human Personality*. Routledge & Kegan Paul, London, 1953.
6b Eysenck, H. J. *The Dynamics of Anxiety and Hysteria*. Routledge & Kegan Paul, London, 1957.
7   Hilgard, E. R. *Theories of Learning*. Appleton-Century-Crofts, New York, revised edition, 1966.
8   Horney, K. *Our Inner Conflicts*. Routledge & Kegan Paul, London, 1946.
9   Hull, C. R. *Principles of Behaviour*. Holt, New York, 1943.
10 Kretschmer, E. *Physique and Character*. Routledge & Kegan Paul, London, 1925.
11 McDougall, W. *An Introduction to Social Psychology*. Methuen, London, 22nd edition, 1931.
12 McDougall, W. *Outline of Psychology*. Methuen, London, 1940.
13 Murphy, G. *Personality*. Harper, New York, 1947.
14 Newcomb, T. M. *Social Psychology*. Dryden Press, New York, 1950.
15 Nunn, Sir Percy. *Education: its Data and First Principles*. Arnold, London, 1956.
16 Pringle, M. L. K., Bossio, V. 'Early, prolonged and emotional maladjustment.' *Journal of Child Psychology and Psychiatry*, 1960, **1**, pp. 37–48.

17 Russell, E. S. *The Behaviour of Animals*. Arnold, London, 1938.
18 Russell, E. S. *The Directiveness of Organic Activity*. Cambridge University Press, London, 1946.
19 Sartre, J. P. 'The meaning of "to make" and "to have".' *In* Moustakas, C. E. (Ed.) *The Self*. Harper, New York, 1956.
20 Sheldon, W. H., Stevens, S. S., Tucker, W. B. *The Varieties of Human Physique*. Harper, New York, 1940.
21 Sheldon, W. H., Stevens, S. S. *The Varieties of Temperament*. Harper, New York, 1942.
22 Thorpe, W. H. *Learning and Instinct in Animals*. Methuen, London, 1956.

PART THREE

Motivation and Children

CHAPTER EIGHT

Basic Needs and Basic Goals

To the question, 'What do plants require in order to grow?' this simple answer may be given: 'Air, water, sunshine and soil with such-and-such constituents'. Plants are so formed that their growth and well-being depend upon their obtaining these basic requirements. In the case of children the problem is more complicated; for them, there is psychological as well as physical growth and well being, so that the question to be asked is, 'Are children so formed in body and mind that certain dispositional states arise which require specific goals for their satisfaction?' In answering this question, the term 'need' will be used to indicate these dispositional states.

The terms *drive* and *conation* have been used to designate the predisposition on the part of living creatures to become persistently active while under the influence of a need. Thus, need inplies conative or drive tendencies (to be active) and a goal (object or situation) to the attainment of which behaviour (called instrumental behaviour) is directed. The term *purpose* or *purposive activity* implies a need, its instrumental behaviour, and its goal.

It has been shown experimentally that a rat deprived of food or water over a limited period of a day or so and allowed to run in a revolving drum makes as many as ten times the number of revolutions of the drum as it does when it is not deprived. The activity of the rat is expended aimlessly under these conditions. In a natural environment, its activity would be more clearly instrumental, and directed towards obtaining food or water. The relation between a state of need and activity is seen in the impetuous, often petulant, restlessness of children and in the wriggling and crying of babies when they are hungry.

Internal or physiological needs—for food, drink and sleep—tend to recur. For the time being hunger is satisfied by eating; but in a few hours it will return. Satisfaction followed by resurgence of a need is sometimes observable with psychological needs: for example, to explore the new and unknown. An explorer will search new territory, then return for a time to the security and comfort of home. But before long he becomes restless, and soon he is off again.

The ways in which many of the needs about to be described are expressed by human beings have their parallel in the behaviour of birds and animals. Birds seek food, find mates, build nests and go through the reproductive cycle. They chirp and sing, play and fight with each other; they live socially, a social life, which, so ornithologists tell us, is an intricate one. Throughout the chapter the parallel will be drawn wherever possible by describing the behaviour of birds and animals under experimental or natural conditions. Hence the discussion that follows will form a picture of children—in both their physical and mental characteristics—functioning as the young of a species belonging to a higher group of primates with all the evolutionary development of primates behind them.

Children, however, are the young of a particular species which has distinctive needs of its own. These make children different from the younger members of all other species. Man's invention of tools and institutions (home, school, church, clubs) makes satisfaction of needs more complicated for children than for birds or animals. It is true that man seeks to provide for the physical necessities of existence, to ensure the continuation of his species, and to be with his fellows; but he also wants to express his individuality—to be original, to create, and to acquire a firmly based self-esteem. For man, therefore, needs sometimes conflict: for example, he wants to be secure, yet to adventure; to be like other people, yet to be unique; to experience a sense of union with other people, yet to be independent of them.

Needs imply goals. For this reason to indicate a state of need we often stress not the need itself but the goal that will satisfy it, by using such verbs as 'desire', 'want' or 'need' with appropriate object—for example, 'I want food', or 'He needs affection'.

In this chapter, 'need' will always be used as a noun to indicate a dispositional state (e.g. the need to be independent); and 'desire', 'want', 'seek' will be used as transitive verbs, the objects of which are the appropriate goals, i.e. situations which, when attained, will end the state of need. Accordingly, the classification which follows is phrased in terms of dispositional states of need and the corresponding goals which will satisfy them.

BASIC BODILY NEEDS AND CORRESPONDING GOALS

The following list of such needs and of the goals which will satisfy them has been compiled by Young (29).[1]

1 Needs arise because of processes taking place within the body. The individual therefore

a) Seeks food and water to satisfy hunger and thirst;
b) Seeks rest and sleep to avoid or reduce fatigue;
c) Seeks to rid the body of waste products by excretory activities;
d) Seeks a member of the opposite sex to satisfy sexual desires.
e) During bodily illness with high temperature and under conditions of heat, cold or lack of oxygen, the body automatically becomes active and perspires, shivers and gasps in an attempt to right the imbalance. When an animal lacks an essential bodily constituent—for example, sugar or calcium—it will seek out the foods which will restore the deficit.

An everyday example of such behaviour is the pregnant woman's craving for certain kinds of foods. A more dramatic instance is the boy, charged in court for stealing huge quantities of sweets, who was subsequently diagnosed as a diabetic.

2 Needs arise because of stimulation by external objects. Resulting behaviour may broadly be divided into

a) approach activities aimed to seek comfort and pleasurable stimulation;
b) withdrawing activities aimed to prevent discomfort and pain.

3 Needs arise for physical activity and for expression of feeling. An individual satisfies such needs through

a) random movement of the arms, legs, hands; gross activity of the whole body, as in running, climbing, swimming;
b) random vocalization, bodily movements: jumping and shouting in excitement or joy; slumping and weeping in sorrow.

[1] page 62.

The need for physical activity is probably greater in children than in adults, and certainly children are less inhibited in expressing it. When they leave the classroom, it is difficult to get them to *walk* along the corridor on the way out to play. They cannot restrain the urge to fling their arms and legs about and to whoop with joy as soon as they are freed from the confines of the classroom. Sometimes we find it exhausting even to watch their careering about in the playground. Their restlessness before a Christmas party or school concert is difficult to suppress.

The division into basic bodily and basic psychological needs arises because some needs, unlike those of hunger, thirst and sex, have no clearly physiological basis. Yet in human beings even the satisfaction of basic bodily needs may become complicated.

Some bodily requirements (such as oxygen, normal body temperature) are usually satisfied automatically; others (such as food, sex) presuppose a complex social organization. Secondly, human beings develop appetites which are not needful to the organism. As the Roman epigrammatist, Martial, put it, 'Man eats when he is not hungry, drinks when he is not thirsty, and makes love at all seasons.' Thirdly, satisfaction of bodily appetites, particularly acquired tastes (beer, wine, tea, smoking), can indirectly satisfy psychological needs. Children who are deprived of affection often start eating a lot, especially sweet things, and for a time they may become quite fat. Adults who are anxious may also over-eat, or smoke more than usual. Because of these complications, the division is by no means clear-cut.

BASIC PSYCHOLOGICAL NEEDS AND CORRESPONDING GOALS

It is not easy to give a complete list of psychological needs and goals. Some psychologists have been content to list only a few, others have listed fifty or more. The six-fold classification below is based on the work of Maslow (17). It presents those needs which, Maslow would say, should be satisfied in order that a child may develop his personality to the full. The everyday examples I have chosen to illustrate the ways in which children and adults display these needs also illustrate what I mean by the process of creative becoming.

1   To experience a sense of union with other people (to belong);
2   To be secure;
3   To be independent of other people;
4   To adventure and to gain new experience;
5   To know, to construct, to create;
6   To experience a sense of personal worth.

The major goals of the first two needs are identity with other people and conservation—keeping things within the environment much the same. The goals of the next three are separateness from other people and change—making the environment different in some way. The last, self-esteem, is derivative in the sense that its satisfaction follows balanced satisfaction of the identity and conservation of the first two, and of the separateness and change of the other three, basic needs.

To experience a sense of union with other people (to belong)

Many experiments with animals have traced the early development of the tendency of living creatures to become attached, especially to members of their own species. It has also been shown that animals and birds can become attached to creatures other than those of their own species. In one well-known experiment, Lorenz took a group of goslings who had become attached to him and another group who had become attached to their own mother. When the groups were mixed and covered with a box and the box was then uncovered, the goslings separated themselves out once again into their two groups. Those who had attached themselves to Lorenz followed him; those who had attached themselves to their mother followed her.[1]

While birds of different species do not usually mate, Craig demonstrated very early in this century that two different subspecies of wild pigeon can be crossed, provided that the young of the one species is reared by adults of the other.

As reported by Hess (12), the conditions in both these instances were experimentally contrived by Lorenz and Craig. The goslings which were devoted to Lorenz had been hatched out in an incubator; the first living creature they saw was Lorenz; and they did not see their mother. The goslings of the other group

[1] Lorenz has used the term *imprinting* (literally meaning 'to stamp a mark on') to denote the sudden acquirement of any fairly complex habit. This experiment on the quasi-maternal attachment of young creatures is a special case of imprinting.

(from the same clutch of eggs) were hatched out and cared for by their mother. Craig held his pigeons in captivity. While, therefore, attachments to creatures of differing species or sub-species can occur under exceptional conditions, it is usually true that under natural conditions birds of a feather do flock together.

De Vore (5) has illustrated how animals live in groups, and seek to remain close to their kin. As a result of his special studies of baboons he points out that a baboon lives the whole of its life in close contact with other baboons. If, in the process of foraging, it gets left behind or finds itself even a few yards apart from its fellows, it hastens to rejoin them. Such behaviour has survival value for both the individual and for the species, since the baboon that does not develop this attachment is more vulnerable to predators and less likely to reproduce.

The tendency to become closely attached has been studied in human babies. In a controlled experiment, Schaffer and Emerson (22) traced the development of a baby's desire to be near to and recognized by others. Up to the age of about seven months, a baby will respond to a familiar person or stranger, though he is more responsive to the former. When he is between twenty-eight and thirty-two weeks, his attachment becomes more specific: to members of the family and more especially to his mother, with the tendency then to show some fear of strangers. The authors speak of the baby's *attachment need*. Their findings are similar to those of Ainsworth (1), who studied twelve East African mother-and-baby pairs. They are also confirmed by Freedman's study (6) of the gradual transformation of the baby's smile after the fifth month or thereabouts, 'from a universal response to all human faces to one reserved only for familiar persons'.

Human beings seek:

a) To be with or in the presence of other people;
b) To be acknowledged individually by another person or persons;
c) To join in co-operative activities with others;
d) To have a specially close relationship with one person or with a few chosen persons.

These headings indicate *relatively* distinct goals of the need to belong. They also represent stages in a progression: from least to most close contact.

TO BE WITH OR IN THE PRESENCE OF OTHER PEOPLE

A baby when put to bed one evening cries and does not go to sleep. His mother picks him up and brings him into the living-room, propping him up against a pillow on the settee. At once his crying stops, his eyes widen, and his head moves slowly from side to side as he follows his mother's movements. He is obviously content; no cries, no whimpers.

When this happens, one of the people in the room may remark that the baby is 'having his mother on': the baby is clearly not in a state of physical need. But the speaker forgets that the need to be with other people may sometimes be as pressing for a baby as the need for food and drink. As she looks back over the day, the mother may recall that the baby had spent most of it by himself and probably wants company for a while.

Children of two or three are playing in the same room. They do not interact; each has his own separate activity (parallel play as it is called, and to be described in more detail later). The nursery teacher calls them, and all except one small boy disappear into another room. He is so busy that he does not hear the teacher. Later on he looks up to find himself alone; he immediately drops the toy he is playing with and hurries to look for his companions.

The reassuring effects of being with other people is more particularly seen when children are anxious. If a thunderstorm awakens and terrifies her children at night, a mother will ask her husband to bring them down into the sitting-room while she prepares hot drinks. In each others' company, the children's fears are eased.

Finally, to take an example from adult life: a young man living alone, who could quite easily watch a film on his own television set, decides he will go to the cinema. To be with other people provides a comforting break from being alone.

TO BE ACKNOWLEDGED INDIVIDUALLY

Merely to be with others is rarely enough in itself; a child seeks individual recognition. When the mother pauses in the midst of her activities to look at her baby who cannot sleep, the baby smiles, moves his arms and wriggles his body. The mother smiles back, shakes her head and says gently, 'You wicked thing. You should be fast asleep.' The mother's tone belies the literal meaning of her words. The baby chuckles, gurgles, thrusts and flexes his arms and legs, and wriggles his trunk with delight.

The lone child, after finding his companions, edges up close to the teacher. She puts her arm round him and he is content. The young man, seated in the cinema, sees someone he knows in the distance. He raises his hand in greeting; his acquaintance responds with a smile. The young man is pleased and settles more comfortably into his seat.

In everyday life, 'Hello', 'Good morning', 'How are you?' are customary greetings; and usually, an acknowledgment received is also reciprocated.

TO JOIN IN CO-OPERATIVE ACTIVITIES

More than just to be with other people, and to be acknowledged by them, children seek to join in co-operative activities with them. The mother may play with her baby 'This little piggy went to market', and the baby's gleeful responses witness to his pleasure. The kindergarten teacher says to the children, 'Let's dance.' Seeing the hopeful look on the small boy's face, she adds, 'Stephen and I will lead you.' When she takes his hand, the pang our small boy experienced earlier on finding himself alone is decisively dispelled.

For older children, their group provides a means by which their energies and skills are organized (much as an institution provides a background of organization and purpose for adults). It also provides excitement and an opportunity for them to express their feelings with zest and in a relatively uninhibited way.

It may be that our young man, on being seated in the cinema, sees a group of close friends. He gestures a request, and in response they beckon him to join them. He does so. His enjoyment of the film is enhanced in that it is now a shared enjoyment.

TO HAVE ESPECIALLY CLOSE RELATIONSHIPS WITH ONE PERSON OR A FEW CHOSEN PERSONS

The need for a sense of union finds its fullest satisfaction when a child has a recognized place within the environment and amongst the people he knows best. This place can be a physical one, for example, the chair at the table which is *his*. The three bears, you will remember, say in turn, 'Who's been sitting in *my* chair, eating *my* porridge, sleeping in *my* bed?' The emphasis on 'my' suggests that, in so far as someone has used what is theirs, an outrage has been committed, a violation of each one's personality.

A brother may tease his sister by sitting in *her* chair. She tries to edge her brother off it, but he tantalizingly keeps his position until their mother, seeing what is happening, says, 'Come now, you know it's her place.' The brother gives way, and the small girl shuffles into the chair with a touch of triumph. She senses, even though she could not put it into words, that her mother's recognition that she has a place of her own implies a recognition of her as a person with legitimate rights.

This need for a place includes a need for an established position in the social order: within the family as son, daughter, sister, brother, eldest, youngest, among companions as friend, playmate, leader, follower. It includes the need for a 'place' in another person's life, to be the subject of someone else's thoughts and tender concern. Even though her mother's affection may have to be shared with a brother and sister, a child likes to be assured that her own position is unique. Recognizing this, her mother may say, 'I love you all, but you, Mary, and you, John, and you, Robert, (pointing to each in turn) each have your special place.' She assures them all that her love is general; she assures each that her love is particular.

Speaking precisely, the need for affection implies this personal recognition, this unique place. Our young man says to himself, 'It's not so good living alone. I'll ask Jane to marry me.' Within our own society it is generally accepted that affection is most perfectly expressed in romantic love.

The need for affection in its precise sense has its complement: to give as well as receive affection, and to feel that this affection is accepted by another.

A gift is often an expression of this desire. The small child picks a flower and gives it to his mother. If she accepts it graciously, he feels assured that the love he bestows on her is valued. But if she happens to be preoccupied and ignores the gift, the child feels unhappy. It is not only that his mother's rejection deflates the joy and expansiveness which accompanies the giving, but that, to the child, her rejection of his gift means rejection of him.

An adult would take a similar point of view. If a person gives a present and then finds that his present has been discarded, he feels he has been rejected. Indeed, in our society there is a relation between loving and giving. Because of this relation between giving and receiving gifts and giving and receiving affection it is understandable that a child who feels deprived of affection may sometimes steal. His feelings of desperation are such that he is compelled, in this symbolic way, to help himself to the affection he feels no one will give him.

The need for affection has generally been regarded as the major psychological need of children. This is understandable, since, when a child is deprived of affection, he loses in many ways.

1   He loses the pleasure of being at one with others, of sharing their activities, their loves and hates, and joys and sorrows.
2   He is without a *place* and, therefore, without a sense of social identity.
3   His self-esteem is imperilled. When he is deprived of affection or when his mother shows obvious preference for a brother or sister, he may experience self-doubts ('Perhaps mother does not love me because I'm not worth it')'. Such self-doubts can become generalized into an overall feeling of unworthiness and to loss of a sense of personal identity.
4   Because of 1, 2 and 3 feelings of security are impaired; so is his capacity to explore and to adventure.

To be secure

Harlow (10) carried out the following experiment with a baby rhesus monkey. He constructed a monkey nursery, consisting of a large box, six feet by six feet, containing a number of things a baby monkey might find interesting: a small artificial tree, crumpled paper, a wooden block, a door knob. It seemed an ideal monkey nursery. Yet when the baby monkey was introduced into the new environment, it curled itself in a corner, hid its head, and would have nothing to do with the nursery or its contents.

Harlow then brought into the nursery a dummy monkey made of soft cloth which he had used in previous experiments and which the baby monkey had accepted as a surrogate mother (see

Fig. 9).[1] The young monkey immediately left its corner and clung to the 'mother'; after a while it began to peer about, then hesitantly made a brief excursion to explore the box and its contents before returning to cling to its 'mother' again. Thereafter, it began to alternate between periods when it explored and periods when it clung to its 'mother', the periods of exploration becoming longer and increasing in frequency.

Harlow took his experiment a step further by introducing strange and frightening objects, for example, a large dog-shaped toy with huge eyes and long antennae. The monkey showed every indication of terror and ran to its 'mother'. Nevertheless, it ventured out after a short time to peer at, explore and even attack the strange creature. When, following these two experiments, Harlow removed the dummy mother, the baby monkey again huddled in the corner with its face hidden.

This experiment suggests (1) that the baby monkey's ability to explore his new environment and to be at ease within it presupposed a secure base from which to venture (2) that the baby monkey was able to cope with a new and strange feature within the environment provided again that there was a secure base from which to venture (and then return).

The behaviour of the baby monkey has its parallel in children's behaviour. A child will often play in the nursery or garden, returning at intervals to his mother, only to go on exploring again when reassured by her continued presence. When out visiting in a strange place, these retreats to mother tend to be more frequent. Older children explore the outside world of street and field as well as the institutional world of school, church and club, with the family as their secure base.

Within the idea of security there is a paradox. The function of security is to enable a child to break away from the early sources of it and find renewed assurance within an ever-widening social circle (28). The child proceeds from the security provided by his mother to that provided by the family as a whole to that provided outside the family by companions and institutions. But the need for security implies a further step on the child's part, namely, to

[1] On pages 190–1 details of other, and related, researches by Harlow with rhesus monkeys will be given in which Harlow illustrates the importance of a mother to a baby monkey. It is true that the experiment described here illustrates the importance of the mother; but the main stress is on *security*.

cope by himself with problems that give rise to anxiety—or at least with some of the less difficult ones. Such 'coping' behaviour is illustrated by the following anecdote.

A group of ten-year-old boys playing in a field come to a fast-flowing stream and decide to cross it. There are stepping stones set at varying distances apart, and sometimes a jump is needed to go from one to another. All the boys cross except for one whom we call Michael. Michael gingerly steps on to the first stone, then back again; he stands immobile, unable to take another step, despite encouraging calls from his friends.

In order not to complicate the illustration, let us assume that his friends do not taunt Michael. They recross the stream, and all wander home.

During the afternoon Michael is obsessed with the painful details of the incident. Suddenly he decides to go back to the stream and try to cross it by himself. As he walks across the fields, his anxiety is shown by a slowing of his walk, his growing confidence by a determined hastening of his steps. The same alternation occurs when he reaches the stream; yet he crosses slowly and carefully. He feels competent, and in his exhilaration gives a whoop of joy and runs gaily home.

Michael feels elated not only because he has mastered a difficult skill (although a sense of achievement comes from this in itself), but also because he has overcome his temerity. He has progressed from fear and anxiety to cautious activity and competence. He has done so through his own effort and independently of other people. For, whereas dependence implies physical nearness and reliance upon other people, independence means taking the initiative, doing routine tasks and carrying out more sustained projects on one's own.

To be independent of other people

Studies of the early social life of animals have described the progressive moves of the young away from their mothers. For example, Rosenblatt and her collaborators (21) have suggested three stages in the social life of kittens. During the first (birth to about three weeks) feeding is initiated by the mother. She 'presents her mammary region', and the kittens actively search and eventually find a nipple and suck. Within a few days, each kitten consistently feeds on specific nipples, some on the anterior, some on the posterior, and some on the intervening ones.

During the second stage (about the third to the sixth week), the kittens initiate feeding, approaching the mother when she is at rest or herself feeding. The kittens now begin to play among themselves and to make non-sucking approaches to their mother. During the third stage (about the sixth to the eighth week), again it is the kittens who initiate sucking as their mother walks about. The mother is not at all co-operative, and may fend them off or wander away and leave them for a time. The kittens begin to feed themselves, lapping milk or biting ineptly on scraps of meat. Socially, the kittens play more and more amongst themselves. Their mother seems to encourage this non-nutritive activity by herself engaging in playful exchanges with them.

Harlow (11) has studied behaviour after separation in rhesus monkeys. He, too, speaks of three stages: one of attachment (lasting about ninety days) when the mother encourages her baby's dependent behaviour; an intervening stage of ambivalence (lasting about twelve months) when the mother resists too much attachment; and a stage of separation (never total) when the young become more attached to juvenile and pre-adolescent play groups. The young of all these animals, through their play and exploratory behaviour, begin to move away from, and to become independent of, their mothers; and in a quiet, half-passive way the mothers seem to encourage this process—though, as Harlow has observed, the rhesus mother will vigorously fend off her off-spring and push him towards his companions if he continues to be attached to her for a longer period than is usual.

As children mature physically, they begin to do things them-selves and to show signs of seeking independence. A three-year-old will pull his hand out of his mother's grasp and run off by himself in the supermarket; or he will demand to leave his push-chair and walk independently.

He may be determined to dress himself before going out, and as he fumbles with buttons and laces, he will twist himself out of his mother's grip. If his mother gives him half an hour to experiment with dressing before they are due to leave, he ends up with shoes on the wrong feet, hat awry and back to front, coat wrongly buttoned with one edge of the collar touching his nose and the other his chest; but he is pleased with his efforts.

Two nine-year-old girls decide that at church the next Sunday they will sit together instead of with their families.

Permission granted, they sit up primly and behave with a studied decorum.

The above examples illustrate the way children seek to be independent, a need also expressed when they seek adventure.

To adventure and to gain new experience

This, like the need for independence, may at first appear to conflict with the need for security; but if there is too much security, an individual will become bored. He will then seek a novel situation to heighten the excitement of living—a dangerous sport to play, a new problem to solve, another detective story to read. Human beings not only want to reduce the strain of too many anxieties, but also to increase tension when life becomes too secure. As one psychologist has put it (4), 'Man desires both the fat of security and the pepper of insecurity.' Thus, human beings seek (a) to court danger (b) to tackle new tasks (c) to adventure in new places.

TO COURT DANGER

Adults climb mountains, explore Arctic regions, race in fast cars, ride on the 'wall of death'. If they do not do these things themselves, they often enjoy them vicariously by reading about them, and by seeing them at a live show or in films.

A young child will take risks without any realization of the dangers involved, and will cause his mother a great deal of anxiety. A two-year-old may seize the opportunity offered by the garden gate, left open by the baker or butcher, to be off and away. Children climb trees, high walls and buildings. They take risks which would terrify their parents if they knew of them. It is perhaps fortunate that they do not know, since in their anxiety they might inhibit this adventurous spirit, and communicate their fears; for anxiety, like influenza, is infectious.

It may be comforting, however, to know that investigations under controlled conditions in gymnasia with school children of varying ages reveal that most children, while active and adventerous in the situation, do not take risks beyond their capacities. Unlike the very young children, older children have an intuitive awareness of what they can do, the risk involved in the proposed task, and the relation between the two. But, as always, there are exceptions to the rule—the timid child who will take no risks, the dare-devil who takes too many, the child who is 'dared' by others and, under this social pressure, takes risks with which he cannot cope.

It is with respect to the reasonable risks involved in satisfying this need that the over-protective parent over-protects. But a stifling over-security is not compatible with growth. It is easy to keep a seed in a box; it will not get wet and it will not get dirty, but it will not grow. A stifling over-security is incompatible with growth.

TO TACKLE NEW TASKS

The goal of adventure includes the desire to tackle new tasks. One task is completed, a skill is mastered and then dropped, but immediately another task is started and another skill learned. An example of this urge to progress is seen when children are taught the same work for a second time. If a teacher comes to a strange class, and starts to teach something that the children have already learned and set exercises that they have done before, the unanimous cry goes up, 'Please, sir, we've *done* that.' If he insists, the children's pride is hurt; it is an affront to be made to perform the task again, and they may do it badly. But this should not make us think that children do not like routine activities which they can do well. The example given was to do with reteaching an isolated, single skill with mechanical practice to follow, such as a single rule in arithmetic, a point of grammar, or a single step in a dance. Ask children to do a test in arithmetic involving a whole range of rules which they know, or ask them to dance a whole dance which they know, and the routine and repetition will delight them. Such activity satisfies the desire for achievement; it provides, too, the 'fat of security'. New adventures are sought from the security of the home as base; new achievements must be attempted against a background of what is known. If used with discretion, routine classroom work restores children's confidence when the assimilation of new work is slow.

The desire to move on to new tasks is exemplified in children's games. There is a craze for marbles, yo-yos or spinning tops. The marbles or tops are ubiquitous and the teacher is obliged to ban them in the classroom. Suddenly the craze stops. I know of no scientific study of 'crazes', how and why they are initiated, or how they proceed and why. The explanation of the sudden cessation of a craze may be quite simply that the children have had a surfeit of the game and are bored. For them, the skills involved have been learned sufficiently for the present.

TO ADVENTURE IN NEW PLACES

The need to adventure in new places—in fields and woods or city streets outside the confines of their homes, or in caves by the sea—is a very special one for children. It is distinguishable from all other needs. It entails the excitement, the fever and the daring movement into the unknown implied in the united declaration by a group of children 'Let's explore'. Yet, like the courting of danger and the tackling of new tasks, it reflects back to the other basic needs. When Harlow's monkey explores its 'nursery' or a toddler rummages round the house and garden, both baby monkey and toddler are adventuring in what is for each an environment as yet largely unknown. When a group of children build a hide-out in the woods, they satisfy the need to belong with their own group, to be independent of adults, and even to be secure; for the very *togetherness* of their adventuring engenders a feeling of security.

The need to adventure anticipates needs yet to be discussed— to know, to construct, to create.

To know, to construct, to create

Everyday observation, as well as experiments with insects, birds and animals, indicate that, in so far as they find themselves in an environment with certain features—terrain, objects, events—they seek to become cognizant of them. This they do as far as their sensory, motor and intellectual equipment allows. They also manipulate parts of their environment, and use them for purposes of survival and comfort. A similar trend is seen from observation and experiments with children. They seek (a) to know and understand the nature of the objects, people and events taking place around them (b) to manipulate some parts of it and so use them for their own purposes. In a more definite way than animals, they seek (c) to do something original with the materials and objects— something that nobody has done before.

TO KNOW AND UNDERSTAND

Hinde (14) has described how animals (e.g. rats, cats, monkeys), on being introduced into a new environment, will move about exploring new surroundings. When they encounter a strange object in familiar surroundings, they will examine it with whatever sensory and motor powers are available to them. They will spend a great deal of time exploring it before they resume their usual maintenance activity. The exploratory activity in rats (2) and chimpanzees (26) has been experimentally increased by introducing one unfamiliar object after another into their known habitat—a wooden cube, a bow with a bell that rings, an object that moves when touched. The exploratory activity of each animal may cease, though the object is still present. This is because the object has, as we say, become familiar. Following the Russian scientist Sokolov, Hinde puts it in this way: as a consequence of his life's experiences, an animal builds up a 'neuronal model' (an organization of cortical cells) in terms of the multitudinous stimuli that have impinged upon it. As a result of its exploratory activity, this 'neuronal model' is modified to assimilate the new object or the strange environment. The discrepancy between the latter and the familiar world is thus reduced. In Hinde's own words, 'the novel stimuli are assimilated and cease to be novel'.

Children will explore in similar ways. Introduce them into a new environment and they are immediately off to explore it. Show them a strange, intriguing-looking object and they will examine it, ask questions about it, look, feel, lift it.

The 'Why's?' of the young pre-school child are incessant and his concentration intense as he watches his father at some task. 'Why are you doing that, Daddy?' After his father has told him, the child may repeat the word a number of times as if to capture the magic of understanding latent within the name itself.

The drive to explore, to know and understand is so significant a characteristic of living creatures that some psychologists have postulated an innate 'instinct of curiosity'; later writers prefer to describe it as 'an exploratory drive'. Perhaps the origin of the drive could be explained in this way: all living creatures need to know about the material and personal culture in which they live. If they do not, they will be seriously limited in their capacity to deal with the environment, to embrace its pleasures and avoid its dangers; and ignorance would leave them perplexed and anxious.

TO MANIPULATE, TO CONSTRUCT

Observation and experiment show that insects, birds, and animals will do much more than explore. They manipulate objects and material for their own use by means of activity that is clearly instrumental—for example, an insect carrying a stick, a rat a rag for its nest. Innumerable experiments in the laboratory show that many of the higher types of animals will press bars or open doors and shutters to obtain a reward: the reward may be food, or merely the chance to poke their heads outside an aperture and peer at the outside world (19).

The instrumental activities of children are far too numerous to list. There are the sustained activities as when they build a four-wheeled trolley, a den in the woods, a house in the trees. These activities are organized towards a particular end (Chapter 1). Materials are collected, and the child persists until his project is completed. The reader may remember the exhilaration he experienced when, after passing the driving test, he drove off alone for the first time. Children experience similar feelings when they first learn to crawl, walk, run, skip, ride a bicycle, and begin to master academic skills.

Animals will often indulge in activities for which there is no extraneous reward. Hill (13) has demonstrated that rats confined in small cages and then placed in a revolving wheel will continue to run in the wheel for one to two hours after their release. The amount of activity increases with the length of previous confinement. Harlow (9) has shown that chimpanzees will persistently play with a complicated six-device puzzle until they learn to unravel it. At no stage of the process were they given a reward.

Such experiments have led to theories which have already superseded the older behaviouristic views. It will be recalled that Hull and other behaviourists conceived learning as a connection between a stimulus and a response, a connection reinforced by a reward (for example, food) resulting in 'need reduction'. In order to study how animals learn, they deprived them of a basic physiological need (food or water or sex) and observed learning under conditions of what they called 'primary', that is, of physiological deprivation. The experiments reported in the last few pages indicate that animals can explore, be active, and learn without such primary deprivation and the appropriate extrinsic reward. The reward is intrinsic—contained within the activity itself and its successful completion.

Children enjoy activities in which satisfaction in solving a problem seems to be the only reward as with verbal or mechanical puzzles. The fascination with manipulating objects is expressed in many small ways: the baby shaking its rattle again and again to produce sounds, the young child pulling or pushing his trolley. Groos (8) spoke of a child's feelings on these occasions as 'the joy in being a cause'. This imaginary incident gives some idea of what he meant.

A mother and child visit a friend whose door bell gives the most enchanting chimes. When they arrive, the mother allows the child to press the button. The child chuckles, and almost wriggles out of his mother's arms in his excitement. He listens, waits, then presses the button again; and the look of wonder on his face clearly shows his delight. Another visit is arranged. But when they arrive at the house the second time, the mother unthinkingly presses the button herself. The child gives way to a tantrum, and the sound of the chimes, though intrinsically engaging, are forgotten.

The mother may be puzzled by her child's reaction. Yet the reaction is understandable, for the child feels that he has been unfairly deprived of the satisfaction of producing the chimes himself, of joy in being a cause.

Realizing children's spontaneous desire to be active, to explore and to solve problems, psychologists have rendered Groos's 'joy in being a cause' in various ways. White (27) speaks of 'the desire for competence', Piaget (20) of a child's desire 'to be the producer of effects'. Stott (24), after studying his own small son, speaks of 'a relation of effectiveness which a child seeks to establish and maintain between himself and his environment'.

Joyce Cary has described the satisfaction children obtain from the process of learning in and for itself (3).[1]

'The child is a born creator. He has to be, for though in sympathy he is one with those he loves, in mind he is alone. He has to do his own learning and thinking. And Nature, for his very necessary good, sets

[1] page 8.

him to enjoy it. Anyone can see how children enjoy discovery and reflection. But also how soon they are bored with what is known. It is as if Nature says to them, "Go on, go on, there's plenty more that you must know" and has made the joy of discovery evanescent; the imagination, like the appetite, perpetually greedy.'

Here Cary suggests a link between the need to know and understand and the need for adventure. This link is understandable because for children new adventure means new learning. Ideally, the converse should also be true.

TO BE ORIGINAL, TO CREATE

A child may experiment with his chemistry set to make compounds, with his meccano to build unusual structures, with bamboo and string to make musical instruments and a miscellany of noises. He may design something exceptional—a kite with stabilizers, a mechanical device made of cotton reels, elastic and match sticks. He reminds us of the scientist who pursues an unconventional avenue of inquiry, of the musician or artist who devises a new art form.

Creative activities are closely related to constructive ones, but the two forms are not identical. Whereas in constructive activities (graphs, maps, woodwork) children are bound closely to the facts of the outside world, in creative activities (free art, spontaneous acting) they are not so bound. For constructive activities the key word is *manipulation;* for creative activities it is *imagination*.

The distinction between the two is tenuous but important. The danger exists, even among teachers today, of stressing constructive activities as 'basic', of regarding gardening, metal-work, woodwork and mechanical drawing as justified, and purely creative pursuits as 'frills'. They may thus inhibit creativity by too great a demand for technical excellence. Neat writing then becomes more important than originality of thought, the ability to analyse a sentence more important than the ability to appreciate the beauty of a passage, the laws of perspective more important than imaginative expression. But it would be unfortunate to undervalue creative pursuits, for there is truth in the paradox quoted by Shaw (23) that we can do without the necessities of life but not without the luxuries. Necessities feed only the body, luxuries feed the spirit. It is not a contradiction, therefore, to say that creative pursuits are necessary luxuries.

To experience a sense of personal worth

A human being desires

> To esteem himself, to feel confident;
> To be held in esteem by others;
> To feel that his work is useful, valuable and necessary.

TO ESTEEM ONESELF, TO FEEL CONFIDENT

Human beings can both over-value themselves and under-value themselves. The first we call conceit, the second a sense of inferiority. Both are coins of similar minting. The conceited person harbours unconscious feelings of inferiority, even as the inferior person harbours unconscious feelings of superiority. A sense of personal worth entails neither over- nor under-valuation. It is akin to what theologians call 'proper pride', best experienced after a piece of work well done.

TO BE HELD IN ESTEEM BY OTHERS

So far, the esteem described has been *self*-esteem, the confidence *self*-confidence, an independent judgment of one's general worth resulting from the worth of a job well done, an afterglow of Groos's 'joy in being a cause'. But a sense of personal worth is not solely a matter of a child's or adult's own independent judgment. His dependence on others makes their judgment of him important in determining his own evaluation of himself. A sense of personal worth is not only built up, it is sustained, by the esteem of others, by affection, commendation, and praise for work done, all of which children seek. When a man is commended for his qualities and achievements or knows of other people's good opinion of him, his sense of personal worth is enhanced. When he is in doubt about the esteem of others, a feeling of uncertainty signifies the opposite: his own feelings of worth are being impaired. 'I don't care what he thinks about me,' says the adolescent girl. But the very vehemence of her protest suggests that she cares a great deal.

TO FEEL THAT ONE'S WORK IS USEFUL

A person's self-esteem is inevitably linked with the work he does. Though self-approval of one's work is sometimes enough, it is not always so. The painting or a page of neat writing must be shown to parent and teacher so that they can confirm the child's own estimate. History suggests that even independent people—artists and musicians like Van Gogh, Gauguin and Beethoven—suffered despair because of the lack of recognition given to their work.

The work must not only be 'good', it must be useful and worth while. Sometimes a very young child will 'dust', 'sweep', empty the waste-paper basket; an older one will help in the kitchen. Realizing that her child is seeking this assurance, a mother says, 'You *are* a useful girl.' If a boy does some gardening or carries the coal, he is commended for the valuable 'man's job' he is doing.

The esteem a man derives from his job is related to his estimate of its usefulness, which, in turn, depends upon the worth which the community places upon it. Studies indicate a serious impairment of the self-esteem of people unemployed for long periods. One of the dangers of retirement lies in the fact that a person may begin to feel that he is no longer useful and his self-esteem suffers a corresponding impairment.

Children imbue their activities with a particular sense of purpose. We are sometimes amazed at the seriousness with which they play. They will pursue a game or project as if their very lives depended upon it. 'That was a good effort' is the group comment on a boy's feat of batting; or, for a suggestion he makes, 'That's a good idea'; and the boy feels a glow of satisfaction.

In summary, for children—and indeed for adults—satisfaction of the need for a sense of personal worth depends upon satisfaction of all the other basic needs. Feelings of worth develop in a secure environment where children are encouraged in their pursuit of new experiences, and of creative and constructive activities.

It is interesting to observe in conclusion that Maslow (17) has proposed a sequence of basic needs constructed according to their relative strengths or 'prepotencies'. He arranges them thus:

1 Physical needs (including the need for physical security).
2 Affection: warmth, acceptance by and approval of others.
3 Self-esteem or feelings of personal adequacy (arising from satisfaction of needs 1 and 2 and also of needs 4 and 5).
4 Development of physical and mental skills through constructive activities.

5   Self-fulfilment (in a broader sense than 4): to know and to
    understand, to explore, to adventure, to create.

The point of Maslow's sequence of needs is this: when physical
needs (1) are satisfied, man seeks enrichment of his life through
need 2; if 2 is satisfied, then he seeks further enrichment in need 3;
if 3 is satisfied, yet further enrichment in needs 4 and 5. Given a
socially secure environment in which physical needs are adequately
provided for, the relative prepotencies of needs is in the order 5
as the strongest to 1 as the weakest.

Under conditions of social disintegration or upheaval, such as
earthquake, war, or pestilence, the relative strengths of 1 increase
and the order of prepotency tends to be from 1 as strongest to 5
as weakest. Investigations of large groups of people suffering such
forms of extreme stress confirm this tendency, which has also been
confirmed in a study of a group of young men volunteers who
were starved under experimental conditions for a period of six
months and then gradually re-established on a full diet during the
following six months (15). Marked personality changes had taken
place in the young men by the 25th week of starvation. They had
ceased to be purposively active, to pursue studies, to do woodwork, to paint, to draw (needs 4 and 5). They no longer cared about
their personal appearance (need 3), were irritable towards each
other, resentful towards the scientists who carried on the experiment and coldly hostile to relatives who visited them (need 2).
They sat or lay around on their beds or in the garden thinking,
dreaming and wanting one thing only—food (need 1).

It would be a mistake to use such findings as these to explain
away man's social, constructive and creative needs and to deride
those needs as a veneer covering man's basically biological nature.
Rather it is the case that when he is biologically satisfied man tends
naturally to move towards the satisfaction of need 5. In that this is
so, he moves towards the generally accepted ideal of what being
human means. As Maslow has put it, 'Man lives by bread alone
only when there is no bread.'

BASIC NEEDS AND GOALS AND THE TEACHER IN
THE CLASSROOM

It is not suggested that this is a complete list of basic human needs
and goals, but rather that it is a classification which may be helpful

to parents and to classroom teachers in their understanding of children. First, like classification in botany, classification in psychology is a valuable aid towards description. This flower is not just a flower, but is one belonging to a particular group of flowers, a species of a genus; this is not just behaviour, but purposive behaviour related to a particular need and in pursuit of a particular goal.

Secondly, the list can be useful for explanatory purposes in that the question, 'Why is he behaving in this way?' may be answered in terms of the satisfaction of one or more of the basic needs. Thirdly, at a simple level, the list may have diagnostic value. A child is 'difficult'—over-submissive, over-aggressive, or very withdrawn—and the causes of his difficult behaviour may be sought in terms of the lack of satisfaction of one or more of the basic goals.

Lastly, the list may be helpful to the teacher in evaluating his work. In doing so, he might give consideration to such factors as:

The spaciousness of classrooms and playgrounds, the adequacy of lavatory and washing accommodation, opportunities for physical activity, timetabling of recreation and lunch intervals (bodily needs).

The way in which he (the teacher) uses his authority to organize and control the children's behaviour without being unduly repressive (security needs).

Activities within the classroom, including ordinary lessons, art, music, dancing, hobby-clubs, visits, and other projects; the degree to which his pupils are personally involved in the activities, and the degree to which the activities provide a challenge, being neither too easy nor too difficult, and give a sense of direction and purpose (the need to know, to construct and to create).

The provision of individual work which can be pursued without help or hindrance from others (personal mastery) and of class and small-group activities (a sense of oneness with others).

The assurance which pupils receive of their progress from the teacher's judicious use of individual praise and blame or from the way he reviews a topic they have already mastered (self-esteem).

The list of basic needs presented in this chapter does, of course, over-simplify the human situation. Children are complex, they live in a complex society, and a teacher does not describe and explain children's behaviour or diagnose children's problems by the magical use of any formula of basic needs and goals. However, provided the danger of over-simplification is recognized, the list may be helpful in assessing school work, describing and explaining children's behaviour and perhaps, on a simple level, diagnosing children's difficulties.

REFERENCES AND BIBLIOGRAPHY

1 Ainsworth, M. 'The development of infant-mother interaction among the Ganda.' *In* Foss, B. M. (Ed.) *Determinants of Infant Behaviour* II, Methuen, London, 1963.

2 Berlyne, D. E. 'The arousal and satiation of perceptual curiosity in the rat.' *Journal of Comparative and Physiological Psychology*, 1955, **48**, pp. 238–46.

3 Cary, J. *Charlie is My Darling*. Carfax edition, Michael Joseph, London, 1951.

4 Conze, E. *The Psychology of Mass Propaganda*. 1939. Unpublished.

5 De Vore, I. *Primate Behaviour*. Holt, New York, 1965.

6 Freedman, D. G. 'The infant's fear of strangers and the flight response.' *Journal of Psychology and Psychiatry*, 1961, **2**, pp. 242–8.

7 Goldstein, K. *The Organism*. American Books, New York, 1939.

8 Groos, K. *The Play of Man*. Appleton, New York, 1901.

9 Harlow, H. F. 'Learning and satiation of response in intrinsically motivated complex puzzle performance by monkeys.' *Journal of Comparative and Physiological Psychology*, 1950, **43**, pp. 289–94.

10 Harlow, H. F. 'Affectional responses in the infant monkey.' *Science*, 1959, **130**, pp. 421–32.

11 Harlow, H. F. 'The maternal affectional system.' *In* Foss, B. M. (Ed.) *Determinants of Infant Behaviour* II, Methuen, London, 1963.

12 Hess, E. H. 'Imprinting in animals.' *Science*, 1959, pp. 133–41.

13 Hill, W. F. 'Activity as an autonomous drive.' *Journal of Comparative Physiological Psychology*, 1956, **49**, pp. 15–19.

14 Hinde, R. A. *Animal Behaviour*. McGraw-Hill, London, 1966.

15 Keys, A. *et al. The Biology of Human Starvation*. University of Minnesota Press, Minneapolis, 1950.

16 Mace, C. A. 'Homeostasis, needs and values.' *British Journal of Psychology*, 1953, **44**, pp. 200–10.

17 Maslow, A. H. *Motivation and Personality* Harper, New York, 1954.

18 Myers, A. K., Miller, N. E. 'Failure to find a learned drive based on hunger: evidence for learning motivated by "exploration".' *Journal of Comparative and Physiological Psychology*, 1954, **47**, pp. 428–36.

19 Nissen, H. W. 'A study of exploratory behaviour in the white rat.' *Journal of Genetic Psychology*, 1930, **37**, pp. 361–76.

20 Piaget, J. *Play, Dreams and Imitation in Childhood*. London, Routledge, 1952.
21 Rosenblatt, J. S., *et al.* 'Early socialization in the domestic cat as based on feeding and other relationships between female and young.' *In* Foss, B. M. (Ed.) *Determinants of Infant Behaviour*, Methuen, London, 1961.
22 Schaffer, H. R., Emerson, P. 'The development of social attachments in infancy.' *Monograph of the Society for Research in Child Development*, 1964, **29**, No. 3 (Serial No. 94).
23 Shaw, B. *Everybody's Political What's What*. Constable, London, 1944.
24 Stott, D. H. 'An empirical approach to motivation based on the behaviour of a young child.' *Journal of Psychology and Psychiatry*, 1961, **2**, pp. 97–117.
25 Thorpe, W. H. *Learning and Instinct in Animals*. Methuen, London, 1964.
26 Welker, W. L. 'Some determinants of play and exploration in chimpanzees.' *Journal of Comparative Physiology*, 1956, **49**, pp. 84–9.
27 White, R. W. 'Motivation reconsidered: the concept of competence.' *Psychological Review*, 1959, **66**, pp. 297–333.
28 Winnicott, D. W. *The Family and Individual Development*. Tavistock Publications, London, 1965.
29 Young, K. *Personality and Problems of Adjustment*. Routledge & Kegan Paul, London, 1947.

PART FOUR

Physical, Emotional, Social and Intellectual Growth

CHAPTER NINE

Ages and Stages

THIS chapter is a short introduction to the study of children's emotional and social development.

Emotional development implies the growth of children's ability to understand and to control the emotions of joy, sorrow, love, hate, anger, fear and so on. *Social* development implies the growth of their ability to co-operate with others in such a way that their social life contributes towards their own growth while, at the same time, their membership of social groups contributes towards the growth of their companions. The main theme (which, it is hoped, will run as a clear thread throughout this study) is that social and emotional development, like the development of any skill, such as skipping or playing with a ball, is a slow, gradual process in which children move from inept to more skilful behaviour.

Take the child learning to ride a bicycle. He wobbles, he falls, he slips on the pedal and hits his shin. Contrast such behaviour with the boy who, having more than mastered the task, trick-rides, feet on handlebars or hands in pockets, so that parents and teachers become alarmed because of his daring in the use of these skills which he has acquired. Or contrast the little four-year-old girl, quarrelling, demanding, impetuous, and the same little girl as a sophisticated young adult during her coming-of-age party. Anyone who attends such a party and who is old enough to reflect back to earlier years may realize with a start that an amazing process of growth has taken place, from lack of emotional control to emotional control, and from an inability to be happily social to an ability to be so.

It is generally agreed by students that there are broad stages in children's social and emotional growth, and that it is important to be aware of these in order to understand children's problems and to provide for their needs according to the stages to which they have developed. Adults often fall into the error of thinking that some child is abnormal, or that he is developing 'bad habits' which, if not stopped, will continue throughout life, when actually the 'difficult' behaviour, the so-called 'bad habits', may be typical of most children of that particular age.

Gesell (1, 2) not only demonstrates the importance of these stages of development, but also says that growth tends to go in cycles of stages and that these cycles are repeated three times during the first sixteen years of life. In the table below an attempt has been made to summarize his main findings; though the table may not correspond exactly to Gesell's concept of ages, stages and cycles, it does approximate to it.

AGES AND CYCLES

STAGES	Cycle 1 Pre-school	Cycle 2 Primary	Cycle 3 Pre-puberty, puberty and early adolescence
A_1	$1\frac{1}{2}$–2	5–$5\frac{1}{2}$	10–11
B	2–3	$5\frac{1}{2}$–6	11–12
A_2	3–$3\frac{1}{2}$	6–7	12–13
C	$3\frac{1}{2}$–4	7–8	13–14
D	4–$4\frac{1}{2}$	8–9	14–15
A_3	$4\frac{1}{2}$–5	9–10	15–16

FIG. 4 Table showing ages, stages and cycles

The main stages as Gesell sees them may be summarized in this way:

A_1 Children tend to be relatively amiable and relatively stable.

B Behaviour 'loosens up', as Gesell puts it; children become difficult and their favourite words are 'no', 'mine'.

A_2 Children are relatively amiable again, and favourite words are 'yes', 'we'.

C Children withdraw into themselves and brood introvertedly; they tend to be moody and anxious. Gesell speaks of 'inwardizing thrusts'.

D Children become extravertedly expansive and boisterous. Gesell speaks of 'outwardizing thrusts'.

A_3 Children achieve a unity between the inner (C) and the outer (D), and are therefore more stable, more self-sufficient.

Gesell would argue that just as physical growth and motor development follow definite sequences (this will be referred to later), so does psychological growth. There are stages, and these alternate between those during which children are learning new things and expanding their personalities when, from the parents' point of view, they are 'difficult' (B, C, D); and those during which they are consolidating their gains, as it were, and seem satisfied with what has been done. At such times they tend to be amenable and stable (A_1, A_2, A_3).

Of course, it is important to realize that such a table is based upon the average responses of a great number of children, and that, since there are individual differences between children in the way they grow, it is not a strait-jacket into which all children must be fitted. Some children may not go through these stages in quite this sequence; some may develop quickly and others slowly so that, for these particular children, the ages and stages do not coincide exactly.

It has been argued against Gesell that while such a predeterministic viewpoint may be applicable to physiological development and to the growth of physical skills, it may not be applicable to psychological development because cultural influences will determine the kinds of problems children will need to solve and the kinds of social adaptation they must take. Gesell would answer that the artefacts through which, and the social context within which, the characteristics of each stage are expressed will vary from culture to culture, but that the stages themselves will be much the same for all cultures.

In the chapters which follow, the general characteristics of children within each age-grouping will be given, followed by more detailed year-by-year sketches. The general trends of these sketches are based mainly upon the findings of Gesell, but also upon the work of others to which reference will be made as this study progresses.[1]

Before going on to consider each age-group by turn, it may be of value to outline beforehand the main principles that will be

[1] Many of the details of the way in which these trends are expressed are based upon the writer's own experience as a teacher and parent as well as upon his own observations of children at play.

used to describe the processes of growth, many of which are related to, and entail a restatement of, some of the basic needs described in the previous chapter.

The first principle is that growth is a progressive move towards independence and self-determination. Children sometimes find these moves difficult to make because they seek independence from adults, the very people who are the main source of their physical and psychological security. Healthy children like to conform and thereby to experience the delicious sense of security which oneness with adults provides; they also like not to conform and so to experience the independence which separation from adults provides. Much of children's erratic, disobedient and obstreperous behaviour can be seen as exaggerated attempts to think and to act independently, and thereby to assert their individuality.

Secondly, activity amongst and association with their own groups give children feelings of security and offset the anxiety which their moves towards independence generate. This oneness that they seek with other children of their own age is expressed in such harmless ways as the secret codes and languages, the secret hide-outs of the nine-year-old, the escapades of the thirteen-year-old, the confidences which adolescents share with each other but not with adults. Sometimes, this togetherness can veer over into a clearer defiance of authority, as in the gang activities of boys at puberty or 'chicken' games at adolescence. Nevertheless, children are often individually assertive and aggressive even within their own groups as they compete one with the other for positions of significance. The swift transitions from amiable and co-operative behaviour to bitter quarrelling and refusals to co-operate show that the conflict between obeying and being a good group member, and disobeying and being an individual, is also manifest in their own group activities.

Thirdly, acquiring knowledge and skills is essential to the process of growth. In order to grow psychologically a child needs knowledge of the universe in which he lives and the skill to manipulate the objects he encounters within it. This statement relates especially to the significance of individual achievements in giving a child confidence to take his place in a very complex society. To achieve is to feel good.

Fourthly, learning to play the role one is expected to play

because one is a boy or because one is a girl is important in the growth of children in our society. There is continual pressure on children, exerted by adults and by their own contemporaries, to behave as a boy or as a girl should. The separation of the sexes from about seven to fifteen expresses children's determination to acquiesce to these pressures and to learn the role appropriate to boy or girl.

Finally, it is a sign of healthy growth when a child feels a sense of personal worth, and the process of growth can be seen as one in which children aim to maintain and enhance their self-esteem. It is this desire for a sense of personal worth that makes a child dependent on the approval and approbation of adults and friends, and fills him with despair if he loses their good-will. Moreover, knowing that he has the affection of others not only gives him feelings of security but also the assurance that he is worthy of affection. Not to receive affection, or to feel that someone else (brother, sister, friend) is receiving more affection than he, fills a child with doubts about his worthiness to receive affection. It is understandable that in such circumstances a child may, in his despair, become difficult—clingingly submissive and over-desirous for affection, silently withdrawn and uncreative, or rowdily assertive and destructive.

REFERENCES

1   Gesell, A., Ilg, F. L. *Child Development:* 1 'Infant and child in the culture of today.' 2 'The child from five to ten.' Harper, New York, 1949.
2   Gesell, A., Ilg, F. L., Ames, L. B. *Youth: the Years from Ten to Sixteen.* Harper, New York, 1956.

CHAPTER TEN

The First Nine Months and One Year

The first nine months

As particular emphasis will be given in the chapters which follow
to the idea of *stages* in the development of children, it is well to
say a word or two about the three stages of intra-uterine life,
namely:

1   the stage of the ovum (or the germinal stage)—the first
    two weeks following conception;
2   the stage of the embryo—from the third to the eighth
    week after conception;
3   the stage of the foetus—the last eight lunar months (or
    thirty-two weeks) of intra-uterine life.

The three stages comprise the gestation period for which the
full term average is forty weeks or ten lunar months. Babies born
before this are said to be pre-mature, those born afterwards post-
mature.

I   THE OVUM

The period of the ovum begins on conception. The minute,
tadpole-shaped spermatozoa, each of which is so small that it
can only be seen under a microscope, travel along the Fallopian tube at a velocity of between 1 and 4 millimetres per
minute. On their journey they meet the ovum and one sperma-
tozoon only penetrates the ovum which is moving very slowly
in the opposite direction towards the uterus. The ovum is
estimated to be in diameter forty times the size of the head of the
male sperm at its widest; and yet it is so small (about $\frac{1}{200}$th of

an inch in diameter) that it can be seen only as a tiny speck. The now fertilized ovum continues to travel down the Fallopian tube towards the uterus.

Some days after conception, though the exact number in the case of human beings is not known, the process of cell division, or of mitosis as it is called, begins. (Before this takes place the fertilized ovum is called a 'zygote'.) The single cell

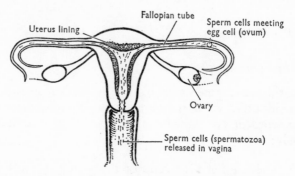

Uterus lining
Fallopian tube
Sperm cells meeting egg cell (ovum)
Ovary
Sperm cells (spermatozoa) released in vagina

FIG. 5 Schematic diagram of the female reproductory system

divides into two cells, the two cells divide into four, the four into eight, the eight into sixteen and so on in rapid geometrical progression. It is estimated that the number of cells in the human body is sixty million millions.

Though cells are rapidly increasing in number, even at this early stage cells are also dying off and being shed.

By the time the journey down the Fallopian tube is completed, two layers of cells can be distinguished, an inner layer of gelatinous cells and an outer layer called trophoblast. The fertilized ovum remains at the opening of the uterus for about two or three days, after which time it enters the uterus and the process of implantation begins. In this process the trophoblast erodes into the wall of the uterus, creating a capillary system through which a more direct contact between the embryo and the mother is attained and through which nutrient material begins to pass from the mother to the embryo. Before this, the fertilized ovum had received nourishment for a very short period from its own yolk and then from the secretions passed into the uterus from the uterine glands.

2   THE EMBRYO

During the stage of the embryo, two processes take place: (a) a 'housing' process, and (b) the continued growth of the baby.

a) *The 'housing' process.* A cavity, called the amniotic cavity, is formed within the layers of trophoblast cells, and the embryo is enclosed within this cavity which is filled with amniotic fluid. During the early stages, the embryo is attached to the roof of the cavity by a 'baby stalk' which is later incorporated into the umbilical cord. The embryo occupies but a fraction of this cavity at first, but when it is full-grown the baby fills the greater part of the sac.

Two points of incidental interest may be noted here. First, the embryo sheds off cells into the amniotic fluid, and when a population of such cells is obtained, it provides a possible technique for deciding the sex of the baby. When treated, 60 to 80 per cent of a population of female cells will show the sex chromatin (particles of X chromosomes that are readily stained) as a small triangular-shaped stain and only 20 per cent of the sex chromatin in a population of male cells will show this when similarly treated.[1] Second, just before birth the amniotic sac breaks, releasing the amniotic fluid as a lubricant to ease the passage of the baby through the vulva.

During the next stage of the 'housing' process tendrils, called villi, grow out of the capillary system mentioned above. These villi intertwine into a flat, disc-shaped mass and, together with the mother's tissue which surrounds them, form the placenta. This is the site of the interchange of nutrient substances and of waste products between mother and child. One side of the placenta is attached to the uterine cavity, the other to the embryo by means of the umbilical cord. The umbilical cord has both veins and arteries; the veins carry nutrient materials and oxygen from the placenta to the embryo (later the foetus) and the arteries carry waste products including carbon dioxide back to the placenta. You will notice that this is the reverse of what happens post-natally. The mother's blood circulatory system is separate from that of the

[1] The technique for obtaining such a population of cells is not yet perfected, and, because of the risk involved to both baby and mother by its use, it is not to date a routine procedure.

embryo and there is no direct interchange of blood. Nutritional substances from the mother are absorbed by capillary action of the villi and conveyed to the embryo by its own circulatory system. Figure 6 shows the 'housing' position at about the end of the embryonic period.

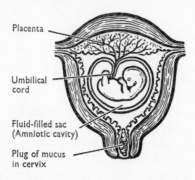

Placenta

Umbilical cord

Fluid-filled sac (Amniotic cavity)

Plug of mucus in cervix

FIG. 6 Diagram showing the 'housing' position at about the eighth week of pregnancy

b) Growth. During the six weeks of the embryonic stage a remarkable process of growth takes place. The cells not only continue to divide rapidly, they also group into different kinds of cells from which specific tissues and organs will later develop. There are three main layers of cells:

1 The outer layer, called the ectoderm cells, which later form more especially the sensory system—epidermis, including hair, nails, sensory organs, nervous tissue.

2 The middle layer, called mesoderm cells, which themselves divide into (*a*) somatic mesoderm cells, and (*b*) splanchnic mesoderm cells. The somatic cells later form the muscular system—muscles, connective tissue, bone, bone marrow, cartilage, also blood and blood vessels; the splanchnic cells form the muscles of the viscera.

3 The inner layer, called endoderm cells, which later form more especially the lining of the digestive system and associated glands, and also the pharynx, larynx, lungs.

By the end of these six weeks of the embryonic period a baby in miniature has developed in that the primordia of all organs have formed even though the length of the embryo is little more than one inch. They are as yet rudiments, but from each will develop a particular limb (arm or leg), or a particular organ (heart, stomach, brain), or a particular system (nervous, respiratory, muscular).

3   THE FOETUS

A month-by-month catalogue of growth during the eight lunar months of the foetal period will not be given here, but only an outline of the broader processes and principles of growth which characterize this stage. The reader is referred to the detailed and interesting account given by Gesell (6).

Development of the foetus illustrates certain principles relating to the direction of growth. First, growth is *cephalocaudal*, that is, structural growth and subsequent movements develop first in the head and then progressively from regions nearest the head to those furthest away. Take, for example, the brain, which during this period develops more rapidly than any other organ, dividing into its three main parts (the cerebrum, the cerebellum and the brain stem) and weighing at birth some ten ounces, that is, roughly 10 per cent of the total weight of the body. At eight weeks, half the foetal length is head; in a newborn baby the head is a quarter of the total length and in a full-grown man, one-tenth. This development from head to limb extremities is seen, too, in the functioning of the foetus, and this has been demonstrated by Hooker (9) in experiments on foetuses that have had to be removed for therapeutic reasons. Thus, at eight weeks skin sensitivity is confined to the area around the mouth and movement in response to stimulation here is a mere flexion of the neck. By ten weeks the trunk and girdles of the limbs move in response to stimulation; by eleven weeks fingers close on stimulation of the palm of the hand. Sensitivity extends over the face, arms and trunk, and movement of every joint in the body occurs at twelve weeks, including flexion first of elbows and knees, then of the fingers and toes.

This last example illustrates the second principle of direction of growth which is generally referred to as the *proximodistal* sequence. Movements begin in those parts of the limbs nearest the trunk and progress to those furthest away, to finer movements of fingers and toes.

At fourteen weeks most of the reflexes have developed (though the sucking, respiratory and grasp reflexes do not appear until the twenty-fifth week) and from this time the development of behaviour results from continued maturation of the sensory and motor organs. The baby spontaneously moves lips and tongue, occasionally moves arms and legs, opens and closes hands. But, by eighteen or twenty weeks there are more distinct 'eating' and swallowing movements; and the movements of the limbs tend to become not only more graceful and flowing but also more vigorous. The movements of the hands and fingers become more clearly a grasp and, as Hooker (9) puts it, the extension of the leg more clearly a kick and that of the arm more clearly a punch. Often at this time, mothers are able to feel these movements which are called the 'quickening of the foetus'.

In studying foetal development, scientists have noticed that movements of the body can be produced experimentally some weeks before they would be expected to occur spontaneously. For example, the movements of arms, legs, lips and tongue appearing spontaneously at fourteen weeks, can be obtained experimentally at ten weeks by stimulating the appropriate part of the foetal body with hairs just stiff enough to exert the slight pressure needed. It seems that structurally the body develops to the point where it could function. Then there is a time lag before it does, under normal circumstances, actually function. In referring to this Carmichael (3) speaks of the 'anticipatory function' in foetal development.

By the twenty-fifth week following conception all the structures and organs essential to life outside have been formed. They require another ten to fifteen weeks to mature to greater strength and so make possible greater efficiency of functioning. Thus, for example, by this time (the twenty-fifth week), the foetus is capable of breathing, but the respiratory muscles are not yet strong enough to expand the chest, so that a premature baby of this age would be unable to supply itself with sufficient oxygen. The foetus can suck but, again, would lack strength in the necessary muscles to obtain enough food for itself. But by twenty-eight weeks the baby is viable; this means that if he is born prematurely at this time, there is an even chance of his surviving.

It is interesting to reflect on the prodigious proportional increase in growth during the gestation period: from an infinitesimal weight at conception to thirty grammes at eight weeks, to three thousand grammes at birth; in length (crown to heel), from ·15 millimetres at conception to 30 millimetres at eight weeks, to 500 millimetres at birth. This means that during the last thirty-two weeks of the gestation period there is a hundredfold increase in weight and over a sixteenfold increase in height. If this same proportional rate of increase continued for every thirty-two weeks after birth up to, say, the age of twelve, a child would in weight be many millions of times that of the earth and in height many millions of feet tall. But of course growth, in terms of proportional weight and height increase, rapidly decelerates after birth.

It has intrigued scientists that the zygote of each species seems to have within it its own self-regulatory processes, a sort of 'growthostat' which regulates both the rate of growth, from rapid to slow, and the sequence of growth, cephalocaudal and proximo-distal. Further, the zygote of each species will develop to acquire the essential characteristics of its species and no other. This has been considered earlier (Chapter 1) when referring to the general notion of potentialities becoming actual.

The picture of intra-uterine life has often in the past been described as one of passive parasitism and perfect bliss, for the baby was considered to be within a stable and equable environment, cushioned within the amniotic fluid and away from the variations of temperature, pressure and sensory stimuli of the outside world, receiving nourishment from the mother without movement or effort. Indeed, it was thought that adults, while not consciously able to remember this state of bliss, nevertheless wished unbeknown to themselves to return to it, especially during periods of mental stress. This strange theory is still held by some psychologists today. But, although the 'housing' process spoken of earlier does provide unique protection, this over-idealized picture of a being separate from the world and in complete security from it is not now generally accepted.

While in a strict physiological sense the mother and child are two distinct beings, since the baby has its own circulatory, respiratory and nervous system and so on, the connection between the two is a close one in that oxygen, water and nutrients are passed from mother to child through the fluid mediums in the blood, and waste products returned. Any event which influences the physical and psychological health of the mother may, therefore affect the well-being of the baby *in utero*. Some of these will now be considered.

Firstly, the baby is influenced by the nutritional status of the mother. Investigations (1, 14) during World War II have shown the effects of maternal malnutrition on infants in Europe. During the siege of Leningrad, 1941–3, the number of premature and still births was significantly high. The incidence of rickets, anaemia and tuberculosis was found to be high in war-time babies in Holland. In England, where it was possible to maintain nutritional levels by preferential rationing for expectant mothers, children did not suffer in this way.

In case of malnutrition there is an interval between the time when the mother first experiences the malnutrition and the time when it will affect the baby. During this interval the mother uses up her own nutrient reserves to maintain the status of the baby and thereby absorbs the stress through her own body for as long as these reserves remain.

Secondly, a good deal of magical folklore has arisen round the possible influence of events occurring during pregnancy, and of the mother's emotional states on the subsequent physical and psychological attributes of the baby. These include such old wives' tales as that a child will have a hare lip if a hare crosses an expectant mother's path; or that a mother can 'mark' her child through being frightened by a snake, rat, frog or other gruesome animal. Many people believed, and many probably still believe, that psychological states are directly transmitted from mother to baby—that, for example, the expectant mother who listens to music will bear a child with a sensitivity for, and appreciation of, music. These are now regarded as superstitions. Yet it is scientifically accepted that the emotional state of the mother can immediately affect the baby. Acute emotional states over a long period—depression, worry and anxiety—retard nutrient metabolism and upset the hormonal balance of the mother's body so that the baby may not be fully nourished and the chemicals secreted by the glands may be transmitted to the baby. Sontag (15, 16) has experimentally demonstrated that after a period of emotional stress the baby is more active and that if the pregnancy is a continuously anxious period, the child when born tends to be under-weight, hyper-active, and to have a good deal of gastro-intestinal trouble, more bowel movements and a higher heart rate.

Thirdly, in the same way as nutrient constituents and hormones are transmitted to the baby so are anti-bodies, viruses, and the products of the drugs which the mothers has taken. These may be beneficial and convey to the baby a temporary immunity, or the beneficial effect of the drugs taken. On the other hand, they may sometimes be harmful, as in the case of the drug thalidomide. In the case of an Rh negative mother who has an Rh positive first child, the anti-bodies created to protect the mother against the Rh positive blood transmitted to her by the first child will, in turn, be transmitted to her second child who may be adversely affected by them.

Finally, particular traumatic events may affect the embryo at critical times, as when a severe psychological shock of some kind in the second or third month of pregnancy may cause a mother to lose her baby. The effect of severe psychological stress occurring as a result of an environmental change has been experimentally demonstrated by Lamond and Lang.[1] They showed that there are substantial embryonic losses in white mice when the mate of each mouse, with whom she has lived for a long time and by whom she has conceived, is replaced by a new and permanent mate some days after conception. Mice whose environment was propitiously maintained and who were not subject to such a drastic change did not suffer such embryonic losses.

However, as regards the effects of pre-natal conditions it is not only what happens, but at what time it happens, that is important. A baby's development is predictable; certain organs develop at certain times and each organ has developmentally its critical stage when extra-uterine influence may impair subsequent growth. The full catalogue of such critical stages and the organs concerned is not available yet, for much further research has to be done in this field. But results so far

[1] In personal conversation with Dr. Lang.

are suggestive. To take two examples: in 1940 Australia had an epidemic of German measles and abnormalities, particularly cataracts, were noted in babies. Subsequent investigation showed that 90 per cent of the babies affected were those of mothers who had contracted German measles in the first eight weeks of pregnancy. Secondly, rickets are found to be frequent in newborn babies when malnutrition occurs in the last months of pregnancy, during which time the process of mineralization of the skeleton of the baby is most active.

In giving this statement of the hazards to the baby *in utero*, the impression may also have been given that at this stage it is dangerously vulnerable, which is in opposition to the idea of total invulnerability critically referred to earlier. But most of the instances mentioned above are exceptional—the starvation and emotional trauma of war, traumatic experiences in the early stages of pregnancy, the complications arising from an Rh negative mother and an Rh positive baby (which can now easily be detected and, in most cases, counteracted). These exceptional instances must not lead us to forget that, in general, the baby *in utero* is well and uniquely protected.

The factors which influence the physical basis of personality before birth are known as *congenital* influences. It is necessary to distinguish between congenital and genetic determinants of personality. The latter operate through the genes and are inherited at the moment of conception; congenital influences are environmental influences taking place *in utero*. Thus, for example, a person cannot inherit syphilis or tuberculosis, but he may acquire these diseases *in utero*— that is, congenital syphilis, or congenital tuberculosis.

The newborn (or neonate)

Much detailed study has been made of babies during the first few weeks following their birth. These weeks are regarded as so distinctive that the baby during this time is given the special title of neonate, literally the new (Gr. *neo*) born (L. *natus*). This special interest is understandable because of the unique physiological changes which are taking place and which effect the transition from foetal to extra-uterine functioning. The length of the neonate stage has been variously given, from as short as one week to as long as one month. Strictly speaking, it is a period of physio-logical adaptation and therefore likely to vary with individual differences between newborns.

An immediate and obvious adaptation takes place with the baby's first gasping breath, and with the change from foetal to adult-type blood circulation. Before birth, the lungs do not function, and respiration is carried out by the placenta through interchange of blood constituents between mother and child. A hole, called the *foramen ovale*, allows blood to pass from the right to the left atrium (that is from one of the two upper chambers of the heart to the other), thus by-passing both the right ventricle, the lower right chamber of the heart, and also the lungs. Any blood that does not by-pass the right ventricle is pumped straight into the main artery or aorta through a duct called *ductus arteriosus*.

At birth two significant changes take place. First, the *foramen ovale* immediately and permanently closes. The heart is thus com-pletely divided into left and right sides, and the way prepared for adult-type circulation.[1] Secondly, the duct also closes so that blood from the right ventricle is diverted away from the main artery and into the lungs which now expand. Thence the blood goes to the left side of the heart, which pumps the newly oxy-genated blood into the aorta and through the body. Patten (10) says, 'The rapid readjustment of the circulation at birth is one of the most dramatic and fascinating of biological processes.'[2] With-in a matter of a few hours a near-normal oxygen level has been established, and within ten days following birth both the pressure and the acid-alkaline balance of the blood are normal.

Some take the view that this first grasp of breath automatically follows the sudden rush of external stimuli which at birth im-pinges on the baby for the first time. This is analogous to the gasps we make when we are suddenly and unexpectedly plunged into cold water. Others take the view that the first breath follows automatically from the sudden and high concentration of carbon dioxide within the blood itself following separation from the placenta, the source of oxygen for the foetus.

Other major changes inevitably follow separation from the mother: the baby's own gastro-intestinal tract must take over the task of ingesting and digesting food and eliminating waste; the

[1] In rare cases it does not close, and we speak of a 'hole-in-the-heart' baby.
[2] page 532.

regulatory mechanisms which maintain the body at a constant temperature must operate to adapt to new variations in the external temperature; and many senses are brought into play for the first time—vision, hearing, taste, smell. These changes necessitate major adaptations and therefore some degree of physiological stress. This is reflected in the baby's loss of weight during the neonatal period.

As for activity, the neonate is asleep for up to twenty hours a day, a sleep which is disturbed mainly by hunger or by some strong outside stimulus, a bright light or a loud noise. A neonate is either quiet and tranquil, as when sleeping and feeding, or crying in apparent distress. As it lies inert, the newborn adopts what is known as the tonic neck reflex position (see Fig. 7). The head is turned with one side of the face flat on the mattress; the arm and leg on the side to which the head is turned are extended and the other arm and leg are flexed. As Gesell points out, looked at from above, the baby appears like a fencer ready to begin a parry.

FIG. 7 Tonic neck reflex position

Sucking is by far the strongest, most developed and most easily stimulated reflex. Three interesting reflexes present at this time suggest man's primordial origin. First, the grasp suspension reflex (see Fig. 8), which is a grip using the fingers only. It is so strong that when a pencil is placed in the neonate's palms and the reflex triggered off, the baby can hang by its hands and support its own weight. This reflex develops to full strength by about four months and is later superseded by the voluntary grip using the thumb. Secondly, if supported horizontally in water, a neonate will perform the alternate and simultaneous movement of arms and legs appropriate to swimming. This swim reflex disappears in a few weeks. Thirdly, the Moro reflex is the neonate's response to a strong stimulus, especially loud noise. He throws arms and legs out wide and then brings them back to a hugging, defensive position. Such behaviour is appropriate in a young sub-human primate, enabling it to clutch to its mother's body or to the limb of a tree. In a baby this reflex also gradually disappears; move-

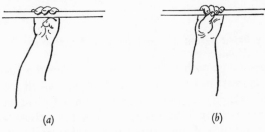

(a)   (b)

FIG. 8 (a) The grasp suspension reflex and (b) the voluntary
grasp

ments of the body in response to loud noises diminish so that by about eight months, the response of the baby is the more subdued start.

So drastic do the changes from foetal to extra-uterine existence appear that some psychologists, especially Rank and his followers (11), have spoken of the 'trauma of birth', and they see all human anxiety as stemming from this trauma or shock. They claim that the shock of birth generates a huge reservoir of anxiety which feeds the numerous activities of later years.

However, there is a very great danger that we will ascribe to a neonate experiences similar to those we imagine we would our-selves experience in such circumstances. In the case of birth it is not possible to check out judgments by asking the baby or by re-flecting back upon our own experiences at birth. It could be argued against Rank's theory that the neonate's physiological sys-tem has not developed to enable it to experience the feelings of an adult; it is certain that the neonate has not developed to the stage where he can consciously comprehend the processes taking place and, by apprehending, generate anxiety about what is to come. It is, of course, very difficult to prove or disprove such a theory. Theoretically one may suggest a designed experiment whereby the relative extent of trauma suffered by many babies is assessed to discover the relation between the amount of trauma at birth and the amount of anxiety in later years. But the difficulty is how to assess the extent of the birth trauma from one baby to another. Psychologists are generally sceptical about Rank's theory. While they would be prepared to say that a difficult birth does seem to make *immediate* neonate adjustments more difficult, they would not, like Rank, subscribe to the permanent effects of normal births.

The first year: a period of dependence and sensuousness

General bodily growth is very marked during the first year—a one-third increase in height to about two-and-a-half feet, a treble increase in weight to about twenty pounds by the end of the year. There is corresponding progress in bodily activity—from the relative immobility of the neonate to the considerable mobility of the one-year-old. Progress towards walking illustrates the cephalo-caudal direction of growth, control of eyes and head first, then trunk, then legs.

Within a few weeks a baby can move its head and lift it a little. Movement of the eyes is at first uncoordinated and the baby often gives the appearance of being cross-eyed. But within four to six weeks he co-ordinates his eye movements and is able to focus on an object, to fix his gaze upon it, and to follow with head and eyes a moving object within limited range. Mastery of the trunk begins later (about three months) when the baby can, with support, sit upright on his mother's lap and control his head. However, it will take another four months before he is able to sit up without support. Soon afterwards, he propels himself along on his abdomen (eight months), crawls on hands and knees (nine months), then stands, holding on to the edge of his cot, a chair, or a table (ten months). Before the year is out, he may take a step or two when gently led.

Progress in the ability to grasp and manipulate objects illustrates the proximo-distal direction of growth—that is, gross activity of arms is followed by finer movements of fingers and thumbs. At first the arms move in circular fashion from the girdles, but by two months the baby reaches out to objects and people. Later he grasps objects and holds on tightly (sixteen weeks), and the tenacity of his hold indicates that his capacity to grasp is more developed than his capacity to release this grasp. Eyes and hands co-ordinate (twenty-four weeks) and the baby gazes at an object as he holds it with both hands. It is about forty weeks before he is able to use the thumb in apposition to the fingers and neatly to pincer objects. As he develops, he becomes progressively more active in grasping, snatching, pulling, poking.

These activities of the baby also illustrate two other principles of growth. First, the Principle of Differentiation which states that finer movements are differentiated out of gross, general movements of the whole body. It is not a case of small movements, like those of the fingers, wrists, feet and ankles, preceding and leading by a process of addition, as it were, to larger movements but, as the principle states, of large movements preceding, and of smaller movements differentiating out of them. The second is the Principle of Integration, which implies that as growth proceeds, fine, specialized movements begin to function together with, and in relation to, other such movements. This leads to behaviour which is at a more complex level of organization and is illustrated, for example, by the baby's co-ordination of hand and eye.

There are individual differences in the rate of development. Some babies walk as early as nine months and some do not do so until they are eighteen months old; some pick up an object between the thumb and forefinger by seven months, others not until eleven months. But although the rate varies from individual to individual the direction of growth and the differentiating and integrating processes involved are the same for all babies.

Accompanying all this is the growth of sensory acuity and of the ability to acquire sensory experience—seeing, hearing, feeling, tasting. Reference will be made to the continued development of these skills when the sensory, manipulative and exploratory nature of children's play is discussed in Chapter 19.

The baby's personality also grows rapidly. For the first few days and weeks after birth, the baby is not a 'person' but 'a strange, fragile-looking thing'. But even during the first year he develops a unique personality, so that he becomes an individual whose idiosyncracies the members of the family have already come to know. To their delight he may have spoken his first two words, 'Da-da', 'Ma-ma'.

The impressions that mothers form about the differences between babies (as when a mother says, 'This one is so much more placid than my first') have been confirmed by experimental work.

These are the constitutional differences already mentioned at the beginning of Chapter 6.

Hadfield (7) [1,2] has called the first year of life a period of 'dependence and sensuousness'. As for the dependence, obviously the baby depends upon the mother for its physical existence and well-being, but the term 'dependence', as used here, includes also psychological dependence.

Investigations would seem to show that a baby's mental well-being depends on the presence or near-presence of the mother and that a baby's emotional state reflects that of the mother. We are aware that anxious mothers tend to produce anxious children and happy, assured mothers to produce happy and assured children. But dependence during the first year has about it a special quality which may arise, first, from a baby's obvious helplessness and lack of autonomy. Most adults and children are aroused to feelings of tenderness and an urge to cherish when they see a baby, or, for that matter, any young creature such as a very young calf or colt, a kitten or puppy. Boys and girls will spontaneously utter gentle, tender sound and, individually, they will seek to hold or stroke the young creature. We sometimes say of young things, 'It's a pity they have to grow up', implying that as they grow they become less attractive. Nevertheless, it may not be loss of attraction as such but that, when older, living things become more autonomous and, therefore, more independent; and this independence, plus their rude health (all attractive in themselves), do not arouse in us the tenderness and the urge to cherish which make young things particularly endearing.

Secondly, as far as children are concerned, the exclusive nature of the mother-child relationship during the first year is lost with age.

For older children the mother-child relationship is certainly important, but relatively less exclusive in that they have other contacts both within and outside the family.

As for sensuousness, the baby, it would seem, takes delight in bodily stimulation. It appears to enjoy the processes of sucking, urination, defecation, the feel of air and water on its body and the kinaesthetic sensations which are experienced in bodily movements—kicking of legs, movements of arms and of head. These pleasures aid the baby in the performance of the biological func-

[1] page 73 ff.   [2] page 82 ff.

tions so necessary for the healthy development of its body; but the satisfaction by the mother of a baby's biological needs has important psychological implications for the baby.

Indeed, you may sometimes wonder why students of children's mental development are concerned about the biological aspects of baby care. It is not the biological aspects in themselves, but the fact that it is in the execution and satisfaction of biological needs that the baby has its first experiences of social living; that is, a human being's first experiences of social living are connected with feeding, excretion, hygiene (washing and bathing). Furthermore, as has already been indicated in studying the child-bearing practices of primitive groups, the regular or haphazard way in which they are carried out, the qualities of slow tenderness or quick brusqueness that the mother brings to these tasks, will influence the feelings which a baby will acquire about the world. Freud placed great emphasis on the importance of these activities in social and emotional growth. More recently, Erikson (5) has re-interpreted Freud's point of view by suggesting that, according to the way in which these are carried out, a baby will or will not develop what he calls 'basic trust', meaning by this the feeling that the world in which he lives is a safe, stable, predictable place. The manner in which these activities are carried out by the mother is important, therefore, for the baby's sense of security and emotional well-being. We will say a word or two about each as they relate to our culture.

Suttie (18) has illustrated what is meant by the quality of the mother's touch and its possible influence on the baby by pointing out the differences in bodily sensation which a baby most probably experiences in the processes of feeding and of excretion, and also the possible differences in the mother's attitude towards the two processes. He states the differences much as shown in the table on page 186.

Because of the mother's usual attitude of tenderness, tolerance and approval, and because the baby, in any case, often slips into sleep almost immediately afterwards, there may be no marked complications for the baby as a result of the process of feeding. However, because excretion is followed by vivid wakefulness, handling and attention by the mother, and because the mother's attitude may be ambiguous, her movements at this time may be abrupt, brisk, quick and, as Suttie has so neatly put it, 'unhappily intolerant'. Such movements contrast with her slow, tender and 'happily tolerant' movements following feeding. (Of course, even with feeding a mother may cause her baby some distress by making him adapt too exactly to the clock; whereas, of course, the periods between a baby's feelings of hunger vary not as the

Feeding	Excretion
Initially the baby experiences a feeling of emptiness.	Initially the baby experiences a feeling of fullness or tension.
After feeding, the baby experiences a feeling of fullness.	After excretion, the baby experiences a feeling of relaxed emptiness.
Feeding is followed by sleep.	Excretion is followed by vivid wakefulness.
The attitude of the mother to feeding is one of total approval.	The attitude of the mother towards excretory activities may be ambiguous, uncertain.

clock but according to the amount of energy he has expended in kicking, rolling and gurgling, and the amount of fresh air he has had since his previous meal.)

Suttie sees bathing as the time when a baby first experiences the delights of playing. In this he implicitly makes a contrast between this time, on the one hand, and feeding and 'pottying' times on the other. While feeding and 'pottying' can have their delights, they are, like work, duties to be done, with their accompanying anxieties—Will he eat? Will he perform?—and the delights are incidental. A mother will sometimes say to her child when encouraging him to excrete, 'Do your duty'. About these activities, then, there is an air of purpose and necessity. But bathing allows more opportunity for unhurried and unanxious play which is beyond that required by hygiene alone—for splashing, for sponging water over the baby's body, for sensations such as the feel and taste of the sponge, for laughter and goo-goo talk with the mother. Suttie dwells long and often on the need for a mother to enjoy bath-time in a leisurely way, and not to be tempted to hurry it in order to get on with household chores.

In Chapter 4, following the work of Mead, a short account

was given of the Arapesh and the Mundugumor peoples, of their respective patterns of culture and of the connection between their differing personalities and the differing ways they suckled their babies. Suttie, too, has studied the personalities of people within industrial cultures like our own and has related these personalities to prevalent attitudes towards babies and towards the way babies are reared.

Suttie suggests two main characteristics that may influence and, from his point of view, impair people's capacity to care for babies. First, he speaks of a 'taboo on tenderness' by which he means a tendency on the part of many people in our society to shun, to avoid the tender feelings and the urge to cherish on seeing small, helpless things already briefly described.

As Suttie sees it, people in industrial societies, especially men, become so caught up in the assertive and masculine activities necessary for the manipulation of objects (and, indeed, of people if this is necessary to their purpose) that their capacity to feel tenderness and to experience the need to cherish becomes impaired. Because of this 'taboo on tenderness' many people in our society become embarrassed by such displays of tenderness as a man chuckling and goo-gooing with a baby. Yet Suttie sees this capacity to feel tenderness, to experience the urge to cherish, and to enjoy both, as essential features of adequate baby care.

The second point he makes is this: in an industrial society in which so often human relationships take the form of contract, as with the buying and selling of goods, of services or labour, we tend to ask of any human relationship, 'Who gets most out of this?' There is, therefore, always the possibility that people will apply this way of looking at human relationships to, and ask the same question of, a mother and her baby.

Suttie points out that such a way of looking at the baby-mother relationship may well impair it, since the comparison made is invidious for the baby, who is seen as the one who passively takes in contrast to the self-sacrificing mother who actively gives. But, says Suttie, the baby gives too. The mother gives the breast, the baby the lips. To chuckling and goo-goo talk, the baby responds with its whole being; it laughs, kicks, waves its arms and shakes its body. In short, the baby gives its all, and has the capacity not only to receive but also to give love. Indeed, Suttie has said that the baby is born only with the capacity to love and that the capacity to hate arises from adults' inability to love the baby in return. While we may not agree with this, for it has tremendous philosophical implications which relate to the problem of good and evil, we may agree that the ideal of baby care is that of tenderness, of the lullaby and the rocking chair.

So much for the interesting way that Suttie looks at the baby's life during its first year. But Suttie wrote in the 1930's. Modern studies have been concerned carefully to observe the behaviour of babies, and, where possible, to test experimentally theories about child rearing, such as those suggested by Suttie. These observations and experiments have centred chiefly around the effects of adequate or inadequate mothering.

Here are some examples of such experimental studies.[1]

First, Professor Harriet Rheingold (12) acted as surrogate mother to a group of eight six-month-old infants living in an institution. For eight consecutive weeks she fed, bathed and changed them, cuddling, smiling at, and talking to them. In this way she attempted to become as real a mother as possible to each. A control group of eight other babies in the same institution was cared for in the usual, routine manner of the institution with several women looking after them as the needs of the babies (mainly the biological ones) and the duty roster of the institution provided.

The most significant result at the end of the eight weeks was the greater social responsiveness of the eight babies whom Rheingold had mothered, when they were compared with the eight babies in the control group who received the usual institutional care. The babies especially cared for by Rheingold smiled more readily and responded with more kicks, wrigglings and arm wavings to Dr. Rheingold herself, to the examiner who did the weekly testing and to a stranger who was brought in at the end of the eight weeks in order to observe the response of each baby to a new and strange face.

[1] These observations and experiments were not of academic interest only but aimed to answer vital practical questions relating, more particularly, to the adoption of children. For example, if a married couple wish to adopt a baby, is it better for the immediate and future well-being of all three that he be taken to his adopted home as soon after birth as possible? Or is it better that he be kept in an institution for up to a year? Answer to such a question as this required knowledge of the differential effects on a baby's progress during its first year of an institutional as compared with a home environment.

The second experiment consisted in part of a comparative study of babies in two institutions in Iran (4). One was a poor institution in which the babies had little personal contact with adults, since there was only one attendant for every eight babies. The babies lay down all the time and were not, for example, lifted to a sitting position for feeding or placed on their stomachs to encourage movements leading to crawling. There were no toys to play with. By contrast, the second institution was a rich one in which the babies received much more personal attention and were placed on their stomachs, given toys to feel, to take and to manipulate.

The progress of the two groups of babies was compared in the early part of their second year. There were marked differences in motor development illustrated by such facts as these: only 42 per cent of the children in the deprived institution could sit alone, only 4 per cent of them could stand alone while holding on to a support; none could walk. By comparison 90 per cent of the children in the richer institution could sit alone, 60 per cent could stand and take a few steps while holding on to a support, 15 per cent were able to walk without support.

The first experiment demonstrated that the personal care provided by Rheingold, her smiles, goo-goo talk and so on, stimulated and encouraged social responses by the babies so that, in this respect, they progressed significantly beyond the babies given no such personal care. In the second experiment, the provision of toys, of appropriate floors for crawling, of supports for standing, and of personal attention so combined to stimulate and to encourage motor development in the babies of the rich institution that they progressed towards walking much more rapidly than did the babies in the poor institution. Other researches have shown the beneficial effects of adequate mothering and of the affection and tenderness that accompany such mothering. These researches have studied the effects of hospitalization of young children, and also the differences of physical health, appearance and behaviour between babies brought up in private homes where they receive much attention, much cuddling and much love, and babies brought up in institutions where there is not a sufficient staff to provide these.

Spitz (17) has shown that children deprived of such mothering fall into a state of apathy and depressive grief which he calls 'anaclitic depression', and that the effects of this deprivation seem most severe when it occurs about six months after birth. The investigations by Bowlby (2) have already been referred to, as a result of which he has suggested that inability to form close, happy and friendly relations with others in later life can sometimes be traced to insufficient or interrupted mothering during the first two years. Ribble (13) made a special study of children who lived in an institution. She speaks of the listlessness, emaciation and pallor of these babies, who are relatively unresponsive to the smiles of adults and more prone to infection than babies brought up in the affectionate surroundings of a home and family.

Experiments with animals also confirm the importance of adequate mothering. For example, Harlow took monkeys away from their mothers at birth and provided them with surrogate 'mothers' mechanically contrived out of wood, wire, cloth and so on. One of these surrogate 'mothers' consisted simply of a bare wire frame, shaped like a body, with a 'face' added. The second surrogate monkey was made of a block of wood covered first with sponge rubber and then with soft terry cloth. Some young monkeys were given both kinds of surrogates, the hard and the soft. These monkeys would spend hours clinging to the cloth 'mother'. Even if food could be obtained only from the wire 'mother', the young monkeys would return to the soft 'mother' immediately after feeding. When frightened they would run to the soft 'mother' and cling to 'her' for protection (see Fig. 9).

It would seem at first that young monkeys so brought up were adequately provided for, since between them the two mechanical mothers supplied both food and protection. As Harlow (8) said, in speaking of the cloth surrogate, 'The result was a mother soft, warm and tender, a mother with infinite patience, a mother available twenty-four hours a day, a mother that never scolded her infant and never struck or bit her baby in anger. . . . It was our opinion that we engineered a very superior monkey'.[1]

But by the time these young monkeys were two years old it was obvious that there was something wrong with them. They showed obvious signs of emotional instability, were socially inept, infantile and unskilful in their play. Some were aggressive, venting their rage on attendants and people who passed by their

[1] page 73.

cages. Some seemed to direct their rage towards their own bodies by biting, scratching, falling, bumping and generally hurting themselves; others remained constantly quiescent, huddled in a corner of the cage or clinging desperately on to the soft 'mother'.

FIG. 9 One of Harlow's monkeys, with cloth surrogate 'mother' (*left*)
and wire surrogate 'mother' (*right*)

Even when placed in a group they played alone and seemingly had no idea of how to play co-operatively.

Eighteen of these monkeys were introduced into a social community of monkeys who had been brought up in the usual way with their mothers. They improved socially, but none of the eighteen acquired the full complement of responses and attitudes to make them socially normal.

Harlow had to conclude that the 'mothers' he devised were not so perfect after all. As he observes, growing up to be a monkey is a complex process. While the two surrogate mothers can between them provide food and protection, neither of them can encourage the baby monkey to learn the beginnings of this complex process of growing up—to groom itself, to jump, to climb, to strike out on its own, to play with other monkeys.

A further interesting feature of Harlow's experiments is that they demonstrate the importance of soft-comforting contact in the growth of love. That the wire 'mother' gave milk was not sufficient to establish 'her' as a favourite. Even though, as the young monkeys grew older, 'she' remained their only source of food, they nevertheless continued to prefer the soft surrogate, going to the hard surrogate only when they were hungry. It would seem that softness of surface facilitates intimate contact between infant and mothers, and provides a rich soil upon which affection can flourish. This is understandable. Softness implies yielding, a pleasurable, non-punishing acceptance; by contrast, hardness means resistance, a painful, punishing non-acceptance. Thus, in times of distress or of fear the monkey can press deeply into the soft cloth, and it gives comfort and protection; by contrast, the hardness of the wire surrogate, its lack of resilience means that the young monkey is as exposed to outside sources of danger as if he were alone.

This desire for soft things is seen in young children's affection for soft cuddly toys. A small child will often carry around with him something soft, like a small woolly blanket, and will hug it and suck it as he would a doll.

Harlow also found that monkeys who were given the choice tended to prefer a rocking 'mother' or a rocking crib to a still one, 'though the degree of preference varied considerably from day to day' (8). He concluded that affection is also enhanced by motion but to a less significant extent than it is by soft, pleasurable contact.

These three experiments indicate what the term mothering implies in the day-to-day life of the baby. For the baby it means opportunities for experiences of the following kind:

1 *Sensuous and sensory experiences:* the touch, feel, smell of the mother's body: bright surroundings, gentle noises, e.g. the sound of the mother as she bustles around.

2 *Exploratory experiences:* to explore objects with hands and eyes; to feel their texture and warmth, e.g. spongy rubber toys.

3 *Manipulative experiences:* these relate particularly to the development of the baby's ability to manipulate his own body. For example a baby can:

sit at about four months (but requires the active support of the mother);

stand at about eight months (but again requires active support of the mother);

pull itself to a standing position at eleven months (but requires appropriate furniture, stands, etc.) Even apart from these opportunities to manipulate his own body, there is the provision of such simple things as a rattle to hold and to shake, a block to move around in one finger, a hanging toy to hit and so on.

4   *Social and emotional experiences:* a baby can respond socially at about three months or before; for example, will smile in response to a smiling adult, babble in response to mother's chatter; laugh, kick legs and roll arms in response to mother's smiles and headshakes, wriggle in response to the mother's tickling.

The simple principle implied in the above classification of a young baby's experiences and of a mother's part in encouraging these is this: a child's body matures, that is, muscles, limbs and trunk get larger, longer and stronger; cartilage matures to true bone; nervous pathways become more complex and acquire fatty sheaths (called myelin sheaths) which separate one pathway from another; the brain grows in size and in the complicated nature of its structure. These maturational changes which progressively take place give rise, at varying times in the child's life, to states of maturational readiness, for example, readiness to smile, to crawl, to stand, to control (e.g. bladder and bowel), to perform intricate movements of the fingers. Any state of maturational readiness needs to be translated into the appropriate physical activity, such as smiling, crawling, standing, walking and so on. This translation of a state of matured readiness into the appropriate physical activity is more likely to take place when the child's physical and psychological environment stimulates and encourages it. If the child is not stimulated and encouraged, then the opportunity provided by the maturational readiness is not taken advantage of, and the baby becomes retarded, at least temporarily, in that particular skill.

One can make an ethical judgment and say that affection, tenderness and cherishing, which the term 'mothering' means, are of intrinsic worth, that is, they are good in themselves. These researchers go further by showing that mothering has practical implications for the mental and physical well-being of the baby, not only during the baby stage itself but possibly even beyond this into later life.

REFERENCES

1 Antonov, A. N. 'Children born during the siege of Leningrad in 1942.' *Journal of Pediatrics*, 1947, **30**, pp. 250–9.

2 Bowlby, J. *Maternal Care and Mental Health*. World Health Organization, Geneva, 1951.

3 Carmichael, L. 'The onset and early development of behaviour.' *In* Carmichael, L. (Ed.) *Manual of Child Psychology*. Wiley, New York, 1954, pp. 60–185.

4 Dennis, W. 'Causes of retardation among institutional children: Iran.' *Journal of Genetic Psychology*, 1960, **96**, pp. 47–59.

5 Erikson, E. H. *Childhood and Society*. Horton, New York, 1951.

6 Gesell, A., Amatruda, C. S. *The Embryology of Behaviour*. Harper, New York, 1945.

7 Hadfield, J. A. *Childhood and Adolescence*. Penguin Books, Harmondsworth, Middlesex, 1962.

8 Harlow, H. R. 'The nature of love.' *American Psychologist*, 1958, **13**, pp. 673–85.

9 Hooker, D. 'The development of behaviour in the human foetus.' *In* Dennis, W. *Readings in Child Psychology*. Prentice-Hall, Englewood Cliffs, New Jersey, 1951.

10 Patten, B. M. *Foundations of Embryology*. McGraw-Hill, London, 1958.

11 Rank, O. *The Trauma of Birth*. Harcourt, Brace, New York, 1929.

12 Rheingold, H. L. 'The modification of social responsiveness in institutional babies.' *Monograph Society for Research in Child Development*, 1956, **21**, No. 2 (Serial No. 63).

13 Ribble, M. A. *The Rights of Infants*. Columbia University Press, New York, 1943.

14 Smith, C. A. 'Effects of maternal malnutrition upon the newborn infant in Holland (1944–5).' *Journal of Pediatrics*, 1947, **30**, pp. 229–43.

15 Sontag, L. W. 'The significance of foetal environmental differences.' *American Journal of Obstetrics and Gynaecology*, 1941, **42**, pp. 996–1003.

16 Sontag, L. W. 'Some psychosomatic aspects of childhood.' *In* Seidman, J. M. *The Child: A Book of Readings*. Rinehart, New York, 1958, pp. 466–75.

17 Spitz, R. A. 'Anaclitic depression.' *Psychoanalytical Study of the Child*. International Universities Press, New York, 1946, Vol. 2, pp. 313–42.

18 Suttie, I. *The Origins of Love and Hate*. Routledge & Kegan Paul, London, 1945.

BIBLIOGRAPHICAL NOTE

Foss, B. M. *Determinants of Infant Behaviour*. Methuen, London.
Volume I, 1961, Volume II, 1963, Volume III, 1965.

Volume I is a very scientific account of the behaviour of infants during their first year. It includes, among others, an article by Rheingold on the responses of children reared at home as compared with those reared in institutions; also one by Harlow giving a detailed account of the behaviour of his monkeys.

Volume II contains, among others, a further article by Harlow: on maternal affection in rhesus monkeys. Human studies include one on mother–child interaction in Uganda, and one on the smiling and exploratory responses of infants.

Volume III is also concerned with relations between mother and child, both animal and human, and presents a variety of studies: a baboon in a domestic environment, two mother–infant pairs in a baby clinic, Israeli children in kibbutzim and family, the impairment of development in children of withdrawn mother, the genetics of the smiling response.

CHAPTER ELEVEN

Pre-School Children
(one, two, three, four)

The second year, like the first, is characterized by very rapid growth, particularly of two very important skills, namely talking and walking. Crawling is replaced by halting steps, then by a steady walk, until by two years the child is sturdy on his feet and able to walk up and down steps (one at a time, of course). By two years, children can manipulate objects more easily, pile blocks one on the other, handle dolls and trucks. They have acquired a noticeable degree of autonomy and do not passively accept the universe, but go forward actively inspecting, touching, pushing, pulling. Inarticulate noises are replaced by comprehensible gestures, single syllables, single words and then phrases.

Toilet training is not completed even by the end of this year, and there may be numerous 'accidents'. Cleanliness training has been referred to in previous chapters but, because the 'formal' training which begins at this time is important in determining the kind of relationship existing between mother and child, we may add to what has already been said.

Sometimes during this period children are fascinated by their own excreta. They may pride themselves on their ability to produce it. As one little boy put it after he had 'produced', 'No more now or none for tomorrow.' They may even attempt to play and to smear objects with excreta. Freud aptly refers to such activity as 'pleasure in the product'; and Gesell has said, 'It may have the novelty of self-discovery and the excreta is naïvely exploited as though it were that much plasticine; it may even be disposed on the doorstep with some respect for design' (2).[1]

[1] page 326.

Researches suggest that too early and too severe toilet training can lead to immediate complications, such as enuresis, aggressiveness and negativism or timidity and fearfulness. It can cause a child much perplexity and confusion. Often, therefore, under the pressure to conform he achieves well while at other times he may lapse badly (8, 11, 14). Further, one unfulfilled demand of this kind can create a resentment which may poison the whole atmosphere and cast a cloud over the total relationships existing between mother and child.

Children at this stage tend too, to be naïve exhibitionists. They will quite unashamedly display their bodies: the little girl will lift her clothes in executing a twirl, while both boys and girls delight to run around without clothes. Sometimes they will play with their genitals quite unself-consciously and often publicly.

Because of this preoccupation with excreta, this exhibitionism and genital play, Freud calls this a stage of 'polymorphous perversion' (Gr. *poly* many; *morphe* shape). The term 'polymorphous' is apt enough but the term 'perversion', while applicable to an adult who behaves in this way, is not applicable to a child of one or two years of age. For the child, to explore, to touch any part of his body or to play with its products, is no more reprehensible than to explore or to touch any other object. Moreover, the genital manipulation of which we spoke is not masturbation in its true sense, for true masturbation ends in an orgasm and is possible only with sexual maturity. The activity of the two-year-old is best called genital play which is sensuously rather than sexually pleasurable for the child.

Exhibitionism, stool smearing and genital manipulation can be trying, particularly for parents who are somewhat squeamish regarding the body in general and the indignities which it casts upon them. It would be unfortunate if parents took the point of view that their child is developing bad habits and that these must be stopped whatever the consequence. We need to discard many of our pruderies when looking after children in their second year (and, indeed, children in their third and fourth years). By so doing, we are psychologically more prepared to encourage children to follow socially acceptable ways of behaviour without having to resort to physical punishment or to arousing those senses of guilt and shame which confuse and terrify young children.

During their second year children make rapid progress in their ability to talk. One investigation (17) has given the following average number of words used: 3 at one year, 22 at eighteen months, 272 by two years.[1] In no other period of one year will a human being achieve anywhere near a ninety-fold increase (3 to 272) in the number of words he acquires, and in no other six-month period will he show a twelve-and-a-half-fold increase (22 to 272). Investigations also suggest that, up to about the age of three, girls are more advanced in their language development than boys (19); further, that progress in motor development (creeping, crawling, standing, walking, etc.) and in speech alternate, so that progress in one tends to be accompanied by a temporary lessening of progress in the other (16).

The main features of children's speech during this second year are these. First, the use of single words. Single words are also used to indicate a state of things; and so 'hot' means, 'The milk is hot', 'foot' may mean, 'My foot hurts'. Secondly, the child has not developed the skill to use difficult word combinations and he overcomes this by inventing his own simpler combinations; and so, 'prepol' means 'pretty polly', 'normum' means 'naughty mummy', 'silou' means 'silly you'.

Children of two improve yet further in the skills they began to master when they were one. They are more mobile; they can walk, quite competently, push and pull toy trains and trolleys. They have acquired a degree of autonomy, meaning that they are able, within limits, actively to manipulate much of the environment of home and garden; also, that they can choose, to do or not to do; and if they choose to do, then what to do and what not to do.

This autonomy has many advantages for a young child. It means that he can explore and get to know the small universe in which he lives; in that he is able to choose, he can begin to experiment with it in a trial-and-error kind of way. For example, he plays with a peg and inserts it in here, then in there; it may be inferred that unconsciously he is reasoning in this way: 'I put the

---

[1] These average numbers must be taken cautiously and not be used as a norm, that is, as a basis to compare the language achievement of individual children. This is because there are such marked differences between children in the number of words they acquire at any particular age (even though they belong to the same socio-economic group) that average figures can be misleading. The main emphasis here is on the *rapidity* with which words are learned during the second year.

peg in here; it doesn't fit. I'll try this hole; it does fit.' It may also be inferred that, when the problem is solved, he experiences a sense of triumph and of completion similar to the click of satisfaction that adults experience when they solve a problem. He may also feel, as a result, that the universe is a sensible place: things go together.

Yet, like many other of the unique gifts of man, growth of autonomy with the ability to choose and to experiment, has its negative as well as its positive side. Many happenings in the life of a two-year-old illustrate this. For example, a two-year-old can go into the kitchen, into the garden or stay where he is. Which shall he do? It is difficult for him to decide. He wants to go on playing and he feels an urge to go to the lavatory; he cannot make the decisive choice and the result is calamity.

The child's growing autonomy seems to bring its own kind of instability. He might oscillate between extremes; from a rush of 'busyness' and excitement to sudden dawdling, from a screaming demand to be dressed to a refusal to co-operate when his mother decides to comply. He is very busy at some job or other; mother notes this and sighs with relief—he's settled for a bit. Then suddenly he tires of it and slumps down in a corner and sucks his thumb with a little squelching noise that sets his mother's teeth on edge. This instability, this tendency towards extremes is seen particularly in the temper tantrums very common at this age amongst children in our society. Graphs compiled by research workers of the number of temper tantrums children have in relation to age show a peak between ages two and three.

We might ask why this is so. The explanation which Hadfield gives (6)[1] is that there arises, at this stage, a discrepancy between the extent of children's needs on the one hand and their power of control on the other. Perhaps in the light of the above discussion on autonomy, Hadfield's point can be put as follows. When a child acquires a degree of autonomy, his world expands and his needs increase. He begins to see more and more objects which attract him and these he wants to hold, to feel, to taste, to examine. There's that cut glass bowl, there's father's gold watch, both objects that are taboo. Again, many large objects are so heavy and awkward in shape, the chair he'd like to push, the stone he'd like to lift, father's spade he'd like to handle. The peg may not

[1] pages 100–1.

fit though he tries it in one place after another. At a time when he is busy experimenting, perhaps at the very moment when a solution is in sight and he is about to experience Groos's 'joy in being a cause', it may happen that he is forcibly removed, to be washed and dressed, to be given a meal or to be put to bed.

In short, as will be explained later in this chapter, children are beginning to enjoy exploratory play and this brings many frustrations, for as yet children have not developed the power to accept the restrictions set by the world in which they live and by their own limited development. Under pressure of these difficulties, children experience extreme emotional frustration which is almost certain to lead to a temper tantrum.

Temper tantrums are very distressing for both children and parents. Two points may help us to understand them more clearly. In the first place, children probably suffer considerable anxiety during a temper tantrum because of the inner feelings of rage which they experience. Perhaps we can compare our own feelings when we suddenly realize that someone has exploited and used us, or has deliberately made us look foolish before others. We experience a sudden surge of anger and feel as if we are going to split in two because of the violence of this anger. This can be a disturbing experience for an adult; we may surmise that a child in a temper tantrum is similarly disturbed.

Secondly, even within the apparent negative of a temper tantrum, there is a positive element. To live in our society we need to be assertive in order to get on, and children need to be assertive too in order to maintain their own amongst the aggressive jostling of their companions. A temper tantrum is an attempt on the part of children to do just this. True, the attempt is a failure, but it would be unfortunate for a father to take the point of view that his particular child is out to master him, saying, 'Either he or I will be master in this house'; or to take the view that this outburst must be stopped because the child may get into the 'habit' of it. Such a superficial viewpoint may lead parents to crush the spirit of the child and his growing ability to assert himself. A child thus crushed may regress, or go back to babyhood: 'I'll be a baby again, because Mummy and Daddy only like babies', which can lead to a refusal to grow up and a continuance of baby ways. It could also lead to excessive conformity: the child is just 'too good'. 'Mummy is good and I am bad. I must do as Mummy says.'

Situations which lead to a temper tantrum can sometimes be avoided. They occur often at meal times, bed times, bath times, 'pottying 'times and often because, implicitly, there is a conflict between what the mother deems to be important and what the child does. For a mother, that her child eats, excretes, sleeps and is reasonably clean is important; it is also important for her that she keeps to some kind of routine even though it may not be an exact one. Not so a newly autonomous child: it is more important for him that he gets the peg in the right hole, the cork into the right bottle, the sand into the bucket. At times like these a mother may judiciously decide to forego for a few minutes one or other of these 'essentials' until the task is done—the peg or the cork fitted, the bucket filled.

But there are times when a mother cannot, or feels she should not, wait. There are times, too, when children have to be denied something—that treasured silver teapot, the new and expensive flower vase—and we must deny with quiet firmness. If temper tantrums occur (and they will), then we need to try to be as calm as possible about them. A calm attitude can reduce a child's feelings of anxiety and generate the kind of atmosphere which will enable him to get over it. It is unwise to meet the aggression of a temper tantrum with aggression.

Sometimes their determination to shape the complex universe in which they live is expressed in a firm obsessionalism. 'Dat dere', 'Dat dere', 'Dat dere' and so on. He is referring to his toys which he has placed 'dere' and which must not be taken from 'dere'; and fierce is the tantrum if a parent does not comply. This obsessional placing of objects often takes place just as he is about to go to bed, at a time when his mother is nearly bursting with impatience to get him out of her hair. Then, to the mother, these rituals may seem to be nothing but a ruse on the child's part to put off going to bed. But the rituals have their purpose; they assure him that all is in order in the world which is important to him; and he can sleep in peace.

Of course, this occasional obsessionalism is confined to his own things. Let him loose in his parents' bedroom or his father's study and the contents of the drawers and desk are scattered with resolute abandon, and the resulting chaos appals even the most complacent of mothers.

202 PHYSICAL, EMOTIONAL, INTELLECTUAL GROWTH

But let us not paint too negative a picture of two-year-olds. They show, too, many charming tendencies. They laugh with others; they are tender with a baby and will touch and stroke it; they show a sturdy independence and resist too much restriction of their movements. If you do not keep an eye on them and do not keep garden gates closed they are off before you know it. They will play alone, sometimes for considerable periods, filling and emptying a bucket or trolley with sand, or with wooden blocks. They will respond socially to a mother's happy and humorous moods when, for example, she chants nursery rhymes, with a particular and nodding emphasis on rhythm, or when she waltzes round the room. A few only of these tendencies have been mentioned here, since the active exploring and learning of the two-year-olds, and of other pre-school children, will be described later in this chapter and a fairly detailed consideration of their play given.

After the temper tantrums of the twos, there follows a period of relative emotional calm. Perhaps the greater emotional control which children show at three is part of a general growth in control. Thus, for example, bodily movements as in walking and running are smooth and less jerky than at two and there is a significant increase in the motor skills, in the finer skills (as in the use of crayon or pencil) and in the more gross bodily skills required for, say, pedalling a tricycle. Perhaps it may also be inferred that, relative to the two-year-old, they are accepting the world of reality a little more, and the limitations set by its size and weight and their lack of either. Certainly by three children have turned the corner away from babyhood and are 'on the straight' with the kindergarten and the Infant School ahead of them. Before the year is out they begin to talk about going to school and to look forward to it.

Children of this age chatter a lot: they chatter to themselves; they will stop in the middle of an activity and chatter away to mother or to any available adult. It is nice to have grandma around because she seems to have more time to listen. But it doesn't matter anyway because three-year-olds talk away happily to themselves. It is as if they are fascinated by the magic of speech and language, especially now that they have gained considerable facility in the use of words. The three-year-old is able to understand others better and to make himself more easily understood. This is possibly why a mother may say, 'He's so much more reasonable now than when he was two.'

But the words of caution here (as contrasted with those given in the above account of the two-year-old) are these: we should not paint too positive a picture of three-year-olds. Relative to the tempestuous two-year-old, the three-year-old seems quiet and controlled. But, at three, the growth of autonomy continues, with its positive and negative components, as does the fierce realization of *me* and *mine*. Group play is still difficult and soon disintegrates into grabbing or pulling toys from each other, pushing, kicking, scratching. He can 'entertain' his parents to 'tea' with more grace and studied decorum than he can his play-mates. Again, particularly at nightfall, or when he is tired during the day, he will run into a temper tantrum and appear once again like a two-year-old in ferment. And, of course, there are the 'issues', for example, eating.

Particularly after weaning and in the years which follow, some mothers become very anxious about the amount a child is eating and force him to eat more than he really requires. Often mothers tend to forget that a small child has his own 'physiologi-cal wisdom', which is possibly a more reliable indicator of his needs that the schedules prepared in books. Mothers, too, often forget that a small child needs only perhaps one-fifth as much food as the average adult, even allowing for the extra required by the child for growth. Many are the battles fought and the Water-loos met in the dining-rooms of homes in our society over this problem of feeding. This is unfortunate because these battles are often unnecessary and arise from a mother's understandable but unwarranted anxieties.

In the case of the three-year-old even if, in general, he eats enough to satisfy his mother and to ease her anxieties, he may still dawdle and play with food as if it were the mud he had been scooping around during his morning's play. This is miserably deflating to the self-esteem of a mother who has spent much time and loving care in the preparation of what is, by all acceptable standards, a most tasty dish. At such moments he appears incon-siderate and ungrateful; but this is not to be taken personally. Just as a child is very concerned with *my* and *mine* before he becomes concerned with *thy* and *thine*, so he is nonchalant and ungrateful before he is considerate and grateful. It is the way human beings grow.

Like the twos, the threes have their little fits of obsessionalism when no toy, no doll can be moved from its definitely allotted place. But now their desire to shape the universe may take the form of ordering adults about. 'You sit dere; you dere' and so on; and if a parent or older brother or sister moves from 'dere', the child will determinedly poke, push and manipulate the erring one back to his proper place. Brothers and sisters can usually take all this ordering about in their stride and laugh about it; but, a father, in a moment of righteousness and impatient exasperation, and feeling, perhaps, that he cannot allow the child to get 'into the habit' of ordering people about, may say, 'Indeed I'm not going to let him tell me what to do.' But such 'ordering' should not be confused with an indiscriminate drive for power or as a habit which must be stopped at its inception. After all, a three-year-old is very much dependent on the will of others, brothers and sisters as well as parents, and most of the time he has to accept their ways of doing things and await their pleasure when he wants something done. The occasions when these huge beings follow his directions and await his pleasure must provide him with the utmost satisfaction, even though these occasions are infrequent and of short duration.

Probably the main hazard for parents with two- or three-year-olds is the impasse, the 'you-will-I-won't' stalemate (sometimes called 'the battle of wills'), that can so easily and so suddenly spring up between child and parent and that can become the prelude to a temper tantrum. Probably, too, the main problem is to avoid this hazard as far as possible (it is hardly possible with these youngsters to avoid it altogether). An impasse can arise from many situations as when the child has a bout of not eating, of dawdling during dressing, bath- or bed-times, of plain refusal to do what he's told.

Were it not, perhaps, for the twos and threes (and, in fairness to the threes, more particularly the twos) not even man's ingenuity would have devised the many wiles by means of which the path to an impasse might be diverted. For example, a child may be more than reluctant to go from the garden into the house as a first step towards the bathroom and a bath. Numerous are the techniques that have been devised, one or more of which can be tried in such an everyday situation as this one. Here are but a few of them:

the 'surprise': the 'surprise' is in the house, of course;
'help me': e.g. to carry something into the house;
'let's play': e.g. hide-and-seek in the sitting-room;
change in tone of voice: the suggestion, 'Let's go into the house' is whispered, as if it were a special secret. It may be sung or even danced to;
change in speed of movement: e.g. skipping once round the garden and then into the house;
competition: e.g. 'Let's race Bobby to the sitting-room door';
personal challenge: e.g. 'Let's see if you can touch your cot before I count ten'.

Even so, such a list is but a counsel of perfection, since frequently not one of them will work. The child may be far too thrilled by the skipping and want to continue it, but round the garden only; he stalls at the steps leading into the house. On the other hand, he may not be thrilled at all by the reward that is promised afterwards, and a five-minute plan seems to mean as little to him as would a five-year one. Also, there is a limit to a mother's patience, to her ingenuity, and to the time she can give to these time-consuming diversions; and the need for a diversion frequently comes at a time when both mother and child are tired. Consequently, a screaming two- or three-year-old can often be seen being carried, like a rucksack, under his mother's right or left arm, his head down, his feet kicking.

It is particularly noticeable that, by four and a half, children have acquired considerable physical and verbal dexterity and even some social acumen. They are so much quicker in their movements and their speech that, by comparison, three-year-olds appear slow and even ponderous. With the greater physical dexterity comes more running, jumping, skipping and, perhaps, occasional balancing on one foot. They dash around the place. Similarly with words: they talk more, and more quickly. At four children begin to learn more about the world just outside the garden gates, to make their way in it and to adapt to companions.

When they become skilled at a task, children will generally make a game of it. Their physical dexterity means more complex

games, expressed individually in more intricate block constructions; and there is great pride in what has been done. He holds
his pencil or painting brush with greater ease and he achieves
greater precision. When he has drawn the outline of an object, he
will look hard at it, and then put in a few details that attract him.
Socially, children still play best in pairs, but they can attain some
success at dramatic group play.

Change appeals to their growing imagination and to their
ability to use their imagination to vary their play. The shop easily
changes into a post office, the post office into a railway station, the
railway station into a hospital and so on. The skilled kindergarten
teacher can smooth the difficulties of change, and the excitement
of the change can neutralize the hostility children so often generate
one towards the other.

Now begins scapegoating, especially when group play is not
supervised by adults. One child is ostracized, and the rest feel
gloriously at one, safe, smug and a little righteous in their condem-
nation of the outcast. Scapegoating is a pronounced feature of
children's social life at all ages, so that references will again be
made to it in the pages which follow.

Greater facility in speech is followed by fun and games with
words—repeating words, rhyming words, and even inventing
new ones such as 'squishy', 'poozy', 'hibitty'. In group play with
words, pepper may perhaps become 'peppitty pep', bib 'bibbitty
bib', boot 'bootomy boot'. Language requires flexibility of the
muscles and skilled control of the movements, of the mouth and
tongue. Such flexibility and such control is a function of both
maturation and practice, as earlier described in this book. Playing
with words—even nonsense words—serves to provide practice in
this form of play. The authority (17) mentioned earlier in this
chapter gives the number of words acquired by the end of the
fourth year as about one thousand five hundred.

However, the four-year-old is essentially an individualist. He
will boast about his ability, and his achievements—'*Mine's* best',
'*I* am clever', '*I* can do that'. He will boast, too, about his possessions, *his* father and what *his* father said. Anything he has is bigger
and better than that of the other fellow and anything *his* father
says is good, is right, is true and shall not be contradicted. But
though so loyal to his parents when with his companions, in the
presence of his parents he may be assertive, and this assertive-

ness may spill over into a temper tantrum or may be expressed in a physical or verbal attack as when he hits his mother's skirts with a few swinging rights or calls his father a 'beast' (or worse, according to the richness of his vocabulary).

But he can be a diplomat, too, especially when he wants something badly and knows that rough stuff will not get him anywhere. It is amusing to listen to a four-year-old boy trying to persuade a reluctant playmate to let him borrow a truck which he dearly wants to play with. 'Now if you give me your truck for a little while, you can have my train for a little while. That would be nice, wouldn't it? And you can have the truck back afterwards and I'll have the train.'

Often, at this stage he acquires an imaginary playmate with whom he plays for hours. He greets his 'friend' in the morning, and talks to 'him' about all manner of things. They get on splendidly together, though sometimes they will argue with one another. He will chat to his mother about his 'friend' (to whom he refers by name) and the wise mother will co-operate in the imaginary venture because the child is getting much joy from it. Furthermore, it probably serves a very useful function. Through it, the child experiments with the skills and techniques of social intercourse in a setting created by himself and which is, therefore, one that he can manipulate. As such, it is preparatory activity for the real world of social give-and-take which he is now beginning to enter.

The child may tell tall stories: the lion he saw in the garden, the uncle from the other side of the world who spoke to him in the street, the tree which he lifted up by the roots. These stories are an offshoot of the child's growing capacity for imaginative thought, as are also the creativity and originality that we see and hear in the games children play and the intriguing things they say. They are not lies in the adult sense of the word but exaggerated fantasies, an expression of the dramatic, of the extraordinary. An adult will often exaggerate in the same way (though not perhaps to the same extent) about some extraordinary event he has experienced or some deed he has executed. In the case of both, the child and the adult, part of the motive is to gain attention and feel important. By four, children's desire for significance expresses itself in assertive behaviour in their play and even in their relationships with favoured adults. These first flights from anonymity sometimes make children boastful and cheeky, sometimes bossy and aggressive.

Researches indicate that, as with the baby in his first year, so during these ensuing years, children need the personal attention, the encouragement and the warmth best provided by a mother's love. Bowlby (1) has described the distress which many young children suffer from temporary separation from their mothers, as when, for example, the children have to go to hospital.

Apart from the studies by Rheingold, Dennis and Bowlby mentioned in the last chapter, other studies, especially those of Goldfarb (3, 4, 5), are consistent in showing that children who have been in institutions permanently or for a very long time, and who have not had this very personal care and attention, tend to be retarded intellectually and socially when compared with children brought up from birth in foster homes. They also show greater emotional instability and an inordinate desire for affection and approval. However, as Yarrow (21) has pointed out in a comprehensive survey of the literature on maternal deprivation, and as the Iran study mentioned in the last chapter shows, the effects depend upon the type of institution it is, upon the number of staff per child, the amount of equipment, whether or not the institution has a kindergarten school with a qualified kindergarten teacher and so on. It depends, too, on the organization of the institution. If organization is based on the cottage system so that children are living in separate houses in a 'family' of others, with a 'mother' and a 'father', the effects are very much minimized.

Yet it is as well for the kindergarten and classroom teacher to know about the possible effects of institutionalization, so that she can make allowance, or, better still, specially provide for the institutionalized child she may have in her class. Undoubtedly, researches do suggest that:

1   Hospitals should be organized to provide for frequent visits by parents, and, for example, for the presence of the mother before and when the anaesthetic is given and when the child wakes up from it. In this way, the effects of the separation inevitable when a child goes to hospital are lessened (12).
2   Generally speaking, if a married couple decide to adopt a baby, it is to the benefit of all three that the baby be taken to his foster home as soon after birth as possible.

3   Children's institutions should be liberally staffed and provided with plenty of equipment.

We understand that children must be adequately fed and clothed and would be critical of a children's institution that did not do this. Perhaps we are not yet so sensitive to the importance of providing for the psychological needs of children as they have been described in this and the previous chapter, and also in Chapter 8.

Despite this need for mother, children are beginning to be a little independent even during these early years. This is seen in the fact that children now play a lot. At the end of the last chapter it was stated that a good mother quite naturally and unself-consciously encourages her baby to practise many kinds of skills as its body matures sufficiently to perform them. These skills were classified as sensory, exploratory, manipulative (mastery), emotional and social. Children's play, a consideration of which is soon to follow, will also be classified in the same way. This is appropriate, since play is a means by which children continue to practise these skills on their own, or with their companions, and independently of their mothers.

So far our discussion of pre-school children has emphasized emotional development and the difficulties which the individual child experiences (as well as those experienced by his parents) in coping with his emotional excesses as he grows up within the family environment. Important aspects of pre-school children's growth have yet to be considered: how and what they learn, and their contacts with other children. These are best understood by observation of their play, because this period is essentially a formative stage in play during which children discover the techniques they will use throughout their childhood. Older children have perfected these techniques and are able to progress beyond the simple beginnings seen during the early years; their play is more sophisticated. This later stage may thus be seen as one during which the techniques acquired earlier are perfected and consolidated and used for the purpose of enjoying more skilled and complex play. Since play is a feature of the whole of childhood, the observations which follow will sometimes be upon children's play in general. Not only will the play of pre-school children be considered, but reference will also be made back to babyhood and forward to play during the Infant and Primary years.

Play as sensory experience

Such play occurs particularly during the first two years, since acquisition of sensory experience through seeing, hearing, feeling, tasting, moving, is a dominant feature of infant activity. The baby delights in looking at brightly-coloured and moving objects. He will follow with his eyes the movements of his mother as she prepares his bath. He will gaze for a long time at the movements of the leaves in the tree under which his pram has been placed. He listens to the tinkling of the tinsel hanging from the ceiling, to the soothing sounds of a lullaby. In more active moments he shakes his rattle and the vigour with which he does this suggests that, for him, it is an assertive reminder that he is able to manipulate this world of sound. A baby will grasp, feel and then taste an object such as the bath sponge; a one-year-old will gently stroke adults and other children as well as objects that are new to him and this exploration by touch is, of course, a mode of discovery. As adults we speak of wanting 'to get the feel of things', aspecially when we enter a strange environment. We may infer that for a toddler also the world is new and strange, and he is out to get the feel of it in a very literal sense. A mother is puzzled and sometimes annoyed because a baby or a toddler *will* put everything into his mouth, but this, too, is an essential part of sensory knowledge. The child's point of view is, 'How can you know what an object is like until you have tasted it?'

From their earliest years, children seem to delight in the kinaesthetic sensory experiences that accompany bodily movements. The baby moves his arms, kicks his legs, rolls himself over and wriggles his whole body. The toddler swings arms and a leg, turns round and round until he is giddy, bounces up and down on a springboard and delights in being thrown up into the air; and the thrill of the swoop of the swing is a new experience and one which will delight him for many years to come.

Play as exploratory experience

Activity more clearly suggesting exploration begins as the baby becomes more mobile. It is the 'into-everything', the 'can't-leave-anything-alone' phenomenon. In the house, a toddler searches and explores; objects that have been put away are found; taboo objects that have been inadvertently left around are seized upon. One of these may especially take the toddler's fancy; it is gazed at, felt, smelt and tasted and then thrown on the floor, picked up and thrown on the floor again just to see what happens. Here is the beginning of experimentation.

A two-year-old expands his horizons and the scope of his activities into the garden and it is fascinating to watch him. He wanders around, skips a few steps, and swings a leg. By turns he picks up a spade and digs, finds a rake and rakes, takes a hammer and hammers—just a little of each action. He finds a stick and pokes it into the soft earth or into a hole in the fence; he looks at a tree intently for some minutes, smooths the bark and plucks a leaf which he puts carefully into the pocket of his shirt; then he pats the pocket to make sure the leaf is safely inside. And so it goes on. The activities may seem pointless to adults because each activity is distinct from any other and the child seems to be accomplishing nothing because no one activity is sustained for any length of time. Yet, he is exploring his universe, obtaining knowledge of its nature and also acquiring practice in numerous small skills.

Play as experience of mastery

Even before they are two children will 'dust' and 'sweep', turn the radio knob and empty the waste-paper basket. But play activities for the purpose of mastery, such as riding a tricycle, are more clearly characteristic of older children, for the ability to master objects presupposes both maturation of bodily processes and learning through experience. At two a child just handles blocks; at three he balances them and uses them to load and unload his truck; at four he makes simple structures, such as a house which he equips with furniture and people for purposes of dramatic play. To take another example: at two a child just pushes his tricycle; at three he rides it in the garden; at four he is so skilled that he is able to ride along the pavement and adjust his speed in accordance with that of his mother's walk.

The manipulative activities of pre-school children are innumerable and are seen, for example, in their use of climbing apparatus (swings, ladders, trapezes), in their constructive activities (making roads and tunnels, sand and mud pies), in their creative efforts through painting and crayoning. The varied nature of the activities of the pre-school child and the fact that these children move quickly from one activity to another emphasize the need to provide plenty of material at this stage.

Van Alsyne (20), in an investigation of children between two and five, found that they spent 98 per cent of their time in play with objects or material. While a group of older girls will be content with one long skipping rope and a group of boys with one ball and four stones for goal-posts, children of four must have a rope or a ball apiece.

The desire on the part of children for achievement has already been referred to when children's need to construct was discussed. We may add here that achievement generates a feeling of self-confidence in a child regarding the complex universe in which he lives. Even apart from the pure joy of achievement, a child who has learned to ride his tricycle becomes a different person because of this. He is now able to manipulate another small part of the world in which he lives and he reminds us of Little Jack Horner, who, you will remember:

> Put in his thumb
> And pulled out a plum
> And said, 'What a good boy am I!'

And, of course, he was 'a good boy', for the rhyme epitomizes the exhilaration, the enhancement of self-esteem which children derive from positive achievement.

In connection with the three modes of play so far described, it is interesting to reflect on the fascination which water and soft materials, such as mud, wet clay and sand, have for children. They seem unable to resist the puddle on the pavement and will walk into it, shuffle their feet and then kick the water in all directions. Mud has an equal appeal. At two they will smear it over their faces and at four make it into balls or pies. After heavy rain, older children have great fun making mud dams in the gutter and diverting the water in every possible direction.

The appeal of these materials may have these three sources. First, both water and mud provide rich sensory experiences for a child when, for example, he plunges an arm into water or a hand into soft mud or sand. (Even adults enjoy such experiences. When sitting on the sand at the seaside, they will often scoop their hands into the sand continuously, letting each handful slide slowly through their fingers). By contrast, wooden blocks provide little sensory experience; rather they are objects for manipulation. Secondly, these soft materials provide opportunities for exploration, as when a three-year-old dabbles in water and squeezes and shapes mud or clay. If you ask him what he is making, he may say, 'I don't know, I haven't finished it yet'—that is, he is exploring the possibilities of his material and for the time being has no definite aim beyond this. Thirdly, these materials are relatively easy to manipulate and therefore are excellent media through which children can experience a sense of mastery. Water does what you want it to do—it can be poured from one container to another and it 'fits' both, it can be kicked and at a whack it moves with a glorious splash. Mud and clay are so easy to shape into a cat, a dog, a man or whatever you will, primitive though these shapes may appear to adults. For older children the damming of water provides opportunity to explore the possibilities of their materials in a more controlled, experimental way and so to manipulate them on a grander scale.

Play as emotional experience

Insofar as its accompaniments are pleasure and pain, laughter and tears, exhilaration and disappointment, play inevitably means emotional involvement for children. We are more concerned here, however, with the expression in play of children's fears and of their feelings of guilt and insecurity.

Even small children enjoy having their fears stimulated when playing chasing, bogey-man and animal games. When he is cornered in the chase, the small child is fascinated by the roar of the lion (who is his father), or the guttural sounds of the 'bogey-man' (who is also his father), and appears to experience a strange mixture of delight and fear. There is a limit to this, of course, and the wise parent intuitively realizes when this limit has been reached and the mixture of delight and fear turns to fear only.

It is interesting to speculate why children like to have their fears stimulated in this way. Because it is as necessary for human beings to learn to know fear as it is for them to know security (absence of fear), the explanation may be that experiencing mild fear is one aspect of children's growth, and that by having these play experiences of fear they are able to cope more adequately with the few actual and the many imaginary fears which beset them, even when they are in a very secure environment.

The feelings of aggression and of guilt that children experience are often expressed in their play. Thus, for example, a four-year-old smacks her doll and scolds her with the decisive reprimand, 'You wicked, wicked girl.' The child may have been scolded and smacked by her mother for some misdeed, and the anger that she felt but dared not express is now diverted from her mother to the doll. The world 'displacement' is used by psychologists to indicate this kind of behaviour—that is, when a person diverts the expression of an emotion from the person or object who is the source of it to another person or object, as the small girl does in the example given here.

It may be, however, that the child has generated guilt within herself for a misdeed which has not been discovered. She has stolen and eaten one of those delicious chocolates from the box hidden in the cabinet and, having experienced the quick delight of tasting forbidden fruit, is now feeling wretchedly guilty. When she calls her doll wicked and smacks it, the vehemence of her reprimands and the ferocity of her smacks may surprise us. Actually, they express her determination to maintain the self-deception that it is the doll and not she who is wicked. This is the phenomenon of projection, that is, the process of ascribing to another the feelings and impulses one finds it hard to accept in oneself.

The same process operates when the four-year-old acquires the imaginary friend of whom we spoke earlier; the imaginary friend may also be seen as a projection by the child of part of himself, and as an early manifestation of what will later become powers of self-awareness and self-criticism. His friend is sometimes 'bad'; 'he' wants to do and say 'naughty' things and has to be reprehended and restrained. The child is not aware that he is playing out his own temptations and that by reprehending and restraining his 'friend', he is reprehending and restraining himself. He will naïvely tell his mother how 'naughty' his friend can sometimes be. But whereas now he argues with his 'friend', in later life he will argue with himself (without the need of this projective aid) about his own past and contemplated deeds, about the pros and cons of a situation, and about the nature of the universe and the people in it.

It is characteristic of children to displace their aggressions and to project on to others their feelings of guilt and the forbidden impulses they feel. We shall be referring to these processes again in Chapter 13 when we consider some specific social and individual problems of young children.

Play as identification

Even apart from fears and guilt, however, children live out both difficult and joyous experiences in their play by ascribing emotional experiences to, and then identifying themselves with, their favourite toys. In comforting her doll when she 'cries', in rejoicing with her when she 'laughs', the little girl is herself comforted and herself happy; in feeding and attending to the toilet of her doll the little girl lives through, at one distance removed, the difficulties and pleasures she has herself experienced or is experiencing. It is said that the way to learn a subject is to teach it. It may well be that in 'teaching' these and other skills to her doll, the small child is also learning them more adequately herself.

Identification goes further than this and is expressed in the tendency on the part of a person unconsciously to mould himself in the likeness of another person or persons. Small children identify themselves with people whom they know and especially with those whom they love and with whom they have sympathetic contact. Insofar as adults make their impression on a child they become part of him and he wants to do as they do. Identification for a child includes not only sympathy and admiration but also the desire to imitate the person with whom he identifies himself. For children it is an active living out of their contacts with other people and is therefore expressed particularly in their dramatic play.

It is expressed in the early years in simply mimes—smoking, telephoning, powdering the face, blowing the nose (using Daddy's huge handkerchief), dusting and putting things on the shelf, or, perhaps, wearing an isolated garment, like a scarf or a tie belonging to mother or father. A three-year-old will spend hours carrying father's umbrella or mother's handbag, and a small object, such as an old watch or brooch, will be clutched and cherished.

We may sometimes be mystified by the tenacity of his sense of ownership and his complete distress when the umbrella has to be taken away from him because it is raining and father needs it. It is only when we see its symbolic significance that we are able to appreciate its value to him and understand the distress and temper tantrum which follow his loss.

By four, children are able more definitely to enter into the playing of the social roles of people of whose activities they are aware—the postman, grocer, policeman, carpenter—and into the playing of the domestic roles of the housewife. Such play is more than mere imitation, for children seem to immerse themselves in the activities of those with whom they identify.

One of the best ways of doing this is dressing up. To be a bus conductor, milkman or engine driver, to immerse oneself in Mummy's or Daddy's activities, means dressing accordingly. To adults clothes are very important; they are more than a means of keeping us warm and of covering our nakedness. When we dress the part, we live the part—thus the flowing gown makes the charming hostess; jeans and sweater make a girl feel ready for hiking and camping because, dressed for the part, she feels more adequate to the masculine exertion needed for such activities. We put on slacks for slacking. Whether we go to church, to a wedding, to sports, or to a funeral, we play the part more adequately when we are dressed for it. To say, 'Do I look all right?' implies more than just, 'Am I nicely dressed?'; it means, 'Am I suitably dressed for the occasion?' A positive reply reassures us, for we know that we can play the role we are called upon to play more appropriately because we are suitably dressed. It is the same for the child. He wishes not only to be like Daddy, but to immerse himself in Daddy's activities, and what better way than by dressing up? By about four a dressing-up box is essential equipment for boys and girls, and Daddy's hat, coat and umbrella are very important. As children develop beyond the pre-school and Infant School stages they move from domestic and familiar local roles to those of cowboys and Indians, or cops in adventurous pursuit of robbers. To this we shall refer again later.

Play as social experience

Play has so far been described in terms of individual experiences—individual sensory, exploratory and emotional experiences—and also in terms of achievement and of identification with others. But play is also a social experience. From her researches with children Parten (12) has classified children's play into five main stages: solitary, spectator, parallel, associative and co-operative play. Her researches indicate clearly that there is a progression in the play of pre-school children from solitary through spectator, parallel and associative play to the early beginnings of co-operative play.

Solitary play occurs particularly during the first two years. The baby, content with his own company, gurgles, laughs, kicks and rolls in his pram. The eighteen-month-old toddler plays alone with a variety of objects—a doll, a teddy, blocks, or a few pots and pans. He may put blocks slowly into a pan, or try to fit one into the doll's eyes. It is a time when the success of play depends not so much on the presence of other children as on, to quote Gesell, 'the presence of interesting playthings and the absence of hazardous equipment' (2).[1]

In spectator play a child just watches other children without taking part himself. This may occur at any age during the pre-school period, but its ideal manifestation is seen during babyhood when the baby sits in his pram in the garden watching a group of children as they run, chase, scuffle, laugh and shout. The baby is 'all eyes' and his head moves from side to side, seeming to observe every detail of what is going on. He will crane his neck to see what is happening behind the hood or underneath the pram. Sometimes, in obvious delight, he will raise his arms, bounce hard up and down in his pram and give a loud shout of glee. Occasionally one of the children will come up to the pram, chuckle and then tickle the baby's chin. This adds to the baby's pleasure, but is not essential to it, for his delight is in watching, listening and being with other children.

Even an older child will sometimes just stand absorbed in watching other children, obviously enjoying the process. He will smile and frown in clear sympathetic contact with the children he is observing. But spectator play, as Parten's observations show, is not very frequent after the first three years, and children who are much older (say seven or eight) are not content merely to watch; they want to enter the group. The older child of whom we have just spoken is happy to accept an invitation to join in

[1] page 150

and, though he is shy and his movements a little stilted when he first enters this group of strangers, he soon loosens up and becomes one with the group in their pleasure and excitement.

In parallel play each child pursues his own activity, even though children are together in the same room. This is typical of a group of two-year-olds. On observing such a group you will see, for example, that one is pulling a little trolley; another is attempting simple manoeuvres with a toy car; a third is pounding clay and pulling off little pieces and squeezing them between his fingers; and a fourth child is feeding and attending to the toilet of a doll, or making sand pies, patting them down and smoothing them carefully. Each child is content to pursue his own individual activity.

By three one sees more associative play, in which activities are still individual but where there is interaction, the recognition of one child by another and simple exchanges between them. Thus, two children may be playing with dolls; each child has her own equipment (doll, bed, pram and so on), but one child may exchange information with the other: 'Bertha is tired . . . Bertha tells me . . .'; or ask a question of the other: 'Bertha is hungry. Is Maria hungry, too?'

By four, attempts at co-operative play become more evident. Such play entails an acceptance of mutual roles, so that activities are reciprocal and success in play depends upon each child carrying out the obligations implied in the role he has accepted. If children play postman, milkman, grocer or mothers and fathers, then there must be those who deliver and those who receive, those who sell and those who buy; there must be parents and there must be children. It is difficult for young children to accept their assigned roles for long, and especially difficult for those who have the 'dependent' rather than the 'key' roles. Therefore, it is understandable that these early attempts at co-operative play fail, and misery, squabbles and tension often ensue. The skilled nursery teacher anticipates this and removes the tension by quickly initiating parallel play. The social skills necessary for co-operative play are acquired only in later years.

To conclude this chapter, here are three important observations regarding children's play. First, there is little differentiation between the play of boys and girls during the pre-school years. It is true that by the age of four boys tend to play more often with

replicas of our technological culture, such as trains, cars, or
lorries, and girls with domestic objects, such as dolls, or prams.
But there is an interchange of these between boys and girls, and
boys are not ashamed to play houses or girls to play with an
engine.

The social pressures on boys to be boys and girls to be girls
come later and are reflected in their separate play activities.

Secondly, children's play activities supply evidence of their
physical development, for during the pre-school years these
activities progress gradually from gross bodily activity to the
beginnings of finer movements. At two a child pulls, lifts,
pushes, scribbles, daubs paint and runs round and round. By four
he tries out skills requiring finer co-ordination. Finer movements
of the wrist now alternate with broad sweeps of the arm as in
painting; the child will try out his skill with scissors and paper
and he is more skilled in the use of objects requiring wrist movements, such as crayon and pencil. He begins, too, to try out
isolated physical skills requiring balance and co-ordination, such
as hopping or balancing on a plank. If he has had the opportunity
to practise, even by four he can become adept on the swing or the
trapeze.

Thirdly, a word of warning: any classification of children's
play is a little artificial, as is the ascription of certain kinds of play
to certain ages. While it is true that certain kinds of play are
predominantly sensory, or predominantly exploratory and so on,
some children's play may combine many or all of these aspects—
as, for example, children's activities together on the sands during
a seaside holiday. Moreover, while pre-school children tend to
progress from solitary to co-operative play, all kinds of play are
in evidence during all ages. Thus, as shown by the work of
Suttie (Chapter 10), a baby will respond co-operatively in play
with his mother and father; on the other hand, a four-year-old
will play by himself or stand absorbed just watching other
children. While analysis has its value in helping us to understand,
we must bear in mind that, as with Gesell's division into ages
and stages, we have spoken here of modal trends in children's
play and that there are always exceptions to any generalizations
made about children's play as well as about their growing
personalities.

REFERENCES

1 Bowlby, J., Ainsworth, M., Boston, M., Rosenbluth, D. 'The effects of mother-child separation: a follow-up study.' *British Journal of Medical Psychology*, 1956, **29**, pp. 211–47.

2 Gesell, A., Ilg, F. *Child Development:* 1 'Infant and child in the culture of today.' Harper, New York, 1949.

3 Goldfarb, W. 'Infant rearing as a factor in foster home placement.' *American Journal of Orthopsychiatry*, 1944, **14**, pp. 162–7.

4 Goldfarb, W. 'Effects of psychological deprivation in infancy and subsequent stimulation.' *American Journal of Psychiatry*, 1945, **102**, pp. 18–33.

5 Goldfarb, W. 'Psychological deprivation in infancy and subsequent adjustment.' *American Journal of Orthopsychiatry*, 1945, **15**, pp. 247–55.

6 Hadfield, J. A. *Childhood and Adolescence.* Penguin Books, Harmondsworth, Middlesex, 1962.

7 Hurlock, E. B. *Child Development.* McGraw-Hill, London, 1956.

8 Huschka, M. 'The child's response to coercive bowel training.' *Psychosomatic Medicine*, 1942, **4**, pp. 301–8.

9 Jersild, A. T. *Child Psychology.* Prentice-Hall, Englewood Cliffs, New Jersey, 1960.

10 Landreth, C. *The Psychology of Early Childhood.* Knopf, New York, 1958.

11 Macfarlane, J. W., Allen, L., Honzik, M. P. 'A developmental study of the behaviour problems of normal children between twenty-one months and fourteen years.' *University of California, Publications in Child Development.* Vol. II. Berkeley, University of California Press, 1954.

12 Parten, M. B. 'Social participation among pre-school children.' *Journal of Abnormal and Social Psychology*, 1932, **27**, pp. 243–69.

13 Robertson, J. *Hospitals and Children: A Parent's Eye View.* Gollancz, London, 1962.

14 Sears, R. R., Maccoby, E. E., Levin, H. *Patterns of Child-rearing.* Row, Peterson, Evanston, Ill., 1957.

15 Sears, R. R., Whiting, J. W. M., Nowlis, V., Sears, P. S. 'Some child-rearing antecedents of aggression and dependency in young children.' *Genetic Psychology Monographs*, 1953, **47**, pp. 135–234.

16 Shirley, M. M. 'The first two years, a study of twenty-five babies.' Vol. II. Intellectual development. *Institute of Child Welfare Monographs* (Serial No. 8) University of Minnesota Press, Minneapolis, 1953.

17 Smith, M. E. 'An investigation of the development of the sentence and the extent of vocabulary in young children.' *University of Iowa Studies in Child Welfare*, 1926, **3**, No. 5.

18 Stone, L. J., Church, J. *Childhood and Adolescence.* Random House, New York. 1957.

19 Templin, M. C. 'Certain language skills in children.' *Institute of Child Welfare Monographs* (Serial No. 26) University of Minnesota Press, Minneapolis, 1957.
20 Van Alystyne, D. *Play Behaviour and Choice of Play Material of Pre-school Children*. University of Chicago Press, Chicago, 1937.
21 Yarrow, L. J. 'Maternal deprivation: towards an empirical and conceptual re-evaluation.' *Psychological Bulletin*, 1961, **58**, pp. 459–90.

CHAPTER TWELVE

Infant School Children
(five, six, seven)

These years may be seen as a time of transition, transition between a life confined almost exclusively within the family (as at four), to one in which children are immersed within the wider society (as at nine). For children, this wider society has two main components: the school, children's own groups.

The description of children's play given in the last chapter demonstrated children's progress: from solitary and parallel play within house and garden (as at three) to co-operative play with companions (as at nine); also, that the nature of their groups changes. Whereas at five children are happy to play in mixed groups and, if a boy to play with a girl, and if a girl to play with a boy, by nine children are willing and happy to play only in groups, or with a child of their own sex.

Group activities with companions imply learning: to see and accept oneself as a member of a group as well as an individual, to be co-operative and friendly, assertive and retaliative, to act in the expected manner according to whether one is a boy or a girl. There are, too, the many skills which children learn within their groups and independently of adults.

The school is orientated towards the total society, not only towards one of its institutions, as the family. Therefore, the school teaches children intellectual and motor skills which are necessary for living within society, and to value those things of which most of its members approve.

These new orientations mean that children are brought into contact with, and acquire knowledge of, the world outside the home; they become more independent of the family and move from the world of fairy tale and fantasy (as at four) to acceptance of the world of social and technological reality (as at eleven or twelve). They acquire experience of relatively more impersonal contacts, such as those with their teacher; because, however kindly they may be, teachers are inevitably more detached and less warm than are mothers; and however conscientious, they can never give quite the personal attention that mothers do.

School and companions now become important means by which children's basic needs, as described in Chapter 8, are satisfied. Further, a child's self-esteem, his feelings of personal worth, do not depend only on what the members of his family think of him, but also upon his ability to perform the skills and to do those things which teachers and playmates expect, and upon their opinion of him.

But while school and companions offer new opportunities for growth, they create new problems. The challenge of the new demands they make may cause the individual child moments of doubt and fear. Therefore, to speak of these Infant School years as a period of transition does not mean that it is static and problem free. Rather, the transition is a dynamic and progressive one during which children are continuing to change and to grow; and where there is growth there is often conflict. In the descriptions which follow, both the progressive and the problemmatic nature of the period will be considered.

The three characteristics of Infant School children now to be discussed are their desire for individual recognition, for individual achievement, and their growing independence. Because the next chapter is devoted to a consideration of some of the prevalent personal and social problems of young children, it will supplement what is said here and also what has been said in the previous chapter.

Infant School children, particularly at five or six, are still concerned to receive the kind of individual attention and the individual recognition they receive at home. They are, therefore, not yet able to pursue stable, co-operative activities with other children. Though they play together, their groups are loose and easily disband. Isaacs (7) puts the point very neatly when she says that the social group is only a background for individual activity and that these children tend to play *in the presence of* rather than *with* other children.[1] Therefore, as Isaacs again stresses, social life among younger Infant School children is an up-and-down process. Their lack of social skill and their desire for individual significance make it very difficult for them to co-operate for long in social pursuits in which some are relatively anonymous. Content perhaps to take a minor role for a while, a child will then revolt in a desire to have a more important part in the play—to be the leader rather than one of the led, to be the driver of the bus or train rather than the ticket collector or a mere passenger, to be the bride rather than the bridesmaid at the wedding. Those taking major roles quite naturally resist any change and the result is quarrelling and social chaos.

The desire for individual recognition is often naïvely expressed in the classroom. Children may be in small groups, each group pursuing the same or separate activities. Then one child slips away from her group to say something to the teacher, some personal detail about a new dress, a new toy or perhaps a new baby who may or may not exist. What the child has to say is probably not important; what matters most is personal contact with the teacher and the pleasure and reassurance that come from this. Infant teachers need to be on the alert for 'wanderers'—children who will be aimlessly ambling about the classroom doing nothing in particular. Perhaps they have lost interest in the task in hand, or they have found it difficult to make a start (as Infant children often do); they then decide on personal contact with the teacher, fail to get this and continue to amble about. The skilled teacher is able to spot this and delicately re-establish the child in some definite task.

Self-admiration is also naïvely and unashamedly expressed. The little girl may stare into the looking glass and ask, 'Am I pretty?' and expect a very positive answer. She may indulge in a little self-praise: 'Aren't I a good girl?' or 'I'm really very clever.' Of course, this should not be interpreted as conceit in the adult meaning of the term, nor need adults assume that the child is developing the 'bad habit' of unblushing self-praise. Rather, the little girl is discovering herself, building up a picture that is acceptable and pleasurable to reflect upon, a necessary and inevitable feature of growing up; for the ability to love others pre-supposes an ability to love oneself. However, in the early stages of

[1] page 83.

acquiring a worthy self-picture, there are times when children may exaggerate the pleasingness of their appearance and the grandeur of their achievements – an understandable exaggeration since, as yet, they are unsure of themselves.

The importance, in the growth of personality, of acts of achievement was discussed with reference to: (a) the implication of the questions 'Who is he?' and 'What does he do?' (Chapter 1); and (b) to know, to construct, to create (Chapter 8).

During the Infant School stage, there is a definite movement from 'who I am' to 'what I am', from an individual with a name and belonging to a family to an individual who is significant because he has achieved this, that or the other. At five, achievement is concerned with improving skills already learned in the past—skipping, jumping, running, swinging, riding a tricycle; school brings new skills into operation—organized group play, the beginnings of reading and writing. Often, while busy with such activities, children will appeal to adults to judge their efforts favourably. 'See how far I can jump!' 'Watch me do this!' 'Look what I've just made!' At seven, such appeals for approval frequently alternate with the more despondent, 'I'm no good', indicating the clear beginnings of self-evaluation; the standards of parents and teachers are now becoming the child's own and he tends to show dissatisfaction with himself for achievements falling below the standard that he is now beginning to demand of himself.

Taking the third general characteristic, namely that children of this stage are much more independent of parents, here the word 'independent' is too definite a term, and it would be more accurate to say that there are perceptible signs of behaviour indicating some independence of home and parents. This is natural enough, for the child has now begun school. The teacher becomes a significant person in his life, the adult bridge spanning the gap between the personal world of home and the less personal world of society at large. Earlier it has been said that we often neglect the fact that parents, too, are forming attitudes as their children are growing up. This thought is relevant here in the sense that, as a child begins to show signs of independence, parents will form their own attitudes towards this growing independence, attitudes which are very important to the future welfare of their children. Thus, the over-possessive mother may try to restrain her child's growing outside interests in order to keep him closer to her, or, in an anxious attempt to reassure herself that she is still wanted, demand from her child more affection than he is able to give. But whatever the outside interests, mothers are still very much wanted, especially at times of emotional stress.

Moore and Ucko (10) have made an experimental study of children's development between the ages of four and six, based on the way in which 118 children (fifty-four boys and sixty-four girls) solved life-situations posed to them individually within a doll-play setting. The results obtained, particularly those relating to the differences in the nature and rate of development between boys and girls, are so relevant to an understanding of Infant School children that they will be considered in some detail.

The eight situations devised by Moore and Ucko included these. Four plates, four chairs and five members of the doll family. A night scene is suggested, one doll has woken up in the dark, what does he (she) think or do? Two dolls fight, two dolls are naughty, the child is questioned about what happens in each case. A baby doll is fed and tended by the 'mother' doll to the exclusion of the doll with whom the child identifies himself.

The results suggest that children between four and six make considerable progress socially, as shown by a general increase in the number of constructive responses between these ages; that is, children of six significantly more often than children of four, 'find solutions to the problems or modify the situation to effect a solution'.

At both ages girls on the whole are more developed in this respect than boys. Girls at four showed an understanding, in terms of constructive responses, equal to that of boys at six. Boys are more aggressive than girls, especially in fighting and naughtiness; they are more anxious than girls of the same age—four-year-old boys for all eight situations, six-year-old boys for seven of the eight situations. Boys also showed greater anxiety in their incidental remarks to the experimenter—they asked, for example, how long they would be kept, whether mother was still waiting or would have left by the time they had finished.

The authors discuss these differences between boys and girls. They cite Tanner (15), who gives evidence indicating that 'the physical development of boys is slower and less predictable than girls', and that this slower and more uneven development makes boys physically more vulnerable than girls. They quote experiments illustrating the kinds of stresses to which boys are more vulnerable than girls: for example, starvation and atomic radiation (4), the hazards of a poor social environment (1), the stress of beginning school (12), childhood illnesses (6).

In discussing their results, Moore and Ucko suggest that growing up in our society, and for that matter in most societies, is more difficult for small boys than small girls. Girls can happily accept the domestic, can enjoy play with dolls; but the pressure is on boys to be assertive and aggressive. Girls can identify themselves happily with their mothers; but boys cannot, even when they are six. To be 'mother's girl'—yes; but to be 'mother's boy' —a very doubtful proposition.

Yet, on the whole, constructive responses far outnumber any other single category of response at both ages both for boys and for girls. The writers seem to introduce a note of caution which means, first, that small boys and small girls should not be contrasted, and girls judged *soft, tender, dependent, vulnerable* and boys *resistant, hardy, independent, resilient:* it is no contradiction to say that all eight adjectives apply to both boys and girls. Secondly, the flat 'taboo on tenderness' should not be imposed too early; rather, small boys should be given time to move from the domestic to the harder, more impersonal and more aggressive world outside.

There are, of course, obvious differences between children within the three age groups, five, six and seven. Children at this stage can in turn be pleasingly conforming, perplexingly petulant and strangely preoccupied: researches (e.g. 3b) suggest that at five they are more conforming, at six more petulant and at seven more preoccupied.[1]

The significant event at five is going to school, and this brings its pleasures and its pains. Children are proud of their new status and of all the personal possessions that go with it—school clothes, satchel, lunch, pencil, rubber. A child's world is now considerably extended for good or ill, and his general feelings of well-being are

[1] Because actual ages are tentative and not necessarily exactly applicable to a particular child, we could speak of three *phases* within this stage of development, i.e. first phase, second phase, third phase. In order to remind the reader of this, the phase to which a modal age is ascribed will sometimes be placed in brackets after a given age, e.g. six-year-olds (second phase). This will also be done in the chapters which follow.

dependent on the behaviour and moods of another adult (the teacher), and on happy or unhappy events in which he and his companions take part at school.

The results of a survey by Stendler and Young (14) of children's reactions on first going to school suggest the following: that nearly all children look forward to going to school; that, having started, the majority (92 per cent) occasionally feel reluctant to go, and a very small number (about 8 per cent) frequently feel this reluctance.

According to the mothers of this study, the general effect on the children of going to school was positive; the children obviously had enhanced feelings of independence, of being 'a big' girl or boy, which was expressed at home as an increased proneness to dress and look after themselves. These children also displayed the usual symptoms of social change—a tendency towards occasional instability at home—disobedience, impatience.

Stendler and Young's findings are based, not on a direct study of children, but on the results of interviews with two hundred mothers. These interviews took place on two occasions, during the first two months after the children had started school, and again eight months afterwards. No control group was used. It is therefore impossible to tell whether there were other causes at work as well as the fact of first going to school (for example, other changes in the environment, the day-by-day processes of maturation) and, if so, the extent to which these causes influenced the personality changes that the mothers felt had taken place. Though these studies are not definitive, they delineate broad trends; in line with these, here is a description of children's possible impressions of school.

When children first go to school, it may well seem a world of new and strange sensations; there are the bustlings of the teacher, the noise of the children in the adjoining classroom, the unfamiliar smell, which an adult will notice so distinctly when she visits the school and to which, if her own school life was an unhappy one, she may react with a vague feeling of foreboding.

These five-year-olds will often look about them with large observing eyes, seeming to assimilate and retain. Small things may catch a child's eye—a mark on the wall, the small boys' ruckled socks and chubbiness, the large cupboard with double doors, the swift entrance of an imposing adult, her earnest conversation with the teacher, very far away and outside the child's comprehension but still part of this new world. The child's gaze may sometimes centre on the teacher. He looks intently at her as if to absorb every detail of this important person and make her part of himself.

When the child's mother comes into the classroom to take him on a special trip she appears out of accord in this new environment. She belongs to a different kind of world—of the personal, the warm, and the close. The new world of school is personal, but not quite so personal; warm, but not quite so warm; and certainly not as close. The child is not yet fully at one with it. Sometimes—when she is marking the register, for instance—the teacher may use the child's full name. This, too, is strange at first; but the child realizes it is 'correct'; he must get used to it. He is not just Timothy; he is Timothy Placing.

Perhaps it would be true to say that during their first year at school children observe rather than attend; and insofar as they are on a threshold looking in, the teacher has to coax them to take part in a collective song or game such as 'London Bridge' or 'Follow my leader'. It can be heavy work, since their singing and movements may sometimes be stilted and wooden. They seem not to put their whole selves into the activity; for, as they chant and sing, they look round, again assimilating. They may be diverted by the apparently inconsequential—a piece of cotton on the jersey of the boy in front, which a child will assiduously try to pincer and remove.

This duality, 'in' but not 'of', gives rise to inappropriate behaviour—when, for example, an Infant School child singing with her class on the stage during 'open day' suddenly sees her parents in the audience, stops her singing, and moves forward to wave a continuous greeting.

The reader will see later that this short sketch of children first going to school contrasts with the sketch (to be given in the next chapter) of 'the society of children' in the middle and later Primary School years. But to learn to become a child in the full sense implied in this later sketch takes time. There are so many games, rhymes, riddles and ceremonials to be learned. One has all the time to watch other children and do exactly as they do. Yet the very contrast between the two sketches highlights the amount of progress children make: from the diffident, distant observations of their first weeks to the spontaneous, concentrated, in-it-up-to-the-neck sociability of Primary School children.

But, of course, this sketch and the observations which follow of five-year-olds at school are very general. They probably describe more particularly children who have been cared for exclusively by their mothers and who, on going to school, have for the first time to be without the very close contact to which they have been used. Amongst other interesting findings, Moore (11), has experimentally demonstrated that children who have attended nursery schools adjust more easily at Infant School and are rather more independent and self-assertive.

Many things may upset the confidence of children's first approach to school. Sometimes, for example, a five-year-old will become a victim of the teasing and bullying of an older child—say, a seven-year-old. This can be quite terrifying for him, yet he will not tell an adult about it and may suffer in silence for weeks until a parent or teacher accidentally gets to know about it. The observant teacher is aware of such a possibility and is always on the look-out for it.

Going to school also entails certain awkward changes in routine. For example, the school lavatories are cold, strange, impersonal places for a child who may therefore try to avoid using them and rush home instead. To small children, schoolrooms are big and the distance from home to school long, even though to grown-ups only very short. Adults become aware, in a dramatic way, of a child's greater estimate of size and distance when they return for the first time to the home town which they had left in early childhood, and find the schoolrooms so much smaller and the journey between home and school so much less than they had expected.

Occasionally, the stresses of the change may show themselves in a stomach upset or diarrhoea. But when the school programme is an interesting one and the atmosphere generally friendly, tensions caused by extraneous factors are eased. It is unfortunate that many of our Infant School classes are far too large, since this makes it very difficult for teachers to provide the varied and active programme that five-year-olds need. As a result, many teachers have to content themselves with a programme that is too formal for children of this age.

Parents may also generate tension by an over-concern, even at this early stage, for their children's academic development. If, for example, a five-year-old's cousin of the same age who attends a different school can read a little, and proudly exhibits her knowledge and ability when she pays a visit, a mother may experience a twinge of jealousy and even of alarm at this. Then, impelled by a conviction that her child too must 'get on' (a very prevalent attitude in our society), she becomes critical of modern readiness programmes and of the drama, mime, stories and play activities which characterize the modern Infant School and which are such necessary preliminaries to more formal work.

However, given a school in which there is much active learning, and parents who are not yet influenced by the bogey of competition, it may be suggested that five-year-olds are likely to be confident as they make this significant move into the outside world.

Fives play best in pairs; increase the number to three or more and there is a tendency for one child to become an outsider. We shall discuss this point again in the next chapter. Boys and girls play happily together and, while boys will build tunnels and bridges, and quickly convert an innocent set of bricks into a menacing tank, they like also to play with dolls and at houses with girls. A father may react with horror to see his son, even though he is only five, playing with dolls, and may thrust a football grimly into the child's arms. Perhaps a child will become a better footballer when he is older if he is allowed at this stage to experience the delight and, indeed, the security which these feminine activities provide. When children play at 'schools', they often tell us more about themselves than they do about what actually happens at school. The exaggerated severity which the 'teacher' shows and the punishments she imposes reflect Piaget's findings (13) on children's punitive concept of justice. Sometimes, the 'pupils' play at being 'bad' at school, and will joyfully play out the disobediences which they dare not express in the actual situation.

As in earlier years, fives still like some things to remain the same. They like to abide by the same routines when, for example, they go to bed or get up and prepare to go to school. They want still to hear the same story over and over again with no omissions and no alterations. Let a mother try, when in a hurry, to miss a sentence or a paragraph and she is quickly reminded that she has done so. She then has to go back and read it precisely as it *should* be read. An old gramophone provides endless pleasure and children will listen over and over again to the same record, the performance being continuous for the better part of a whole morning.

It would seem that these exact repetitions give children a feeling of security by providing unchanging routines in a world that is, for them, constantly changing. Change generates anxiety, but what is new can be assimilated with less anxiety against a stable background of people, objects and events that do not change. In this connection, it would seem also that when they bring things to school, such as a rag doll or a favourite toy, children provide themselves with a familiar and well-loved object. This reassures them in a strange world that has not, as yet, been quite assimilated. Similarly, when going to the loneliness and darkness of sleep, it is comforting to have a doll to hug. By soothing the doll's fears, by assuring the doll of his abiding love, the child is himself soothed and himself loved.

Fives (first phase) find it difficult consciously to accept self-blame and they tend to blame others for what they themselves have obviously done. Yet, paradoxical as it may seem, they suffer feelings of guilt about things for which they are obviously not responsible. When a friend falls down and is hurt, or a brother is punished, a child may feel a vague disquietude. It is *he* who is responsible for the hurt, or it is *he* who should be punished. In the past he has had an impulse to hurt the friend and, when the friend falls down and *is* hurt, he is unable to dissociate his own impulses as mere impulses from the accident and unable, therefore, to see clearly that he was not the cause of it. Again, in an undifferentiated way (which he certainly could not formulate) he registers that he has many times committed, in fantasy at least, the forbidden deed for which his brother is being punished, and that he is no less guilty. Inability to distinguish clearly between what actually happens on the one hand, and his own mental states and fantasies on the other, may also lead him to elaborate events and to tell tall tales.

The five-year-old tends to conform and is generally docile, amiable and contented. There are the occasional outbursts when he will call his mother names and contradict in a recalcitrant way. He can, too, be dogmatic and bossy with younger siblings and with children of his own age. During periods of anxiety, tensional outlets such as thumb-sucking, sniffing, nose-picking, or nail-biting are more frequent. Mother is still the child's main bulwark against anxiety and so, at such times, he still shows a clinging dependence on her, expressed as a refusal to let her out of his sight.

Nevertheless, speaking generally, Gesell depicts this phase as one during which 'the assimilative, organizing forces of growth are in ascendancy' (3b).[1] Of the five-year-old Gesell also says, 'If not a super-man, he is at least a super-infant. He is an advanced version of delightful three-year-oldness' (3a).[2]

There follows at about six, or even some months earlier, a period when the individualism spoken of as a general characteristic of Infant School children seems to be at its height, and children's behaviour becomes unstable and unpredictable. They argue and quarrel with companions; they seem almost insatiable in their demands to be recognized, to be commended and praised by teachers and parents; and they may grizzle when they fail to get recognition and praise.

Perhaps the most significant characteristic of the sixes (second phase) is their tendency to fluctuate—in mood, behaviour and even in the acquirement of skills. With this fluctuation goes a tendency towards emotional extremes—of excitement or disappointment, of joy or sorrow. Sixes behave well at one moment and are kicking in protest at the next; or they are amenable and co-operative, then suddenly stubborn. It is difficult to predict how they will behave on any particular occasion, as host or guest for example. This unpredictability also applies to their school work. What they do well today, in writing a few letters or reading a few words, they cannot do tomorrow. They may even for a time write backwards. In behaviour and in the performance of skills there is not always the consistent progress parents and teachers like to see, and at this stage we should not demand it. Sometimes a child will lead two lives, one of which contradicts the other, as when at school he is 'very, very good' and at home he is 'very, very bad' (or vice versa).

Children are now becoming even more aware of the importance of their possessions in any bid for individual significance; they are proud of their number, and the words 'my' and 'mine' figure significantly in their vocabulary. They will still unceremoniously grab the toy that a friend has borrowed or one that a friend refuses to lend. But the value of an object is decided by its

[1] page 68.   [2] page 248.

appeal for them rather than by its cost in money. An older child may take advantage of this by persuading a younger child to exchange one of his possessions for one of much lower commercial value owned by the older boy. The younger child is pleased about the 'swap'. But when his parents hear of it, they become indignant with the older boy, because they judge according to the economic criterion (as the boy himself has done), and enforce the return of the object.

Children may have little fits of kleptomania and will take things. Often on searching the pockets of her six-year-old, a mother will find a trinket belonging to the child next door, or some small toy which has been taken from school. This is not stealing in the adult sense of the word and probably the best way to deal with such a problem is for the mother to restore the trinkets herself or, in a neutral way, to ask the child to take them back. If a mother finds herself taking a stern moral attitude to this, or fears that the child is forming 'bad habits' which must be dealt with decisively and with punishment, she should cast her mind back to her own early childhood and remember that she probably 'took' objects in much the same way.

There is, too, the difficult problem of choosing between alternatives. What would you like to do? Go to the shops or to the swings? Which would you like to have, chocolate or ice-cream? This problem was mentioned when discussing the two-and-a-half-year-old. At six it can be even more complicated because of the widened horizons of the child's experience. For adults, choice can be difficult and even a source of mental distress. For example, during war-time we were glad to have spectacles, a pencil, a rubber, or some such item irrespective of colour, size, shape, as long as the object fulfilled the purpose we had in mind. But with increasing availability of goods, a wider choice became possible. After long deliberation, we may choose a pair of glasses, let us say, and having paid for them and taken them home, we feel disturbed and brood on whether we have really chosen the right ones, or whether the green oval pair would not have suited us better. We may infer that having to make a choice can also be disturbing for children. It may cause them confusion during the act of making the choice and distress because they regret the choice they have made. Perhaps at this stage it is better for parents and teachers not to offer too many choices.

Life now takes on a new complexity, as it did at two-and-a-half. Children are getting caught up in the competitive jostlings of their peers and with the school and its demands. But it takes a little time to get used to this jostling and the child may be as old as nine before he is at home with others of his own age. Sixes are frequently socially inept. Two is still the ideal number, except when children are in the hands of a skilled teacher; increase this number and the bickering and the scapegoating also increases The play of boys and girls tends now to differ more obviously; boys are interested in toys which are replicas of the machines of our technological society (tractors, aeroplanes, engines) and girl. keep to domestic pursuits (dolls and houses). Boys engage in rowdy, explosive, gross bodily activities—cowboys and Indians, cops and robbers. These, like the game of tag amongst boys and girls, are an expression of sheer exuberance rather than *organized* games in the more clearly defined sense as with children at ten. But if some six-year-old boys still like to play at dolls and houses with girls, there is again no need for fathers to be concerned or worried about this.

Children's gross bodily activity and their enthusiasm make control of bodily movements difficult for them and often give rise to domestic accidents. Put a bowl of water on the floor for a moment and the six-year-old is sure to put his foot in it (and it's not much good asking him not to). A sweep of the arm at the meal table and, before you know it, the tea is spilt.

Children seem to experience numerous fears—of dogs (a very prevalent fear among children in our society), of thunder and lighting, of the shadows on the walls. A child may resolutely refuse to go on an errand and his mother may be surprised at the determined vehemence of his refusal. It may then turn out that, in order to fulfil the errand, the child has to pass a house with a dog which snaps, or the house of an older child who persists in bullying him. Mothers need to be aware of such possibilities and not to jump to the immediate conclusion that her child is being wilfully disobedient. Some six-year-olds ask for a light when they go to bed after being without one for some time. It is wise to accede to this request.

Gesell uses these terms, among others, to describe the six-year-olds: 'impulsive', 'undifferentiated', 'volatile', 'dogmatic', 'compulsive', 'excitable'. Perhaps these characteristics reflect the tensions of change as children move (1) towards the outside world, and (2) towards the world of fact and away from fantasy. There are cultural pressures on children to make these moves. To take some examples: school is an institution which encourages them in this; adults remind children more often now of the difference between their imaginings and actual events; a boy is teased into discarding behaviour that is domestic and feminine, that is, behaviour which suggests that he is still a 'mummy's boy'.

These moves are all part of the child's growth towards independence and individuation, and to achieve these he must move away from the family and also learn to assess events in the real world and to cope with them. However, parents and teachers must be careful not to destroy completely the world of fantasy and imagination in their zeal to make their children 'practical'.

By seven, children are 'settling in' to this process of change and appear to be developmentally poised (third phase). They are not quite ready for the indiscriminate sociability of typical eight-year-olds and yet they have matured beyond the petulance of the sixes. They are active and vigorous enough—boys at the 'rough stuff', shooting it out in the style of the Westerns, and yelling and shouting at each other in the process; girls at less aggressive pursuits, such as skipping, hopping, swinging. But there is not the organization and the relative willingness to accept rules as at nine or ten. The rules of the game can be happily accepted by a seven-year-old when they apply to others, but are still difficult to comprehend when applied to himself. When others insist that rules do so apply, the response is, 'I'm not going to play (with you) any more.' Group games are still, therefore, precarious affairs and they often end in chaos. A seven may then settle for a best friend—of the same sex.

It is interesting that at this stage children have periods when they are preoccupied. A seven-year-old will play by himself more than he has done before; he may become suddenly a little shy in the company of others, particularly of adults, and may walk on the other side of the road to avoid greeting an adult. Possibly mothers say more often at seven than they have before, and certainly more often than they will for many years to come, 'He's very quiet.' Because of this tendency to withdraw and to brood, the child may appear to be heedless or forgetful from the point of view of parents and teachers. A parent may say, 'You're getting deaf, boy!' or may think the child is deliberately not hearing in order to escape some household chore.

However, these broodings and preoccupations can be seen developmentally as a lull ('inwardizing thrusts', as Gesell says) before children take a plunge into the social activities ('outwardizing thrusts') of Primary School pupils. Moreover, in our extraverted society we tend to look with alarm or suspicion at any tendencies towards introspective behaviour. Yet such behaviour is a very necessary part of the process of growing up, for it is a means by which we get to know ourselves and are able to assess the significance of new experiences, to assimilate new learnings, to perfect new skills.

This preoccupation, this ability to be alone may be connected with the seven-year-old's tendency towards perfectionism and towards persistence in the pursuit of perfection. Children will now, alone and away from others, practise to improve their skipping, swinging, painting, colouring and their skill in spinning tops or shooting marbles. The rubber is used vigorously and in a determined way and, because of this drive to get things *right*, Gesell has aptly referred to seven as 'the eraser age'. This desire for perfection may be, in part, a spontaneous desire and akin to the desire to know, as discussed in Chapter 8. It may also be, in part, an expression of the process of introjection, that is, the acceptance by children of adult standards as if they were their own. The desire for perfection may make children appear conceited, as when they say 'Mine's best!'; it may also lead them to feel a little self-righteous when they are good and behave as a parent or teacher has told them; and so they will tell tales on each other.

We are sometimes annoyed by children's tale-telling, but, as I have said elsewhere, 'in telling these tales, are they not also reminding us that they have accepted and followed our codes of behaviour and are therefore entitled to their feelings of virtuous indignation towards the one who has infringed the codes, and entitled also to their implicit demands that he be punished? Perhaps the real source of our annoyance is that they are accepting our codes too much, which is precisely what introjection means, and are becoming a little priggish in the process' (2).[1]

All seven-year-olds are not, of course, amenable and obedient at all times. A seven can be stubborn and refuse to do what he is

[1] page 95.

told. This stubbornness takes the place of the temper tantrum of earlier years. Seven-years-old do not like to be disturbed when engaged in a task and, if they are disturbed, will become irritable. Younger brothers and sisters who, pristinely innocent of the creative value of a project, irreverently daub hands or feet upon it are likely to receive a clout. An incident of this sort often brings an elder child into strife with his parents who feel they must side with the younger one. A seven-year-old may, too, be sensitive ('touchy' as we say in everyday life); he may rush from the room and slam the door because he has been teased or laughed at. It is a good idea for parents to restrain older siblings from playing unmercifully upon this weakness.

Children still fear the shadows on the wall, or going into a dark room, and they are still very impressionable so that parents need to protect them from films and news likely to stimulate their anxieties. But anxieties tend now to be more related to events which could possibly happen in the real world, and may arise from (1) imaginative broodings in retrospect, as in the exaggeration of the possible consequences of the child's own misdeeds (he may, for example, throw a stone blindly over a hedge and run away; then for days he broods upon the possibility that the stone he threw has broken something or hurt someone); (2) imaginative anticipation (for example, that he will be late for school, that his spelling test will be too hard, that the steamer or the train in which he is travelling will sink or crash).

To conclude this study of children up to about seven years of age, their sexual development will be referred to more specifically and this will be done for each stage of development which follows.

Two points by way of introduction: firstly, Hadfield (5)[1] has made a distinction between the terms 'sensuous' and 'sexual'. The point of this distinction is that, for young children, what is often called 'sexual' activity might more aptly be called 'sensuous' activity—the delight is in the soft or hard, warm or cold, rough or smooth, and the motive is often curiosity.

Secondly, research findings on the 'sexual' life of children are few, and for the descriptive accounts of children's sexual development which are contained within this and the chapters which

[1] pages 82–4.

follow, the findings of Kinsey *et al.* (8, 9) are relied upon. Kinsey's results need to be taken with caution for a number of reasons. One, they are based on an American population and are not necessarily applicable to any other national group. Two, Kinsey's sample consisted of people who were prepared to talk about their sexual experiences; some of these allowed him to interview their children. Not all parents would be prepared to do either, and the sample may, therefore, be biased—that is, not representative of the American population as a whole. Three, much of the data on which his accounts of the sexual experiences of children are based were obtained from recollections by adults of their childhood experiences. Such recollections can often be mistaken ones.

Yet the findings provide data about boys and girls, including data on the differences between the sexual activities of children in various socio-economic groups, which are, to date, the most comprehensive available.

During the pre-school and Infant School years 'sexual' activities are incidental and casual; for example, the genital self-manipulation of the baby during the first two years, the innocent curiosity of boys and girls of three and four regarding differences in their anatomy. This curiosity may lead them to exhibitionism, the mutual genital manipulation by boy and girl or by a couple of the same sex, the occasional game of doctors or of mothers and fathers amongst five- and six-year-olds which may have a marked sensuous component and be accompanied by mutual feeling of bodies.

How children will regard these activities will depend upon the reactions of adults. Such activity is neutral for little children, but for an adult it may be coloured by cultural and emotional overtones derived from his/her upbringing. Because of these emotional overtones a mother may fill children with dread, that is, with an undefined anxiety about something which they cannot comprehend. Kinsey's evidence suggests that this can be detrimental to children's sensuous and later sexual development. To this point we shall return in the next chapter.

Kinsey sums up his findings about the 'sexual' activities of the under-eights as follows: 'Much of this sex play is purely exploratory, animated by curiosity . . . and without the recognition of the emotional possibilities of such experiences' (8).[1]

[1] page 163.

One final word: teachers and parents of children of this age-group have the delicate and difficult task of being firm and yet, at the same time, of not pricking the bubbling spontaneity of Infant School children. These children need the outer control which adults can provide to protect them from uninhibited and extreme expression of their feelings of love and hate and of their impulses to deride and to hit their companions. They also need teachers who are good organizers, who can provide a background for constructive 'busyness' which is nevertheless flexible so that it can be changed often and quickly. Teachers of Infant children must be unshockable, ready for the unexpected remark (maybe crude and rude by adult standards), for a sudden outburst of temper, of stubbornness, for a 'sexual' incident, and yet not be drawn to moralizings because of these.

Thus it is that the school can do much to help the six- and seven-year-olds to develop by providing a varied curriculum which gives opportunity for group co-operation, creative and constructive work, for reading and reading-readiness programmes, and for general bodily activity. It is a curriculum that provides for both fact and fantasy.

REFERENCES

1   Acheson, R. M., Hewitt, D. 'Stature and skeleton maturation in the pre-school child.' *British Journal of Preventative and Social Medicine*, 1954, **8**, pp. 59–65.

2   Gabriel, J. 'Resolution of opposites and the teaching of children.' *The Australian Journal of Education*, 1960, Vol. 3, No. 2, pp. 91–105.

3a Gesell, A., Ilg, F. L. *Child Development:* 1 'Infant and child in the culture of today.' Harper, New York, 1949.

3b Gesell, A., Ilg, F. L. *Child Development:* 2 'The child from five to ten.' Harper, New York, 1949.

4   Grenlich, W. W., *et al.* 'The physical growth and development of children who survived the atomic bombing of Hiroshima and Nagasaki.' *Journal of Pediatrics*, 1953, **43**.

5   Hadfield, J. A. *Childhood and Adolescence.* Penguin Books, Harmondsworth, Middlesex, 1962.

6   Hewitt, D., Westropp, C. K., Acheson, R. M. 'Effects of childish ailments on skeleton development.' *British Journal of Preventative and Social Medicine*, 1955, **9**, pp. 179–86.

7   Isaacs, S. *The Children we Teach.* University of London Press, London, 1932.

8   Kinsey, A. C., Pomeroy, W. B., Martin, C. E. *Sexual Behaviour in the Human Male*. Saunders, London, 1948.

9   Kinsey, A. C., Pomeroy, W. B., Martin, C. E. *Sexual Behaviour in the Human Female*. Saunders, London, 1953.

10 Moore, T., Ucko, L. E. 'Four to six: constructiveness and conflict in meeting doll play problems.' *Journal of Child Psychology and Psychiatry*, 1961, **2**, pp. 21–47.

11 Moore, T. *Children of Full- and Part-time Mothers*. Mimeographed, 1964.

12 Olson, W. C. 'The diagnosis and treatment of behaviour disorders in children.' *In 34th Year Book of the National Society for the Study of Education*. Public School Publishing Company, Bloomington, U.S.A., 1935.

13 Piaget, J. *The Moral Judgment of the Child*. Harcourt, Brace, New York, 1932.

14 Stendler, C. B., Young, N. (a) 'The impact of beginning first grade upon socialization as reported by mothers.' (b) 'Impact of first grade entrance upon the socialization of the child: changes after the first eight months of school.' *Child Development*, (a) 1950, **21**, pp. 241–60, (b) 1951, **22**, pp. 113–22.

15 Tanner, J. M. *Growth at Adolescence*. Blackwell, London, 1955.

CHAPTER THIRTEEN

Problems and Questionings

THE purpose of this chapter is to consider some specific problems of children under seven. The word 'specific' has been used deliberately, for the problems to be considered are not intended to exhaust all those that children experience, but are chosen as representative of the kinds of difficulties which parents and teachers need to understand. These problems can broadly be classified as follows:

A Those which relate more to children's social life and which arise particularly in connection with:
the possession of objects;
the 'possession' of people, i.e. gaining the exclusive affection and attention of favoured adults;
the coming of a new child into a group;
the ostracism of an individual child by a group of children.

B Those of a more individual nature which arise in connection with:

young children's inability to accept self-blame;
their inability to accept the inevitable.

C Young children's fears.

Beginning with those problems listed under A: in a superficial way it may be said that they indicate psychological growing pains and are, as stated earlier, an indication that children have not yet learned to be social so that these forms of behaviour show a lack of social skill, just as wobbling on a bicycle or falling off it indicates a lack of motor skill. Ineptness precedes aptitude in the process of acquiring social and mental as well as physical skills. But one can go further than this in an attempt to explain these social problems.

In what follows, a parallel will occasionally be drawn between the behaviour of children and the behaviour of adults in comparable circumstances, for, by doing so, we should be able to understand children's behaviour more clearly. Indeed, the better we, as adults, are able to understand our own behaviour, the better we can understand the behaviour of children. Further, the more tolerant we are of our own weaknesses and failures, the more tolerant we shall be of those of our children.

To take the problem of sharing: as pointed out earlier, the process of development is partly the process of increasing the concepts *my* and *mine*. 'It's *mine*, it's *mine*, it's *mine*.' 'It's *my* mother!' 'It's *my* train!' 'It's *my* bicycle!' To have exclusive possession of objects or the exclusive affection of people is to be significant. I am not merely I, I am the person who has a mother, a train, a bicycle. To share these objects with another is to lose the pride, the esteem, the uniqueness which the individual child feels because he has them.

Sometimes, children will fight over an object until the object itself is destroyed. A parent says, 'Well, there you are. It is broken and neither of you can have it now.' But, puzzling as it may at first seem, the children are content with this state of affairs. That they are content is not really so puzzling in the light of the pride which possession gives. For example, a mother may, in such circumstances, decide that the object belongs to one of the children and give it to him. The child who has been given the object glances at the other child and tilts his head—just slightly— in triumphant pride. The mother catches sight of this and hastily admonishes the child with, 'Don't *do* that.' As far as the two children are concerned, it is better for neither to have it (even though this means that the object is destroyed) than to run the risk that one should be given it and proudly triumph over the other.

It is good, too, to have the attention and affection of a loved adult, to snuggle up close to him or her and to feel the warmth which such a close relationship brings. To share this affection and attention is to destroy its delicious exclusiveness. As long as it *is* equally shared, children can accept the inevitable necessity of having to share parental affection within the home and the attention and affection of the teacher in the classroom, but, as will be shown later, it is often difficult for a new child to be accepted into the family or play groups.

Such feelings about possessions may be related to ourselves; for, as adults, we gain significance not only because of who we are and what we are, but also because of what we possess. To lose even part of our property leaves us depressed and anxious, and the request to share may fill us with doubt. A woman buys a new dress, goes to a dance, and there is another woman at the dance with an identical dress. She is filled with dismay, for the dress is now 'shared' and has lost its power to make her feel significant.

We feel much the same about the 'possessing' of people. I resent a third person not only because I have now temporarily to share *my* friend but also because I fear that this third person will take my friend away from me. If this happens, then not only shall I feel deflated because of his ability to do this, I shall also lose the satisfaction that accompanies the *exclusive* possession of *my* friend. Sharing or losing property and people is often difficult for adults to endure. It is probably even more difficult for children.

All this is closely connected with the third problem, distrust of the stranger. We adults are wary, a little dubious, about the newcomer. He is someone new and we have to learn a little about him. He sets us a little problem. We wonder to what extent he may want to change the way of living (*our* way of living) to which we have become accustomed. We resent it if he is too ostentatious, too vocal at first. Similarly for children, the new girl or boy is an unknown quantity who has to be sized up, a potential rival for toys and for the affection of people. It is understandable if children show resentment against a new child, and that this resentment should be seen especially in the small group—as, for example, the family when a new baby, an adopted child, or an orphaned cousin enters as a permanent member of the group. In the larger class groups, hatreds and hostilities are not as pointed and can more easily be overcome, for a lot of sharing takes place in any case, and one extra does not make very much difference. The skilled teacher, too, can introduce the new child into the group and watch unobstrusively for the possible rise of jealousies, hatreds and hostilities.

Children sometimes 'take it out' on another child by forming a close group which excludes this one child and by then proceeding to make disparaging remarks about him. 'He is ugly.' 'He is dirty.' 'He smells.' All this adds to the infinite distress of the one excluded. Sometimes we feel angry, indeed righteously so, at the way children will, on occasions, persecute another child in this way, and we may ask ourselves, 'What satisfaction do they get from this?' Actually, they get a number of satisfactions. First, hatred of an outsider by all members of a group cements group solidarity and gives each individual member the feelings of security which come from being an accepted member of a unified group. Secondly, the outsider provides an easy means by which each child can ensure his continued membership of the group and this he does by agreeing with everyone else on the complete badness of the outsider. To question, to doubt the views of most members of the group or even to mention any of the good qualities of the one excluded is to invite social disapproval. Indeed, a child is intuitively aware that, if he does this, he might find himself in the place of the excluded one. The third advantage that children derive from this making of a scapegoat of one child is that it enables them to feel superior at his expense.

Of course, adults sometimes do the same. A group of people get together and talk is aimless; then one of the group mentions a person who is generally disliked. Eyes sparkle and tongues wag furiously as the mean ways of the despised one are discussed. Unity has been attained and rapport established between all members of the group. Few children or adults would be courageous enough under such circumstances as these to suggest some virtues in the outsider and thereby to run the risk of the general censure of the group, and perhaps, as has been suggested, of being oneself excluded in place of the outsider.

As will be emphasized later, children have yet to prove themselves by their achievements and therefore they are unsure of themselves as they jostle amongst each other for position. By criticizing another, by persecuting another, they feel more confident, more righteous, and more secure in the group to which they belong.

Taking now the first of the two individual problems given under B, namely the inability to accept self-blame: children will often blame other children for something which they have obviously done themselves. For example, a child can be playing with a little truck when he smashes it against a wall: a wheel is broken and his delightful game is at an end. If another child is near, he may hit him, or he may run to tell his mother that it was 'him' who broke the wheel.

Adults may not be as crude as this in their reactions, but, if you observe the everyday behaviour of people, you will notice that self-blame is difficult to accept. We forget to carry out a promise and we say, 'I was busy at the time.' The nail that we are hitting into the wood bends because we did not hit it squarely on the head, and we say, 'Really, this hammer!' The housewife burns the cake and she says, 'It is the children; they make so many demands on one's time.' The tennis-player 'muffs' a shot. He looks at his racket, makes a swift stroke in the air and mutters, 'This racket really does want restringing.' It is not easy, and requires a degree of integration to accept self-blame and to say, 'I did it, and it's my fault.' It is very tempting to find some small excuse and, if there is no obvious one, then in the last extremity we may say, 'But I was tired at the time.'

It is very much the same for children. The child who breaks the wheel of his truck could 'kick himself', but it is much easier to displace these aggressive feelings on to the little boy standing near and to kick him instead. He could himself accept blame but how much easier to blame the other boy. Even this apparently simple sequence of events is complex in its psychological structure.

> John breaks his truck.
> He feels angry with himself.
> He would like to punish himself ('I could kick myself!' as an adult would say).
> Instead, John kicks Alex who is standing near by.
> It is then so easy for John to answer his mother's question, 'Why did you kick Alex?' with, 'Because he broke my wheel.'

This is a simple example of displacement and projection. John displaces on to Alec the anger he feels towards himself and he then projects on to Alec the blame that is really his. One needs, in these circumstances, to avoid the charge of 'deliberate lying'. Gentle explaining probably helps more towards the learning and acceptance of social behaviour than a charge of lying (and it is surprising how much of his own behaviour you can get a child to understand through conversational questions and answer, and through suggestive explanation).

The second problem under B was children's inability to accept the inevitable. Frustrating events are often hard to bear and to accept, even when they are outside the control of any person—the rain that spoils our holiday, the car that breaks down at a crucial moment. By getting emotionally perturbed, by running into a tantrum, we merely add to the inconvenience and the suffering we just have to endure. For small children, such frustrations are probably even more difficult to endure, partly because of children's limited understanding of themselves and of the world in which they live. For example, a child and his mother decide to go out, but it suddenly comes on to rain and they cannot go. The child feels hopelessly frustrated and he may dissolve into tears, or hit wildly at his mother's skirts. It is difficult for him in such circumstances to understand that nothing can be done, for his understanding is too inadequate to enable him to differentiate between that which is an inevitable result of impersonal forces and that which is within the power of the mother personally to engineer or to remedy. It is easy, therefore, to stamp feet and to attack mother because she is the source of the frustration or because she refuses to do anything about it (according to his vague understanding of the situation).

Problem C, children's fears and anxieties, is a difficult one, and it is not possible to encompass all its complexities in a short statement. The reader is referred to a detailed account (6) and to three surveys (1, 5, 7).

These surveys show that children differ in their propensity to fear, and that their fears take many forms: fear of situations, objects and people actually met—the dark, water, storms, cars, trains, the bully, dogs; of possible hazards—flood, fire, 'bad men', burglars; of unfamiliar animals—lions, tigers, snakes; of imaginary creatures—spooks, witches, ghosts; of loss of self-esteem—to fail a school test, to have a bad school report, to be admonished by a teacher.

They show, too, children's tendency to anticipate the possibility of danger (maybe a most unlikely one), and in their imagination to exaggerate the dire nature of the danger and its consequences—for example, the little girl who is anxious about going to sleep because she worries that she will not wake up in time in the morning, and will be late for school and scolded by the teacher. 'Imaginary fears', 'irrational fears' are terms often used by parents to designate such anxieties.

Studies of children suggest the onset of fears about certain situations over a span of years, their decline, then the assumption of fears about other, and different kinds of, situations. A young baby shows signs of apprehension when there is any sudden change in the environment caused by such things as loud noises, sudden flashes of light, loss of support when suddenly dropped, the abrupt appearance of an over-demonstrative and excitable person or of a crowd of strange people. But though showing this immediate apprehension, a baby soon recovers when silence and calm is restored. When he is away from home, a baby will often appear restless and distressed, even though the new environment is peaceful and propitious; and a mother will remark on their return that the baby 'has settled down again'.

The second year sees the development of other fears: of high places and of falling, of animals, and, in a few cases, of the dark and of being left alone.

Research work suggests that children do not become afraid of the dark until they are two or more years old (5, 6). Perhaps darkness means different things for a baby in its first year from what it means for an older child. For a baby, darkness means lack of the presence of other people as described earlier (page 142); but it may also mean deprivation of sensory experience—lights, sounds, talking, activity. Take, as an extreme example, a dull, foggy English November day the whole of which the baby has spent in the half-dark living-room under conditions of low and unchanging stimulation. Mother puts on the light at 4.30, a bright light casting intriguing shadows. Things in the room are now clearly visible, and the baby can move his head from side to side and take notice. But, alas, within an hour or so, he is taken to bed and plunged into total darkness. He may then whimper and cry for more of the sensory satisfaction provided by the lights and movements.[1]

But when a child's capacity to imagine begins to mature, darkness means loneliness and emptiness. The emptiness could, of

---

[1] Suggestions about the motives of a baby must always, of course, be tentative. But Hebb, a leading psychologist, has spoken of a class of fears due to sensory deficit and has included in this class fear of darkness and solitude (4). Important experiments done under supervision (2) have shown that depriving adults of sensory stimulation—sound, light, touch—over a period of a day or more causes them to become seriously disturbed.

course, be filled with delightful fairy fantasies; but if the child is anxious, he may conjure up frightening possibilities, and the movement of a curtain and the shadow it causes begin to take on frightening possibilities.

Perhaps an analogous situation for an adult is to be alone at night in an empty house when every sound becomes ominous. It is good to have a dog on these occasions, even a fox terrier. It could not, of course, cope very effectively with a marauder; but the lone adult knows that he is misinterpreting the sounds that startle him. He looks at the dog; it is making no move.

When their child of four, five or six suddenly wants a light when going to bed parents, in their surprise, may comment that he has never asked for a light before. But the request is understandable enough, since anxiety about the dark is a function of a child's maturing imagination and not merely of his chronological age.

Other fears that develop up to the age of about seven are of animals, imaginary creatures, possible hazards, dreams and nightmares; some fears are acquired because of unwise threats by mothers: the policeman, the 'bogey' man, and, worse of all, that his mother will run away and leave him.[1]

Anger and the conflicting feelings of love and hate mentioned earlier give rise to impulses which are hard to restrain and which become further sources of anxiety. Other impulses arise, too, which fill the child with anxiety and guilt—to touch the forbidden, to steal a chocolate, to destroy some object. The anxiety accompanying these impulses may be accentuated because, if the impulses are expressed, the child may incur the displeasure of a cherished adult.

With the development of social life come further fears—of the bully, of loss of the social support of companions, of being made a scapegoat, of being 'sent to Coventry'. With the development of a self-concept, of self-awareness and of the ability to assess the universe more objectively (between the ages of about six and twelve), many past imaginary fears decrease in frequency and intensity. New fears are acquired by the child relating to loss of self-esteem through failure of some sort—to lose the approval of

[1] In their study referred to earlier the Newsons found that 22 per cent of the parents in the sample threatened their children with policemen, teachers and doctors, and 14 per cent that they would desert the child or send him away.

adults and of his fellows, to fail in an examination, to have a poor school report, not to be promoted to the next class, to be humiliated by a teacher. Thus, as children grow older they move away from highly imaginative fears of the objective world to fear of situations which give rise to feelings of personal inadequacy (5).

Whereas a baby shows immediate fear of a sudden noise and settles down again, in later years children anticipate the possibility of fearful situations and will anxiously brood about what *might* happen. And imagination may work at full steam so that the mild nature of the dog is forgotten as the child looks at its teeth and imagines the potential dangers inherent in such sharp instruments. Children will not only brood about the possible repetition of a past experience of fear, they will anticipate a fear that is a most unlikely one. Even bright children may become anxious about the possibility of being kept back a class at a school in which children are kept back only in exceptional circumstances such as long absence through illness.

It would be presumptious to suggest that there is any easy way to deal with children's fears and anxieties. As Jersild says, if children's fears are irrational, then 'it is natural and normal for children to have irrational fears' (5).[1] Or, as Gesell puts it, 'From the point of view of child guidance, fear should not be too much feared. Fear is normal, Fear is natural' (3b).[2] It may be added that fear and anxiety are an inevitable part of the human condition, of the growing as well as the grown human being. One of the strange paradoxes that beset man is that his imagination, which is the source of his originality and creativity, is also the source of so many of his fears; and the more imaginative a child is, the more likely he is to develop imaginary fears.

Nevertheless, whereas one social environment will engender very considerable anxiety, as among the Dobuans and the Mundugumor, where violence and competition rouse anxieties which they seek to reduce by magical formulas, another will not generate so many, as is the case with the peaceful and co-operative Arapesh or Zuni. Children also 'catch' fears from their parents and under exceptional circumstances parents communicate their fear or their calm to their children. During the Second World War, it was seen that the extent of children's fears of air raids depended on their parents' response. If the parents were anxious and fearful, so

[1] page 868.   [2] page 296.

were their children; if the parents remained calm and carried out the necessary precautions in a cool, business-like way, the children were also calm. Further, parents can help a child over his fears by tolerant reassurance. Intolerance or impatience with this 'silliness' (as a father may sometimes put it) would be most unfortunate.

A mother, too, may try a direct approach by making the child come with her into the cupboard under the stairs. The difficulty of such a direct approach is that the child's feelings are subjective and it is hard to judge whether one is increasing or decreasing his fears. Probably it is best to try an indirect approach, creating conditions (by, for example, leaving the door of the cupboard under the stairs open) in which the child can try to overcome his anxiety about a particular situation on his own. When a child does overcome fear on his own, it is very likely that he will gain confidence to deal with future fears. This achievement is independent of outside approval because, in his own heart, the child knows he has achieved a small triumph. The illustration given on page 147 and the indirect approach illustrated above exemplify the sequence of overcoming fears suggested by Gesell, namely, shock and withdrawal, compulsive return, final resolution.

Children's fears are sometimes expressed in their dreams. Parents are often alarmed by these because, in dreams, the expression of an emotion is acute and uncontrolled. Parents, too, may have been unaware before this that the child had these fears. While they need to take cognizance of such dreams and seek to right possible outside sources of anxiety (such as being bullied by another child), or to reduce them by, say, providing a nightlight, parents must expect the occasional anxiety dream and not be alarmed by it. Gesell has suggested that with five- to ten-year-olds fear dreams far outnumber anger dreams.

It is interesting to reflect on why children conceal their fears. A child may be tormented by another child, or fear the dog up the road. He will say nothing about these fears and only by accident will parents get to know about them. May the explanation be this? A fear situation is one with which a child cannot cope, and so he is helpless and feels personally inadequate. Since his concept of himself is dependent on what cherished adults think of him, he cannot afford to reveal his fears because he feels that in so doing he will lose their esteem and his own feelings of personal inadequacy will

252 PHYSICAL, EMOTIONAL, INTELLECTUAL GROWTH

be further increased.[1,2] Such an attitude is especially engendered if parents, not sympathetically in tune with the child's fears, admonish him (even if they do so gently) by saying, 'Surely you are not afraid of a dog at your age?' A more positive approach would be to encourage a child to talk about his fears so that he realizes that his parents accept them and in no way disparage him because of them.

Two questions will now be asked, and answers attempted concerning the emotional and social development of children.

Question 1. Why do children enjoy the more gruesome fairy stories?

Children develop considerable feelings of hatred towards other people and they experience sudden urges to be aggressive and hostile. They want sometimes to hit out at friends who interfere with their individual activities (frustration), who have toys they want (jealousy), who want the toys they have (fear of loss). Again, they want sometimes to hit out at parents or teachers because of the frustrations which these adults may quite legitimately have to impose.

Feelings of hatred are dangerous, for such feelings are accompanied by impulses to hostile actions which may threaten the child's rapport with others and therefore his feelings of security. Because of this, a child may *repress* both the feeling and the impulse—that is, he is not consciously aware of their existence. But, although the feeling and impulse have been repressed, they do influence his behaviour and do need to be expressed. Fairy stories provide a means by which this can be done.

Take some of the well-known fairy stories: in Hansel and Gretel the witch is pushed into the fire; in Jack and the Beanstalk the giant is ruthlessly slain; the fate of the ugly sisters in Cinderella is a little pathetic, but children rarely express pity for them. A case

[1] Of course, a small child does not argue things out consciously as this way of putting things seems to imply. He probably feels a vague disquietude, but he is unconscious of the reasons for his behaviour. His feelings and not his reason direct him.

[2] It is interesting to reflect that children of ten or eleven will talk freely about the anxieties they experienced when they were younger, at, say, six or seven, even though they are diffident about admitting present ones. To admit anxieties experienced when they were 'little kids' does not lay them open to a charge of weakness.

has been reported of a group of children who were brought up
without hearing any of the conventional fairy stories because their
parents took the view that they were far too gruesome. But by the
time they were seven the children had made up their own, which
were of so gruesome a nature that, in comparison, Grimm read like
a gentle bed-time story. As one writer has put it when she spoke
of this fascination which children show for the gruesome and
cruel, 'It is meat that is almost too strong for many adults to
take' (8).[1]

The main characteristic of fairy stories is that in them the good
are very, very good and the bad are very, very bad: there is a very
clear division into the 'goodies' and the 'baddies'. One hates the
'baddies' and loves the 'goodies'. Thus, fairy stories give children
an opportunity to identify themselves with the good and to reject
the bad. Through them children can love in purity without any
trace of hate and they can hate in purity without any trace of love.
By hating and rejecting the 'baddies', a child feels easier in himself;
by loving and accepting the 'goodies', he feels secure in his own
goodness. Both feelings enable him to be a little righteous.

It is said of the little girl in the nursery rhyme that:

> When she was good,
> She was very, very good,
> And when she was bad,
> She was horrid!

In all probability children feel themselves to be as the rhyme
says the little girl is (sometimes good, sometimes horrid). Fairy
stories help to maintain the balance of feelings towards the good.

Of course, adults derive similar kinds of satisfaction from
many of the films they see, especially Westerns, and also from
many of the books they read.

Question 2. Why do children hate so wholeheartedly and love
equally wholeheartedly?

A child sometimes expresses direct hatred of an acquaintance
of his own age. Mother informs the small boy that Edward is
coming with his mother for an afternoon visit, and the small boy

[1] page 675.

taking a very determined stance, says shortly but unequivocally, 'I hate him.' Mother sighs and wonders what will happen. Such an attitude can be explained in much the same way as were the fairy stories. Edward takes the place of the witch, the giant, the ugly sisters and is the 'screen' upon whom the child projects his own horridness, for, by making Edward horrid, he is not so horrid himself. One could add, too, that the child shows an inability to balance, to weigh up the merits with the demerits of a person. As integrated adults we know A whom we like for qualities a, b, c and dislike because of qualities x, y, z. We can co-operate with him because of a, b, c, and we may say of x, y, z, 'He annoys me sometimes', or, if we are feeling very benign, 'Nobody is perfect and he, like everyone else, has his faults.' Sometimes we only see x, y, z and we become hostile; sometimes, at an opposite extreme, we see only a, b, c and we indulge in indiscriminate hero-worship. In this we are rather like children, for they see in terms of either black or white with no shades in between.

REFERENCES

1   Angelino, H. J., Dollins, J., Mech, V. 'Trends in the fears and worries of school children as related to socio-economic status and age.' *Journal of Genetic Psychology*, 1956, **89**, pp. 263–76.
2   Bexton, W. H., Heron, W., Scott, T. H. 'Effects of decreased variation in the sensory environment.' *Canadian Journal of Psychology*, 1953, **46**, pp. 95–8.
3a   Gesell, A., Ilg, F. L. *Child Development:* 1 'Infant and child in the culture of to-day.' Harper, New York, 1949.
3b   Gesell, A., Ilg, F. L. *Child Development:* 2 'The child from five to ten.' Harper, New York, 1949.
4   Hebb, D. O. 'On the nature of fear.' *Psychological Review*, 1946, **53**, pp. 259–76.
5   Jersild, A. T. 'Studies of children's fears.' *In* Barker, R. G., Kounin, J. S., Wright, H. F. (Eds.) *Child Behaviour and Development*. McGraw-Hill, New York, 1943, pp. 329–44.
6   Jersild, A. T. 'Emotional development.' *In* Carmichael, L. (Ed.) *Manual of Child Psychology*. Wiley, New York, 1954, pp. 918–74.
7   Maurer, A. 'What children fear.' *Journal of Genetic Psychology*, 1965, **106**, pp. 265–77.
8   Murphy, L. B. 'Childhood experience in relation to personality development.' *In* Hunt, J. McV. (Ed.) *Personality and the Behaviour Disorders*, Vol. 2, Chap. 2. Ronald, New York, 1944.

BIBLIOGRAPHICAL NOTES

Many examples of children's behaviour illustrating the kinds of problems raised and questions asked in this chapter, as well as Isaacs's insightful comments on such behaviour, will be found in:

Isaacs, S. *Social Development in Young Children*. Routledge & Kegan Paul, London, 1933.

A selection from these examples of children's behaviour (and Isaacs's comments) are contained in:

Isaacs, S. *The Children we Teach*. University of London Press, London, 1932.

CHAPTER FOURTEEN

Primary School Children
(eight, nine, ten, eleven)

General physical growth

B Y general physical growth is meant growth of the body as a
whole, visible externally as an increase in height, weight, and
muscular strength. It is with these that we are mainly concerned,
although the visible changes are also accompanied by internal
changes, such as increases in blood volume and in size of heart,
kidneys, respiratory and digestive organs (31).[1]

During the Primary School years, although the *rate* of
general physical growth becomes less than it was during the preceding years and less than it will be during the spurt which
follows, growth certainly does not stop. Its cumulative effect is
obvious to the casual observer. The rate of increase in weight
(about 10 per cent each year) is usually greater than the increase
in height (about 5 or 6 per cent each year). Yet two features
of children's growth contribute to the long-legged, long-bodied
appearance of the average boy or girl—the more rapid growth of
arms and legs as compared with head and trunk, and the tendency
for the trunk to grow in length more than breadth. But there are
marked individual differences in rate and type of growth; some
children are tall and slight, others short and heavy.

Strength also increases. A child of twelve is twice as strong as a
child of six, measured by strength of grip (18). The speed and
accuracy of movement and the ability to control and to co-ordinate these also increase. The walk at eleven is no longer the shuffle
of the pre-school child, but a spring from the feet; it is mainly
from the feet and legs that movement emanates. When a seven-

[1] Chapter 2.

year-old boy kicks a football, his whole body is involved: the movement is a molar one. The power generated is only partly communicated to leg and foot, and the ball travels only a short distance. When he is eleven and kicks a ball, the essential movement is of the leg and foot. The power is concentrated within these. A flick of the foot and the ball travels further and is more accurately aimed. Children become more skilled in throwing a ball, aiming at a target, and at games, like fivestones, which require dexterous movements of hands and fingers.

The principles of growth described earlier continue to operate during this stage. This applies to the cephalo-caudal principle— that growth develops first in the head and moves progressively from regions nearest the head to those furthest away. The head has attained 90 per cent of its growth by the age of eight; the trunk is still large in relation to the rest of the body. During the subsequent Primary School years, the arms and legs have their turn to grow at a relatively greater rate.

Improved skill in throwing, aiming and playing fivestones exemplify the operation of the proximo-distal principle—that movements progress from those parts of the limbs nearest the trunk to those furthest away. The boy kicking a football at seven and then at eleven illustrates the Principle of Differentiation—that larger movements precede smaller, and that the smaller movements are differentiated out of the larger. The greater co-ordination shown by older Primary School children exemplifies the operation of the Principle of Integration—that fine, specialized movements begin to function together with, and in relation to, wider and more general movements. The emphasis children place on speed and accuracy illustrate how they enjoy and spontaneously practise the kind of skills which further their own growth. Unknown to themselves, they are capitalizing on the physical maturation that is taking place.

It follows that the school, in its Physical Education programme, should encourage general bodily activity, and provide practice in ball throwing and aiming skills. A child's natural stance expresses readiness for movement. As one authority puts it, 'The natural attitude for a child is one which he adopts when playing. He stands with feet apart and knees bent, and delights in squatting' (39).[1] At these ages, therefore, children should not be

[1] page 27.

compelled to stand like soldiers at attention, nor to sit perfectly still for long periods of time (39). Because the increasing flexibility of the body and its limbs is best expressed in quick expansive movements, fine writing and needle-work, which demand slow and laborious movements, should not be overdone, especially during the early Primary School years. Such close work can cause children harmful fatigue.

The growth of girls is slightly more rapid than that of boys. In girls skeleton growth is some days earlier during the pre-natal stage, some weeks earlier in babyhood, and nearly two years earlier at puberty. Towards the end of the Primary stage girls begin to shoot ahead, since at this time they usually begin their growth spurt. By thirteen girls have attained 75 per cent of their final strength as measured by arm thrust, boys only 45 per cent (39). This difference does not mean that girls are actually stronger than boys during the Primary stage; boys are just a little stronger.

By twelve, second teeth have replaced first teeth and there are no more intriguing gaps about which young children are so refreshingly unconscious. Infectious diseases and fevers—whooping cough, chicken-pox, scarlet fever, diphtheria—become less frequent than during earlier years.

Children's mental development

The principles of teaching to be considered later in this chapter will be based on the relation, and the distinction, between concrete forms and abstract forms of thinking. This relation and this distinction will now be considered.

Let us suppose that in front of us is a square red box made of hardwood. Through vision, touch and hearing (if tapped) the box and its qualities can be perceived. These percepts represent the concrete in its simplest form. The box and its qualities may be named—'box', 'square', 'red', 'hard'. The words designate concepts, since they imply a universality which the percepts do not have. In using them we relate the box to other boxes, and to 'redness' and 'hardness' in general, and so move one step from the concrete to the abstract, still in a simple form.

Suppose that a second box is put beside the first. This box is rectangular, red and made of tin. The second box provides an opportunity to generalize (they are both boxes), to describe the relations of similarity (colour and straight edges) and of difference (in material and shape). Although we may say, 'You can see they are the same colour', what actually we see are sensory qualities. Some relations are conceived; that is, by an active mental process we go beyond the percepts to say in effect, 'These two sensory qualities,—this particular red and that particular red—are similar.' These relations are abstractions, and again special nouns are used to denote them.

Mathematics and science furnish a more precise language which facilitates the transition from the concrete to the abstract. Mathematics arises from measurements—length of sides, areas of surface, volume, length of light waves, the use of formulae. Science provides theories—of colour, of molecular structure, with special reference to wood and tin.

Up to the age of two children are clearly at the stage of the concrete. They acquire knowledge by their senses; and by their own actions they learn that they can make objects move, or change them in some way. Piaget (27) calls these first two years a *sensori-motor* stage.

After the age of two, children's learning of language is the learning of names and labels that symbolize objects and their qualities—'box', 'red', 'hard'. But their use of words is still confined to the concrete, and amounts to little more than a pointing to or describing this or that particular object. They cannot conceive of a class of objects, and so distinguish between 'all' and 'some'. The slug the child sees on the road may be for him the same slug he saw in the garden. Therefore, Piaget calls it a stage of *pre-conceptual* thinking.

At five or so, children can make the distinction between a particular object and a group of objects. They delight in the word 'another'—'*another* butterfly', '*another* bird'—and there is one moon. They are still unable to detach themselves from their perceptions and feelings to consider facts independently of them.

They cannot as yet comprehend the notion of physical constancy, of size and quantity. When sticks of equal length are placed exactly alongside each other, children will judge them to be equal; but when one stick is moved ahead of the other, they sometimes describe the one moved forward as longer. They will say that the number of marbles in two identically shaped short wide jars are equal; but when the marbles from one of the jars are emptied to fill a tall thin jar, some children will say there are now fewer marbles 'because it is thinner', some that there are more marbles 'because it is higher'. They seldom conceive of the whole as being conserved. Because of children's dependence on their perceptions and feelings, Piaget calls the years between four-and -a-half and seven one of *intuitive* thinking.

The accurate use of concepts requires several more years. A very young child will ascribe 'life' to anything that emits a noise: the clock that ticks, the telephone that rings, the bag that squeaks when trodden on, like Little Claus's sack in Andersen's fairy tale. Young children appreciate Little Claus's deception. It is one they understand; surely anyone, they think, could be made to believe a thing was alive if it squeaked. Later, life is ascribed to that which moves: the sun, the moon, both of which young children like to see depicted, and will themselves depict, as a man's face. It is late in the Primary stage before children ascribe life only to man, animals, plants and insects.

As children grow older, there is progress in the way they explain events. Stern relates how a highly intelligent child of four explained to him that a magnet 'has long thin arms (so thin that you cannot see them) and tiny hands with tiny fingers (so tiny that you cannot see them). The long thin arms stretch out, the tiny fingers grab the nail and pull it towards the magnet.'

Piaget would call such explanations 'animistic', since children ascribe life to inanimate objects. Children of nine or ten would laugh at such an animistic explanation; but they watch with interest as the teacher shows them how various kinds of magnets work, and explains the differences between a copper clad and an iron clad, between the short-pull and the long-pull magnet. They would be still more intrigued and enlightened if the teacher showed them a film, or took them to see a pot magnet lifting sheets of iron as much as ten times its own weight.

Because Primary School children learn mainly from their experience of objects and the way they work, Piaget has described this stage as one of *concrete operations*. For the nine- and ten-year-old the concrete is what can be seen, touched and manipulated, so that the way an actual mechanism works can be understood, and the principle applied in another context. Relations—'same', 'different', 'opposite'—are also understood. Objects can be ordered in series from 'less' to 'greater'. They can be classified. Quantifications and simple arithmetical calculations can be made.

Annett (1) made a detailed study of the ways in which 300 children, aged between five and eleven, classified cards. Four of the cards depicted animals, four plants, four pieces of furniture, and four vehicles. The children were asked to sort the cards 'os that those which belong together are in the same group . After sorting the cards, a child was asked to say of each of his groups, 'How do these belong together?'

Annett found that the five- and six-year-olds were very confused about the sorting; their most frequent response was to make no sorting at all. Between the ages of eight and eleven, there was a clear increase in the frequency of sorting according to the above categories. But a perfect 4 by 4 sorting into groups of animals, plants, pieces of furniture and vehicles was achieved by only twenty-four of the three hundred children.

The tendency of the five-year-olds who did sort their cards in some fashion was to give no explanation. In reply they simply said 'don't know', or repeated 'they go together' or 'they belong'. At six, there was a tendency for the children to *enumerate* the objects or give facts about them—'this is a tree', 'this is a cow', 'this is a bird', 'the cow is in the field'. At seven and eight, they tended to explain their sorting in terms of *contiguity* by saying that the objects are generally found together—'the clock goes on the desk', 'you sit in a chair to watch television', 'the bird builds a nest in the tree'. By nine, the predominant mode of explanation was the use of *similarities;* that is, they mentioned a characteristic common to the two or more objects grouped—'they both fly', 'they both grow', 'you sit on them'. The same kind of explanation was most frequent with children of ten and eleven. But more frequently than the nine-year-olds, the ten- and eleven-year-olds gave the more abstract and all-embracing explanation in terms of *class names*—'plants', 'animals', 'furniture', 'machines'. Younger children sometimes used class names, but of an inappropriate kind; for example, animals were called 'pets', the vehicles 'toys'.

Primary School children are able to understand constancies of size and quantity, and usually have no trouble with the problem of the sticks and of the marbles. Most of them can think in terms of cause and effect, but they are unable to understand abstract theories, or make calculations involving intricate formulae. This comes later during the next stage, which begins at about twelve and which Piaget calls one of *formal operations* or reflective thought. As children proceed through this stage, the more intelligent are better able to reason about hypotheses and deduce conclusions without the help of concrete objects.

Piaget thus classifies thinking into five major forms—sensori-motor, pre-conceptual, intuitive, concrete operational, and formal operational; and he ascribes approximate ages to each. The significance of this classification (and of Annett's findings to some extent) is to show that thinking proceeds from 'the concrete' to 'the abstract', that is, from dependence on perception, feeling and manipulation of objects and situations to consideration of relations between them and of the structure and form of propositions and formulae. The principles of teaching to be considered at the end of this chapter and of Chapters 16 and 17 are based on the distinction, and the relation, between 'the concrete' and 'the abstract'.

Children's activities and interests

During the Primary School stage children's activities become more sustained and more organized (9, 10). At eight boys play at wild running, chasing, wrestling, war games, commandos, cops-and-robbers. Their attempts at organized play are sporadic and short-lived. Since rules are hard to accept when they go against oneself, and since the boys have not learned the rules of many of the games they play, there are many upsets. The rules they actually follow are usually their own; differences that arise are argued out between one individual and the rest of the group or between two opposing groups, each of which argues to its own advantage. Consequently there is much squabbling and shouting. Often groups disintegrate, and activities end with cries of 'I'm not playing with you any more.'

By the age of ten boys settle down to plan—an excursion, a project such as a hide-out to be sited, furnished and sorties plotted. Having now learned the rules and realized their value, they are able to play a continuous game of cricket or football, with sides. There are inevitable protests, but a ten-year-old can accept a decision implying finer points, such as an lbw. in cricket, even though it goes against him.

For girls the transition from the less to the more organized is not so obvious, since they are more-co-ordinated than boys to begin with. Still there is progress: from doll-play, cut-outs and acting in small plays at eight (often ending in disaster and tears) to more sustained activities at ten, such as planning a picnic, writing stories and plays, and acting them. There are the usual street games: skipping, hop-scotch, tops, roller-skates. Their indoor games show a similar advance. The ludo, the snakes-and-ladders and 'snap' played at eight are replaced at ten, by the longer-lived dominoes, card games and complex jig-saw puzzles.

Primary School children are objective, meaning that their orientation is outwards—toward understanding and manipulation of their environment. Their interests are practical: to make, or put together and mend, things that work (an electric door bell, an alarm clock). Blocks are materials to be used for building churches and castles with battlements and arches. Meccano sets are means for constructing cranes and vehicles of all kinds. They like toys that move: kites, scooters, bicycles. They make things that are useful: bows and arrows, fishing tackle, aprons, knitted scarves and hats.

Like their reading, children's drawings at this stage are full of action and incident. The vigour and power of their painting indicates that for them this mode of self expression serves many functions. It is a means of expressing their feelings and desires for movement and action, and of representing the knowledge they have acquired. Children are good actors and actresses; their relative unself-consciousness makes them so. Much of the play of boys is a form of make believe—Wild West games, cowboys-and-Indians, soldiers on parade. Much of the play of girls is acting in its usually accepted sense—dressing up, dancing, reciting. Every aspect of puppetry—making the puppets, planning the shows and producing them—provides scope for imaginative Primary School children.

Children's collections

The progress from the less to the more sustained and organized applies to children's collections. The miscellaneous collection in an eight-year-old's pockets—nails, pebbles, pieces of string, paper clips, pencils—is replaced at ten and eleven by the specialized collection of stamps, coins or shells. A mother, emptying her small son's pockets, may wonder what possible purpose the collection of 'junk' inside them can serve. She dare not throw it into the dustbin where, as far as she can see, it rightly belongs. The urge to collect is so characteristic of Primary School children that its nature and incidence will be considered in some detail.

Charles Darwin commented on the innate tendency to collect or hoard manifested by many birds and mammals, and indicated its obvious survival value. He suggested that a similar tendency might be an important ingredient in the sense of ownership characteristic of man. Later zoologists have studied the tendency to collect in magpies, jackdaws, squirrels, monkeys, and, most remarkable of all, in the Californian wood-rat. Herbert Spencer, on the other hand, tried to explain collecting as an effect of association. Pleasure is associated with collecting: pleasure in looking at pretty or curious objects, in finding them useful for weapons, food, and for attracting the admiration of others, for example, hanging ornaments about the person to attract the opposite sex. James, in his *Principles of Psychology*,[1] criticizes the associationist view. In support of the theory of an inherited instinct he points out that collecting occurs in higher mammals, that it is manifested early and spontaneously in children before associations have been formed, and that it is a feature common to almost all human beings.

Stanley Hall and his students investigated children's 'passion for collecting' as early as 1886. They found that 90 per cent of a large population of students had formed collections during childhood. Valentine (36), in a later inquiry among 300 students, gives 98 per cent. One of the earliest and most thorough studies of collecting, by one of Hall's collaborators, is that of Caroline Burk.[2] She traces its development as follows. Pre-school children show a marked tendency to appropriate things that might in fact be useful, but without realizing their utility. Later, subsidiary motives play a part: curiosity in its various forms (collecting shells, fossils, pets, books, pictures), exchange and barter and the value of collections therefor (coins, marbles, stamps), a sense of ownership (pride and rivalry). By the age of ten or eleven children's collections become more systematic and a stimulus for acquiring

[1] pages 422–4.
[2] *Pedagogical Seminary* (later called *The Journal of Genetic Psychology*), 1900, **7**, pp. 179–207.

knowledge. Children will seek information about their collections in catalogues, encyclopaedias and dictionaries.

Burk noted that, although girls indulge in collecting almost as much as boys, their interest is sentimental and aesthetic rather than practical. What Burk implies is that the joy girls obtain from collecting is the joy of cherishing and caring for the objects collected. The motive of pleasure by association, as Spencer would put it, may perhaps apply: for example, the girl who collects her theatre tickets and writes on the backs the name of the pantomime, film or ballet she saw. Boys' collections are more clearly related to a semi-scientific interest. They go hunting for curios and swap them with each other. Girls collect what is given to them or what comes automatically: miniature dolls, picture-postcards, bits of dress material and so on. They do not swap as frequently as boys.

Hall's co-workers discovered that the focus of children's interest in their collections changes: from the items themselves (as with young children) to their classification and the relations between the items upon which the classification is based, the explanation of their peculiarities (as at thirteen). This observation provides an interesting example of the way children spontaneously move from the concrete (the items) to the abstract (classification, relations, explanations).

Collecting is also associated with a child's sense of identity in that possessions can be stored and so become comforting reminders of his own personal and special existence. The small boy's miscellaneous collection, however extrinsically worthless, has for him an intrinsic and symbolic value. When his mother tries to persuade him to throw the objects away, he will have none of it. To lose these possessions is to lose a little of the 'I, me, my, mine.'

This motive is especially evident when collecting takes delinquent or pathological forms, and things are collected in order to restore a lost sense of identity: the child deprived of affection who steals, the miser, at odds with his fellow men, who stores up possessions, the patient in a mental hospital who does the same. Children's collections also have an educational value. To take a few examples, stamp collections, botanical specimens, pictures of countries and cities quite obviously have such value. No teacher compels his children to collect. Rather he makes suggestions here and there, and so tries to stimulate the children's natural tendency to do so. When they respond, he advises them on how to improve their collections, classify and relate items, and explain their significant features.

Television and children

Most of the children studied by Himmelweit and her co-workers (16) in their survey of children's television viewing habits were aged between ten and eleven. Supplementary studies were made of children aged eight to nine and of a smaller group aged thirteen to fourteen. Himmelweit reports that, in the early stages of the Primary School, children preferred puppets, nature, animal and how-to-make programmes; those between ten and eleven preferred crime thrillers, request programmes, family series, Westerns and hobbies programmes in that order. The first four of these are favourites also with pubescent children, only a few of whom view children's programmes. The viewing of the rest is almost wholly confined to adult programmes—crime, adventure, comedy.

A study by Olley (26), which includes data on the favourite television programmes of Sydney children between ten and fifteen, shows that the types of programmes preferred are much the same as those chosen by the English children of Himmelweit's study. Adventure and mystery drama takes first place, comedy second, children's programmes third (with Western and adventure stories preferred), stories of family life fourth. In both the English and Australian investigations the number of girls favouring stories of family life is twice the number of boys; sports programmes are favoured by twice as many boys as girls.

Pitty and Kinsella (28), in the last of nine studies of American children, report a similar pattern of viewing. Animal stories (*Rin-tin-tin, Lassie*), animated cartoons (*Disneyland, Mickey Mouse*) are favourites during the Infant and early Primary School grades, and lead on to an interest in adult crime (*Maverick*), thriller (*Shock Theatre*), adventure (*Zorro*), domestic comedy (*Father Knows Best*). The amount of viewing is greater among American than English children, especially at the younger ages: twenty compared with eleven to thirteen hours a week at the Primary stage, thirteen compared with eleven to thirteen at pubescence. In both countries less intelligent children view for longer than the more intelligent.

Himmelweit points out that there are wide variations in taste between individual children. Even the most popular programme was mentioned by no more than one-third of her sample. There were wide differencies in amount of viewing, which varies with the number and kinds of other interests. The wider a child's interests and the more active his outdoor life, the less time he has for watching television. As Himmelweit puts it, 'For all children, outdoor play, and in adolescence in particular social activities, proved television's strongest rival. For the average child viewing took second place to these' (16).[1]

In a changing society like our own, each generation of parents in dealing with their children has fresh problems to face. Some are the result of technological changes: radio during the twenties, cars and motor bicycles during the thirties and forties, television in the fifties. When television came, teachers and parents were alarmed over its possible effects. Many felt that it would interfere with children's school work and play. At first television was alleged not only to have these effects, but also to cause eye strain and nervousness.

Research has not confirmed these opinions. Television does not greatly interfere with school progress. Campbell's analysis of the effects of viewing in the early days of television in Sydney (7) shows that the time given to watching television was taken from other forms of amusement such as cinema, variety theatre, radio, skating, 'doing nothing in particular'. Himmelweit, however, concludes that the school work of children of high intelligence may be adversely affected by an addiction to television. She found that no more children among her viewers than among her non-viewers wore glasses or complained of eye headaches.

As to whether television makes children more prone to be violent or delinquent or to be passive or withdrawn, the general answer given is that it depends upon the child. The less intelligent, the more neurotic and those who have poor relations with their families are most likely to immerse themselves in television and to be adversely affected by it. The more stable, more intelligent and those with good home conditions are less likely to become television addicts and to be so affected. 'Television may contribute, but it is very unlikely to originate' (29).[2] Of course, with children whatever their intelligence and degree of stability, viewing, like the cinema or reading, can become a soporific during a time of

[1] page 12.   [2] page 168.

stress. A child, at odds with his companions, may seek refuge in television. In a case like this, addiction is a symptom, not a cause.

Himmelweit and her colleagues report data on the fears aroused in children by television programmes. She suggests that young children like suspense for the sake of the relief which follows. 'The point at which pleasurable suspense becomes fear depends both on the maturity and emotional balance of the child as well as on the nature of the programme' (16).[1] If children realize that it is fiction and that all will come out well in the end, they can watch without feeling threatened. It would appear that, when there is a clear division between the bad people (who are very bad) and the good people (who are very good), and when the fights are of the more fantastic type seen in Westerns, children show little fear. Real fear experienced when viewing a horror film, like *Frankenstein* or an Edgar Allan Poe story, may haunt an older Primary School child for many days.

American studies report that fighting at close quarters with knives is more alarming than gun-fights; a bitter verbal battle which suggests deep hatred between adults is more alarming even than knives. Where they identify themselves with characters—a young child with an animal, an older one with another child—the suffering to the animal or child either by fortuitous circumstances or by the deliberate cruelty of human beings, cause children great distress. As one child said, 'When I thought the dog (Lassie) was going to step in that old bear trap, I just about died!' (29).

Criticisms have been made of the quality of programmes, 'the narrow range of imported drama with emphasis on crime, violence, and dreary domestic situation comedy . . . the adult models presented on television are disparaging and destructive for girls and inadequate and one-sided in the view of life presented to boys' (40). American mothers, in making up their ideal programme, have suggested more opera, travelogues, great plays, good music, news, and science programmes (28). Himmelweit says that even when such programmes are available, children will not choose them of their own accord, and suggests that mothers should guide children's viewing, that teachers should examine programmes in advance and give children advice on what to view, and that the *Radio Times* and the *T. V. Times* should be

[1] page 207.

more specific in indicating which programmes are or are not suitable for children.

Himmelweit's general conclusion is that television is neither as black as it is sometimes painted, nor 'the enlightened harbinger of culture'; that, as a mass medium influencing children's lives, it is not 'spectacularly different from any other mass medium'.

It is not possible within a short space to deal fully with the problem of television and its impact on children. The research techniques are complex, and the findings often conflict. The reader is referred to the many observations and comments, made by Himmelweit (16), Schramm (29) and their associates, upon which this account has been mainly based, and to Sir Cyril Burt's critical note on Himmelweit's study (6). Professor Burt's note, though brief, covers Himmelweit's main findings. It is also a considered statement of the general problem of television and the child in modern society.

Sociability: children's own groups

A baby may satisfy his basic and play needs either in his mother's company and with her encouragement, or by himself as he looks around and finds out about the objects within his reach. For the toddler, his mother, the house and garden are enough. The social activities of Infant School children are uncoordinated and transitory, with shifts in interest and no stable leadership, activities which Isaacs (17) has aptly described as 'temporary alliances for the purposes of play'.

During the Primary School stage social life expands in a new bid to satisfy basic and play needs. The home, though still the secure base from which these social activities are pursued, is now too confining, and can satisfy these needs only in part. Children's desire for a sense of union with others now includes union with their companions. Their feelings of security lie partly within the certainty of their group membership; their adventuring is outside the home; their growing desire to know, understand, and create cannot be fully expressed without the company of their fellows; through their groups they seek to organize their lives independently of adults. Nevertheless, this independence is only partial. Particularly if he fails in some venture, or suffers some emotional stress, the child returns to the security of his home, and seeks the help, sympathy and affection of his parents.

For our purposes a children's group may formally be defined as a collection of three or more children, constituting its members, each of whom interacts with each and all the rest; consonant with the harmonious nature of the group, each member will have a sense of belonging, of being accepted by, and attracted to, each and all other members.

Experimental studies show that at the age of nine children's lives are for the most part centred on the family. In ranking their preferences for members of their family and friends, two-thirds of ninety-one nine-year-old children ranked parents first, brother or sister second, and a friend third (24). Experimental studies also show that, as children proceed through the Primary School, they become more influenced by their companions. Whereas nine-year-olds reversed 26 per cent of their original judgments of pairs of pictures in favour of the opposite judgment of a popular child, eleven- to twelve-year-olds reversed 48 per cent, a significantly higher number (15).

Young children are prone to tell tales one on the other. It may be that the gradual transition to group-mindedness is reflected in the decreasing frequency with which children tell tales as they move through the Primary School, and in their changing attitude towards those of their number who do. I know of no controlled study of children's tale-telling behaviour, but suggest that it proceeds somewhat as follows.

Infant School children are unabashed at telling tales. The indignation of a group of little Infant School girls—stiff, wide-eyed and righteous—coming to report the enormity of Johnny's offence and pointing fiercely towards 'him' is a problem with which an Infant School teacher often has to cope. But the young 'culprit' does not reproach the tale-bearers; he accepts the tale-bearing as part of the order of things. So, by and large, do eight-year-olds. By nine, distinct murmurs of disapproval express the children's changing attitudes. By the age of ten, and more certainly by eleven, the code is clear and decisive; you should not tell tales. It could be suggested that, as children become more closely identified with their own groups, they tell tales less and become more censorious of those who go on telling tales.

Primary School children's groups include the relatively informal play groups of younger children, aged about eight and nine. These groups tend to be formed spontaneously. The choice of companions is incidental to the accidents of school, class in school, street and family. Thereafter, the nature of Primary School children's groups gradually changes, so that by ten or eleven the groups become more structured, more distant from adults, its members chosen deliberately and for specific purposes. These factors allow for more complex, expansive and selected activities (22).

Children's groups: the purposes they serve

An individual's personality has already been described as 'always in a process of change or becoming', a generalization which is true of the developing personalities of Primary School children. As we have seen, children have now become capable of more complex processes of thinking and more complex physical movements. As a result of social experiences—at home, at school, and in the wider community—they have acquired new interests, new purposes, new goals, and more clear values, beliefs and opinions.

Children naturally seek to exercise their developing physical and mental capacities, to further their new interests and to fulfil their new purposes. This they can do most readily in groups, since these provide them with an opportunity to engage in activities more complex and varied than is possible when playing alone or with a single companion.

Children now want to express themselves without too much restraint: to assert, submit, co-operate, sympathize, to be frank and sometimes derogatory in their remarks. Playing always in the presence of, or with, adults would inevitably restrict them.

When a group of boys are playing, and one of them sees an adult approaching, he whispers a quick caution. Suddenly there is silence, which continues until the adult is out of sight. When a child gives vent to his outraged feelings about the foolishness of one of the members of his group as they play together and a teacher passes by, the boy is put out and feels disconcerted. This is an aspect of himself that he does not want his teacher to see.

The point of these two illustrations is that children's own groups provide them with a social environment of equals within which they can express themselves. True, there are some who are more skilled, some who lead and others who follow. But it is a group, all the members of which are equal before the law and within the wider society to which they belong; all are subject to similar restrictions and similar freedoms. A child can be 'himself' in his group (of course, a child can be 'himself' with his family, but not quite in the same way as he can be with his contemporaries).

The growth of personality entails progressive moves towards independence and self-determination. Children are still dependent on parents for their material welfare, and still psychologically dependent on them for comfort, especially at times of emotional stress. But as Isaacs (17) has emphasized, they are nevertheless able, through their group activities, to build and manage a small world of their own, within the security which membership of a group provides. Children, like adults, feel safer when they belong to a group than when they are alone. Furthermore, children's growing desire to organize and their acceptance of rules makes the world they create ordered and predictable. In this respect it is like the one provided by benign adults, but with the crucial difference that it is they themselves who do the organizing and rule-making. In that they provide security and organized activity, children's own groups are a bridge making easier their early moves toward independence and self-determination.

That children form relatively exclusive groups is also determined in part by the technical nature of our society. In a primitive society, children can 'potter around' quite usefully with adults as they till the fields, fish or build a hut or a boat. In this way there arises a close relationship between children and adults, based on the tasks required to keep the society going. As Margaret Mead has observed from her studies, children in primitive societies do not form tight, exclusive groups. Speaking of the children of the Manus tribe of New Guinea as they existed in the 1930's, she says (23):[1]

'They had no sort of formal organization, no clubs, no parties, no codes, no secret societies. If races were held, the older boys simply divided the children up into fairly equal teams, or selected pairs who were matched physically, but there was nothing permanent about these teams, no continuous rivalry between the children. Leadership there was, but only the spontaneous, free sort due to intelligence and initiative. Very loose age-groups, never exclusive, never permanent, tended to form about special activities, as a fishing trip a little afield of the village for part of an afternoon.'

[1] page 122.

By contrast, ours is a highly technological society, and children cannot take a real part in producing its predominantly machine-made products. That this is so is reflected in changes that have taken place even within the last three or so decades. On the farm, for example, the horse which a boy could feed, harness and lead through the fields has been replaced by machinery. For a city boy, the baker and the milkman, who used to make their rounds with horse and cart, have lost their appeal. They now use motor vans. Moreover, the law, mindful of the extent to which children can be exploited, rightly imposes conditions on their working.

Consequently, unlike the Manus children, our children are remote from the productive process; satisfaction of their desire to be useful is less certain, and the gap between play and work is wide. And so there arises a separation between children and youths who are virtually unproductive, on the one hand, and productive adults, on the other.

Children's groups: maintaining their exclusiveness

Children have various simple devices for maintaining the isolation and exclusiveness of their groups. They surreptitiously acquire boxes and old sacking in order to make 'hide-outs', dens which are theirs and in which they can organize existence as they please. Sometimes they devise secret signs and passwords. By these means they are able to communicate with each other without anyone else knowing what is going on.

In the security of their groups, aided by discussion amongst themselves, they weigh up the strengths and weaknesses of adults, particularly those in authority over them. They assess adults' reactions and moods, and discuss their possible sources. They acquire skill at this weighing up, and do it with some insight. The nicknames children of ten or eleven will devise are often most apt. By becoming objective about adults, children who have reached the Primary stage no longer look upon adults as omnipotent and omniscient.

Such critical exchanges are healthy enough. They help to make grown-ups seem fallible in children's eyes, thus reducing the pressure of the authority which adults exert, and loosening the dependence created by uncritical adoration or fear. But though critical, children at the Primary stage, unlike thirteen-year-olds, are not antipathetic towards them.

Yet, in seeking independence of adults and family, children find a new dependence—on their fellows. As a child grows older, he wants more and more to think, act and feel like the members of his group; his feelings of self-esteem become progressively more dependent upon the esteem in which he is held by his companions and upon their acceptance of him (38). It is understandable, then, that children are distressed when they are 'sent to Coventry' or made the scapegoat of their group, and that they should fear situations which may lead to these gestures of disapproval, as, for example, when they are put 'on the spot' by a teacher or any adult with authority, to 'tell' on a companion. As Isaacs puts it (17), 'He is much more sensitive now to the praise or contempt of his chums. Giving away their secrets or becoming a "sneak-thief" will cause him more pangs of shame than defying a teacher—or even telling him a lie.'[1]

Children seek adventure

Children now look for new experiences outside the home. Here the reader is referred back to the discussion of children's need to know and to adventure (Chapter 8), which concluded with the observation that children learn through their adventurous activities and that, ideally at least, learning should be an adventurous activity for them. Obviously, learning and adventuring are part of the process of emancipation. The more a child knows and the more he can do for himself, the less dependent he is on adults. He does not have to wait for a busy parent to help him, he can mend a puncture, blow up his football, and do a hundred other jobs for himself.

The relation between children's growing independence and their adventurous pursuits is perhaps suggested by the stories which appeal to children at different ages. For example, this is typical of the kind of theme which appeals to Infant School children. Here is a family of bunnies—mother bunny and father bunny and six little bunnies. One of the little bunnies is restless and thinks he would like to go into the outside world to see what it is like. When his mother is not looking, he bounces off. For a time every-

[1] page 98.

thing is exciting, and the bunny opens his eyes wide at all the things he sees. When he comes to a garden full of lettuces, he settles down to a fine meal. But suddenly along comes a huge dog and the terrified bunny runs away with the dog after him. He manages to hide amongst a pile of logs. There he waits, trembling, until father bunny comes along and takes him home where mother has been anxiously waiting. She is so relieved to see them that she even forgets to scold. The little bunny vows to himself that he will never, never leave home again.

Contrast this story with a type commonly enjoyed by Primary School children. A group of boys and girls are on holiday at the seaside. One afternoon they take a boat and go to explore an island about a mile off shore. They find that the island is the hide-out of thieves (or smugglers, or kidnappers). After a series of adventures, the children help to capture the thieves and re-trieve the booty or the victim. They return home in triumph to tell their parents all about it. The spirit of this age-group has been captured by the many writers whose stories contain a major theme of adventure and triumphant return.

If Infant and Primary School children are prepared to hear these themes and their many variations over and over again, then such themes must have an appeal for them. It would seem that whereas Infant children have one eye on the outside world but are rather fearful about venturing too far, Primary School children, with the support of their group, happily embrace adventurous activities away from home.

The society of children

The characteristics so far described combine to produce a society of children with a pattern of its own, a society that is closed to adults and not quite the same as that of pre-school or of pubescent children. It is one which has its own rituals and ceremonials, its peculiar kind of humour, its peculiar kind of toughness. In that many of the games played at eight, nine and ten have been played by children throughout the ages, this society is timeless and in some senses independent of the larger society of which it forms a part. It is known that many of these games—fivestones, for example—were played by children in ancient Greece and Rome, and a close study of the picture by Bruegel (c. 1520–69) 'Children's

Games'[1] will show that many of the games depicted there are played by children today. Bruegel's picture catches the spirit of this society of children—active and busy playing at hopscotch, marbles, hide-and-seek, dodge-ball, knuckle bones, tops, hoops and so on.

This is a world of ritualistic rhymes ('Lady-bird, lady-bird, fly away home', 'Rain, rain, go away', 'Eeny, meeny, miney, mo') and ritualistic chants with their ceremonials ('London Bridge', 'The farmer in his dell').

Adults do not teach children these games, rhymes, and chants. The children teach each other, and the rituals and ceremonials connected with each are handed down from one generation to another. If a teacher, during a play break, suddenly joins a group of boys who are playing marbles and plays with them, or if he 'jumps in' and, as the rope turns, skips with a group of girls, the children are highly amused. He is entering a world that is not really his, and the children laugh at the incongruity of his action. But if the teacher plays cricket with a group of boys of, say, eleven or twelve, the children accept it. Here adult and children meet in an activity that is congruent to both.

It is a world, too, of tricks, riddles, puzzles and jokes. Conjuring tricks fascinate these children. Riddles are tried out on adults and on other children. 'When is a door not a door?' 'Why did the chicken cross the road?' Their favourite humour is the play on words, the 'caught you' answer. Wolfenstein (37) has discussed the possible psychological features of children's humour and given many examples of the kinds of humour they enjoy.

It is a world of magic and superstitious observances—to count the number of palings in a fence, not to step on the cracks in the pavement, to touch every lamp-post passed. Sometimes these ceremonials are played as games, and so a group of children may decide to touch all lamp-posts, or not to step on a crack all the way to school. If a child is anxious about going to school for some reason, he may compulsively carry out one or more of these rituals all alone. He is anxious and dreads the imagined result of not following the exact procedure. But when these obsessional

---

[1] Grossmann (12), whose book contains a reproduction of the painting and four reproductions of details from it, states in his commentary that eighty games have been counted and that a list of these is given by Gluck (11).

activities are pursued as a group, the element of dread disappears and the procedures become a light-hearted game.

This society of children can be a tough one at times. The physical peculiarities or idiosyncrasies of individual children are often seized upon, are teasingly pointed out, or become the source of accurate (and sometimes cruel) nicknames. Criticism is personal and forthright: 'If I had a face like yours, I'd join the zoo.' The less competent are not spared confirmation of their incompetence. They are chosen last when two sides are picked to play a game, and the obvious reluctance to have the incompetent one in the team is emphasized by some such disparaging remark as, 'Come on. I suppose we've got to have you.' The boy who unwittingly picks up the ball in the middle of a soccer game is subjected to a barrage of abusive comments. It is an exacting society, for the child must know the 'right' way to do things and must do them in that way. If he does not, he may be excluded from the group or feel the kind of despair that the primitive man feels when he misses a vital step in the tribal dance.

It is interesting to speculate upon the reasons for these rituals, ceremonials and obsessions. The games, the rhymes, the riddles and the tricks demand considerable dexterity. There are two main criteria of competence. One is accuracy, but the other is the speed with which the game is played, the rhyme chanted and the answer given. Often the game, as in dodge-ball, skipping or hopscotch, is speeded up; and so may be the pace at which the rhyme is chanted or an answer demanded. The measure of one's dexterity then becomes accuracy with speed. The one who makes a mistake or who is last is 'out'. As Stone and Church (30)[1] have pointed out, mastering of the skills demanded by all these activities gives children a sense of achievement, of being able to cope with the world of sight, sound, thought and movement. Probably the fascination of the professional conjuror for children of this age is in the capacity to manipulate the universe of balls, sticks, boxes and so on which he displays, a capacity revealed in the speed and accuracy of his performance.

But despite the obvious exuberance of children and the enjoyment they get from their group activities, there are moments of individual anxiety. These may arise because of a child's growing self-awareness, his desire to be competent in many

[1] Chapter 8.

skills, to keep his place in the group, to obey his parents and to do well at school. The obsessional ceremonials performed individually help to allay these anxieties, for at heart the child believes in his magic and obtains reassurance from it.

Boys and girls play separately

Sex gives rise both to physiological and social differences. Most societies prescribe the kinds of behaviour appropriate to men and women; and adults daily influence their children to behave as a boy or a girl 'should' (2). Adults will say, 'Boy's don't cry' 'Boys should stand up for themselves', 'Girls don't fight', 'Girls should not be rough and run wild.' They will give children toys appropriate to their sex. For a boy scientific and technical toys like engines, cars, lorries, football and cricket gear; for a girl domestic toys—dolls, dolls' houses, prams, dresses, a miniature sewing machine.

One American study (21) shows that middle-class mothers do not make such clear distinctions as working-class mothers between the behaviour and character appropriate for boys and girls. Nevertheless, in general, the 400 mothers who were questioned, both middle- and working-class, wanted their ten- and eleven-year-old boys to be dependable and ambitious, and to do well at school. They wanted their girls of the same ages to be well-behaved, neat in appearance and popular with their friends.

Research indicates that boys in particular are aware of how the behaviour expected of them differs from that expected of girls (25). Forty-one eight- to eleven-year-old boys gave these examples, among others, of the behaviour respectively allowed to, tolerated in, and expected of boys: to be outside more than girls, to be noisy and get into more trouble, not to be 'softies' and not to get behind in school. On the other hand, they thought that for girls things were different. Girls could be afraid and cry when they were hurt, they need not be good at spelling or arithmetic, should play quiet games and not be rough (13).

When children are observed at play or are asked about their favourite games and toys, it is generally found that boys and girls play the types of games and choose the types of toys appropriate to each (3, 4, 14). Girls oscillate in their choices, sometimes choosing boys' games and toys rather than girls'. Boys are more decisive. There is no doubt in their minds as to what kind of games and toys are appropriate for them and what kind are appropriate for girls. Hartley and Hardesty (14) suggest that one reason why boys are aware of the roles of girls is because they want to avoid such roles so as not to engage in activities which might risk their being called 'cissies'.

By the middle and late Primary School stage, boys and girls accept these differences in attitude and behaviour. This is reflected (a) in their different interests: for ten-year-old boys, sports, gross motor skills, mechanics, science; for girls, sewing, cooking, music, art, and (b) in their choice of friends: boys give as their favourite the 'real boy', one who is restless, quarrelsome, bossy, never shy, takes chances, and is good at sport. Their ideal is competent in athletics, daring, and a good leader. Girls give as their favourite the girl who is quiet, popular, full of fun, does not show off, is friendly, good-looking, a good sport, not bossy. Their ideal girl is congenial, well-behaved, good-humoured, composed, non-aggressive (33, 34, 35).

Boys and girls tend now to go their separate ways, but the separation takes place without any marked antagonism between them. Boys may make disparaging remarks about girls and their activities and vice versa; but these remarks are without the antagonistic 'bite' which may characterize those of older boys and girls about each other. A distinction, too, may be made between the play of the two groups. The play of boys tends to become more 'masculine'—that is, boys tend to be analytical, to pull things to pieces to see what they consist of, or to see how they work. They are more assertive, and more aggressive in their approach to people and objects. This masculine activity takes varying forms— mad careering about in the playground, wrestling and rolling together on the floor, cowboys and Indians, camping, the living out of an adventure story they have read or a film they have seen.

The play of girls, on the other hand, tends to be 'feminine'— towards synthesis, understanding, construction—and is related to family and school, rhythmical and dramatic activities. Girls become especially adept at games of skill, as we see when we watch the variations girls will introduce into their games of skipping, hopscotch, swinging. They delight in decorating and designing, in making things out of everyday objects such as clothes pegs, pipe-cleaners and cotton reels. Insofar as they are more constructive and less playfully 'puppy-like' in their activities, they show a greater maturity than boys, particularly by about ten.

In speaking of sexual development, Kinsey (19[1], 20[2]) has pointed out that during these years sensations can arise from diverse forms of bodily stimulation (fast movement, physical punishment, genital friction), from diverse emotional experiences (excitement, anger, fear), as well as from more specifically sexual situations (seeing boy/girl/self naked). Perhaps a boy and girl of nine or ten may be together and both be roused to an ecstatic mood by other than a sexual stimulus (excitement, movement), and this may lead them suddenly and impulsively to caress each others' bodies. How they will react will depend upon the attitudes they have already acquired, so that the strangeness and depth of their experience will affect them in either a pleasurable or a confused and guilty way.

If adults get to know about these things, it is best that they do not bring to them the emotional overtones which so many of us attach to such activities. Because of these overtones, parents and teachers may become harsh and unsympathetic and feel that it is their duty to punish, or at least to admonish very severely.

It is well to remember that children are very busy at this stage with all the activities we have described and that for most of them such sexual diversions are rare and incidental; so much so that Freud spoke of this as the 'latency' stage because he considered that, during these years, sexual activity was sublimated to the acquisition of knowledge and the adventuring sociability described in these pages.

From the information obtained from his subjects, Kinsey (19)[3] concludes: (a) that if children are 'caught in the act' by adults, and are reprimanded or punished, this can be a traumatic experience which may deter later sexual adjustment; (b) that if children are not 'caught in the act' (or if they are caught, their parents treat the whole matter in a neutral way), the experience does no damage to later sexual adjustment.

Eight, nine, ten and eleven

Obviously most children who are just eight years old behave differently from most children of eleven years eleven months. To

[1] page 164.   [2] page 106.   [3] page 115.

cater for such differences four phases of development within the Primary School group will be described. Researches (9, 10) tend to show that these phases correspond roughly with the chronological ages eight, nine, ten and eleven years. We will, therefore, speak of the eight, nine, ten or eleven-year-old instead of the first, second, third or fourth phase. However, for any individual child, a phase and a chronological age may not coincide in quite this way. Indeed, regarding the generalizations being made about children in these five current chapters (Chapters 12–17), the reader must remember the maxim that any statement about a group always admits of individual exception.[1]

Imagine a young married woman, keen that the home she is about to make should be as beautiful as possible, who finds herself suddenly in the midst of an ideal homes exhibition; or imagine a young man, whose main enthusiasm is cars, finding himself in an international motor show. The chances are that at first both will be so excited by all they see that they will not know where to start and will dodge from one exhibit to another, briefly inspecting each, but making no intensive study of any one.

There is a sense in which the eight-year-olds (first phase) resemble people in such situations. It is as if they have suddenly discovered how fascinating the world outside home and school is; and they are so amazed by the multitude of things to see, do, and learn that they cannot decide quite where to start.

The eight-year-olds tend to flit from one activity to another and from one topic to another. They seem as if they are always poised to do and think something other than what they are doing and thinking now. An eight-year-old may be completely absorbed in some solitary pursuit when in comes a companion with an idea and off they both run. To the question, 'Where is he?' the answer is usually, 'Why, he was here only a minute ago!' It is appropriate to say of them that they are 'always on the dart' and that their darting only ceases during sleep, sleep which is usually immediate and very deep. For this, mothers are most grateful.

The range of their interests is very wide and stretches, as we have already indicated, from the surface of the earth to the moon and stars, and from their own particular spot on the earth's surface to any place where there are people or over which an aeroplane

[1] See note, page 227.

can fly. In short, there is little about their environment which does not interest them; but it is, of course, a superficial interest, like the housewife's first quick inspection of the ideal homes exhibits. Specialization of interest comes later.

Eight-year-olds do not usually persevere at any one task. This inability to apply themselves for long to any one thing is not so much a fault as an understandable stage through which children go, and is consonant with their wide range of interests. Yet despite this, children certainly make great progress socially, emotionally, and in creative and academic skills during the eight to nine period. This progress can be seen when we contrast the more co-operative play, the more controlled movements (shown not only in more skilled physical activity but also in greater dexterity in the finer movements required for writing and figuring), the more skilled drawings and paintings of the just nines with those of the just eights.

Ethically the eight-year-olds are more stable. They know when they have done wrong and are not so subject to the fits of kleptomania of the six- or seven-year-olds. However, they still find it difficult to accept blame and to control their feelings of aggression. They may blame another for what they have done themselves, and take it out on another child when they feel 'just plain mad' at a parent or teacher. An eight-year-old may impulsively slap a younger brother who interferes with what he is doing, and he generally makes things uncomfortable for the younger brother when his mother has decided that he *must* take care of him.

Psychological growth is probably even more rapid and more consistent between the ages nine and ten (second phase). It is as if children of nine know where they are going and are determined to get there. Growth at this stage contrasts with the patchy unevenness of growth between six and seven.

The eight-year-old was compared with a young man who has been set down amidst exciting automobiles at an exhibition. As the young man stands there amazed and bemused, not knowing what to look at first, he sees a group of friends, and off he goes to join them. His finding of this group of friends is opportune because his confusion is dispelled, and he is able to explore the environment in which he finds himself, guided by his friends and with the added zest and security which congenial companions provide.

This seems to be precisely what the nine-year-old does.

Executive ability develops. Children of nine want to run many of their own affairs, and they do not want any interference from adults. As has been mentioned, they have their secret hide-outs and they will prepare plans for a day's outing, organize games and draw up a set of rules for their group, a constitution to which all members must adhere. Individually, children show a need to improve their performance in favourite skills: for instance, a child entirely on his own initiative may practise a stroke in cricket, a kick at football, or even mechanical arithmetic or a page of handwriting. In this ability to persevere at favourite tasks, nine-year-olds are greatly superior to eight-year-olds.

Eight-year-olds have been described as 'always on the dart'. Of the nine-year-olds it can more truly be said that they are 'always on the move', implying that there is much activity and much rapid movement but that these are more controlled.

For boys in our society the concept 'being a good sport', implying fair play and fair dealing, becomes the dominating ethical ideal. A nine-year-old may try to avoid punishment when he can; but, if he knows he deserves it, he will accept it without having to take it out on another child. If he is sent to bed, however, he may feel unjustly treated and very sorry for himself, and indulge in a fantasy of running away from home because 'then they will be sorry for what they've done'.

Perhaps we can sum up this second phase by saying that, insofar as children now stand midway within 'the society of children' (aged seven to eleven), they epitomize the enthusiasms, the quickness of thought and action, the ritualistic ceremonials, the humour and the toughness of this 'society' .

Ten-year-olds (third phase) are at a stage of transition between the earlier instability of the eights and the excitement of the nines on the one hand, and the rebellious boisterousness of the elevens and twelves on the other. As such, they tend to be without the emotional excesses of the later period. At school they work well and, given reasonable conditions and an understanding teacher, find school very pleasant. They are more consistently persevering and show a more controlled ability to run their own affairs than even the nine-year-olds, and they have not yet developed the tendency towards a 'don't care' attitude and a loss of enthusiasm which can infect twelve-year-olds. Gesell, summing up, says of this period that it is 'a golden age of developmental equipoise' (10).[1]

However, it is well to remember that individual differences in development become evident by this time. In a group of, say, forty ten-year-olds, some may be nearer nine in social and emotional development, some nearer eleven. Teachers and parents need to be on the watch for these individual differences.

To return once more to the analogy of the car enthusiast, it would seem that he has done a good deal of searching and exploring with his group of friends. Now the extreme excitement has gone; he begins to slow up and to inspect individual items more closely and in a more leisurely way. This is analogous to the behaviour of the ten-year-old. He, too, slows up and there is a relatively relaxed approach to existence which may be contrasted with the unstable darting of the eights and the zeal and intensity of the nines.

This does not mean that ten-year-olds are not physically active. They enjoy physical activity, respond to the rhythmical work of the physical education lesson, enjoy organized games, and appreciate the control imposed by a teacher. They may even invite an adult to referee one of their games. However, their prevailing stability does not preclude occasional emotional outbursts of anger or enthusiasm. Children of this age are obviously less dependent on their parents, but sometimes the ten-year-old will demonstrate with a quick hug a burst of affection for them. This may express a sudden feeling of tenderness or acute anxiety that suddenly overcomes him. A very young child will experience a similar feeling, but he will be more demonstrative and will rush and bury himself in his mother's skirts.

Fears and anxieties are more objective now. By the age of ten, the child can laugh at former fears, such as fear of an old woman (as at six), of thunder and lightning (as at seven), of the shadows on the wall (as at eight) and of burglars (as at nine). But he now fears situations that are real possibilities and less the products of his imagination—failure in school examinations, for example, or not being chosen for the school team. He also fears situations in which there is a danger of severe loss of self-esteem.

Differences between boys and girls are now greater. Boys tend towards more boisterous activities and 'supermanism'; they

[1] page 37.

wrestle and fight; they form secret societies with initiation ceremonies. Girls tend towards more 'back-yard' activities such as
skipping and jumping in groups, hopscotch, and tennis against the
wall. Boys are inordinately shy of girls and, perhaps because of
this, they are sometimes rough with them. They may interfere
with their play, pulling their ropes or spoiling their hopscotch.
The girls defend themselves, but the squabble is soon over, and
the boys are off again, leaving them to resume their activities in
peace. Mixed parties are no longer a success, for boys are uncomfortable in the presence of girls, and become noisy and obstreperous in their attempt to hide their confusion.

Eleven-year-olds are difficult to place because, as a group, they
are in between. This is so for physiological, psychological and
educational reasons. Physiologically most eleven-year-old boys
are only on the threshold of pubescence, since no more than about
25 per cent of them have begun the growth spurt. Researches
indicate clearly that girls are more advanced: for more than 50 per
cent of them changes begin to occur before twelve. But for boys
and girls, marked individual differences make grouping according
to age hazardous. Thus the growth spurt which begins now in the
few early maturers will not begin for the few late maturers until
another two years have passed. On the one hand, because of the
breadth of their activities and interests, their enthusiasms and
emotional impulsiveness, eleven-year-olds (fourth phase) bring
to mind the nine-year-olds. On the other hand, because they show
more antipathy towards adults and because the antipathy between
boys and girls is very marked at eleven, they bring to mind the
twelve-year-olds. Educationally, most children are just twelve
when they enter Secondary Schools, although some are under
twelve.

I have placed the elevens here rather than with pubescent children, with the above precautions in mind.

Eleven (fourth phase) may be described as a period of continued and even accelerated search for knowledge, adventure and
social experience. Children's curiosity extends to what adults are
talking about and what they are doing. An eleven-year-old will
interject in the middle of a conversation between adults, or he will
burst into the room demanding to know what people are talking
about. His interference is often annoying, but it is understandable,
since it suggests the beginnings of what will become a more

serious interest in the world of adult activities. When he inspects what an adult is doing, he is not merely being a nuisance: he wants to *know* what is going on and try his hand at the job.

The marvels of science become a frequent topic of conversation. It is interesting to observe that often when conversation turns to scientific achievement, old people tend immediately to speak of the first aeroplane, they saw, of the first motor car that came to their village. The conversation moves from the present to the past. Young people, on the other hand, will move quickly from the present to the future, to the wonders which science has yet to make possible.

Group activities tend to be more thoroughly planned and executed. The hide-out is more elaborate and may even have locks and keys, while the activities within it are organized, whether they be concerned with eating, playing cards, or discussion. Precise and organized devices for consolidating the group are more prevalent. Groups have names—the 'Demons', the 'Wolf Pack' or the 'High Street gang'. They have secret signs and special handshakes; they have group symbols—a badge, a flag, a token. Not only may a constitution be drawn up, but weekly dues may also be demanded, with a treasurer to keep accounts. There is much concentration when the treasurer outlines the financial position and decides how much money will be spent. More primitively, groups may have initiation ceremonies which demand the performance of an act of daring or the ability to withstand pain or endure ridicule.

Girls, too, like outdoor activity, and may build a den or a house in the trees. But they, unlike boys, are content to have their den in a garden shed quite near home. A group of boys will return from an adventure, and peer through the door and windows or otherwise intrude on girls' privacy. They will make fun of the girls who, like indignant hens, will become ruffled and try to 'shoo' them away. Girls are generally more domestic. They have acquired some skill in sewing and will engage in an advanced stage of doll play by sewing dresses and sometimes dressing the dolls in national costumes. A girl may even now be proud of the variety and number of dolls she has accumulated, and have them arranged in a row in her bedroom. This is the final stage before dolls are given up for ever.

Girls will also play games in a more adult and 'real 'way. For

example, a girl may form a 'library' of all the books she can collect, making and issuing cards systematically. She may even
play shop, but with a more realistic basis—real scales and weights,
real goods and real money. Girls will dress up, but the dressing up
goes beyond mere identification and is now not an end in itself
but a means of dramatic expression, of depicting an historical
occasion. It may involve putting on a play written by one of
their number or by a slightly older girl.

With all these activities goes an intensity, and the extremes
include emotional experiences of joy, enthusiasm, excitement
and also anger. In short, the feelings children experience towards
what appeals and what repels are intense and are expressed
in their play in whoops of joy, loud laughter, aggressive behaviour,
argumentativeness and contempt for the child who bungles.

Home appears on the surface to be more and more incidental
to existence. It is a place where the eleven-year-old sleeps, eats,
leaves things around, and occasionally gives vent to his anger.
When a parent asks him to do a chore, his intensity, zeal and
enthusiasm disappear and a pained inertia takes their place. It is
not much use moralizing on these occasions. One can offer him a
choice of a number of chores so that at least *what* he does is of his
own choosing. Probably the best way to get a job done is to catch
him at a time when he wants something put right that is crucially
important to him. For example, he wants you to mend his torn
football jersey or, in the case of a girl, to fix the collar of the blouse
she is making. You can then say, 'I will do this while you mow
the lawn (or wash up).' Here is a practical situation in which
the justice of the position is clear. Children understand this and
will do the lawn or the washing up efficiently and willingly even
though with no undue enthusiasm.

They do not scuffle or wrestle on the floor as much as they
did when they were nine, but they still push and grab in school
lines. And the individual eleven-year-old *will* have his joke, such
as pulling a book away from the arm of the fellow beside him;
taking the tail of the coat of the boy in front and using it as a
lever to heave himself ahead while walking into school; removing
pen, pencil, or book during the short absence of the owner. For
the teacher and parent these are 'irritating habits' and older
adolescents, who are often the victims of these jokes, regard them
disdainfully as indicating the childishness of 'kids'.

Boys are noisy and loud, and will yell at each other during group activities. A puzzled adult, hearing the din, may ask quite politely, 'Do you *have* to shout like that?' The boys may be at a loss for an answer to this question, but, if they only realized it, the correct one is very simply, 'Yes!'

At home, they could be called 'quarrelsome'; their impulsiveness, shown in their lack of control over their feelings, and their restiveness, make them impatient, quarrelsome and 'nasty' to younger brothers or sisters. They can, too, be annoyingly argumentative with their parents and often have fits of 'dramatic rudeness'.

We have to be careful not to see all this in the negative sense only; for there are positives within the apparent negatives of the eleven-year-olds. They are restlessly active, but this indicates self-motivation; their questioning is an active urge to know; their impatience has a positive quality in that they have places to go to and things to do, and so they wish not to be interfered with; their jokes are part of a developing sense of humour. Even their argumentativeness is an attempted assertion of personality. Eleven sets the stage for pubescence, and activities may be seen as a final fling into indiscriminate expansiveness before the specialization of interests, which will have its beginning during pubescence and which progresses to the vocational specialization of late adolescence.

The self-motivation of Primary School children means that there is much they can do on their own, and the parents' task is to provide their children with the materials, to interfere as little as possible, and not to demand too much in terms of shopping and household chores. This does not mean that Primary School children should be excused from all duties, but that the parent, while getting them to help in the house, should try to estimate the importance to the child of the activity of which he is temporarily being deprived. If it is obviously tremendously important, then he should be excused. Similarly, the teacher who keeps in a child, or a group of children, after school should realize that this is a punishment the severity of which depends on factors outside the teacher's control. These he should try to assess. Sometimes to be kept in is severe punishment; sometimes it does not mean very much. But, because children are so active, being kept in after school is almost always hard for them.

The education of Primary School children

Insofar as Primary School children are enthusiastic, and insofar as much of their activity is directed by and amongst themselves, they do much of their growing and learning independently of adults. But to stress children's learning through group play, as has been done so far in this chapter, may give a false impression, since we may be led to underestimate the work of the school. A society like ours could not function at its high technical level without the work of the schools in preparing children for it.

Two of the major purposes of the Primary School are to make children literate and to imbue them with a sense of what is real and useful, so that they become more competent to deal with practical problems. Ability to read, write and compute is essential. Without it a child would be seriously handicapped, and his self-esteem would become precarious. Imagine how humiliated a backward reader feels if he has to ask a friend the meaning of a caption beneath a picture or a public notice. As Erikson (8) has put it, a child has now reached a stage at which he says in effect, 'I am what I learn'.[1]

Children's education is decided not only by the nature of our society and the skills it demands, but also by the nature of the children themselves. As we have seen, physically, children are active, quick and dexterous; their thinking is in terms of the concrete. Their interests—in the physical and in what works and is useful—accord with these physical and mental characteristics.

Much of what goes on in today's schools may appear to the layman 'mere play'. In actual fact, school work is, and must be, more organized and formal than a child's solitary or group play. The confusion of the layman probably arises from the fact that he cannot see that the Primary School teacher's task is to approach the abstract by means of the concrete, and to seize on the concrete to illustrate abstract principles. To do this, school work has to be related to children's everyday experience: for example, everyday words like 'post office', 'bus stop', 'danger', and everyday require-ments— to receive and give change, to weigh, to measure, and to compute. Reciting the multiplication tables is not just rote learning; it is a quick way of adding, illustrated by the number of squares on a draught board or a sheet of stamps. Yards, feet and

[1] page 84.

inches are not abstract measures, but standardized derivations from body movements and measurements—of arms, feet, fingers. The teacher takes advantage of the accidental and the contemporary to illustrate an abstract principle—the finding of a cast-off snake skin in the school garden (a rare occurrence but one I myself experienced), a crane at work near the school, the displacement of water by a stone dropped into the school aquarium, the flight of an astronaut. There are also the stories of the chance discoveries of great scientists, for example, Archimedes, Galileo and Newton. These are apocryphal perhaps, but they illustrate the principle of a curiosity ever on the alert.

During early years, much of children's activity consists of the learning of simple skills—lifting, packing, pouring, fitting. In the early school years simple academic skills are learned—reading, writing and figuring. Children obtain satisfaction from this learning as an end in itself. But as they grow older, although they recognize that there are many new skills to be mastered, they also desire to put to practical use the skills they have already learned. This practical work serves the double purpose of extending their knowledge and experience and of making them more proficient in the skills they have learned. At ten and eleven the desire to *apply* their knowledge and skills is more clearly seen. This shows itself in their own activities. To take an example from this chapter: at eleven, dressing up is not satisfying in itself, as it was at four, but is only satisfying as part of a larger whole, a dramatic production. The same applies to work in the classroom, more and more of which becomes an application of skills already mastered as well as the learning of new skills. A well-chosen project can give children an opportunity to apply known skills in a more realistic way than can further examples from the text-book and more formal exercises. It enables them also to satisfy their extensive interests and co-operate with others.

With eight-year-olds a teacher can tap a wide range of interests within such subjects as social studies, English composition and free drawing. The enthusiasm of nine-year-old children is greater than their executive ability, and they often become discouraged. The school can provide a planned environment from which they can profit, one that is extended beyond the solely academic to include art, crafts and hobby sessions. It is an environment in which children are encouraged to express themselves in drama, mime, poetry, story writing and music. By means of these children retain a sense of make believe.

Primary School children can take a good deal of drill—tables, mechanical arithmetic, spelling—but the teacher should take care not to capitalize too much on this and so to neglect meaning. Nor should he be deceived into believing that his children's ability to repeat a passage word perfect must mean that they 'know' it. Understanding aids learning by heart; but, in turn, learning by heart may well aid understanding. For, when a passage of prose or poetry is known by heart, one may return to it in order to ponder the knowledge or wisdoms it contains.

Interest in the technical and scientific should be encouraged; nor should it be thought that such lessons are for boys only. Investigations (e.g. 32) have shown that girls can become as interested in solving technical problems and as capable of doing so as boys. History and geography offer many opportunities for children's desire to make things—models of mediaeval villages, native implements.

The school class is not a social group in the way that children's own groups are. The classroom is a place where children share social experiences planned as a means towards their academic growth and development. Physical education is not just play. It comprises a series of bodily activities and of organized games planned as a means towards children's physical growth.

The preferences children show for school subjects accord with what has been said about their desire to make things, to express themselves, to know their environment. Primary School boys choose handwork, drawing, nature-study, singing, geography; girls choose singing, dancing, drawing, nature-study (39). Handwork and drawing are more than just subjects in themselves; they are vehicles for teaching other subjects.

In order that these children may be educated in a way that is consonant with their own needs and those of society, Primary Schools should have small classes, adequate equipment and buildings. Educationists must, therefore, always be alive to these requirements, and always strive to persuade a society, at present all too reluctant to provide them, that it is important to do so.

REFERENCES

1   Annett, M. 'The classification of instances of four common class concepts by children and adults.' *British Journal of Educational Psychology*, 1959, **29**, pp. 223–36.

2   Barry, H. A., *et al.* 'A cross cultural survey of some sex differences in socialization.' *Journal of Abnormal and Social Psychology*, 1957, **55**, pp. 327–32.

3   Brown, D. G. 'Masculinity – feminity development in children.' *Journal of Consulting Psychology*, 1957, **21**, pp. 197–202.

4   Brown, D. G. 'Sex-role development in a changing culture.' *Psychological Bulletin*, 1958, **55**, pp. 232–42.

5   Burt, C. 'The differentiation of intellectual ability.' *British Journal of Educational Psychology*, 1954, **24**, pp. 76–90.

6   Burt, C. Critical notice; 'Himmelweit *et al.*, Television and the child.' *British Journal of Educational Psychology*, 1959, **29**, pp. 173–5.

7   Campbell, W. J. *Television and the Australian Adolescent.* Angus and Robertson, Sydney, 1962.

8   Erikson, E. 'Identity and the life cycle.' *Psychological Issues*, 1959, **1**, pp. 50–171.

9   Gesell, A., Ilg, F. L. *Child Development:* 2 'The child from five to ten.' Harper, New York, 1949.

10 Gesell, A., Ilg, F. L., Ames, L. B. *Youth: the Years from Ten to Sixteen.* Harper, New York, 1956.

11 Gluck, L. *The Large Bruegel Book.* Schroll, Vienna, 1953.

12 Grossman, F. *Bruegel.* Phaidon Press, London, 1955.

13 Hartley, R. E. 'Sex-role pressures and the socialization of the male child.' *Psychological Reports*, 1959, pp. 457–68.

14 Hartley, R. E., Hardesty, F. P. 'Children's perception of sex roles in childhood.' *Journal of Genetic Psychology*, 1964, **105**, pp. 43–51.

15 Harvey, O. J., Rutherford, J. 'Status in the informal group: influencibility at differing age levels.' *Child Development*, 1960, **31**, pp. 377–85.

16 Himmelweit, H. T., Oppenheim, A. N., Vince, P. *Television and the Child.* Oxford University Press, London, 1958.

17 Isaacs, S. *The Children we Teach.* University of London Press, London, 1932.

18 Jones, H. E. 'The development of physical abilities.' *In Adolescence, 43rd Year-book of the National Society for the Study of Education.* University of Chicago Press, Chicago, 1944. Part 1, pp. 100–22.

19 Kinsey, A. C., Pomeroy, W. B., Martin, C. E. *Sexual Behaviour in the Human Male.* Saunders, London, 1948.

20 Kinsey, A. C., Pomeroy, W. B., Martin, C. E. *Sexual Behaviour in the Human Female.* Saunders, London, 1953.

21 Kohn, H. L. 'Social class and parental values.' *American Journal of Sociology*, 1959, **64**, pp. 337–51.

22 Mead, G. H. *In* Strauss, A. (Ed.) *The Psychology of George Herbert Mead*. University of Chicago Press, Chicago, 1956.

23 Mead, M. 'Sex and temperament in three savage societies.' *In From the South Seas*, Morrow, New York, 1939.

24 Mensh, J., Glidewell, J. 'Children's perception of relationships among their family and friends.' *Journal of Experimental Education*, 1958, **27**, pp. 65–71.

25 Moreno, J. L. 'Changes in sex grouping of children.' *In* Swanson, G. E. et al. (Eds.) *Readings in Social Psychology*. Holt, New York, 1952.

26 Olley, A. K. *Post-television Social Survey*. School of Applied Psychology, University of New South Wales, Sydney, 1962. Mimeographed report.

27 Piaget, J. *The Psychology of Intelligence*. Routledge & Kegan Paul, London, 1951.

28 Pitty, P., Kinsella, P. 'Children and T.V.—a ninth report.' *In* Seidman, J. M. (Ed.) *Adolescence*. Holt, New York, 1960.

29 Schramm, W., Lyle, J., Parker, E. B. *Television in the Lives of our Children*. Stanford University Press, Stanford, 1961.

30 Stone, L. J., Church, J. *Childhood and Adolescence*. Random House, New York, 1957.

31 Tanner, J. M. *Education and Physical Growth*. University of London Press, London, 1962.

32 Torrance, P. E. 'Changing reactions of pre-adolescent girls to tasks requiring creative scientific thinking.' *Journal of Genetic Psychology*, 1963, **102**, pp. 217–23.

33 Tuddenham, R. D. 'Studies in reputation: III. Correlates of popularity among elementary school children.' *Journal of Educational Psychology*, 1951, **42**, pp. 257–76.

34 Tuddenham, R. D. 'Studies in reputation: I. Sex and grade differences in evaluation of their peers, II. the diagnosis of social adjustment.' *Psychological Monographs*, 1952, **66**, No. 333.

35 Tyler, L. E. 'The development of vocational interests. The organization of likes and dislikes in ten-year-old children.' *Journal of Genetic Psychology*, 1955, **86**, pp. 33–44.

36 Valentine, C. W. *Psychology and its Bearing on Education*. Methuen, London, 1950.

37 Wolfenstein, M. *Children's Humour*. The Free Press, Glencoe, Illinois, 1954.

38 Zelen, S. 'The role of peer acceptance, acceptance of others and self-acceptance.' *Proceedings of Iowa Academy of Science*, 1954, **61**, pp. 446–9.

39 Report of Consultative Committee on The Primary School. H.M. Stationary Office, London, 1931.

40 Working Party on Mass Media—Final Report. Australian Psychological Society. From Conference Notes, Monash University, 1966, pp. 31–8.

CHAPTER FIFTEEN

Early and Middle Adolescence (physical and mental development: interests)

PHYSICAL DEVELOPMENT

A significant event in the physical development of children during adolescence is the growth spurt. This is of about two years' duration and generally takes place from about eleven to thirteen in girls and thirteen to fifteen in boys; but there are marked individual differences, and it may occur at any time between ten and sixteen in girls and eleven and seventeen in boys.

Externally, the growth spurt takes the form of an additional increase in height and weight, in the amount of subcutaneous fat (especially in girls), and a broadening of the shoulders (especially in boys); at the same time the forehead becomes a little higher and wider. The rest of the face increases in size, particularly the jawbone, which now completes the last quarter of its final length. The relatively receding chin of the younger child becomes the more jutting chin of the older one—a feature more apparent in boys that in girls. The growth of the head is not as marked as the growth of the body as a whole. Hence the size of the head and the face becomes smaller in proportion.

At birth the brain has attained 25 per cent of its adult weight, by one year 60 per cent, by five years 90 per cent. It takes ten years to complete the last 10 per cent. Tanner (25) suggests that, although the length and breadth of the head increase during the growth spurt, the brain itself probably grows at a fairly steady rate after the age of five and has no growth spurt.

Internal bodily changes also occur during this period and the two or more years which follow it: there is an increase in the size and strength of the heart and in lung capacity. There is, too, a rise in the number of red corpuscles, and therefore in the amount of haemoglobin in the blood, and the amount of oxygen which can be carried from the lungs to the tissues of the body.

The rate of growth of muscles, heart, and lungs is parallel to that of the skeleton as a whole. Growth is rapid until the age of four, less rapid between five and twelve; then comes the growth spurt. The reproductive system, however, does not grow at a parallel rate: there is little development up to the onset of puberty, after which growth is rapid.

The period of about two years that precedes puberty is usually called 'pubescence'. During this time the biological changes are taking place which will culminate in full sexual maturity. Puberty is the specific moment at which the reproductive functions reach an effective stage. For girls, it occurs with the first menstruation (the menarche). Researches quoted by Horrocks (14) in America and by Tanner (25) in England put the average age of the menarche at between thirteen years one month and thirteen years four months.

It is much more difficult to determine the exact moment of puberty in boys, since for them there is no single event to mark it. The criterion adopted by Crampton (quoted 14) is the development of pubic hair to the point at which a kink appears. However, researches in which this criterion has been used are by no means unanimous as to the moment of puberty, the average ages varying from thirteen years one month to fourteen years three months. Kinsey found that his subjects reported rapid physical development at the time of the first ejaculation. The latter is sometimes accepted as the point of puberty in boys. Kinsey gives these ages for the first ejaculation: 13·71 years for boys who go to college, 13·97 for those who do not go beyond high school, and 14·48 for those who leave school at fourteen (16).[1]

Primary sexual characteristics now develop. In boys, the external genitals rapidly increase in size, and the testicles enlarge and become pendulous; this growth reflects the internal growth of the male sex glands, the testes. The shaft of the penis also increases in length and circumference. Erections are now more frequent and occur in response not only to erotic stimuli or fantasy, but also to pressure—caused by tight clothes, for example —and to emotional experiences like excitement or anger. In girls

[1] page 187.

the ovaries develop, but do not reach their full weight until about twenty. The uterus increases in size, weight and length.

These primary changes are accompanied by the appearance of secondary sexual characteristics, for example, in boys and girls, pubic and under-arm hair, and in boys enlargement of the larynx and the breaking of the voice. By early adolescence, some of these secondary changes provide a clear indication of the physical differences between the two sexes. Up to nine years of age there is little difference between boys and girls in rate and type of growth; both have a flat, stick-like appearance—though some, of course, are thicker, some thinner, some taller and some shorter. After the age of nine girls begin to get taller and bigger, a trend that is accelerated by their growth spurt. When boys start their growth spurt, they begin to overtake and surpass girls. Certainly by sixteen, boys, compared with girls, are on the average taller and more muscular. Their skin has hardened, their necks have thickened, and their shoulders appear broad, especially in relation to the relatively narrow waists. In girls growth of breasts and of subcutaneous fat, widening of hips, thighs and pelvis, combine to give them the typically feminine appearance.

The internal changes—of heart size and lung capacity—are also very much greater in boys; and the differences in the relative strength of boys' and girls' muscles, only slightly greater in boys during earlier years, becomes marked after thirteen. These internal differences combine with the external to give boys greater athletic potential. Sporting records are accordingly calculated separately for men and women, since men's performances are uniformly higher (25, 26).

The changes described are determined by certain of the ductless (endocrine) glands which pour their secretions (called hormones) directly into the blood stream. The glands chiefly responsible for the changes are the pituitary, the adrenals and the gonads (testes, ovaries—see Fig. 10).

The pituitary gland secretes two hormones, one of which stimulates general bodily growth and the other the growth of the gonads. The amount of both hormones greatly increases just before and during the growth spurt. When they have developed far enough, the testes produce the male hormones (called androgens), and the ovaries the female hormones (called oestrogens), which are the chemical bases of the primary and secondary sex characteristics. The male and female hormones in turn inhibit production of the growth hormone from the pituitary, so that, as the gonads mature, general physical growth tends to slow down. Androgens and oestrogens are found in about equal amounts in boys and girls before the age of nine; but, as the gonads mature, boys produce more androgens and girls more oestrogens.

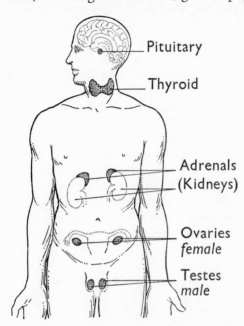

FIG. 10 The location of the glands chiefly involved in the physical changes connected with the growth spurt and with the development of primary and secondary sexual characteristics

The process is complicated. First, the relative importance of the adrenals and gonads in secreting the sex hormones is not clear, nor is the exact nature of the interaction which takes place between these glands and the pituitary. Secondly, males produce some oestrogens and females some androgens, and the proportion may vary from individual to individual. Thus it is that a woman who has an above-average secretion of androgens may show some of the harder, muscular features of the male; and the male who has an above-average secretion of oestrogens may show some of the soft, rounded features of the female.

Thirdly, the process of sexual development actually begins in the hypothalamus, a small region within the thalamus, the upper part of the brain stem. Chemical secretions from the hypothalamus stimulate the pituitary to commence the process. The production of these initiating substances is held in check by counteracting substances (also in the hypothalamus) until the body is mature enough to absorb the physiological changes which sexual development entails. In exceptional cases, the restraining substances cease to function, and the releasing mechanism becomes prematurely active. The result is precocious puberty, i.e. sexual development at an early age, perhaps at six. One further point: the earlier maturation of girls could possibly be explained in terms of the preservation of the species, since it is more important that girls develop quickly to the point where they can reproduce, especially when births are single and where life expectancy is short.

Individual differences and children's physical growth

As has been said, there are individual differences in the rate of physical growth and therefore differences between children in the ages at which they reach puberty. Attempts have been made to discover why this is so. Interesting interrelations have been found.[1]

London children reach adult height and weight eighteen months to two years before most African children (Roberts). The warmer the climate, the less is the average weight when growth is completed. Within most societies, girls in the highest socio-economic group menstruate before girls in the lowest economic group; a study of the ages of the menarche of English girls gives a difference of three months (33), a study of South African Bantu girls a difference of five months (4). Standard of nutrition, though related to race, climate and socio-economic status, most decisively affects growth rate (Acheson). It is probably the most important single environmental factor (3).

The improved standards of living during the past hundred years almost certainly account for what are called secular changes, that is, changes in the stature of adults and the rate of children's growth from one generation to another. In the United States, adolescent boys are 6-8 per cent taller and 12-15 per cent heavier than boys of the same age fifty years ago. The average age of the menarche in girls, now given as just over thirteen, was probably between sixteen and seventeen a hundred years ago. Evidence indicates a similar increase in the rate of maturing of both English

[1] The symposium papers, contained in the following book and written by scientists whose names are given here in parentheses, discuss research findings on the major genetic and environmental influences which affect rate and completed status of growth in man.

Tanner, J. M. (Ed.) *Human Growth*, Vol. III. Pergamon Press, London, 1960.

and Northern European girls (Boyne). A recent study (20) suggests that the average age at which girls in Western societies first menstruate has now stabilized at about 13 years 4 months, since there has apparently been no reduction in the average age of the menarche in English girls since 1949.

Genetic factors play a significant part in determining the rate of maturation. Identical twins frequently menstruate for the first time within a few weeks of each other (Tanner); the ages of menarche of mothers and daughters is not unrelated (correlations of about ·40 have been reported). Family resemblances as well as statistical correlations give support to the part played by heredity in physical growth: children come more to resemble their parents in height, weight and general bodily stature as they mature and as their growth potentialities are realized (Tanner).

The results of research suggest that muscular or mesomorphic boys begin their growth spurt earlier than linear ectomorphs, and that round endomorphs show no definite tendency one way or the other. In terms of the three descriptions given in Chapter 6, this means that Peter is likely physically to mature earlier than Paul, while no prediction can be made for William (25[1] and 26[2]). Sheldon anticipated this finding during the early forties by demonstrating that, in older youths between eighteen and twenty-two, the mesomorph matures most rapidly. A more recent study (15) shows that, when compared with boys who mature late, boys who mature early are taller, heavier, have a stronger hand grip, and are in advance in skeleton age by about two years. These differences were in the same direction for each set of measurements made annually on the boys' twelfth to seventeenth birthdays.

MENTAL DEVELOPMENT: *Growth of intellectual ability*

Ample evidence—observational, experimental, physiological, and statistical—has confirmed Galton's classification of abilities into two main kinds: (1) a general ability entering into all we do, say or think, and (2) a set of specific abilities limited to relatively special fields. Individual differences in these abilities, particularly the former, appear to be largely innate. We are thus led to the concept of an 'innate, general, cognitive ability', which for brevity has been termed 'intelligence'. *Innate* implies that intelligence is

[1] page 73.   [2] pages 48–53.

inherited, *general* that it is manifest in many kinds of adaptive behaviour which involves coping with everyday problems and meeting novel ones, *cognitive* that it is concerned with reasoning as distinct from striving (conation) and feeling (affect).

Like the body, general intelligence grows continuously throughout childhood and during adolescence. This we realize from our everyday observations of children. When compared with most ten-year-olds, we see that most fifteen-year-olds can plan more, make maturer judgments, and do more advanced school work. The nature of intellectual growth can be understood in the light of what has been said in the last chapter, since it means the increasing capacity to progress from concrete to abstract modes of thinking, from perception of particular objects and events to perception of similarities and differences between them, and to understanding of the laws of their structure and movement. It means, too, the growth of the ability to think hypothetically, to use reasoning of the type 'If x, then y'. 'If I drop the stone into this tumbler, the water in the tumbler will overflow.'

Piaget's stages of mental development, also described in the last chapter, constitute his sequential view of the growth of intelligence. They depict new kinds of thinking, from sensori-motor to concrete to formal operations, each kind growing out of, yet superseding, the earlier.

Tests of general intelligence measure a global intelligence rather than the emergence of any specific form of thinking. A child's score on a test of general ability indicates the level of development he has reached at the time the test is given. When such tests are given to the same children at intervals, from their earliest years to late adolescence, the results indicate that intellectual growth is continuous and steady up to about fourteen, by which time it has attained about 80 per cent of its full growth. The rate of growth then begins to slow down, and growth ceases somewhere between twenty and twenty-two. After this an individual will acquire more knowledge and many skills; but his capacity to acquire, and his rate of acquiring, will no longer increase.

Besides general intelligence, there are special abilities—verbal (to use words, to understand concepts stated in words), numerical (to use numbers, as in computation, to understand number concepts and relationships), spatial (to visualize shapes and forms, and imaginatively to manipulate them), mechanical (to understand the interplay of mechanical parts, and physical and mechanical principles), and many others. Vernon (30) has classified them into two main groups: verbal–numerical–educational, and practical– mechanical–spatial. It has been found that scientific ability cuts across these two, leading some psychologists to suggest a division of the former into literary-linguistic ability and mathematical-scientific ability. This gives a three-fold classification of special abilities, the latter two and the practical—mechanical—spatial.

These special abilities are distinct from one another, yet in one sense they are related, since a person's level of performance in each is partly dependent on his general ability. It is understandable that this is so. A person can acquire skill in dealing with actual objects, as a child does through his sensori-motor activity. But beyond this 'practical' level, his performance on any task is better or worse according to whether he is able or not to deal with the abstract notions which appertain to the special ability involved. The carpenter works with wood; he also reads the plan (an abstract conception) of the job he is working on and makes a sketch-plan of one he is soon to begin. This capacity to conceive the abstract is, as we have seen, the essence of general intelligence when fully developed. Because of the common influence of general ability, children who are above or below average in one special type of performance (or work) tend to be above or below average in the others. There is a common fallacy that a child who is backward in school work must by that very fact be good with his hands. Sometimes he may be, but such a child is the exception (29).

Research with tests of general ability and the special abilities have led psychologists, including Burt and Vernon, to suggest that abilities are organized as a hierarchy[1], forming a pyramid of abilities on four levels, thus:

I First-level abilities (the level of behaviour) at the base of the pyramid: these comprise the innumerable specific skills that we use in our everyday lives, such as using words—talking, finding the right expression, understanding other people's conversation, reading, and writing; using numbers—the four rules, calculating costs and change, measurements, etc.; physical activities—hand and eye co-ordinations, use of hands and feet; practical ability—using tools, fixing, mending.

[1] See definition of hierarchy given earlier on page 128.

2   Second level abilities, each embracing its own group of
     first-level abilities: for example, verbal ability embracing the
     many word skills, numerical ability the many number skills,
     manual ability the many practical skills.
3   Three third-level abilities, each embracing its own group of
     second-level abilities: literary ability including verbal ability,
     verbal reasoning, multi-language skills, ability in literature;
     mathematic-scientific ability, scientific reasoning; the practical
     and spatial abilities.
4   At the summit of the pyramid is the all-inclusive general
     ability, which enters every activity at the other three levels.

Tests show that special abilities—like general ability—also
grow continuously throughout childhood and adolescence, but
mature much later and at different ages. Thurstone (27) has compared the rates of growth of special abilities, and finds that these
rates vary. For example, most adolescents reach 80 per cent of
their adult performance in verbal fluency by the age of twenty, in
verbal comprehension by eighteen, in perceptual speed (the ability
to recognize likenesses and differences between objects and symbols
accurately and quickly) by twelve; memory, spatial and numerical abilities reach 80 per cent of their adult level between ages
fourteen and sixteen.

Three features of children's mental growth during adolescence
are important if we are to understand their personal development
and educational needs. First, whilst pre-adolescent children do, of
course, vary in general intelligence, the variation between children
becomes greater during adolescence. For example, a child with an
I.Q. of 100 when six years old and so with a mental age of 6·0
would be expected to have, when he is twelve, a mental age of
12·0. A child with an I.Q. of 125 would at six have a mental age of
7·5, at twelve a mental age of 15·0; that is, the difference in the
mental ages of the two is 1·5 at six, 3·0 at twelve.

Secondly, this increasing variability with age is true of special
abilities. Here again Primary School children vary; and occasionally one sees the Primary School child who shows a remarkable
precocity in one of them. But in general it is at adolescence that
these specific differences between children become most marked.
Then special abilities begin to play a decisive part in determining
their scholastic achievements. Therefore, a profile which shows a

student's relative standing on a variety of special abilities is more meaningful than a total score or I.Q.

But the part played by special abilities, though greater with Secondary than with Primary School children, is never as great as the part played by general ability. Burt (5) has estimated that in a group of children at about twelve to thirteen general ability is still three times as influential as verbal ability, twice as influential as arithmetical ability, and four times as influential as manual ability.

Thirdly, there is no difference in average intelligence between adolescent boys and girls; but boys begin to show greater mechanical, spatial and numerical ability, and girls greater linguistic and literary ability. It is not yet known how far these differences are genetically determined, and how far they are due to social influences. It is possible that the differences reflect what parents, teachers and other influential adults expect of each sex.

Heredity, environment and intelligence

Hebb (12) makes a distinction between what he calls Intelligence A and Intelligence B. Intelligence A, he says, is an individual's basic, genetically determined intelligence, 'an *innate potential*, the capacity for development, a fully innate property that amounts to the possession of a good brain and a good neural metabolism' (12).[1] Intelligence B is an individual's manifest intelligence as it is expressed in the way he solves problems and, for a child, in how well he does at school. Since a test of general intelligence represents a sample of this behaviour, the score obtained could be called Intelligence C, that is, a measure of Intelligence B, which in turn is related to Intelligence A.

Intelligence A is a concept; it is not directly observable and not directly measurable. Since it is the result of physical attributes ('a good brain and a good neural metabolism'), it is wholly a product of heredity; it cannot therefore be improved or impaired by the child's environment. Intelligence B and C are much more direct inferences from behaviour. They are determined partly by A and partly by the environment. For, to understand and cope with the problems of one's environment, or more, specifically, to answer questions in an intelligence test, presupposes some

[1] page 294.

acquired knowledge and some acquired skill in using objects, symbols, language, number and so on.

Those who construct tests of intelligence try to do so in such a way that the scores obtained offer a tolerably accurate indication of the child's innate potentiality, i.e. of 'Intelligence A', as Hebb would call it. Nevertheless, wherever possible, it is desirable that the crude test-scores, particularly if obtained with the ordinary group-tests, should be submitted to the teachers for criticism; wherever doubts arise, the child should then be interviewed, and, if necessary, tested on a different occasion and in a different way. When this is done, the evidence for inheritance stands out far more clearly.

First, the correlations amongst children who are reared together or apart, as presented below, agree fairly closely with the theoretical values that would be expected from the Mendelian Theory of genetics (6).

	Reared together	Reared apart
Identical twins	·925	·876
Siblings	·538	·517
Unrelated children	·269	·07

In the second place, even in the case of students at school, college or university, the rate of intellectual growth, as measured by intelligence tests, begins to slow down at fourteen and to cease at about twenty. This happens in spite of the intellectual stimulation students receive during these years.

Thirdly, children who are coached on these tests improve on average only about 6 points—an improvement that takes place after the first three hours or so of coaching, and then ceases. Vernon (29) suggests that such improvement is highly specific to the type of items and to the form of test used; and that probably most of the improvement comes from the child's familiarity with the mechanics of the particular test.

Yet the correlations given above also indicate that the resemblance in scores on intelligence tests is related to similarity of environment. They show that the resemblance between each group is greater when its members are reared together than when they are reared apart.

Burt has calculated that, when innate intelligence has been assessed, not (as is more usual) by the test-scores taken as they stand, but after careful checking with teachers (as described above), then only 12 per cent of the variations between individual children represent the effects of environment, and 88 per cent that of their genetic endowment. Charlotte Burk's American findings—of 20 and 80 per cent respectively—were based on test-scores alone (derived from the most reliable types of tests). Though these are American figures, they agree with those obtained in Britain for the unchecked scores obtained with the better type of test.

When a comparison is made between the unchecked test-scores of identical twins brought up together and apart, the effect of environment is sometimes obvious, especially if the test used is of a purely verbal type. Where there are marked differences (of a dozen or more points) between twins who have lived their lives apart, these features of the environment and the personality of the twins with higher I.Q. were to be seen: longer and/or uninterrupted schooling, a foster home on a higher socio-economic level, one or more favourable personality characteristics, for example, more persistent, less anxious, more serious, more confident (23). Both Burt (6) and Vernon (29) have commented on the influence of better schools and better foster homes in raising children's I.Q. scores as obtained with ordinary tests. Clarke and Clarke (7) have shown how a stimulating environment can lead to higher scores on certain types of intelligence tests even in persons who are mentally deficient. Honzik (13) has shown that children whose scores with tests fluctuated considerably had had many ups and downs in their lives, with periods of happiness alternating with periods of unhappiness.

An English study (17) has found that, by five, a clear and significant trend appears, namely, for the I.Q.s of lower class children to show a steady fall and those of middle class children to show a steady rise. The study is important in showing that the impairment of children's intellectual development imposed by an impoverished environment shows itself clearly even before children start school.

Since, therefore, measured Intelligence C, from which an I.Q. is derived, is an indirect estimate of Intelligence A and dependent on environmental as well as hereditary factors, to speak of an individual I.Q. as absolute, exactly measurable and remaining unvaried from infancy to old age is misleading. An I.Q. is only 'approximately constant'.[1]

[1] The subject of I.Q., its nature and the question of its constancy, will be considered further in Chapter 23.

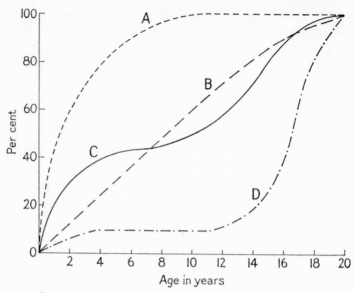

A =Weight of brain and its parts
B =Intelligence
C =General bodily growth
D =Genital

Fig 11. Types of postnatal growth

What has been said so far in this chapter about physical and intellectual growth implies four distinct sequences. These are depicted in Figure 11.

The spurt that characterizes general physical growth does not affect general intellectual growth. It is true that children who mature early physically also tend to have a higher I.Q.; so do children who are physically superior. But when allowance has been made for the fact that early maturing, physical superiority and high intelligence are related to high socio-economic status, and also for the fact that both physical and intellectual growth depend on chronological age, the correlation between general physical and general intellectual status is low—between ·10 and ·20. Nor has any appreciable relation been found, in the fully grown person, between size of head or height of forehead and intelligence. It is hazardous, therefore, to draw conclusions about a child's intellectual ability from his physique (2, 18, 19).

INTERESTS: *General*

An interest is usually thought of as a freely chosen activity which holds the attention and is a source of pleasure and satisfaction. Interests are related to basic needs, in that they imply activities in the pursuit of goals through which such needs are satisfied; but interests have a specificity which the basic needs have not. Children may, indeed, want to know and understand their environment; but the numerous superficial interests of Primary School children develop into the less numerous but more specialized interests of the adolescent. Anderson (1) discovered a relation, in the case of pre-adolescent children, between breadth of interests and happiness and adjustment, but for adolescents a relation between depth of interests and happiness and adjustment. Children may wish to be with other children and to join in their activities; but the sociability of Primary School children becomes more discriminating. An older person usually wants to be with particular people—those who share his attitudes and interests, and belong to the same recreational, political, trade or professional groups.

The factors which determine an individual's interests are likely to be many and varied: his sex, general intelligence and special abilities, his socio-economic status, the place where he lives, his physical endowment, opportunities and experience, the period of history, and his parents' restrictions and taboos (28). Heredity plays its part. Shields (23) illustrates how identical twins had similar interests, even though reared apart and uninfluenced one by the other.

These interests included (for separate pairs of twins) drawing and playing chess; collecting brass and making ornaments out of silver paper (both had won prizes in flower shows); reading tastes and archaeology; oil painting and playing wind instruments; classical music with the same favourite composers. In one case, both of forty-year-old female twins were still enthusiastic cyclists. That heredity may play some part in determining interests is understandable. Inherited characteristics such as motor dexterity, sensory acuity, general and special abilities predispose a person towards interests which are in accord with them. In developing these characteristics a child may be persistent and enthusiastic; and persistence and enthusiasm are the very essence of interests. Thus it is that interests and abilities should be the main determinants in choice of vocation (9).

The range of interests among a large group of children of the same age is likely to be wide. Yet there will be an agreement which will enable us to suggest lines of development. For, as children grow, some interests are discarded, the pursuit of others becomes more complex, and new interests arise.

As a result of the greater strength and greater capacity for well-integrated control of the body that adolescents acquire after the growth spurt, the range of their sporting activities widens, and the level of their performance increases. They play competitive games (football, tennis, for instance) and are physically active (cycling, hiking, climbing). A clear division tends to appear during adolescence (24): there are those—the stronger, predominantly mesomorphic adolescents—who play games competitively, and who aspire to high achievement; then there are those who play in a relatively non-competitive way, and for whom the game is less important than the social activities that go with it. Many become spectators; some relinquish all interest in sport. For 33 per cent of a group of English adolescent boys, playing games was their favoured activity on a Saturday afternoon; 31 per cent watched games. For over 60 per cent sport was given as a very strong interest; only 7 per cent were not interested at all. Girls' activities were less energetic: the meetings of cliques, conversations, telephoning and window-shopping (32).

The desire for incessant physical activity lessens with age. The irrepressible darting of Primary School children becomes the slower walk of the seventeen-year-old. Whereas, when young children meet, they will say, 'Let's play' and will express their compatibility in a physically active way, adolescent exchanges are conversational. In some a new and absorbing interest develops: gossiping. Adolescent gossiping, like that of adults, is probably a mixture of fact and fantasy, of love and malice. The most frequent topics of conversation are, for girls, clothes, teachers, boys; for boys, sports, sportsmen, cars, girls (8).

Interest in the opposite sex follows sexual maturation and takes many forms: surreptitious passing of scandalous novels, bawdy jokes—particularly among boys—search for the descriptions and references in stories, magazines or the Bible. Socially there is progression to mixed groups, and learning to dance.

Because they develop earlier, girls want to make the transition before boys, and at a time when boys of the same age are still content to pursue their exclusive activities. In one investigation, boys and girls of fourteen—all members of a youth club—were asked to say what they enjoyed doing most. Only 11 per cent of the boys, as compared with 60 per cent of the girls, chose mixed social activities (11).

Children's intellectual development is reflected in the elaboration, or the more realistic pursuit, of their earlier interests. Collections are systematic; toy cars and models are discarded for real engines, or a motor bike, to tinker with. Social interests are common to most adolescents at all intellectual levels; but the less intelligent tend to be the more sociable. They spend relatively more time in gang or group pursuits. In developing their special abilities, adolescents who stay at school begin to acquire a corresponding way of life. For example, of three adolescents, all with high general intelligence, one may have good verbal ability and his life may revolve around the study of language and literature; another may have good mathematical ability and ability to reason inductively, and his life revolves around science. Yet a third may have good mechanical and practical ability, and his life and interests centre around engineering.

In summary, a great change takes place in children's interests and activities during the years between later Primary and upper Grammar School. The society of children described in Chapter 14 is the world of childhood—of children who roller skate, skip and play hopscotch on the pavement, their two groups, boys and girls, quite separate. The world of seventeen, if not totally adult, is a clear preparation for being grown up—girls and boys, who have their sophisticated and mixed social activities and their boy-girl interests, some of whom pursue sport, organized and competitive, and some their special interests in a systematic way.

Reading

Even though there is individual variation, it would appear that children read more between their twelfth and fifteenth birthdays than they do at any other time during their childhood and adolescence. An investigation in the Practising School of the University of Chicago gives a range, per year, of 5–79 books at twelve, 1–108 at thirteen, 1–155 at fourteen (reported in 31). Gesell (10) confirms this trend, and speaks of 'general variability'. The most frequent reply of children over fifteen to his inquiries about their reading was that they did not read as much as they used to. The books the sixteen-year-olds said they would read, if they had the time, included *War and Peace*, *Anna Karenina*, *Pride and Prejudice*, *Of Human Bondage*.

There are a number of possible reasons for the increased reading between twelve and fifteen. By twelve most children have considerable skill and facility in reading, and between these years they have more time in which to do it. Later on, homework and social activities will absorb more of the leisure-time of those who stay at school, and social activities the leisure-time of those who go to work. The latter also lose the opportunity and the stimulus to read, which the school provides. A survey showed that just over 50 per cent of Secondary Modern boys and girls belonged to a public library before they left school; only 16 per cent still belonged two years after leaving (34). In the account which follows, the reading interests mainly of children about twelve to fifteen are considered.

These children's reading reflects their desire for adventure. Investigations in various countries and at various times reveal that they enjoy adventure and mystery stories. A study of 8,000 English children (36) shows that boys prefer fast-moving adventure stories, such as the *Biggles* books, and that detective stories (Conan Doyle, Agatha Christie) and escape stories of the last war are popular. Old favourites such as Dickens, Ballantyne, Stevenson and Rider Haggard are also widely read.

It is a good plan for the teacher of boys to keep an adventure story in his desk, ready for reading to the class as a treat, or to clear the air after a difficult period when the class is mulish and the teacher irritable from his ineffectual attempts to stimulate them. Differences are smoothed again within the atmosphere of masculine adventure.

Girls also enjoy adventure stories, but of a less fantastic kind than *Biggles*—those of Arthur Ransome, for example. Ransome's books are also read by many boys. They tell of children who are sturdily independent of adults and able to do practical things, such as sailing boats, and all the jobs required in camping—pitching tents, making fires, cooking meals. Rosemary Sutcliffe's combination of history and adventure is popular, as in *Dawn Wind* or *Warrior Scarlett*. Detailed descriptions of historical times, good characterization and human interest, shared loyalty, an animal that is almost human in its qualities, happy endings, all combine to give the imaginative child the kind of story he seeks.

To talk together about adventure stories is to share experiences, to renew the enjoyment obtained in their reading of them and to enhance the close identification each child felt with the heroes. But while girls put adventure stories, Dickens and Agatha Christie near the top of their lists, their reading also reflects an interest in domestic and personal events. The major theme of their favourite books is of girls growing up within the family. Often the main character is an orphan who endears herself to her foster parents, as in *Anne of Green Gables*, *Heidi*, and *Pollyanna*. A variety of persons is introduced, each with unique characteristics.

There is the good, saintly girl, and the tom-boy, Beth and Jo in *Little Women*, for example, and Clover and Katy in *What Katy Did at School*. Some romance is included, but only incidentally, to show that the ideal culmination of childhood is a happy marriage.

Connell's study (8) indicates a similar trend in the reading of Australian boys and girls. From his study of New Zealand children, Scott (22) shows that boy's reading is very much limited to adventure, detective and humorous stories. They do not read girls' books. Girls, on the other hand, have wider tastes in reading than boys. Though they read books depicting life within a family setting, they also read boys' adventure books, such as *Tom Sawyer*, *The Three Musketeers*, and *Tom Brown's Schooldays*.

Scott was particularly struck by his finding that significantly fewer girls than boys read humorous stories, such as those of Leacock, Jacobs, and Wodehouse. As he says, one can only make guesses about why this should be. His own is this: that girls are gentler, and temperamentally and physically more sensitive than boys. 'When, therefore, girls read humorous books in which characters are made to look ridiculous, their natural tendency to feel sorry for such people hinders their enjoyment of the humour, especially where the ridiculed person, as in *Pickwick Papers*, is the hero of the story' (22).[1]

Some children of this age—more especially girls—enjoy

[1] page 58.

stories of life at boarding school. Three reasons for this may be suggested. First, boarding-school life has a kind of magic for children who are at day schools. In the stories boys or girls have adventures away from home without the restrictions that home imposes. Although the boarding-school life is idealized in the stories, the children reading them are constantly reminded of the authority vested in the head and the staff. But the restrictions imposed are the well-defined categorical restrictions of teachers in authority, and are easily understood. The restrictions imposed in the home, on the other hand, are bound up with the deep emotional ties of family life; they are sympathetic restrictions, tenuous and ill-defined. In contrast to these, categorical restrictions have a fascination. Perhaps children who are not in boarding schools are as eager to experience these categorical restrictions vicariously through their reading as children in boarding schools are eager to go home at the end of term to the emotional ties and sympathetic restraints of the home.

Secondly, the stories have an appeal because they are about *groups* of children having adventures together. The groups are closely knit and hierarchical in structure, with a strong, admired leader who is captain of the school. Thirdly, there is a fairly clear division of characters into the good and the bad. The leader and his group are always on the side of the right, the true and the good, and their enemies personify those who sneak, cheat, gamble and smoke. Such stories give children of this age the same kind of satisfaction that fairy tales give younger children (page 253).

Wickens (31) has reviewed the research literature on the reading interests of pubescent children in America. She mentions only one book (*Little Women*); but, to judge from her descriptions, the reading habits of American children resemble those of English, New Zealand and Australian children. American boys choose stories of adventure, mystery, athletic prowess, inventions, and mechanics; girls choose stories of home and school life, and biographies of famous women. *Little Women* is a special favourite. Like English, Australian and New Zealand girls, American girls will sometimes read the less 'grim and desperate' boys' adventure stories. But boys will not read girls' books. Children's reading, like their play, conforms to a pattern appropriate to their sex, with girls again being more variable in their choices, and boys sticking rigidly to their own type of books.

Wickens reaches the following conclusions. Children of very high intelligence read four times as much as children of average intelligence; and the latter read more than dull children. The higher the children's I.Q., the higher the quality of their reading. Girls, whether dull, average or bright, read more than boys of the same intelligence. This may be due to the looser structure and the less active nature of girls' groups compared with boys'. Girls' groups are less demanding and so leave more time for reading. Television has stimulated many types of children's reading: biography, travel books, and science. In this space age, astronomy is apparently becoming a favoured topic of reading and study.

Television

The time spent watching television also reaches a peak between about twelve and fifteen—an average of just under three hours a day (21, 35). Older adolescents watch it less, even though they stay up later. Less viewing, like less reading, is probably due to the many other calls on their time: homework, examinations, social commitments and sport. The movement towards adult programmes, which is a significant feature of older Primary School children's viewing, continues. By early adolescence, children's programmes are discarded almost entirely. Adult science fiction, adult Westerns, crime mystery, jazz are now most popular, especially among boys, with girls showing greater preference for jazz and popular music, romance and domestic comedy.

The description given in the last chapter of the viewing of Primary School children, and the statement above, suggest a sequence in children's television preferences which, understandably enough, is similar to their reading preferences. Infant School children, and those a little older, like animal and marionette programmes; also stories of humanized creatures with whose desires and impulses they can identify themselves. The child of ten finds satisfaction from the adventure stories about children, such as those written by Enid Blyton, which have an element of fantasy but are not fantastic. During later Primary School years, the fantastic type of adventure, for example, *Superman* or children's Westerns, have appeal. These provide a great deal of action and some suspense. To children of thirteen or fourteen, *Superman* appears childish; they prefer adult mystery and adventure programmes. These provide a great deal of suspense and some action.

Older adolescents enjoy plays as well as variety programmes and comedy. The more intelligent ones begin to use television, as they do radio and reading, as a source of information and education, and begin to look critically at programmes (21).

Television has now to compete with other media. When pupils and students were asked which one of the four media—television, radio, newspaper, magazine—they would retain if they were allowed only one, the percentage choosing television was 91 per cent at Primary School, 56 per cent at High School, 38 per cent at College (21). But as Schramm reminds us, despite this falling off, television is still the medium that would be missed by most children, whatever their age.

REFERENCES AND BIBLIOGRAPHY

1   Anderson, J. E. 'The prediction of adjustment over time.' *In* Iscoe, I., Stevenson, H. W. (Ed.) *Personality Development in Children*. University of Texas Press, Austin, 1958.

2   Boring, E. G. *The Physical Dimensions of Consciousness*. Dover Publications, New York, 1963.

3   Breckenridge, M. E., Vincent, E. L. 'Nutrition and growth.' *Child Development*, 1955, pp. 116, 119–26.

4   Burrell, R. J. W., Healy, M. J., Tanner, J. M. 'Age at menarche in South African Bantu girls living on the Transkei Reserve.' *Human Biology*, 1961, **33**, pp. 250–61.

5   Burt, C. 'The differentiation of intellectual ability.' *British Journal of Educational Psychology*, 1954, **24**, pp. 76–89.

6   Burt, C. 'The inheritance of mental ability.' *American Psychologist*, 1958, **13**, pp. 1–15.

7   Clarke, A. M., Clarke, A. D. B. *Mental Deficiency—the Changing Outlook*. Methuen, London, 2nd edition, 1965.

8   Connell, W. F., Francis, E. P., Shilbeck, E. E. *Growing Up in an Australian City*. Australian Council for Educational Research, Melbourne, 1957.

9   Evans, K. M. *Attitudes and Interests in Education*. Routledge & Kegan Paul, London, 1965.

10 Gesell, A., Ilg, F. L., Ames, L. B. *Youth: the Years from Ten to Sixteen*. Harper, New York, 1956.

11 Hammond, W. H. 'An analysis of youth centre interests.' *British Journal of Educational Psychology*, 1945, **15**, pp. 122–6.

12 Hebb, D. O. *Organization of Behaviour*. Chapman & Hall, London, 1957.

13 Honzik, M. P., McFarlane, J. W., Allen, L. 'The stability of mental test performance between two and eighteen years.' *Journal of Experimental Education*, 1948, **17**, pp. 309–24.

14 Horrocks, J. E. 'The adolescent.' *In* Carmichael, L. (Ed.) *Manual of Child Psychology*. Wiley, New York, 2nd edition, 1954.

15 Jones, M. C., Bayley, N. 'Physical maturing among boys as related to behaviour.' *Journal of Educational Psychology*, 1950, **41**, pp. 129–48.

16 Kinsey, A. C., Pomeroy, W. B., Martin, C. E. *Sexual Behaviour in the Human Male*. Saunders, London, 1948.

17 Hindley, C. 'Social class influences on the development of ability in the first five years.' *Proceedings of 14th International Conference of Applied Psychology*, Copenhagen, 1961, Vol. 3, pp. 29–41, Munksgaard, Copenhagen, 1962.

18 Lassek, A. M. *The Human Brain*. Springfield, Illinois, 1957.

19 Munn, N. L. *Evolution and Growth of Human Behaviour*. Houghton Mifflin, New York, 1955.

20 Poppleton, P. K. 'The secular trend in puberty: has stability been achieved?' *British Journal of Educational Psychology*, 1966, **36**, pp. 95–100.

21 Schramm, W., Lyle, J., Parker, E. B. *Television in the Lives of our Children*, Stanford University Press, Stanford, 1961.

22 Scott, W. J. *Reading, Film and Radio Tastes of High School Boys and Girls*. New Zealand Council for Education Research, Wellington, 1947.

23 Shields, J. *Monozygotic Twins*. Oxford University Press, London, 1962.

24 Stewart, M. 'The leisure activities of grammar school children.' *British Journal of Educational Psychology*, 1950, **20**, pp. 11–34.

25 Tanner, J. M. *Growth at Adolescence*. Blackwell, Oxford, 1955.

26 Tanner, J. M. *Education and Physical Growth*. University of London Press, London, 1962.

27 Thurstone, L. L. *The Differential Growth of Mental Ability*. Chapel Hill, N. C.: University of North Carolina, the Psychiometric Laboratory, 1955.

28 Valentine, C. W. 'Adolescence and some problems of youth training.' *British Journal of Educational Psychology*, 1943, **13**, pp. 57–68.

29 Vernon, P. E. 'A new look at intelligence testing.' *Educational Research*, 1959, **1**, pp. 3–10.

30 Vernon, P. E. *The Structure of Human Abilities*. Methuen, London, 1964.

31 Wickens, A. R. 'Reading interests: grades seven through nine.' *In* Seidman, J. M. (Ed.) *Adolescence*, Holt, New York, 1960.

32 Wilkins, L. T. *The Adolescent in Britain*. H.M.S.O., London, 1958 (mimeographed).

33 Wolfenden, R. C., Smallwood, A. L. Annual Report of the Principal Medical Officer to City and County of Bristol Education Committee, 1958.

34 *15 to 18*. Report of Central Advisory Council for Education, England, Volume I (Crowther Report). London, H.M.S.O., 1959.

35 Survey: Granada. *What Children Watch*, 1961.

36 *Survey of Boys' and Girls' Reading Habits*, W. H. Smith and George G. Harrap, London, 1957.

CHAPTER SIXTEEN

Early Adolescence: Pubescence to Puberty (twelve, thirteen)

INVESTIGATIONS into children's social groups have been carried out in many countries—for example, of boys in working-class families (10) and adolescents in a country town in the United States (12), children in Israel (29) and Australia (3), and boys in the poorer parts of English cities (21, 22). The results of these investigations confirm the increasing tendency of children to form groups as they grow older, a tendency that reaches its peak at about thirteen. The studies describe the structure of pubescent groups and the kinds of activities the children enjoy. In both respects boys' groups differ from those of girls.

The organization and activities of boys' gangs

The Oxford English Dictionary defines a 'gang' as 'a band of persons who go about or act in concert, usually for criminal purposes or for a purpose disapproved of by the speaker'. The definition implies that a gang is a group that is closely-knit and ready for action; and the word has depreciatory implications as when we speak of 'a gang of thieves' or 'a gang of hoodlums'.

This book, however, is concerned only incidentally with delinquency and so only incidentally with delinquent gangs. Yet, as will be realized, members of a tightly-knit group of pubescent boys engaged in socially approved activity, like football, may suddenly organize themselves for some socially disapproved purpose. To cover this possibility, and to distinguish between the spontaneous play group of eight-year-olds and the more consciously formed and structured groups at twelve, some writers,

including Wolman (29) and Helanko (10), use the word 'gang'
when they refer to older boys' groups. This usage is followed
here.

Boys' gangs have a definite structure, and consist of a leader,
his immediate deputies, and his followers. These gangs centre on
some favoured activity—usually football or cricket—while other
pastimes are treated as incidental. The leader of a gang is chosen
because of his ability in the most favoured activity and for his
qualities of leadership. The status of other high-ranking members
also depends upon the possession of these qualities. For some boys,
however, a place in the gang is assured because of a specific kind of
knowledge or skill which is useful and which adds colour and
variety to group life—a wide general knowledge, an ability to
scale heights, to go through small spaces, to act as the group
joker. According to the particular activity, there is a cry for 'The
Professor', 'The Skylark', 'Titch', 'Fatty'; and the individual so
called is proud of the significant part he momentarily plays.

The stability or instability of the gang, and its continued existence or dissolution, depend partly on factors external to it.
Gang activities unite and preserve; so does the presence of 'enemy'
gangs close at hand. In the poor parts of cities, children play at their
favourite activity within a gang (the 'in-group' or 'we-group').
In a nearby street or on the opposite side of the street, there is
usually another gang (the 'out-group' or 'they-group'). Sometimes
the gangs are competitors in their favourite activity, or 'enemies',
each of whose territory and property are raided by other gangs;
sometimes they are friends who unite to challenge another and
more distant 'out-group'. It is easy for such activities to become
anti-social—when there is no 'they-group' upon which to work
off hostility, or when a 'we-group' and a 'they-group' combine to
steal or to deface a building representing a respected institution,
such as a school, church, war memorial.

In a suburban environment, community-approved organiza-
tions, such as Scouts or church clubs, provide group activities for
these children. In this environment, too, there will be 'private'
gangs, which function independently of adults, and organized,
like the slum gangs, for football, cricket and 'we-group' versus
'they-group' competition. The members of these gangs, too, may
embark upon daring acts which border on delinquency; they
may, for instance, enter an empty house, and break a few windows,

or steal one or two small objects as a token of their daring. For days afterwards, their feelings will swing between delight at their daring and anxiety in case the escapade be discovered.

Boys have many natural outlets for their energies if they live in the country; but even there desire for the forbidden makes an isolated empty house or an orchard a tempting target.

Smoking among boys serves a double function: it is an indulgence in the forbidden as well as a participation in the world of adult magic. It is more safely practised in groups, and more exciting then. If you discover boys smoking, the cave, tent or room reeks like an opium den. This is evidence of their compulsive determination to smoke, despite the unpleasant taste and the feeling of sickness, rather than of their enjoyment of smoking for itself.

We adults often laugh when we hear of these things—provided we are not responsible for the behaviour and upbringing of the children concerned. If we are responsible, we may feel perturbed. But despite our fears, boys are not necessarily acquiring anti-social habits which will continue into adolescence, nor is this behaviour necessarily the beginning of delinquency proper. Crane's study, for example, shows that over 60 per cent of his subjects (all students in Colleges of Education) had taken part in some such activity; but none had been brought before the courts, and all had pursued their studies successfully during adolescence, and were preparing themselves for a vocation, as their entry into Colleges of Education showed (3).

But wherever pubescent boys live, and whatever their supplementary activities, the favourite pastime is competitive sport. The ideal boy, and the one who has high prestige, is good at sport (24). Boys who are accepted by their group express the opinion that they play games 'better than average', those who are not accepted that they are only 'just average' (4). Mays (21)[1] says of English boys living in the poorer parts of large cities:

'The boys who play for the street teams are bound together in a variety of subsidiary ways. They are often close personal friends or classmates or neighbours in a particular street or block of flats. But their interest and delight in football is the permanent integrative force, and outsiders who are known to be exceptionally good players are sometimes drafted to their ranks to raise the prestige and standard of

[1] pages 48–9.

play. Above all other sports, football occupies a paramount position in the estimation of these youngsters. They will play football whenever they get the opportunity. Wherever there are a few yards of space available on waste land or in car parks or on bombed sites they repair with a ball. The younger boys play in the streets after school hours and the workers and apprentices during tea break or lunch hour.'

Internal factors also play a part in preserving or disrupting the gang. Maintenance of the gang's internal structure gives stability when each member accepts his own status and performs his appropriate role. But the play of power between members of the gang may disrupt it, or cause changes in status and role.

Self-esteem is related to the esteem in which an individual is held by his group; for this reason the self-esteem of the accepted leader is usually high. Usually, too, he is successful in his attempts to influence his followers who, by contrast, are diffident when they are trying to influence him; they do so circumspectly (18). The leader initiates projects and directs his followers; and thereby his self-esteem is further enhanced. This process of double enhancement has its dangers, both for the leaders and for the stability of the group. The leader may become too inflated and abuse his power. His followers then resist, and any of a number of things may happen. The leader may modify his attitude, or a new leader may be chosen. In either case the gang continues to exist. On the other hand, it may be split in two, the original leader retaining leadership over one of the new groups, and the members of the other group choosing as leader the main instigator of the revolt.

There is evidence to suggest that during the second half of this stage social behaviour begins to change and to anticipate behaviour more typical of adolescence. Wolman's study (29) shows that, between the ages of thirteen and fourteen, Israeli boys begin to regard the features of close-knit gangs—dictatorial leadership, group names, secret codes and secret signs—as 'childish'; so they do the pranks played in earlier years, such as ringing door bells or breaking windows. Groups and members are now drawn together by friendship and common interests.

Consequently, the changes which begin now and continue into adolescence have two main features. First, gangs tend to become cliques. A clique may be defined as an exclusive group the members of which are bound together by common likes and dislikes, a common pride in belonging to an exclusive group, and by the pleasure they take in each other's company. As we have said, in gangs the emphasis is laid on the favourite pastime (sport) and on infrequent semi-delinquent behaviour; in cliques, however, activities are less dramatic, and incidental to the boys just being together—talking, joking, standing around, looking, going to the cinema. Whereas a place in a gang is very much a function of a boy's position in it, a place in a clique is, to a larger extent, a function of the bonds of friendship which unite a boy to each of the other members.

Secondly, some boys will begin to form *special interest* groups, that is, groups which meet for a specific purpose—chess, photography, radio, making models, for instance. Making radios or electrical systems, tinkering with bicycles and, later on, with car or motor-bike engines, have a fascination for many boys. In this they express their determination to learn empirically the intricacies of machines. It indicates their continued interest in technology pursued at an advanced level, with books and magazines read for scientific and mechanical information.

Horrocks and Thompson (13, 14) have shown that, between the ages of ten and seventeen, children in both rural and urban areas of the United States had fewer friends as they grew older, but that the friendships they made were more stable. Wolman sums up this trend when he says that 'instead of submission to the strong, a more mature and selective sociality develops. The pubescent seeks friends that suit him' (29).[1] It is good to have many friends, but better to have a few, all of whom are close friends (8, 11).

There are social class differences in the activities and the changes so far described. In the first place, the majority of boys, whatever their social class, value sporting activities. But when compared with middle-class boys, those in the lower socio-economic groups fight more and indulge in rougher play; they are less prepared to accept the studious boy (24). Secondly, middle-class boys are more likely to have hobbies, and, encouraged and perhaps pressed by their parents, are more likely to be working hard at school. Boys in the poorer parts of large cities, on the other hand, tend not to pursue hobbies, perhaps because they are not given the opportunity; they have little garden, no shed, no spare rooms, no encouragement from their parents to do so. Nor

[1] page 179.

do they have to do school work during their leisure hours (2). For these boys gang activity is not only pleasurable in itself but also a substitute for individual pursuits. Their dependence on the group is, therefore, great. Thirdly, numerous studies carried out in the United States (e.g. 6, 25), and May's investigations in England (e.g. 21, 22) show (a) that the gang continues for many years longer among boys who live in the poorer parts of large cities, (b) that playing games—football especially—remains the preferred non-delinquent activity, and (c) that out of these gangs much of the delinquency in modern societies stems.

The organization and activities of girls' groups

The groups formed by pubescent girls have many of the features of cliques (girls rarely form gangs). Therefore, it would be more apt to say of girls that they congregate (12, 26). Their groups lack much of the paraphernalia of social solidarity which characterizes those of boys. They are bound by friendship and by an antagonism towards adults and towards boys. Each girl usually has a close friend within her group, and, because of this, the groups generally consist of pairs or trios of friends:

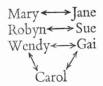

Because friendship between individuals takes precedence over loyalty to the group, there is less team spirit than among boys. A girls' group may quickly disintegrate because of petty differences among its members. Each group will tend to have its core of stronger members with the rest of the group as 'hangers-on'. These 'hangers-on' may be 'floating' and drift from group to group as alliances and activities attract or repel them. Unlike boys' groups, girls' are most evident within the school. After school they tend to break up into pairs or trios of best friends. A group seldom consists of more than six or seven girls. Hollingshead (12) gives five as the modal number of the 259 cliques he studied. The members are usually in the same class at school, have similar social backgrounds, and share the same likes and dislikes.

The activities involve being together in specially allotted places. The members of a clique prefer to sit together in the classroom, to have their own corner of the playground, and their own secret signs and colloquialisms. Their anti-social behaviour takes a more personal form, since making scapegoats of particular children seems to be more usual among girls than among boys. This is directed not so much at one girl for a long period, but more frequently at each of a number of girls for relatively short periods. A girl from another clique is not often chosen because the members of her clique will immediately come to her rescue. Instead, the victim is usually the one who does not belong and who has no protection. Girls tend also to be individually argumentative and defiant; they do not gang up against a teacher or another group in quite the persistent way boys do.

Out of school, girls sometimes come together in small groups of two, three or four, and chatter about their school and teachers. These groups often become special interest groups. The girls dress up, write and act plays, make useful things—table mats, tea cosies, or simple knitted garments. By this age they have acquired enough control and persistence to finish longer tasks such as the making of a small woollen rug.

Some girls will of their own accord look after groups of small children as they play in the street or the park. Often a little girl of six or seven will take more notice of what a thirteen-year-old girl says to her than of her mother. This is not necessarily thoughtless heroworship. A girl of thirteen may be in more sensitive touch with a young child than an adult.

Sex-role adaptation

Lynn (20) has described the ways boys and girls adapt themselves to their special roles. Since the mother plays a more significant part in the home than the father, especially during children's early years, and since teachers in Infant Schools are almost invariably women, a girl first finds herself in a same-sex culture. As she grows up, however, she moves into a society controlled predominantly by men. She may notice the many ways in which boys are favoured. They are allowed to be more active, aggressive, and ambitious; they are given more freedom to explore away from home; they are allowed to rebel occasionally and be 'real boys'.

(A father may punish his son for a misdemeanour; but as he reads his paper at night and his son is safely asleep, he may register some pride that his son should have dared so risky an escapade.) By contrast, the girl is expected to conform more closely to the tidy pattern of social living.

Yet paradoxically girls have greater freedom to deviate from their defined sex-role. They can sometimes wear boys' clothes and play with boys' toys. This freedom to deviate, and her envy of the greater freedom allowed to boys, may lead a girl to become a tomboy, playing with boys and dissociating herself with some disdain from the activities of girls. Some time later, and almost equally abruptly, she again changes her role; and one day we are surprised to see her walking down the street, neatly dressed and looking the very essence of youthful feminity.

For boys, the pattern of adaptation is different. They first find themselves in an opposite-sex culture, then later in a same-sex one. There is a great deal of social pressure on boys from adults and even more from their companions to play a masculine role. They cannot wear girls' clothes or play with girls' toys. Some boys overstress their role. They pour scorn on girls' activities, on creative pursuits, and on the romantic ('mushy') aspects of books and films. 'Too much love and not enough war for me,' commented a thirteen-year-old about a film called *Love and War*. When a boy is made to sit by a girl and is told by the teacher, 'She won't eat you', his look of extreme discomfort suggests that he is not quite sure. Boys' concept of the ideal boy—aggressive, talkative, boisterous, daring, loyal to his group, indifferent towards dress and appearance—and their scorn and exaggerated assertiveness again indicate that they are on the defensive in their determination to avoid any suggestion that they are 'cissies' (28).

Girls see boys as rude and nasty, and many of their activities as plainly childish. In general, writers agree that at this stage girls show greater stability than boys. Perhaps boys are hostile to girls because they sense this, and so feel inferior to girls. Or possibly it is more of a strain for boys to learn masculine roles than for girls to learn feminine roles. A girl is more protected, and learning her role is an extension of her past life at home. Even today, if she is not getting on well at school, we may say, 'Well, she can leave. It isn't so important for a girl.' But for a boy the pressure is to prove himself: 'to be a man', 'not to be a cissy', 'to get on'. Boys' instability may partly arise from the insecurity they feel because of this pressure (7).

Yet, even though boys and girls have pursued their separate activities during the last five years or so, and have frequently shown mutual antagonism, antipathy begins to give way to a more positive awareness of members of the other sex when boys and girls approach the age of fourteen. By this time neither are so certain that members of the other sex are 'silly', 'childish', 'soppy', or quite as redundant in their scheme of things as they had thought. Boys are expected even by their companions to look to their grooming and to acquire some of the social graces. So one day a near fourteen-year-old boy may appear at school with hair, formerly unruly, held neatly in place with brilliantine.

Kinsey speaks of 'homosexual' and 'heterosexual' activities among young children, even when he refers to relatively simple sexual behaviour such as mutual exhibitionism, mutual feeling of bodies and genitals.

Even so his figures show that sexual experiences before puberty are comparatively rare, and that most of them are trivial. His results apparently imply that in the United States about 57 per cent of boys have had some sexual experience by the age of fourteen, and indicate a progressive increase yearly, from 10 per cent at five years of age to 35 per cent at thirteen (15).[1] About 50 per cent of his sample had had a single experience, and very few developed a pattern of frequent or regular sexual activity.

The cumulative incidence for American girls up to the age of thirteen is less. Just under half (48 per cent) of Kinsey's sample had had a 'sexual' experience by the age of fourteen and, in contrast to boys, the figures suggest a progressive decrease year by year, from 13 per cent who had such an experience at nine to 7 per cent who did so at thirteen. (16)[2,3] For over half the girls the experience was a single one, or only a few experiences. Even fewer girls than boys had developed any pattern of frequent or regular activity.

Kinsey's results indicate considerable differences between children of different social classes. For example, among boys who reach only the lowest educational level (up to eighth grade) three times as many have had sexual intercourse during the pubescent

[1] pages 162 and 169.
[2] pages 107–8.   [3] pages 129.

period as compared with boys who reach higher educational levels (up to thirteenth grade). If the boy of low educational level has this experience, the chances are 3 to 1 that he will continue heterosexual activities in adolescence. If the boy of high educational level does by some chance (such as contact with an older girl) have sexual intercourse, the chances are 4 to 1 that he will not continue heterosexual activities into adolescent years (15).

There is always the possibility of forbidden activities, and a probability of sexual references in the conversation of groups of children at puberty. Occasionally amidst their many other activities the attention of boys will be diverted to sexuality; a sexual reference may cause roars of laughter and a spate of smutty jokes follows. During a single conversation nearly every word spoken, even the most innocuous, is given a double meaning. This is a form of collective boasting, an exaggerated attempt to air a sophistication which the boys do not yet possess.

With girls such behaviour is less marked; but by the age of eleven there may be a sudden fascination in swearing, and by twelve or thirteen the infrequent smutty joke. Occasionally this may be done with delighted deliberateness, calculated to arouse a shocked or admiring response from other children, perhaps older ones, particularly older brothers or sisters. It may be too risky to try out on parents, but older brothers and sisters are the next best thing. The interest which the bolder girls show in the boys of a nearby school arouses scandalized admiration from the less daring. Occasionally friends may relate experiences of a mildly sexual nature shared with boys. The stories may be wholly fictitious; and in any case are much improved in the telling. In these ways girls anticipate their later attractiveness as women, and assure themselves they are no longer the small children their parents and teachers sometimes seem to think.

Children and adults

The separation between adults and children becomes more marked now. The pubescent group provides much for its members (recognition, support, the pride of belonging, protection); its secrets must be kept, even though this means defying an adult. Pubescent children realize that there are things you do not talk about to adults—the near-delinquent escapade, a sexual experience, making a scapegoat of a child—and they become touchy when they feel that parents and teachers are prying into their affairs. When their mothers say, 'Where have you been?' the reply is usually 'Nowhere'; when they ask, 'What have you been doing?' the answer is 'Oh, nothing'.

Lesser and Abelson (17) measured the extent to which children between ages six and thirteen tended to agree with parents, teachers and companions. The children were shown pictures of pairs of unfamiliar objects, and asked which of the two they preferred; they were asked a number of questions, for example, 'Which would you rather watch, a sunrise or a sunset?' First, however, they were told what a parent, teacher, or child (according to the source being tested) had answered. The study showed that children between seven and nine usually agreed about the same number of times with adults as with their companions. From nine onwards, and particularly between the ages of eleven and thirteen, they agreed more frequently with their companions. By early adolescence, their companions were the most important of the three influences.

According to one research (19), the problems parents face with their pubescent sons are as follows: to urge them to be clean and tidy, to remind them about gardening jobs, to stop their outbursts of temper, their dilatoriness (especially at meal-times), their teasing of younger brothers and sisters; with their daughters the chief problem is to urge them to give more help with domestic chores, to tidy up their rooms and belongings, and to organize their leisure in such a way as to have time for things, like homework, which are so often left to the very last moment.

At this stage parents are probably going through a period of indecision. Whereas during the Primary School years they have relatively few doubts about the control they must impose on their children, they now feel uncertain about when it is best to stand firm and when to give way.

The children also enter on a phase of indecision in their acceptance of their parents' control. During the Primary School years they do not on the whole question their parents' right to control them. Now they begin to have doubts as to how much, and on what issues, to resist and on what to accept their parents' directive. In the mutual uncertainty that exists between parents and children, parents think their children 'touchy', unreasonable and resentful, and children think their parents lacking in understanding.

A child's impelling bid for autonomy, and his determination not to give way, make him insistent and uncompromising. It is *he* who is right. Parents feel, with some justification, how unreasonable he is. Yet at times he actually feels relieved when his parents do make a stand. A twelve- or thirteen-year-old, for example, asks permission to go out with a group of older boys on some escapade. He really fears that he'll get out of his depth; but he cannot say 'No' to his friends. His parents' refusal relieves him of the responsibility and provides an escape from the pressure of the group which he could not withstand alone.

Two points may be suggested here. First, children do not necessarily want to offend, annoy, and run into bouts of irritability, but their urge towards independence is too insistent and their feelings of insecurity about it too great. Secondly, there is often conflict between love for their parents and the demands of the group. From a boy particularly, the group expects willingness to take part in an escapade or two, to smoke occasionally, to stand up to adults in authority, and to play a game of 'chicken'. Even if parents and teachers are fairly reasonable beings, it is etiquette to criticize them as 'awkward' and 'unreasonable'; although, of course, if the mood changes, all members of the group may agree that parents are 'sometimes all right, though'. This grudgingly-given compliment expresses genuine affection for parents and teachers who are understanding, and relieves the sense of guilt the children feel because of their criticisms, which they know are sometimes unjust. Further, when all the members of the group agree, they can be complimentary about parents and teachers and still be good members of the group. They are thus able to have their cake and eat it—a rare but enjoyable experience.

Therefore, as various studies remind us (e.g. 9), it is well not to emphasize the conflicts at the expense of the bright moments of co-operation between children and their parents. Their co-operation may be displayed in many ways: gradual lessening of control; discussion of plans, or just discussions, between a child and an adult; the freedom implied in such things as a 'say' in choosing clothes, freedom to spend own money; or the sudden asking by parent or teacher of the child's considered opinion—

'What do you think, Jim?' Jim feels good, to the point of a confusion that, at first, makes a considered reply difficult.

The two phases of pubescence

Because individual differences in physical and emotional growth as well as in intellectual ability and in specific skills, now become more marked, it is even more hazardous to ascribe ages to the two phases of pubescence to be described. It is important, therefore to repeat yet again that, for any one child, the phases and ages may not coincide in exactly this way.

The twelve-year-old (first phase) shows the enthusiasm and vitality of the eleven-year-old, but he is much more able to control the extremes of anger and impulsiveness. He combines an interest in other people with a more helpful concern. This interest may be a part of a growing attempt to learn about himself—'Are your thoughts and feelings the same as my thoughts and feelings?' Generally he is more agreeable and pleasant at home—more tolerant of his younger brothers and sisters, and less explosive. But with all this, he has a sensitivity which quite suddenly may upset the relations between himself and his parents. A request is refused; in an unguarded moment a mother gives her daughter an order in a tone of voice more suited to a small child, or criticizes a new hair style. The rapport is then destroyed.

There are the characteristic traits of transition, such as restlessness, intensity, and sparks of anger. The transitional nature of this phase shows itself also in swings of mood; from gaiety to depression; from confident and expansive activity to gloom and discouragement; from enthusiasm to apathy. But these swings are not so frequent or so intense as they will be in later years.

Twelve-year-olds are attached to their groups and find it difficult to withstand group pressure to perform some delinquent act, such as entering an empty house, stealing from a chain store, or ragging a teacher. They may now start to have periods when they just hang around. This may be the first sign of a need for rest (as distinct from sleep), for recuperation from continuous activity. Individual creative activity (making things, such as radios, model aircraft and ships) is popular. This is especially satisfying for the boy who is not good at sport, which is the main group activity at this time.

Girls stop playing with dolls, and will often find an advanced substitute for doll-playing in making puppets and staging puppet shows. They turn now to creative work that has practical applications—making rugs, woollen scarves, a simple smock.

Girls will voluntarily care for a group of small children and act, for example, as 'teacher'. It is fascinating to see little children's response to this 'play' situation which the older girl organizes in a realistic way. There is a timetable, 'real' sums, and 'real' writing, which the small children pursue with an earnestness and diligence which would cause a professional teacher to be envious. But, of course, it does not last very long. The 'pupils' tire quickly, even though for a time they meekly submit to the discipline.

Many girls menstruate for the first time during their twelfth year. If they have not themselves begun to menstruate, they know of girls who have. The mother's function is vitally important in making sure that the child knows exactly what will happen and why, and in teaching her what she should do. Insufficient knowledge can, of course, make the menarche an extremely frightening experience. Gesell (5) says that the earlier the menarche occurs, especially if before eleven, the more difficult it is for the girl to accept it. He does not suggest a reason for this. It may be that, because menstruation begins so early, a girl has not been properly prepared by her mother or teacher. It could also be that she is the first in her group to menstruate, and feels different. This would fit in with what Gesell says of the thirteen-year-old, namely, that at this age concern about menstruation occurs when it has not begun. In this case, the girl feels different because she is among the last in her group.

At thirteen (second phase) children may begin to slow down and take stock. Instead of trying their hand at everything, as at eight or nine, they begin to specialize. A thirteen-year-old may find that he has a particular aptitude—for drawing, photography, mechanical work, or music—and will begin to spend most of his leisure-time in its pursuit. This reflects growing individual differences and the beginning of children's desire to become specialists in a society of specialists.

Thirteen-year-olds tend to be a little distant and pre-occupied. This may reflect the necessity to make choices and the beginnings of a more acute self-awareness. Their preoccupation may worry their parents in a culture like ours, in which even healthy preoccupation is so easily confused with morbid introspection. But there are many things to get straight now—new personal and social problems to solve, and new choices to be made. The younger child does not think. He acts. It is a sign of growing maturity that the thirteen-year-old broods about things as well as acts.

Interference from outside may irritate thirteen-year-olds when they are introspective. They then find their parents' nagging annoying (because of untidy room, pre-occupation, jobs not done), and may snap back. But generally their reactions to adult criticism are not so violent as this. They are less likely to become angry or insolent, and more likely to withdraw, to put up an emotional barrier between themselves and adults. Parents (or teachers) and children then arrive at an impasse: Some adults may then feel they have failed; others reject any such suggestion and point to the 'unreasonableness' of the children. But thirteen-year-olds can be unreasonable.

The growing self-awareness of thirteen-year-olds includes a growing awareness of the *objects* which are extensions of themselves (see Chapter 3). They are not only more critical of their own behaviour and achievements, but also of the behaviour and achievements of the members of their families. A girl wants her mother to be attractive; a boy is proud to remind his friends of his father's achievements. There is an interesting reversal of roles when mother or father dress for the School Open Day. It is the child now who says, 'Oh, not that dress!' 'Not that suit!' She nearly explodes when her mother or father says, 'Why, what's wrong with it?' From the child's point of view, *everything* is wrong. It is usually kindest at times like these if parents take orders from their children.

Insofar as their own personalities are unformed, children tend to live vicariously in the reflected glory of other people. This is expressed in their reading, which has progressed from the poor little rabbit who had adventures and fails to the self-confident heroes and heroines who succeed. It is expressed, too, in the 'crushes' which girls develop for teachers, in children's collections—photographs and clippings of film-stars, ballerinas, sportsmen, and singers.

During this phase some children may become a little blasé and adopt an 'I couldn't care less' attitude. This may affect their progress at school and their relations with their teachers and parents. Their defiance is expressed in a tilt of the head and an almost imperceptible shrug of the shoulders. This behaviour is very hard for adults to take, but if we are able to realize that it is an attempt to maintain a precarious personal dignity, we may be less concerned with the affront to our own dignity. This blasé attitude may also be a defence against the real concern children of this age are beginning to feel about the world and the people in it. By the inverse process of showing apparent lack of concern, they reveal their deep concern.

Towards people in authority boys feel an antipathy, and the separation into 'we' (children) and 'they' (adults) is accentuated. Their curiosity about adult life is often tinged with this hostility. Curiosity and antipathy may be expressed by defying a teacher, especially one who cannot assert himself. They may discover some weakness in him, and deliberately play on it. This is both an experiment to see how the teacher will react, and an expression of opposition to authority. They can do all this without feeling individual guilt, since any guilt would be shared by the whole group. Few teachers are without some weaknesses, and teachers of thirteen- (or fourteen-) year-old boys need to be on their guard, and not fall into the net boys sometimes set. The defiance of the over-dominant teacher may show itself as a group sullenness or as passive resistance to his demands.

Sometimes boys will experiment at home with a few shock tactics. They use a swear word, mention something to do with sex, dogmatically express an attitude or opinion knowing it to be contrary to that of their parents. A girl, writing to a friend about her thirteen-year-old brother, put it like this: 'Bill is up the pole, never looks at a book, never stops letting out terrible *remarks* in front of Mummy and Daddy. Did Roddy ever go through a period of juvenile delinquency?'

When in the classroom, these children like to move about urged perhaps by a need to stretch their growing arms and legs, to satisfy an impulse to tell a friend something not told during recess, or to look for information about their work. When desks are of the old fixed type and movement is prohibited by the teacher, epidemics of note-passing may sometimes break out. If a teacher does intercept an occasional note, it is probably wise to destroy it and leave well alone.

Education and pubescent children

Though pubescent children learn and enjoy learning, on their own and in their groups, the role of the school in their development also needs to be stressed. Because of the blasé attitude towards school and the tendency to defiance, pubescent children may be considered a difficult group to teach (younger children are rarely blasé, and older children more controlled). Against these disadvantages are set many advantages.

Pubescent children have boundless energy, have acquired considerable academic skill, can sustain attention and concentrate more than during their Primary School years. They are more likely to tussle with a problem in arithmetic, and may even want to stay on for a time during recess to finish a job. Increased verbal ability and an increased ability to compromise, to see shades of grey between the blacks and whites, make fruitful discussions in class possible. They are still insatiably curious about the world.

Boys are growing more and more keen on science. Their special interest in astronomy, 'rockets' and travel to the moon prepares them to be at home in the new space age. But they are quite happy to start at the beginning with simple laboratory experiments which involve controlled manipulation of materials and a definite result. The predictability of the explosion when a small jar of hydrogen is exposed to the air and ignited, delights them.

The interest that boys have in science is complemented by the interest girls have in personal relations and in living things. This is a time when many of them begin to acquire pen-friends. Although I know of no investigations to confirm this, girls seem to have pen-friends far more often than boys. To have a pen-friend provides that personal contact which brings alive their interest in other countries. These complementary interests are reflected in the curriculum: physics and chemistry for boys, biology, botany, literature for girls. But the contrast should not be over-emphasized. One authority puts it bluntly: 'It is sometimes almost implied that no girl is interested in physics or mathematics, and no boy in biology, or English literature. This is, of course, nonsense' (30).[1]

The urge to make useful things leads boys and girls at twelve to look forward to beginning woodwork, metalwork or domestic science. But they do want to *make* something. It is acutely disappointing for them if teachers are too formal, and demand the accurate drafting of a plan, or an analysis of the vitamin constituents, before allowing them to make a model or bake a cake. Twelve-year-old boys are not very persevering, and like to make quickly something that can be used. It may be well to accept a rough finish at first and leave finer details until later.

By this stage most children from the middle classes will usually have been taught the value of academic education, so that the school examinations become disciplinary agents to the passing of which considerable energy must be devoted. There are individual differences in the degree of conformity. Some children settle down to work and give up the adventurous escapades mentioned earlier. Others may not settle down until they are about fourteen and start to be nagged by their anxious parents about homework that has not been done. A programme which is less academic may be a suitable interlude for children like these. Indeed, the value of informal learning—by means of excursions, discussions, camps, for example—for the education of most children is consistent with the characteristics described in this and the preceding chapter.

These statements presuppose that the children are reasonably secure socially. A teacher who attempts a positive and creative programme for children from poorer homes at even this stage may be thwarted by the children themselves. They are more aware now of their non-privileged position and are antipathetic to the teacher—not personally, but because he represents a more privileged group. Their antipathy may be very insistent, and may make it difficult for a conscientious teacher to succeed. The despairs and triumphs of such a teacher have formed the theme of a number of novels and films (e.g. 1, 27).

Individual differences in intelligence and special abilities render it still more necessary to make provision for such differences now than during the Primary School stage. Varying kinds of institutions have been devised to cope with the problem: Gram-

[1] page 113.

mar, Technical and Secondary Modern Schools, on the one hand, or Comprehensive Schools on the other (as in England), Intermediate Schools (as in New Zealand), Junior High Schools (as in the United States). It may be said with certainty that whatever the administrative method adopted, it should always be possible for children to move easily from one school to another, if there is more than one, and from one class to another within the classes of each age level, if the school is comprehensive; and the period of transition should extend over several years—from ten to thirteen, say. For, as we have seen, the intellectual growth of some children may be uneven. A child may not mature in a way which fits a system based inflexibly on chronological age (23).

The distinction between learning and applying skills already learned was made in the preceding chapter. During this stage teachers should concentrate largely on the application of skills already learned. An academic programme which moves continuously from one new abstract skill to another may lead the children to ask, 'What is the good of it all?' The school should include activities which are concentrated on the application of a wide variety of skills, as in carefully chosen projects, debates, excursions, and dramatic productions. These activities will appear less remote from the children's everyday lives.

But his stress on the application of skills already learned should not lead us to forget that academic discipline is necessary for children because of the rational and scientific nature of the culture they are preparing to enter. They should therefore be made gradually aware of the value of abstract modes of thinking, not so much through direct or formal teaching, but incidentally, as a respite from learning, say, a new theorem or an equation (a child will often gain much insight from the incidental asides and apparent digressions of the teacher).

To illustrate: even apart from the use of formulae for solving practical day-by-day problems, children may be asked to put equations, such as $(x + y)^2 = x^2 + y^2 + 2xy$, into words. The difficulty of stating in precise verbal terms all that is implied in such an equation, and the large number of words needed to do it, will enable the children to see the economy of thought achieved by symbolic expression. Or the teacher can raise a question as to the value of the zero digit, then discuss the problems that would remain unsolved if it did not exist. In geography, he can work from a set of facts about one area with a Mediterranean climate for example, to other Mediterranean areas, and, in doing so, point out the common geographical features—climate, products and so on—irrespective of the features specific to each area.

The point of these illustrations is that such techniques give children an idea not only of the economy, but also of the ability to predict and control which abstract conceptions introduce.

With children of lesser intellectual ability there is a special need to relate abstract principles to actual situations, that is, to augment their knowledge by means of practical activities in the classroom, workshops or the domestic centre. But though pitched on a less difficult level, the aim is again to enable them to apply the abstract, and to see its value in obtaining control and power over the concrete.

REFERENCES

1   Braithwaite, E. R. *To Sir with Love*. Bodley Head, London, 1959.
2   Chisnall, B. 'The interests and personal traits of delinquent boys.' *British Journal of Educational Psychology*. 1942, **12,** pp. 76.
3   Crane, A. R. 'Pre-adolescent gangs and the moral development of children.' *British Journal of Educational Psychology*, 1958, **28,** pp. 201–8.
4   Feinberg, M. 'Relation of background experiences to social acceptance.' *Journal of Abnormal and Social Psychology*, 1953, **48,** pp. 206–14.
5   Gesell, A., Ilg, F. L., Ames, L. B. *Youth: the Years from Ten to Sixteen*. Harper, New York, 1956.
6   Glueck, S., Glueck, E. T. *Unraveling Juvenile Delinquency*. Commonwealth Fund, New York, 1950.
7   Gray, S. W. 'Masculinity–feminity in relation to anxiety and social acceptance.' *Child Development*, 1957, **28,** pp. 203–14.
8   Gronlund, M. E., Anderson, L. 'Personality characteristics of socially accepted, socially rejected and socially neglected Junior High School children.' *Educational Administration and Supervision*, 1957, **43,** pp. 329–38.
9   Hawkes, G. L. *et al.*, 'Pre-Adolescents' view of some of their relations with their parents.' *Child Development*, 1959, **28,** pp. 393–9.
10 Helanko, R. 'Peer groups and personality: sports and socialization.' *In* Smelser, M. J. and W. T. (Ed.) *Personality and Social Systems*. Wiley, New York, 1963, pp. 238–47.
11 Hicks, J. A., Hayes, S. M. 'Study of the characteristics of 250 Junior High School children.' *Child Development*, 1938, **7,** pp. 219–42.
12 Hollingshead, A. B. *Elmstown's Youth*. Wiley, New York, 1949.
13 Horrocks, J. E., Thompson, G. G. 'A study of friendship fluctuations of rural boys and girls.' *Journal of Genetic Psychology*, 1946, **69,** pp. 189–98.

14 Horrocks, J. E., Thompson, G. G. 'A study of friendship fluctuations among urban boys and girls.' *Journal of Genetic Psychology*, 1947, **70**, pp. 53–63.

15 Kinsey, A. C., Pomeroy, W. B., Martin, C. E. *Sexual Behaviour in the Human Male*. Saunders, London, 1948.

16 Kinsey, A. C., Pomeroy, W. B., Martin, C. E. *Sexual Behaviour in the Human Female*. Saunders, London, 1948.

17 Lesser, G. S., Abelson, R. P. 'Personality correlates of persuasibility in children.' *In* Hovland, C. I., Janis, J. L. (Ed.) *Personality and Persuasibility*. Yale University Press, New Haven, 1959.

18 Lippitt, N. *et al.* 'The dynamics of power: a field study of social influence in groups of children.' *In* Maccoby, E. E. *et al.* (Eds.) *Readings in Social Psychology*. Holt, New York, 1958.

19 Loomis, M. *The Pre-adolescent*. Appleton, New York, 1959.

20 Lynn, D. B. 'A note on sex differences in the development of masculine and feminine identification.' *In* Seidman, J. M. (Ed.) *The Adolescent, a Book of Readings*. Holt, Rinehart, New York, 1960.

21 Mays, J. B. *Growing up in the City*. Liverpool University Press, Liverpool, 1956.

22 Mays, J. B. *On the Threshold of Delinquency*. Liverpool University Press, Liverpool, 1959.

23 Nisbet, J. D., Entwhistle, N. J. *The Age of Transfer to Secondary Education* (Scottish Council for Research in Education, Publication No. 53), University of London Press, London, 1966.

24 Pope, B. 'Socio-economic contrasts in children's peer culture prestige values.' *Genetic Psychology Monographs*, 1953, **48**, pp. 157–222.

25 Shaw, C. R. *et al. Juvenile Delinquency in Rural Areas*. University of Chicago Press, Chicago, 1942.

26 Spaulding, C. B., Bolin, R. S. 'The clique as a device for social adjustments among high school students.' *Journal of Educational Sociology*, 1950, pp. 147–53.

27 Townsend, J. *The Young Devils*. Chatto and Windus, London, 1958.

28 Tryon, C. M. 'The adolescent peer culture'. *In Adolescence 43rd Year-book of the National Society for the Study of Education*. University of Chicago Press, Chicago, 1944. Part I, pp. 214–39.

29 Wolman, B. 'Spontaneous groups of children and adolescents.' *Journal of Social Psychology*, 1951, **34**, pp. 171–82.

30 *15 to 18*. Report for Central Advisory Council for Education, England. Volume I (Crowther Report). H.M. Stationary Office, London, 1959.

CHAPTER SEVENTEEN

Middle Adolescence
(fourteen, fifteen, sixteen)

GROWING up takes place within societies which vary in their complexity, and which differ in their purposes and values. How an individual will cope with the problems of growing up will depend partly upon the culture in which he lives. In some simple societies, the transition from child to adult is recognized in ceremonial rites. Just before these rites are performed, he may be required to live in seclusion from the rest of the tribe for a period of weeks or months, to undergo tests of physical endurance. He is instructed in the codes, laws, morals and customs of his tribe, and in matters of sex. Rituals which suggest rebirth are often observed; for instance, a boy may be tied inside a sack and the sack ceremonially cut open, a girl confined in a dark cave or hut and allowed ceremonially to emerge. The purpose of these rites is to teach children the lore of the tribe, to fit them for their work, and to instruct them in the behaviour, dress and adornment appropriate to the tribe and to their own status in it.

It is interesting to note two distinctive features of these rites. First, the change the children make—from the status of a child to that of an adult with its privileges and responsibilities—is almost immediate. Secondly, the emphasis is on conformity to tribal customs and on transference of allegiance from the family to the tribe. The essence of training is unquestioning obedience to tribal customs and the restriction of individual idiosyncrasies, so that, although a new self is born at puberty, it is tribally moulded. This playing down of individual initiative makes for a society that remains much the same from generation to generation.

In a complex society like ours, however, the opposite is true.

The change from child to adult is not immediate because our children need long preparation in which to become proficient in their vocation, before they assume the responsibilities of full citizenship, and marriage and children. Again, in our society we encourage individual initiative; we approve of the person who can think originally, make choices, and fully accept the consequences of the choices he makes. It is partly the original contributions of individuals that make the changing society which we know today. In short, a new set of characteristics becomes manifest during adolescence; but their growth is gradual and takes a number of years. It has individual as well as social components, and takes place within a highly complex social setting. We will consider this process with emphasis on three main aspects, (a) self-absorption, (b) social absorption, and (c) sexual behaviour.

Self-absorption

Development during adolescence may be regarded as a process of ever-increasing realization of the concepts 'I', 'me', 'my', and 'mine' (see Chapter 3). By self-absorption is meant an adolescent's concern with himself as a self-conscious being who evaluates his own appearance, behaviour, and achievements, and the feelings he experiences as a result. Pressey (23) confirms this self-absorption by noting that adolescents are worried mainly about their self-consciousness, their looks and their achievements, and that each of these worries increases in importance from the years fourteen to nineteen.

Self-absorption becomes more common than before, and is enriched by new experiences. Physiological and psychological changes lead to increasing self-awareness, to new reflective and imaginative broodings, and a heightened self-consciousness. There are more frequent moments of inordinate shyness, and often a tendency to blush easily.

Through self-criticism, as well as through the judgments of other people, the adolescent develops an overall evaluation of himself. This has been referred to earlier as the 'self-concept'. Just as a person likes to build a house or to arrange a room in which he can live and be at home, so an adolescent wants to develop a conception of himself that is lovable and worthy, one with which he can live and feel at home. If he does not do so,

feelings of unworthiness give rise to a sense of disunity and un-
knowingly may lead him to become his own worst enemy.

Adolescents are, therefore, beginning to experience the sort
of problems to which we adults are subject. They know more
acutely than before what it means to be bored, and the feelings of
dull emptiness that follow a period of excitement or strain, or
during a long school holiday with no stimulation.

Adolescents now begin to question existence, to ask what its
purpose is. Such questioning may leave them puzzled and confused. Imaginatively they begin to soar and to realize the great
gulf between the world of their ideal and the world as it actually
is. They may feel a keen sense of the inadequacy of things as they
are. Most of us adjust to this as we get older, perhaps because the
discrepancy is too painful to contemplate. But for creative artists
it is probably an ever-present difficulty.

Because of social differences and differences of temperament,
the acuteness of the problems which accompany emerging self-
awareness will vary between individuals within the same culture.
The more highly educated an adolescent, the more reflective and
self-critical he is likely to become; the same is true of the student
who studies literature and humanities rather than science and
engineering. Paul (the cerebrotonic) is likely to become more
reflective than Peter (the somatotonic) or William (the viscerotonic).[1]

Self-reflection may be expressed in engaging ways as when
adolescents spontaneously reminisce. They will talk of past
events and feelings, of how they loved or feared particular
people, about small acts of delinquency they committed when
they were little children, and the fears and tremblings they had
about them. Through such reminiscing they absorb past experiences and look at themselves objectively—but from a safe distance in
time.

They begin now to use the words 'character' and 'personality',
and to realize the importance of outside influence on the formation
of personality. They speak proudly of the powerful influence of
their school. Entries in their diaries and autograph books combine
reference to 'self' with the idealism typical of adolescents.

[1] See Chapter 6.

PHYSICAL IMAGE AND SELF-FEELINGS

The adolescent's image of himself is in part the image he has of his body. A sense of identity, of being himself, arises from the impulses, sensations, pleasures and pains that his body evokes, and from the enhancement or deflation of self-esteem that the sight of his body arouses. The physical changes taking place give rise to new bodily characteristics, feelings and impulses, particularly those which relate to sex. All these have to be evaluated and accepted.

Because the body is important in the life of the adolescent, many things follow with regard to it, four of which will now be considered. First, the body must be tended and cared for. Whereas a boy of nine or ten is as little concerned with his physical appearance as parents and teachers will allow, a boy of fifteen looks to his grooming and will spend much time combing his hair and cleaning his teeth. Girls become even more concerned with their looks. Getting ready for a party, or even for a visit to the cinema round the corner, is a major operation. They will spend hours brushing their own, or each other's, hair.

Secondly, the body must be appraised. The standard for this appraisal is usually a mental impression of the ideal physique, an impression adolescents acquire from many sources—magazines, advertising, films, television, and so on. The contemporary prototype of feminine beauty has the following main characteristics: she is of average height, slender, yet with some feminine curves. For boys, the ideal reflects the predominantly mesomorphic boy of above average height, who is athletic in appearance, well built, strong (8). Having formed this mental image, adolescents will judge both themselves and others as worthy or unworthy insofar as their appearance accords with it.

Thirdly, bodily defects noted during this appraisal become a matter of concern. Whereas a man of fifty will pat his bald head with some resignation, and may laugh with his children about his flat nose, at adolescence bodily defects, real or imagined, occasion moods of self-depreciation and depression. Such concern is exemplified in the sixteen-year-old who brooded over the thought that her ears were too big, and then drew a face with large ears, calling it 'Self-portrait with ears'. Another sixteen-year-old girl said, half in joke, 'I don't think I'll eat this chocolate biscuit. It may go to my legs and they're too big already.' For girls particularly the concern can be exaggerated, since the increase in weight which sometimes occurs during adolescence is often only a temporary condition. By trying to reduce their weight adolescent girls may distort this temporary condition in order to conform to the prototype. It is so easy for an adolescent when feeling depressed to dwell upon one small defect, and so pleasant when elated to forget the defect in the light of the pleasing appearance of the whole.

Mirror-gazing, a good deal of which is done during these years, is a way of getting to know the new body and its image. It can also be a means of reassurance in moments of anxiety. You may notice that adults, too, look at themselves more during times of stress. Then it is reassuring to learn that one's body-image does not reflect one's mental anguish.

There is yet a fourth problem—the rate at which the body matures. The possible age-range of the growth spurt (10–16 in girls, 11–17 in boys) gives some idea of the extent of individual differences in rate of growth. Such differences are brought vividly home to us when we see a very tall girl, from the top class of a Primary School, walking beside a boy of the same age and from the same class, who hardly reaches her shoulder; or a very short boy in the third class of a Secondary School, trotting beside a big, tall boy of the same age who is already showing a dark down on his upper lip and cheeks. One would surmise that it would be best to mature neither too early nor too late, and to be comfortably in accord with the majority. In fact, research studies (13, 21) suggest better too early than too late. Adolescents who mature early and whose appearance accords with the accepted ideal show a relaxed unaffectedness and assurance. On the other hand, the lack of self-confidence of late maturers is often revealed by their impulsive, attention-seeking behaviour (13).

Adults can sometimes intensify the problem of the child who matures late; for example, an adult may tactlessly say in a boy's presence, and to his great discomfort, 'Fourteen! He's rather small for his age!' It can be very disturbing to be out of line developmentally with one's companions, to be taller or shorter, fatter or thinner than some ideal decrees is 'right and proper'. Parents and teachers could perhaps help children who are distressed by explaining to them that people just do differ in appearance, and that differences are not necessarily deficiencies, as the social norm would sometimes have us believe.

ACHIEVING AND SELF-FEELINGS

Adolescents reflect; they have a whole life in front of them. It is natural, then, that the gap between the present and old age should be dwelt upon. Job possibilities are vicariously explored by reading career novels, especially popular among girls. But child-like ambitions are abandoned—to be a train or bus driver. At least one investigation (26) suggests that the lives of many Secondary Modern boys, as imaginatively planned, are modestly in tune with reality: a job with good prospects, simple recreations (fishing, cycling), marriage (at twenty-three), children, retirement (on a reasonable pension), pleasant pursuits in the country. The plans of girls complement those of boys: a job until marriage (at twenty-one), husband and children, a return to the job, a cottage in the country, grandchildren (17).

Stern (24) asked twenty-four Grammar School boys, aged fifteen to sixteen, to write brief forecasts of their personal and vocational futures. Nine years later he sent them a questionnaire, and found that they had predicted very accurately. Their fore-casts covered a range of careers, including accountancy, engineer-ing, teaching, the R.A.F., and even being a fire-fighting officer in New Zealand. The boys also accurately predicted personal details such as marital status, number of children, leisure-time interests.

The delights of hero-worship—of teachers by pupils, of skilled craftsmen by apprentices—may in some ways be related to the desire to achieve and to acquire competence, to be where the admired person is, and to be as skilled as he.

As well as the imaginative future, there are immediate day-to-day triumphs—in sport, in music or dancing, or winning a prize at school or for newspaper competitions. There are, too, the failures and the fears of failure. Examinations are often a source of worry. They are the chief criteria for the child's success and form stepping-stones to higher achievement and higher social status.

The conclusions reached in a series of five experiments with college students, confirmed afterwards by repetition, suggest a way in which anxiety about examinations may be reduced (4, 18). College students were given class tests under less formal conditions than usual. They were asked to comment on each question—on its clarity, relevance, ambiguity—and to say where they felt it to be confusing. This procedure made no difference to the marks or degree of anxiety of the students who were doing well at college and who were generally confident during class tests; but students who were not doing well and who were usually anxious during class tests got significantly higher marks when 'free to comment'. In addition, they were far less anxious. The investigators concluded that an informal procedure reduced the implicit threat of a class examination, and that the energy formerly expended in anxiety could now be directed to answering the questions. Relative freedom from anxiety probably enabled the students to be more flexible in their thinking, and so better able to comprehend the nature of the questions and to deal with difficult points. A supplementary finding showed that the students also obtained higher marks and were less anxious when they subsequently took class tests under the usual conditions.

Children see the work of the school in relation to their future. This is illustrated by Musgrove (20) in a study of over 350 Secondary Modern and Grammar School pupils. In the opinion of these children, the school should provide intellectual training—preparation for examinations and a career. They also thought that the school should provide the opportunity for discussion and exchange of ideas, and satisfy social needs in associations with fellow pupils and teachers. Even here the pupils emphasized the practical, seeing this function as a preparation for getting on with people when they left school.

Speaking of this practical emphasis that adolescent children give to school work, the Crowther Report (27)[1] says:

'Inevitably there is a strong vocational flavour to what boys and girls value most in secondary education. Before the end of their present secondary course they have reached the stage when they desire to see the relevance of what they are doing at school to what they will be doing when they leave school. They are anxious to see a purpose in education, and this anxiety seems to us wholly natural. It should be neither ignored nor played down, but used to enlist their co-operation.'

Social absorption

As children proceed through adolescence, the single-sex cliques tend to coalesce to form small mixed crowds of a dozen or more

[1] pages 111-12.

boys and girls. Like the clique, the crowd satisfies adolescents' need to be with and to be accepted by their fellows; but it has a looser structure. In it the two sexes intermingle; the presence of girls casts a civilizing influence over the aggressiveness of the boys and obviates the boys' tendency to 'gang up'; and the presence of boys and the attraction they have for girls prevents the girls from forming cliques closely knit, exclusive, and ready to make scape-goats, as at pubescence. But the crowd has within itself the seeds of its own dissolution, since from out of it develop what Cooley has called *intimate pair groups*. Children within a crowd tend to pair off, while still remaining members of the crowd. Two children of the same sex become close friends; later, boys and girls pair off to become adolescent sweethearts.

These crowds may meet informally at a rendezvous, such as a café. They chatter away, bantering and chaffing one another; two of them may join up and quietly leave; two of the same sex may engage in earnest conversation. There is a delightful informality. The pairings of the boy and girl, and the coming together of the two boys are accepted as part of the new human scene. There is little of the teasing and insensitive guffaws with which thirteen-year-olds greet boy and girl attachments. These crowds may meet under more formal conditions—at the church, youth or Scout clubs under the supervision of adults. Ideally such clubs provide the opportunity for creative and social pursuits within a more sheltered environment than can be provided by the street or café.

Early adolescents often get together in single-sex groups. Girls gossip about clothes, boys, film-stars, teachers. One topic leads to another, one girl comments, another contradicts, another makes a compromise suggestion for which they all settle. The girls try out make-up, exchange clothes, experiment with new hair styles, often in imitation of adults and amidst bursts of laughter.

Boys meet as a group in some appropriate spot, often near home—a field perhaps, or a corner of the street. They chatter about girls, cars, radios, television and football. They may suddenly start throwing and catching a ball, seeing who can hit a chosen spot with a ball or a stone, or they may attempt to carry out some individual stunt on their bicycles. Then one of them discovers that he has enough money to treat the others to an ice-cream. Activity is disbanded, and sucking and gossip intervenes.

American studies (e.g. 11, 12) confirm that early adolescents tend to have a best friend of the same sex. These pairs of friends usually have similar interests, I.Q.s and background, and are alike in confidence, dominance and sociability. Although there is this general tendency, however, investigations also reveal marked differences between certain couples. Sometimes one of the two is more competent in some field, more attractive in appearance, or more dominant in manner. The other may then become dependent, and live vicariously in the exploits of his partner.

These close friendships provide an opportunity for the exchange of confidences about all the 'self' problems previously referred to—the changes of feeling and mood, and sex.

Group characteristics can annoy parents and teachers. At fourteen, even children who belong to the more formal clubs and Scout troops have a tendency to break out into wild behaviour. Boys may be busy about some co-operative activity (such as preparing a hot meal in a camp) when one of them with unerring aim throws half a potato at another, and this becomes the signal for everybody to start throwing things. In a few moments, the whole place is in an uproar and the shouts of the adult leader sink to impotent mutterings against 'these barbarians'. But the chaos ceases as suddenly as it began. Once again the boys are their most engaging selves.

By sixteen the game of 'chicken' may reach absurd proportions. An individual is dared to perform a dangerous feat—one infringing a sensible social rule—for example, to cross a very busy street by other than the pedestrian crossing, or to be called 'chicken' if he does not. The explanation of this is probably much the same for older as for younger children. As they become more independent of adults, adolescents, like young children, derive security from their group activities and from rapport with their fellows; because they are also unsure of themselves, their self-judgments and feelings of self-esteem tend to rise and fall according to the opinion of the group. They cannot therefore, risk the censure and ridicule which being called 'chicken' implies. Their desire to tilt against established order further contributes to make the game of chicken a fearful and exhilarating experience for them.

Adults are sometimes annoyed by adolescents' rituals and crazes, by crushes on 'pop' singers; they are sometimes amazed, too, by the group displays of this admiration at airports or outside theatres. The hoards of adolescents at an airport probably consist of a number of these crowds, gathered together to form a much larger group. The rituals, the adoration and the mass displays probably serve a number of purposes. First, they assure adolescents of their group identity, since the rituals and the adoration are *theirs*. Secondly, in these mass displays, mutual stimulation heightens each individual's emotionality; and within this heightened emotionality the self-awareness and conflicts of individual living temporarily disappear. Thirdly, the crushes on 'pop' singers, film-stars and so on may well be an expression of an adolescent's idealism; and within the crowd the myth of his idol's perfection is confirmed. 'If so many other people think and feel as I do, then I must be right.'

Finally, adolescents want to do and say the 'right thing', but are so self-consciously concerned about it that often they commit *faux pas*. A young adolescent says the most foolish things and antagonizes someone—perhaps a girl—whom he wishes to impress; he trips on the rug and hits a woman's arm as she holds a cup of tea; he blushes in front of a group of girls. When he goes home and thinks about all these things, he feels the excruciating pain and remorse that adolescents especially experience from such a series of mishaps. He digs his fingers into the palms of his hands, and bites his lips in an agony of self-hatred.

Parents and teachers

The problems that arise between early adolescents and their parents range widely. Yet most are related, on the one hand, to the adolescents' search for freedom and autonomy, and, on the other, to their parents' maintenance of control. There are the niggling day-by-day problems: for girls, permissions—to go out in the evening, to go out with boys, to wear nylons, to use make-up, to go dancing, to go to bed later (and not appreciably earlier than one's friends) (10); for boys and girls, reminders about noisiness, getting school work done, table manners, eating proper food (3).

There are the things adolescents should have done, but have not. Father comes home expecting the lawn to have been cut, but finds it uncut and his son idly chewing a piece of grass and chatting to a group of friends. Mother arrives home to find the washing up not done, the kitchen in a mess, and her daughter sprawled in a chair reading a book, or twirling her hair and 'just thinking'.

There are the things they have done which they should not have done. An adolescent will decide to make a milk shake (an innocent enough occupation); but she leaves the kitchen be-speckled with drops of milk shake, and an amazingly large number of kitchen utensils scattered all over the place unwashed.

Their very self-absorption may make them appear 'forgetful', 'selfish', 'ungrateful' at the very time when parents feel that they are old enough to help about the house and to be more consider-ate, and when parents are becoming more conscious of the money and self-sacrifice that having children has meant and still means. The argument, 'Look at all the things we do for you and you won't even do this little thing!' seems eminently sensible. Adolescent over-concern with the 'self' is probably inevitable when the 'self' one has is changing and a new one forming. If you are not sure of your possession of a valued object, you usually hold on to it all the harder. The same applies to the self.

Adolescents are especially sensitive to slights and reprimands. To be reprimanded in front of the family is to be treated as if one were still a child, to be scolded in front of friends or strangers is to be subject to the greatest humiliation. It is often difficult for parents to realize that their children are growing up, and to change their behaviour accordingly. For example, a mother may reprove her married daughter as if she were still a child. The daughter laughs about it afterwards with her husband and says, 'Mother still treats me as a little girl.' But she can laugh because as a wife and mother she has a firmly established status and is secure in it. Not so adolescents who cannot laugh because they have no such sure status.

Investigations suggest that the relations between parents' personality and behaviour and those of their adolescent sons and daughters are very much in accord with those outlined in Chapter 5 when speaking of younger children and their parents.

Children of warm democratic parents tend to be friendly and ready to accept social rules; they usually have a conscience that is stable but not over-rigid (22). Those with ambitious mothers, who urge them to high endeavour, tend to have strong drives to do well in technical, athletic or intellectual pursuits—particularly the last (14).

The tendency to rebel against the vexatious control imposed by over-protective mothers, and to be rude, irritable and stubbornly independent, which appears in younger children, seems also to be apparent during adolescence. Investigations demonstrate the effects of the punitively authoritarian parent. A hostile control by nagging mothers is reflected in their adolescent daughters, who tend to be gloomy, unhappy, sulky, hostile (2, 3, 22).

The studies by Bandura and Walters (1), mainly of aggressive and anti-social boys, suggest that as a rule the parents of these boys are punitive and aggressive; that the more hostile a father is towards his son, the more hostile the son is towards his teachers; and inversely, that the greater the warmth the father shows towards his son, the less hostile the son is towards his teachers.

The reminder given in the last chapter should be repeated here: one should not exaggerate the difficulties between parents and their adolescent children, nor the frequency with which they occur. For the general picture would seem to be a positive one. Musgrove (19), in the study of 350 adolescents mentioned earlier, found that only 10 per cent of his sample mentioned restrictions and frustrations at home. Ninety per cent depicted the home as fulfilling its true aims as the children saw them. These were to provide a place where they can express their opinions, feel secure, wanted (boys and girls), where they are encouraged to get on in the world (especially boys), and to learn domestic skills (especially girls). Musgrove concludes that 'the home emerges as a pre-eminently satisfying institution'. These findings have been confirmed by a number of other studies (e.g. 5, 7). Evans (6)[1] reports an interesting study conducted and presented by sixth-formers (*Sixth Form Opinion*, June 1962). She says:

'The results showed that these young people, all highly intelligent, were of the opinion that their parents had made a good job of bringing them up. Asked to give their parents a mark out of ten, the average for the group was eight.'

The position as far as parents and their adolescent children is concerned may be summed up as follows. Adolescent children tend to be happy and well adjusted when their parents are warm and allow them reasonable freedom and autonomy. When their parents are cold and over-controlling, the children are less happy

[1] pages 51-3.

and less well adjusted. Yet even the most good-natured parents feel a responsibility to guide and restrain their adolescent children. Their difficulty, as they themselves know, is to preserve a fair balance between necessary control and reasonable freedom.

What has been said of the child's parents holds for his teachers. For much of the skill of the teacher of adolescent children lies in his ability to balance freedom and autonomy, and to relinquish much of the control he would exercise over young children. This thought is reflected in the changes in children's concept of the good teacher as they proceed from the top classes of Primary Schools to the fourth forms of Secondary Schools. These changes are described in a study by Taylor (25).

Eight hundred children, between the ages of ten and seventeen, indicated what they considered were the characteristics of the good teacher. They gave greatest weight to good teaching—to the good teacher's ability to encourage, explain, give interesting lessons, and mark work regularly and fairly. There was one main difference between the replies of the youngest and oldest children.

Primary School children ranked a good teacher's ability to control the class (to be firm, to keep order, to be fair, and have no favourites) higher than his personal qualities (being friendly, cheerful, good-tempered); whereas children at the middle of the Secondary School ranked personal qualities above the ability to control. It would seem that children in the Primary School realize that they must be controlled if they are to be taught efficiently. Having recognized this, they say, in effect, let's have a control that is fair, firm and kind. By contrast, Secondary School pupils feel that less control and discipline is needed, and that too much would hamper their wish to plan their own lives and develop their individuality.

In a changing society such as ours, there will nearly always be marked differences between the members of different generations. By the time their children are adolescent, parents will probably have arrived at a settled age, and they may not welcome change. Adolescents, on the other hand, are adaptable and are not afraid of it. They are idealistic and ready to accept new ideas; they may admire a person who is unconventional or a rebel. In a sense we should be pleased that they do.

We can understand this more clearly when we meet a child whose problems are the opposite of those we have discussed—the very quiet, obedient, studious child who is no trouble at all, but who is shy and unable to mix with others, particularly girls. His fear of self-assertion may impede his originality of thought and may, later on, prevent his undertaking the responsibilities of a new job or marriage.

One final thought: probably a very fruitful way for us parents and teachers to help adolescents is to study ourselves, looking for and guarding against our resentments because of their youth, our demands for obedience because we wish to remain in authority over them, our desire to over-protect because of our affection for them.

Sexual experience

As a result of the physiological changes that take place at puberty, boys and girls become attracted to each other. The sexual episodes in the lives of younger children are, as we have seen, incidental to the host of other activities in which they indulge; but in early adolescence sex becomes a more important aspect of existence. According to Kinsey, in America most boys begin to masturbate during this period, and by the age of sixteen 83·7 per cent of his sample had some such experience (15).[1] Some of those who have had this experience may suffer from guilt and remorse. They may worry about possible depletion of their strength and future virility, not only because of their masturbating but also because of the increasing frequency of nocturnal emissions.

Masturbation is by far the most frequent sexual outlet for boys during this period, and its frequency does not vary between boys in different socio-economic groups. Among those who continue their education beyond the minimum school leaving age, the incidence of sexual intercourse is so small as to be negligible. Among those who leave school at fifteen the incidence is rare during these years, but more frequent than among the boys who still go to school.

Kinsey denies that at this stage girls are more precocious sexually than boys (16)[2]; within a year of the physiological changes of puberty, he says, most American boys achieve regular orgasms through masturbation, nocturnal emissions, and, in rare cases only, through intercourse. For girls up to sixteen, on the

[1] page 408.   [2] page 125.

other hand, there does not seem to be this sudden upsurge. Indeed, females mature to full sexual responsiveness much later than males. Masturbation and sex dreams are less frequent for girls than for boys. Whereas 87 per cent of boys have masturbated by sixteen (according to Kinsey) and sex dreams are common to most, only 20 per cent of the girls in Kinsey's sample had masturbated, and under 2 per cent had had sexual dreams; and this is three or four years after the menarche. Moreover, whereas 60 per cent of boys who masturbate at puberty continue to masturbate during early adolescence, only 8 per cent of girls do so (16).[1]

The fact reported earlier (page 309) that girls are ready before boys for mixed social activities might seem to contradict Kinsey. However, the precocity of girls during early adolescence is probably social and romantic rather than sexual. Other factors may also operate. Girls are under the more careful supervision of their parents and the other adults who are responsible for them; and they are themselves more alive to the possible consequences, and so more cautious in initiating sexual activity. Yet they may still be annoyed by the restrictions to their social life which adults, with their protective feats, impose.

Because of the antipathy between the two sexes which characterizes earlier years, boys and girls may be shy and awkward at first. A new kind of social relation has to be learned, which involves friendliness rather than antagonism, and, for boys, tenderness rather than toughness. Gangs with their smutty jokes and emphasis on masculine assertiveness, and the taboo on tenderness which these imply, are not ideal antecedents. New and tender feelings may not be easy to express. As a fourteen-year-old said in a letter to his girl-friend, written during a long holiday away from her, 'I want to write some slop so much I'd better stop.'

The problem of sexuality is not an easy one. Anthropological reports indicate that in some primitive societies adolescents have their love affairs and marry early. Indeed, this was so in our own society in the past. In the Middle Ages, for example, a man's expectation of life at birth was little more than twenty-five years, and early marriage was usually encouraged. Many of the heroes and heroines of our legendary love stories belong to the age group which we are describing—Romeo and Juliet, Acis and Galatea, Helen and Paris. But it is unwise to draw inferences from

[1] pages 143, 200, 206.

these societies to our own more complex one, in which adolescents cannot take on the responsibility of marriage and children before they have learned a vocational skill and acquired a general working knowledge of its social, economic and technical organization.

There is, therefore, the inevitable lag between physical maturity and marriage. Further, sexuality has so many non-physical implications. Even at this early stage it may represent, for some, entry into the world of adult magic, like smoking at twelve and drinking at eighteen; and the precocious or delinquent child may be tempted to go further than most adults would wish. The emotional overtones that surround sexuality, as well as the exploitation of sex films and advertising, may well stimulate this attitude.

There is no easy solution which can be applied to all adolescents. However, the very cultural complexity which sets the problem also supplies a partial solution. This is the period when vocational and academic skills, all of which entail much time, thought and energy, are rapidly being acquired and developed. School and society provide diversions in sport, dramatics and clubs. Absorption in these pursuits helps to make the period of adolescence, despite the physiological maturity, one of preparation, so that for persons in our culture there is a gradual easing into full participation in adult sexuality. It could be said, therefore, that the more society provides for the educational and recreational needs of adolescents, the more it enables them to negotiate these difficult years.

Three phases of middle adolescence[1]

Gesell (9) paints a favourable picture of fourteen-year-olds, describing them as robust, vigorous, expansive, frank, communicative, self-contained, relaxed, and with a new self-assurance. The typical fourteen-year-old (first phase) has reached a stage of integration following the self-absorption, shyness and touchiness of the thirteen-year-old. He gets on well with other people—the other members of his family (except perhaps his eleven- or twelve-year-old brother), and his companions. Gesell says (9)[2]:

'At his typical best he presents a fine constellation of maturity traits and potentials, which are in propitious balance. He is exhuberant

<hr>

[1] See note page 227.   [2] page 181.

and energetic; but reasonable in temper (notwithstanding the loudness of his voice). He has a fair measure of wisdom and philosophy, often expressed in wit and humour.'

For most fourteen-year-olds the number of their activities and the calls on their time far exceed their capacity for organizing them. There are sports, the club, the gang, the big match, or a shopping spree. Homework is scrambled through at the last moment. This also happens at twelve and thirteen, of course; but parents feel that by fourteen their children should have accepted the advice, 'Homework first.' Not so; and the condition has still to be imposed, 'provided you have done your homework'.

Fourteen-year-olds are avid for social experience. Their greatest wish seems to be to communicate with others of their own age—a wish collectively expressed in the chattering and laughter of groups of boys and girls, individually in incessant phone calls. A fourteen-year-old girl is busily at work, apparently absorbed. You look up. She's gone, and you hear her dialing a number. As she worked, a thought flashed through her head about something outside her work that she feels *must* be passed on at once. She cannot restrain the impulse, and chatters away for half an hour. Parents of fourteen-year-olds become resigned to a large rise in their telephone bills. They may even have to restrict all calls at examination time (9).

Children's greater verbal fluency aids their growing desire to converse, discuss and debate. 'It's a good *synonym*, if you know what I mean,' said one fourteen-year-old speaking to her parents. Informal contacts are more conversational, and fourteen-year-olds are happy now to sit around in groups and talk. Boys, though, will often break up the conversation to have a friendly spar; or they may suddenly start fooling around, as in the camp example given earlier in this chapter. They may do so in mixed company—they may annoy a café proprietor, for example, spoil a party with sudden larrikin behaviour, or deflate the tyre of a car in the street. Such behaviour makes girls uneasy in boys' company, and they move away. Even though they are becoming more civilized, many boys cannot yet be trusted socially.

At home fourteen-year-olds seem to get on better with their families. Towards older brothers and sisters they adopt an air of cheerful self-confidence and towards younger a benign condescension with a trace almost of smugness, a sort of 'I have arrived' attitude. Yet despite the general air of banter there are still tussles between parents and children.

It takes time for the child to get used to his fast-growing inches and to know what to do with those arms and legs. Thus fourteen-year-olds tend to sprawl and appear physically awkward. To see an adolescent carrying ink over the new carpet provides an anxious moment even for the least houseproud of mothers.

Gesell suggests that the promise shown at fourteen is not fulfilled at fifteen. The typical fifteen-year-old, sometimes despondent, shut in and morose, seems to have lost the exuberance, openness and humour of the fourteen-year-old. Heightened self-consciousness and self-awareness make him self-critical and insecure. He can feel a fit of depression more acutely than he has ever done before. He may acquire small mannerisms and bouts of incessant fidgetiness—playing with his fingers, tapping with his feet or with a pencil, or twirling a clump of hair. He can be irritating at table. Gesell described a mother who kept a bowl of nuts and a nut-cracker nearby to keep her fifteen-year-old son busy, and so save the table cloth and table from the jabs of his knife and fork.

At home the fifteen-year-old's drive for independence and his moodiness render him difficult—sensitive, touchy, with a tendency to make biting remarks. Such attacks may be expressed in loud outbursts following the imposition of a restraint or a complaint by a parent that a son or daughter is not doing his or her bit. When worsted in an argument the fifteen-year-old may rush into his bedroom, slamming the door hard as a gesture of defiance. Sometimes hostility may be expressed by a cold stare, or by a verbal quip, as with the girl who said, 'I see you are reading that book on the sixteen-year-old. Well, I'm going to read it too, and when I'm sixteen, I'll act just the opposite to what the stupid book says.'

It would be incorrect to paint a wholly adverse picture of the fifteen-year-old and his parents. There are too many positives for that. The keen observer notices subtle changes taking place in parents; for example, a mother's gesture of deference to her son's greater knowledge when she asks for information on a technical matter which he has been studying. Such gestures please fifteen-year-olds immensely, and are probably an excellent way of reducing difficult behaviour of the kind described.

There is a sense in which the family is an embarrassment to a fifteen-year-old. It is a symbol of dependence. During a family outing (to the sea perhaps, or to a concert) he separates from the other members to join his own clique or his best friend. It is part of the inevitable move towards independence.

In contrast to his tendency to isolate himself at home, with his clique he is active, vigorous, and talkative. When he is with them, if he feels an underlying despondency, it is only occasionally expressed. His clique—usually a small one, four or five of the same age and sex—is important to him, as are the mixed informal gatherings at café or club. Conformity with contemporaries is the rule; clothes, speech and tastes must be just right.

Boys and girls are now on much better terms. Girls feel more comfortable in mixed groups because boys have left the pubertal 'fooling around' stage. They can talk and co-operate together in joint ventures. As one girl said, 'You can talk to boys now as if they were just like you. It is so nice.'

In summing up, Gesell says of the fifteen-year-old that he is more complex than happy.

An adolescent in our society could be compared with a person who goes to live in a new city. In many senses he has to acquire a new identity. He has to take over a new job, grow used to new surroundings, to new people and events. During this time he is likely to become a little more reflective. He may express doubts, and even be critical, about the way things are done in the new place. He has many moments of uncertainty, is sometimes irritable and sometimes depressed. As he reflects on his first year or two in the new city, he may say, 'I couldn't settle at first; but I'm finding my way around and getting to like it now.' This is how the sixteen-year-old may feel. Sixteen is, in many senses, an age of arrival. Schoolchildren have 'got there', have reached the top of the school, even though the hurdle of the leaving examinations is just ahead. They have 'arrived' emotionally and socially. Socially they show surprising poise in greeting adults and speaking to visitors. There is still a slight suggestion of affectation; or perhaps it is not so much affectation as 'text-book' behaviour carried out in a studied way.

Social life with contemporaries is changing, too—from the excited, uncontrolled chattering of the fourteen-year-old to the controlled conversation which may be limited to a single subject for quite a long time. There is gaiety without giggling among girls, and among boys conversation without the aggressive shouting down of the eleven-year-old or the sparring of the fourteen-year-old.

Emotionally sixteen-year-olds are usually much more amenable. They still do not help spontaneously in the house, but they are less touchy, and less impulsive and compulsive in their drives to defend their rights. They do not protest so much as they did at fifteen, perhaps because, as Gesell has put it, they have by now acquired a sense of independence.

If they sometimes judge adults harshly, they are also concerned to understand them. A group will often become friendly with an elderly man who is a 'character' in the district. They will urge him to relate his experiences, and will later chat together about them, or about some skill he has—such as tying knots or making model ships. They laugh tolerantly about his tendency to exaggerate, feeling a genuine affection for him because he is not a person in authority over them. As yet, they are insensitive to the puzzlement and confusion which life might have imposed on the old man. They are unable to see that his skills and tricks may have a poignancy about them and represent compensation for a generally untriumphant life.

Most of those who are at school have accepted the need to pass examinations, and parents do not have to urge them quite as much. During the leaving certificate examination, many adolescents present a picture of strained maturity, which is accompanied by symptoms of tension—twirling hair, biting nails. Fortunately they are young and resilient; and after a holiday they lose their tense look, and again become their bright, youthful selves.

The individual differences in general and specific abilities, in rate of maturity and in temperament, which show themselves more especially by sixteen, make generalizations hazardous. Sixteen is an age when those who have qualities applauded by society are especially envied by those who have not. The firm, muscular Peter of Chapter 6 becomes the sportsman, admired by girls and boys alike. He shows a tendency to be too sure of himself. Paul may envy him and may tend to be unsure of himself. A girl who has a figure and appearance that is regarded as right may also become a little conceited and be the envy of girls less well endowed. It is reassuring to know that one's physical appearance is pleasing to other people, especially when one is still insecure in one's moves towards achievement. But as one matures, esteem based on physical appearance loses its importance and esteem based on achievement takes its place.

Education and the adolescent

To return to the problem of learning: the relation between the concrete and the abstract and the function of the latter has already been emphasized; the principles of teaching desirable at this stage will now be illustrated, with special reference to the teaching of science and of English.

The experiments which children perform in the laboratory and the results they record are concrete experiences. As such they are merely a preliminary, and designed to lead to abstract formulations, to a generalization expressed in the form of a scientific law. Every laboratory experiment should also illustrate the broader principles of scientific method, such as the control of all relevant variables except the one that is being investigated. This principle is demonstrated when, for example, pupils are studying the relations between the temperature, volume and pressure of a gas, and their teacher explains that in the experiments one of the three variables must be kept constant so that the relation between the other two can be properly investigated.

People may perhaps wonder how teachers and children can cope with all the new facts that scientists are discovering by means of the experimental process. The answer is, of course, that children can learn only a fraction. But the teacher need not be dismayed. His job is to teach principles—the laws governing the behaviour of bodies, of gases and so on, and the techniques of scientific method. In order to teach principles, he must teach facts; but, in planning a series of experiments, he selects his facts to exemplify the scientific law demonstrated by each experiment, and the general rules of scientific method which the series illustrates.

Mathematics is a deductive process; that is, it is a process of reasoning from definitions and axioms (as in geometry) or from a formula (as in algebra) to a new generalization and a new formula, each of which is more specialized than those from which it has been deduced. Only if they arrive at an understanding of the processes and interrelations will the formal teaching of mathematics become meaningful to children.

The same principles of teaching apply to arts subjects, such as English. Children need first to be steeped in the concrete: to read the novel, to act the play themselves, or to see it acted, to hear the poetry read aloud. Here technical aids like radio and television enable the teacher to present the material in a realistic and dramatic way. From these facts—the story of the play or novel, the theme of the poem—the more abstract analysis follows—of structure, form, style, characterization, and so on.

Formal grammar is best taught within the context of concrete examples, the work of famous writers and of the children themselves. In this way punctuation, parsing and analysing can be made more than abstractions for children. The structure of the simple sentence, which parsing gives, the structure of the complex sentence, which analysis gives, and the use of punctuation marks to delineate the clauses can thus all be seen as means towards greater clarity and precision of expression. Earlier in this book statements were made to the effect that too great emphasis on neatness, on technical excellence and conformity to known shapes and sizes can impede the creative efforts of young children when they write, draw, paint or do handwork. There is no inconsistency in saying that with these older pupils the absence of these techniques can impede constructive and creative work. Without such techniques no good production in arts or crafts is possible, and no clear expression in writing. Through instruction, and by their study of the work of those more skilled, adolescent youths and girls can be helped to realize the need for techniques; and out of this realization grow children's desire and eagerness to learn them.

The findings from the experimental study of examinations described earlier in this chapter (pages 342–3) suggest that the use in class by the teacher of more informal examination procedures may prepare the more anxious student to face formal situations with greater equanimity and to achieve better results.

What has been said so far in this book about pupil's learning may be summarized as follows:

1   The sequence of teaching should be from the concrete to the abstract, from particulars to general laws: from this and that

little dog has a tail to all little dogs have tails (Kindergarten); from the coloured rods varying in length and in value, as in the Cuisenaire method, to simple sums (Infant School); from rods and counters, measuring and weighing to the rules of multiplication (Primary School); from this particular geographical region to the general features that hold good of all similar regions, from this particular experiment to the formula, from this play, novel or poem to the structure and form of plays, novels, poems (Secondary and Grammar School).

2   At the Infant and Primary School stages, learning is made meaningful by a predominant emphasis on the concrete. Later, generally beginning at about pubescence, children are able to understand the function of the abstract, of principles and formulae.

3   Since the dichotomy between concrete teaching and abstract teaching is never absolute at any stage, it follows that much of a teacher's skill in presenting his material lies in his ability to assess the correct balance of emphasis, between the concrete and the abstract, according to the age and intelligence of the children he is teaching.

REFERENCES

1   Bandura, A., Walters, R. H. *Adolescent Aggression*. Ronald Press, New York, 1959.
2   Bayley, N., Schaefer, E. S. 'Maternal behaviour and personality.' *Psychiatric Research Reports*, 1960, **13**, pp. 155–73.
3   Block, V. L. 'Conflicts of adolescents with their mothers.' *Journal of Abnormal and Social Psychology*, 1937, **32**, pp. 192–206.
4   Calvin, A. D. *et al.* 'A further investigation of the relationship between anxiety and classroom examination performance.' *Journal of Educational Psychology*, 1957, **48**, pp. 240–4.
5   Elkin, F., Westley, W. 'The myth of adolescent culture.' *American Sociological Review*, 1955, **20**, pp. 680–4.
6   Evans, K. M. *Attitudes and Interests in Education*. Routledge & Kegan Paul, London, 1965.
7   Fletcher, R. *Britain in the Sixties. The Family and Marriage*. Penguin Books, Harmondsworth, Middlesex, 1962.
8   Frazier, A., Lisonbee, L. K. 'Adolescent concerns with physique.' *School Review*, 1950, **58**, pp. 397–405.
9   Gesell, A., Ilg, F. L., Ames, L. B. *Youth: the Years from Ten to Sixteen*. Harper, New York, 1956.
10   Hemming, J. *Problems of Adolescent Girls*. Heinemann, London, 1960.

11 Horrocks, J. E., Thompson, G. G. 'A study of friendship fluctuations in rural boys and girls.' *Journal of Genetic Psychology*, 1946, **69,** pp. 189–98.

12 Horrocks, J. E., Thompson, G. G. 'A study of friendship fluctuations among urban boys and girls.' *Journal of Genetic Psychology.* 1947, **70,** pp. 53–63.

13 Jones, C. J., Mussen, P. H. 'Self conceptions, motivations, and interpersonal attitudes of early- and late-maturing girls.' *Child Development,* 1958, **29,** pp. 491–501.

14 Kagan, J., Moss, H. A. 'Stability of achievement and recognition seeking behaviour from early childhood through to adulthood.' *Journal of Abnormal and Social Psychology*, 1961, **62,** pp. 504–13.

15 Kinsey, A. C., Pomeroy, W. B., Martin, C. E. *Sexual Behaviour in the Human Male.* Saunders, London, 1948.

16 Kinsey, A. C., Pomeroy, W. B., Martin, C. E. *Sexual Behaviour in the Human Female.* Saunders, London, 1953.

17 Mace, C. A. *Foreword* to Veness, T. *School Leavers.* Methuen, London, 1962.

18 McKeachie, W. J. *et al.* 'Relieving anxiety in classroom examinations.' *Journal of Abnormal and Social Psychology*, 1955, **50,** pp. 93–8.

19 Musgrove, F. 'The social needs and satisfactions of some young people 1. At home, in youth clubs and at work.' *British Journal of Educational Psychology*, 1966, **36,** pp. 61–71.

20 Musgrove, F. 'The social needs and satisfactions of some young people 2. At school.' *British Journal of Educational Psychology*, 1966, **36,** pp. 137–49.

21 Mussen, P. H., Jones, C. J. 'The behaviour-inferred motivations of late- and early-maturing boys.' *Child Development,* 1958, **29,** pp. 61–7. **B,** pp. 446–53.

22 Peck, R. F. 'Family patterns correlated with adolescent personality structure.' *Journal of Abnormal and Social Psychology*, 1958, **57,** pp. 347–50.

23 Pressey, S. L., Kuhlen, R. G. *Psychological Development through the Life Span.* Harper, New York, 1957.

24 Stern, H. H. 'A follow-up study of adolescents' views of their personal and vocational future.' *British Journal of Educational Psychology*, 1961, **31,** pp. 170–82.

25 Taylor, P. H. 'Children's evaluations of the characteristics of the good teacher.' *British Journal of Educational Psychology*, 1962, **32,** pp. 258–66.

26 Veness, T. *School Leavers.* Methuen, London, 1962.

27 *15 to 18.* Report of the Central Advisory Council for Education, England, Volume 1 (Crowther Report). H.M. Stationary Office, London, 1959.

PART FIVE

Three Special Topics

CHAPTER EIGHTEEN

The Dichotomous Nature of Children's Growth

EARLIER it was emphasized that children wish to be like other people, to be at one with them; alternatively, that they wish to be distinct and separate from others. Their development is consequently a process involving both conforming and non-conforming behaviour. This dichotomy may be summed up in the following two statements:

1   Growth is a process the results of which tend towards identity with others, to social conformity and to the words 'we', 'us', 'ours', 'yes'.
2   Growth is a process the results of which tend towards difference from others, to lack of social conformity and to the words 'I', 'me', 'my', 'myself', 'mine', 'no'.

The amplification of these two statements which follows may help us to comprehend some of the complexities and the apparent contradictions within children's behaviour.[1]

Referring back to statement 1:

Growth is a process the results of which tend towards identity with others, to social conformity and to the words 'we', 'us', 'ours', 'yes'.

The processes by which a child becomes like other children and like the adults whom he loves are empathy, sympathy, suggestion, imitation, identification, introjection.

[1] I have elsewhere (1) dealt in more detail with these statements and related them more precisely to the problems of the teacher. In what follows I have reproduced much of this article (with some emendations) and again thank Professor W. F. Connell, Editor, *Australian Journal of Education*, for permission to do so.

Empathy is the unconscious imitation of the bodily movements and/or the facial expressions of another. The boy gives a kick as he watches his friend taking the penalty which may decide whether the school wins or loses the match; some members of an audience may open their mouths, lift their chests and raise their hands a little as the amateur concert singer is about to attempt a high note; we look at a building and feel that the thin columns which support it must be groaning under so heavy a weight. Small children empathize when they strain their bodies and emit faint grunts as their father lifts a heavy weight, or when they pucker their faces and contort their bodies as he turns hard at the screw he is twisting into the wooden toy that has been broken. In the classroom, children empathize when, too absorbed even to be aware of it, they react bodily to a teacher's graphic account of the Volga boatmen heaving on their rope, or of the hero's plight as he approaches a place of mortal danger. They feel the tensing of their muscles in the first case and the holding back of their bodies in the second.

Sympathy implies a more definite realization of the emotions of others, especially those of sorrow and pain. Even small children seem to have the ability to infer the state of mind of others from their own in similar circumstances. A small boy will seek to console the little girl who is crying by hugging or gently stroking her. Small children tend to be indiscriminate in their sympathies, meaning that they sympathize not only with people but also with pets, toys and even familiar domestic objects, like a chair or table. Thus, the toy truck that has smashed into the wall is hurt; so is the poor golliwog that has fallen off the table, and mummy who has hit her hand. A child will smooth down the truck, hug the golliwog and kiss mummy's hand 'to make them better'. The doll who is being tucked into bed is happy—'just look at her smiling'. Similarly, if people around the child are laughing in happy mood, he laughs too and he jumps up and down; adults may notice him and renew their own laughter in response to his.

Young children tend also to be suggestible to the opinions, beliefs and ways of behaving of those whom they love, and of those who have authority over them, particularly parents and teachers. There is a sense in which it may be said that parents and teachers have not consciously to proclaim their authority. It is theirs by reason of circumstances, for the young child is dependent upon his parents, and their affection is very necessary to his well-being. Moreover, the very size of parents, the skill and knowledge they possess impress the young child who therefore looks upon them as all-knowing and all-powerful. Murphy (2),[1] in elaborating Piaget's point of view, says that a child's mind works somewhat like this :'If father can mend my toys, if he can lift such heavy things; if he can drive a car through whizzing traffic; if he can do all these wonderful things, then surely he knows such a simple thing as what is right and what is wrong.' Of course, there are no shades of difference; what father says is right, is true, is good.

Such tendencies are, in part, transferred to teachers, especially during the first years of children's school life. 'My teacher said . . .' and that means there can be no argument. The child might have obviously misunderstood what the teacher actually did say, but nevertheless he construes our attempts to clear up his confusion as an attempt to undermine the authority of the teacher; he will have none of this and is quite adamant. 'My teacher said . . .'

These processes of empathy, sympathy and suggestibility to parents' opinions and beliefs are linked with the process of identification, for children empathize and sympathize more readily with, and are more susceptible to suggestion from, those people with whom they identify. Identification, as it is expressed in children's play, has already been described, particularly in their playing of imitative roles—father and mother, postman, bus conductor and the like—and also in their dramatic activities and dressing-up games. Adults identify, too, and perhaps we see the process most clearly when a man, who becomes acquainted with a person of some local or national fame, uncritically accepts the celebritys' ideas and without realizing it imitates his mannerisms, his way of walking or talking.

Children express their identity with parents in activities other than play and are naïvely unaware of the fact that they are doing so. For example, a husband will smile across the table at his wife when their small son unconsciously reproduces some characteristic gesture or mannerism of his mother's. Mother returns the smile when, a moment later, the child reproduces with fascinating exactness one of father's favourite mannerisms. Identification is shown, too, in children's constant repetition of phrases such as, 'I

[1] page 498.

have curly hair (or dark eyes) just like Mummy's.' 'I have brown shoes (or grey trousers) the same as Daddy's.'

Finally, identification implies the child's acceptance of his parents not only as loving, protective and generous beings but also as lawgivers and punishers of those who disobey their laws. A child obeys his parents not merely from fear of punishment and because of his suggestibility, but also because of the positive, affectionate identification which he does not wish to lose. This identification is expressed, too, in children's willingness to do practically anything for their teacher. They will work so hard at a monitorial task that the teacher must be careful not to exploit them. They will identify themselves wholeheartedly with a class effort to collect for this, that or the other.

A further significant process takes place when the child accepts as his own, and demands of himself, the standards of work and behaviour that his parents have set him. This is the process of 'internalization' mentioned many times throughout this book, a process which Freud called *introjection*. The early influence on behaviour of introjected standards may be seen, for example, when the small child calls himself 'naughty' and smacks himself on the hand or bangs his head on the wall or floor as punishment for some misdemeanour. By as early as six or seven, children begin to criticize their own work—'It's not proper!' 'I'm no good!'—and we have to console and reassure in order to protect them from the mental distress which results from their failure to live up to the standards we have ourselves imposed. In the classroom, a child who demands absolute perfection of himself at all times may be inconsolable because of one small blot in an otherwise perfect exercise book. He begs his teacher to tear the page out.

The processes so far described are those by which a child develops as an amenable, conforming being, the way he learns the words 'we', 'us', 'ours', 'yes'. The cumulative effect of the processes can be intriguing, as when we see an adolescent boy who is a replica of his father. Physically he is like his father, and when he speaks he expresses his father's opinions and prejudices. This similarity may suddenly strike us very forcibly and we say, 'He's not even a chip off the old block. He's the old block all over again.'

But it is obvious from everyday observation of children that this is a very one-sided picture of children's growth. It makes no allowance for lack of conformity and occasional (or frequent) disobedience. If children are in sympathetic contact with, susceptible to suggestion from, and identified with adults, particularly their parents; and further, if they introject parental standards and accept them as their own, then peace should reign eternally between parents and children, and there should be no change in the ways of believing, feeling and behaving from one generation to another.

Such conformity does not always occur and such peace does not always prevail, and so, to continue this account of children's growth, the second generalization will be considered:

> *Growth is a process the results of which tend towards difference from others, to lack of social conformity and to the words 'I', 'me', 'my', 'myself', 'mine', 'no'.*

This complements rather than contradicts the first statement which relates to social conforming behaviour, to the child's oneness with others. By contrast, this second generalization relates to the growth of a child's ego, his individualism, his separateness from others.

It was suggested in Chapter 3 that growth of personality entails a progressive realization of the personal pronouns 'I' and 'me' and of the possessive adjectives 'my' and 'mine'. Speaking more specifically of children's development, even by three a child is established with his possessions and he knows the objects and people that are his—*my* mother, *my* father, *my* house, *my* tricycle, *my* engine. By five he has developed considerable skill in bodily movements and physical activities, such as skipping, jumping, running, hopping, manipulating toys and riding tricycles, and these achievements also add to his feelings of 'my', 'mine', 'I' and 'me'; it is *my* jumping, *my* skipping, *my* running. Constantly, there is the boast, '*I* can do this!' or the appeal, 'Watch *me* do this!'

This growth of 'I', 'me' and 'mine' has a further aspect, namely the development of executive ability, meaning the ability to make decisions and to act upon them. It is expressed early in the decisive statement of the two-year-old, '*Me* do it!' and later in that of the five-year-old who stamps his foot in anger and says, 'I want to do it *myself.*' A more mature expression of this is reached in later years when, for example, an adolescent decides on a career and, in a determined way, sets to work towards this end. Executive ability is seen in the stand a child will make against another child or group of children who attempt to exploit him, in the assertiveness required to master a skill, to manipulate difficult material. This may be called the 'I-my-no' aspect of growth and contrasted with the 'We-ours-yes' of the first statement.

The 'I-my-no' is positive in that, through it, a child is learning to value property in a culture which lays great store by it, to sustain effort, to stand up for himself. It enables a child to have ideas of his own, to think and to judge for himself, to be imaginative, creative, spontaneous. In short, it is the source of his uniqueness, of his individuality of expression, of his originality of thought. And in our own society, which is a dynamic and changing one, initiative and originality are valued and encouraged.

But two points should be noticed. Firstly, whereas 'We-ours-yes' leads to similarity, to oneness with others, 'I-my-no' leads to difference, to separateness from others. Therefore children want to think, to feel and to behave as other children do, to be like and to be liked by them. They also want to be different from others, to fly from the painful emptiness of anonymity and to be significant in the small universe in which they live. Because this is so, a child will often behave in apparently contradictory ways. For Susanne (see example on page 44) the way in which her hair is done must be just so, precisely the same as that of other little girls—and many may be the tears if she must wear plaits when all her friends have bobbed hair—but she is delighted with her new shoes; they are different and distinguish her from others.

The second point is that each aspect within the duality of growth is dichotomous and has a negative as well as a positive within it. 'We-ours-yes' can be positively expressed as genuine enjoyment of communal experience, of thinking and doing with others—that is, as co-operation towards constructive and creative ends. Negatively it can be expressed as subservience to the group when the 'I-my-no' is sacrificed for the sake of over-conformity and over-compliance, as in the chicken games of adolescents; also as co-operation *against* something or someone. The negatively-toned term 'ganging' is used to describe this latter process.

The 'I-my-no' also has its dichotomy. Positively, it is expressed in exploratory activity, in experimenting, in creating original thoughts and ideas. Originality of thought as in philosophy, originality of expression as in music, poetry and painting, originality of execution as in administration and technology are the results of being different, of questioning (or saying 'No' to) the long established ways of philosophers, artists, scientists and administrators of the past. But the 'No' of the original thinker has a constructive component; it clears the way for an alternative solution. Yet 'No' without this constructive component is the decisive negative, the 'No, I won't' of the completely uncooperative man. This we call negativism.

Thus, each aspect of growth is double-edged. Because they have not securely established an 'I', 'me', 'mine', 'myself', children especially are very unsure of themselves and therefore, in expressing 'I-my-no' and 'We-ours-yes', they often go to excess. Their determination to hold on to what they have makes them appear selfish; they will not lend their property even though they are not using it themselves; their assertions tend to move over into aggressions, their admonitions of other children into what, from an adult point of view, is frankly rude and abusive. The most raw expression of these tendencies is seen in those situations where competitions for status and recognition is most acute, when children jostle with each other for a position or a possession which is significant. If a boy is called a 'cissy' or a 'cry-baby', if a girl is called 'selfish', 'naughty', 'mean', he or she may turn upon the child or adult who does the name-calling and shout, 'No! No! No!' These qualities must be vehemently disclaimed because to accept them is to suffer the pain which accompanies loss of self-esteem.

Within each of the cycles as Gesell describes them (pages 165-6), the play of the opposite yet complementary processes of growth is evident. During some of the stages within each cycle 'I-my-no' predominates. Then children are asserting themselves as they acquire new skills, more possessions, and as they establish a place among their contemporaries. But with the positive 'I-my-no' come also the negatives and, at these times, children are more often difficult, both as individuals and as groups. In short, the more children are learning to be social, the greater the danger of 'ganging' (negative 'We-ours-yes'); the more children are learning to be individuals, the greater the likelihood of negativisms (negative 'I-my-no').

At other times, children seem to be having a period of relative rest from this expansion of their personalities and to be quietly consolidating their gains: improving on mental and physical skills already learned, enjoying social activities with a group in which they have an established place. At such times, children tend to be relatively more amiable, more stable and easier to handle from a parent's and a teacher's point of view.

Thus it is that, although, when scanning a period of many years, we realize that growth has taken place, and although, when scanning one or two years, we can speak of stages of development, the day-to-day process of children's growth is indefinite and variable. Gesell's comparison of this growth with the progress of the tight-rope walker is most apt. Balancing with his pole, he swings from one side of the rope to the other, just as children swing emotionally from love to hate, joy to sorrow and, socially, from friendly co-operation to hostile antagonism. In much the same way as the tight-rope walker takes three steps forward and two back, so children regress temporarily in their acquisition of social, mental and bodily skills.

Because of this variability in the day-to-day growth of children, it is a mistake to think, when a child behaves well or does a task well one day, that he can automatically do it equally well the next day and that if he does not, it is because he is being deliberately obstreperous. It is for this reason that teachers should evaluate children's exercise books from one term to another and preferably from one year to another, not from day to day. Often we say to children, 'You did it yesterday and therefore there is no reason why you cannot do it today.' This statement, which seems so eminently sensible and logical, cannot be fairly applied to children's growth. We must accept the backward steps, even as we do those of the tight-rope walker, for they are the prelude and impetus to further progress.

These are the complexities of children's growth that make them sometimes fascinating and interesting to be with, sometimes trying and difficult. But despite the ups and downs of obedience/disobedience and 'We-ours-yes/I-my-no', the people and the places that a child knows, the toys that are his, become part of him. His emotional experiences are determined by, and reflect the emotional experiences of, those who are *his*; and through them, he can express his own thoughts and feelings. Mother, father, brother, sister, house, garden, toys form his world. He finds a niche of his own in this world, and his feelings of security depend upon its stability.

REFERENCES

1   Gabriel, J. 'Resolution of opposites and the teaching of children.' *Australian Journal of Education*, 1957, **4**, pp. 91–105.
2   Murphy, G. *Personality*. Harper, New York, 1947.

CHAPTER NINETEEN

Children's Play

MANY theories have been put forward to explain children's play, none of which seems to embrace all aspects of the subject. It is difficult to make a list of the games children play and then to classify them; nor is it easy to define the words 'play' and 'game'. Nevertheless, we can point and say, 'This and similar things are called "games" '; and when a person says, 'Children play games', we know what he means.

The word 'game' comes from the Old Teutonic *gaman* meaning 'joy'. 'Play' is the English verb corresponding to the noun 'game', the Old Teutonic form of which is *plegan* meaning 'to be glad'. Two distinct present-day uses of the words 'play' and 'game' can be distinguished. In a broad sense, they both denote any activity indulged in for the sake of the pleasure it affords rather than for any purpose it achieves. In a narrower sense, they denote a contest carried out according to recognized rules and decided by the strength, skill or luck of the contestants.

No such distinction is absolute. But the play of pre-school children and the ritualistic games, rhymes and chants of Infants and younger Primary School children, as described in Chapters 12 and 14, afford the best examples of the first sense. Play in its second sense is exemplified by the organized games of older children. When the researches on very young children by Parten and Moore are combined with those on adolescent boys by Helanko and Mays, we see that playing develops out of the predominantly individual, spontaneous and imaginative games of young children into the competitive games of older children and adults, which are predominantly carried out in groups and governed by recognized rules.

The motives and the mood of children's play vary according

to whether it belongs to the first or second type. When children play ball games, sometimes the social motive seems to be predominant (they are playing as a group), sometimes the competitive (two groups have formed sides and are playing a match). A child will play by himself throwing a ball up into the air or against a wall and catching it. He may be practising his skill, or just 'having fun', feeling sheer joy from the bodily movement and the skill he has acquired. His fantasy may reveal a social motive (he is 'taking turns' with an imaginary companion) or a competitive one (he is 'taking turns' with a rival and 'beating' him each time).

Play can be fun, its predominant mood gay and light-hearted; yet it can be serious and the mood intense. Play is generally regarded as spontaneous and free; yet many games have rules. Play often implies pretence; yet children's absorption in their play causes them to lose this sense of pretending.

It would seem that most children are aware of the distinction between the 'real' and the 'pretend'. They will sometimes speak of a 'pretend' house, or, when frightened in play with too realistic a representation of a witch or an ogre, will seek reassurance and say, 'It's not real, is it?' Moore (10), in his study of realism and fantasy in the play of four- to six-year-olds, has illustrated children's awareness of this opposition. In one game, the children put dolls into a doll's house which had no roof. One little girl said, 'We'll *pretend* that it's dark.' Whereupon a six-year-old boy put his coat over the house, and with obvious pleasure said, 'It *is* dark, really.' As Moore observes, the more 'real' the pretence can be made, the more acceptable the 'pretend' always is.

Sometimes no such easy solution for narrowing the gap between the 'pretend' and the 'real' is possible, and the pretence must be maintained imaginatively. The child who refuses to accept the pretence endangers the illusion and may dispel it. This is unforgivable and he is considered a 'spoil-sport'.

Play is linked with the tangible artefacts of the culture: a chair, a table and the space beneath it, large boxes and so on. Yet make-believe transforms them into something other than what they really are (a steam engine, a ship or a house, for example). Such play takes the child imaginatively beyond his limited capacities and outside his restricted status as a child. He is an engine driver, a captain, a father or mother.

Play is conceived as activity carried out for its own sake. It is

not 'necessary' in the sense of directly serving an obvious biological need; yet it serves many purposes. The urge to play, like
the urge for food and drink when hungry or thirsty, is very powerful. Children *must* play. One sure sign that a child is physically ill
or psychologically distressed is that he does not play.

Throughout this book, descriptions are given of children's
play at varying ages. This chapter is a more formal consideration of
the chief theories, and of contemporary studies upon the general
nature, of children's play.

The surplus-energy theory

Simply stated, the theory is this: because children and young
animals do not expend their energies in self-preservation (food-
gathering, hunting, defence) or in preservation of the species
(reproduction), they have a large surplus of energy which finds
vent as play. The theory is based on the notion that the energies of
the body are designed for, and appropriately directed towards, the
fulfilment of physiological and practical goals—food, drink,
safety, shelter, etc. There are other, somewhat extraneous goals,
such as the basic psychological goals (described in Chapter 8) to
the fulfilment of which any energy remaining can be devoted.

Children, however, are in a privileged position: adults provide for their physiological and practical needs. So, having more
superfluous energy at their disposal than adults, children play
more.

The theory reflects the thinking and attitudes of a nineteenth-
century industrial society. Play is tolerated, but at the same time it
is a little suspect—a wasteful expenditure of energy which we must
put up with until the energy can be channelled into the industrial
process. Play is positive in the sense that through play excess
energy, which might otherwise be used for obstreperous or
destructive purposes, is expended in harmless ways. Herein lies
one of the early justifications (a negative one, it is true) of games
and physical exercises in schools and colleges, and of playgrounds
in city schools.

It can at least be said for the theory that teachers are all too
aware of the restlessness on wet days at school when the children
cannot go out to play. We speak of their pent-up energies; and on
such days children can become boisterous and difficult to con-

trol. But the theory says little more than that children play because they have the energy to do so. The word 'surplus' does not help much, since it suggests that the non-physiological and the non-practical is extraneous and incidental—a viewpoint contrary to that so far presented in this book and at variance with the evidence given in Chapter 8. It in no way accounts for the variety of the games children play nor for the complexity of motives that impel them to play.

The surplus-energy theory has become associated with the names of the German poet Schiller (1759–1805) and the English sociologist Spencer (1820–1903). In fairness to Schiller, it must be added that the theory does not do justice to his treatment of play, nor even to Spencer's, superficial though his treatment is. Schiller linked adults' pursuit of art and poetry with what he called 'the impulse to play'. He saw in all three an element of freedom and spontaneity. It is interesting to record that Spencer (18)[1] writes thus:

'Many years ago I met with a quotation from a German author to the effect that the aesthetic sentiments originate from the play impulse. I do not remember the name of the author . . . but the statement itself has remained with me, as being one which, if not literally true, is yet the adumbration of a truth.'

The 'German author' was almost certainly Schiller. The few pages Spencer devotes to play are contained within a chapter entitled 'Aesthetic sentiments'.

It is doubtful whether the surplus-energy theory can in fact be ascribed to Schiller. His point was rather that play presupposes an abundance of energy, the joy of living when 'superfluous life presses for activity'. Far from regarding play as 'useless' and 'surplus', he describes it as the expression of man at his noblest. Speaking of the athletic contests at Olympia and the Greeks' delight in combats of strength, speed and agility, he says (16),[2] 'Man plays only when he is in the full sense of the word a man; *and he is only wholly man when he is playing*' (Schiller's italics).

The recreation theory

The recreation theory, the origin of which is generally attributed to the German philosopher Moritz Lazarus (1824–1903), empha-

---

[1] page 626.   [2] page 80.

sizes the restorative value of play: change to an interesting and absorbing activity is more recuperative than complete idleness. Patrick (12) has developed the theory and attempted a justification along the following lines. As society becomes more industrialized, so people, in their work on machines, execute small movements which involve skilled co-ordination of hand and eye. These differ from the more expansive movements demanded by agricultural work. With the ever-increasing amount of schooling, children also do more close work. Consequently a person in an industrial society tends to become fatigued in specific parts of the body, though he has an abundance of energy left within his body as a whole. This finds expression in large-scale bodily activity characteristic of much of adults' and children's play.

The recreation theory has been used to explain the leisure-time activities of adults: teachers and academics who climb mountains during their vacations; students and office-workers who camp, hike, cycle and so on; statesmen who play golf and fish. It has also been used to justify physical exercises, games and play-time in schools, but for a more positive reason than a mere release of energy which might otherwise be used for obstreperous or destructive purposes. Large-scale bodily exercises are held to provide a respite for children from close work in writing, reading and computation. Here again, in fairness to the theory, teachers know all too well that when games, Physical Education and play-time have to be cancelled on wet days, school work—compositions, English exercises and arithmetic especially—tends to become careless and slipshod.

At first glance it may seem that the recreation theory is in opposition to the surplus-energy theory, since the latter emphasizes the consumption, the former the restoration, of energy through play. In fact, the theories are similar in that both postulate, though in different ways, the idea of a surplus of energy which is responsible for play. But this second theory, like the first, fails to explain the variety of kind, and overlooks the complex motives that characterize children's play.

Nevertheless, in stressing that activity is more restorative than idleness, the theory is in accord with an important finding of modern psychology already mentioned (page 151–5) and considered later in this chapter—namely that living creatures are essentially active beings, always 'on the go'. If there is no problem

obviously present for them to solve, they will seek one; if no
trouble is immediately at hand, they will search elsewhere to find it.

The instinct-practice theory

Groos (1861–1946) devoted himself assiduously to the study of the
play of animals (5a) and children (5b). He observed both; he read
the literature on the play of children in primitive groups. His
theory, which has variously been called the instinct-practice and
the preparatory theory, may be summarized as follows.

Animals and human beings have instincts—a term which is
used to mean an innate tendency to be active (to see, to feel, to
behave) in ways which subserve essentially preservative ends:
self-maintenance, self-preservation, preservation of the species. In
the case of creatures low on the evolutionary scale—insects, for
example—the behaviour subserving these ends begins immediately
after birth, is relatively perfect when first expressed, and tends to
remain relatively stereotyped throughout life. Higher in the
evolutionary scale, though some instinctive activities appear
immediately—for example, sucking, swallowing, grasping in
human babies—others mature at a later stage. All are imperfect
when they are first carried out. But the initial imperfection is com-
pensated for by a greater capacity to learn and by the flexibility of
behaviour that results. Activities do not remain stereotyped but
improve with practice, the length of practice varying according
to the evolutionary status of the species: for the kitten, dog, lamb
a few months, for the chimpanzee a year or so, for the human child
many years. Play is a means by which these instinctive activities
are practised and perfected. As Groos puts it, 'Animals cannot be
said to play because they are young and frolicsome, but rather
they have a period of youth in order to play.'

It is understandable that Groos's theory is called both the
instinct-practice theory and the preparatory theory. Play in his
view is preparatory in two aspects. Generally it involves the
practice of bodily skills and their co-ordination, that is, mastery of
the physical self; and more specifically it provides practice in
miniature of the roles the animal or child will fulfil when grown
up—the kitten with peg or bean, the girl with doll and doll's
house, the boy with his meccano or chemistry set.

Groos also studied children's imaginatively symbolic play. In such play, children convert everyday objects—a chair or table or the like—into whatever takes their fancy; or they create a whole environment—domestic, school or hospital. The place is not just a living-room; it is a hospital. The settee is not a settee, nor the length of rubber tubing just rubber tubing; one is a hospital bed, the other a stethoscope.

Groos, like Moore, saw that, although children can and do distinguish between the real and the 'pretend' in such play, they still maintain the illusion that what is pretended is real. They do so, Groos argued, because the illusion allows greater freedom. By maintaining it, the child can in fancy turn any object into whatever he wishes. For Groos, the components inherent within children's symbolic play are the essence of pictorial, plastic and dramatic art—the illusion, the freedom which this illusion confers, the easy play of imagination which results, the joy that is experienced. Like Schiller, Groos saw art as an adult expression of children's play.

Groos's theory had a strong influence on educationists, particularly on Maria Montessori (1876–1952) whose methods of teaching kindergarten children were revolutionary. The basis of her teaching was to allow freedom of action in order to encourage children to do things for themselves. Provided with furniture and equipment of appropriate size, children were encouraged in small-scale adult activities: to lay meals, wash up, and so on.

This completes the summary of Groos's theory, which has been considered in some detail because the strictly instinctive and preparatory side of it, as distinct from his theory of art and play, has been quoted with approval by contemporary scholars (e.g. 11).

To conclude, here is one brief criticism. In accord with Groos's theory, play can justifiably be regarded as preparatory in a general sense, since it is one means by which a child acquires flexibility and skill in bodily movements and obtains experience in coping with the physical and social world. That play is preparatory in a specific sense is very much open to question.

Consider, for example, a little girl playing with her doll. She gives the doll an imaginary drink and scolds or encourages her; then she solemnly tucks her up in bed. Does this behaviour represent pre-exercise of the maternal instinct, as Groos's theory would imply? Or, to put the question in another way, will the little girl become a better mother because she plays with her doll in this way? Again, take the small boy who drives his chair-constructed car. Will he, because of such play, drive a car better when he grows up? It would obviously be difficult to obtain a scientific answer to these questions. But the questions themselves raise doubts as to whether the preparatory nature of children's play can be accepted in any specific sense. It is true that a child may develop interests and a favourable attitude towards play of a kind that has a vocational bias: but when he acquires such an interest and pursues it, he is approaching the 'real'.

The recapitulation theory

According to Stanley Hall (1846–1924), the games children play form a sequence of age stages. These stages follow one another in the same order as the course of human evolution. Through play, children recapitulate man's ancestral past. The crawling baby relives man's primate origin when he crept around on all fours, the six-year-old, dabbling with mud and creeping into holes and boxes, the experiences of the cave man, the nine-year-old playing Red Indians those of men as hunter and fighter. The function of play, Hall considers, is to liberate the child from these atavistic residues of behaviour. Having lived through them in his play, the child is then able to discard them and progress to the highest stage of social evolution represented by the industrial society of which he will become a part. Hall goes so far as to compare this recapitulation process in play with a tadpole's inheritance and subsequent discarding of a tail. He says (6):[1]

'Play exercises many atavistic and rudimentary functions, a number of which will abort before maturity, but which live themselves out in play like the tadpole's tail, that must both be developed and used as a stimulus to the growth of legs which will otherwise never mature.'

The theory is no longer accepted. It implies the questionable doctrine that acquired characteristics are inherited. Empirical studies have shown (8, 15) that the games children play do not follow, age by age, the evolutionary order, as suggested by Hall. They have many determinants: the general nature of the society

[1] page 202, Volume 1.

(industrial or agricultural), local conditions (urban or rural), the round of the seasons, important national events, the general nature of the culture, the stresses a child may have to endure (e.g. severe toilet training, overstrict parents, war), whether a boy or a girl.

Everyday observation certainly suggests that children in our society enter the 'industrial era' at an earlier age than the recapitulation theory would suggest. Small girls as well as small boys 'drive' cars, trains and buses, symbolized by pieces of furniture or replica toys, 'change gear' and 'tinker' with the broken down 'engine' even during their pre-school years.

The recapitulation theory was taken seriously in its day. Hall had made substantial contributions to psychology and education, even though they lacked scientific precision. The most that can be said for the theory is that it reminds us that much of boys' play has the characteristics of the primitive: wrestling, fishing, gaffing for eels, tracking, stalking, chasing, stealing. The virtues boys extol are toughness, endurance, bravery, and loyalty.

Psychoanalytic studies of children's play

Freud formulated no distinct theory of children's play. He was interested in it as an expression of children's emotional life and as a possible clue to their emotional problems. He attached particular importance to its repetitious and symbolic nature. In what he had to say about play he was influenced by the writings of Groos. When considering children's tendency to go on repeating words and phrases when first they hear them, he agrees with Groos. He actually quotes Groos, saying that this play with words 'probably obeys one of the instincts which compel children to practise their capacities' (3a).[1] To explain children's desire to repeat the same games or to hear the same story over and over again, Freud invokes his pleasure principle, the sheer pleasure the child obtains from these repetitions, an idea not unlike the joy which Groos sees as an essential component of most of children's play. Freud goes on to suggest that these repetitions reassure the child that the world in which he lives is a stable and predictable one.

Freud wrote of children's fantasy and imaginative play, and

[1] page 128.

of the possibilitity of interpreting such play in the same way as he interpreted adults' dreams. For, to Freud, a child through his fantasy play relives and attempts actively to master experiences which he has found or is finding emotionally painful. In Freud's own words (3b):[1]

'Children can master a powerful impression far more thoroughly by being active than they can by experiencing it passively. Each fresh repetition seems to strengthen the mastery they are in search of.'

Erikson (2)[2] likens this repetition in play to 'the way in which we (adults) repeat, in ruminations and in endless talk, in day dreams and in dreams during sleep, the experiences that have been too much for us'.

Such points of view form the theoretical basis of play-therapy. Play is a natural way by which a child expresses his feelings. The play-therapy situation is one in which a child is given opportunity to 'play out' his problems, much as an adult may 'talk out' his difficulties with friend, doctor or therapist.[3]

But whereas Freud stresses repetition, Erikson speaks more specifically of the 'ego-strength' acquired through individual play in general and its repetitious nature in particular. A child assembles a small world of manageable objects and gains control over it. When feeling disturbed, he returns to this world and, in exercising his power over it once again, acquires strength to cope with his difficulties. This process is analogous to what an adult may do. When troubled, a man may work in garden or workshop, a housewife spring-clean and rearrange a room, an artist express his anguish through painting, sculpture, music or whatever mode of art he follows.

Erikson touches on the social significance of play. Through it a child discovers 'a world shared with others'. But study of the social significance of play takes us beyond psychoanalytic thought proper to characteristics of children's play that are more appropriately considered under a special heading.

[1] page 35. [2] page 85.
[3] Gilmore (4) has demonstrated in an experimental study that children who had recently been in hospital for a tonsillectomy played many more doctor-nurse–hospital games than did a control group of children who had never been in hospital.

The social significance of children's play[1]

In their play, children often take the roles of adults. When playing
by himself a child may alternately take complementary roles;
for example, he may be both bus conductor and passenger, shopkeeper and customer, or teacher and child. Or he may invent an
imaginary companion with a name of his own, to whom he
assigns one of the roles while playing the other himself.

Within such play there are elements both of freedom and of
control. The child is free to take any role he wishes; but having
taken it he is bound by the behaviour appropriate to it. Sometimes
a child will tire of the restraint involved in taking on alternate
roles and will laugh them away, throwing tickets, goods and
chattels sky high and 'acting funny'. But, by ceasing to 'play
properly' he dispels the illusion and with it the freedom, and the
play disintegrates.

In their early years children use other children not so much as
persons but as objects—to be pulled, pushed, felt, coerced, and so
on. When two children get the idea that each can take a separate
role—as, say, mother and father—the social potentialities of play
gain significance and the possibilities within it are widened. Each
child is then 'set' to behave in a way appropriate to his role. Each
has expectations that the behaviour of the companion will accord
with the companion's role. The child's play is now organized in
relation to another. Here we have the nucleus of what social
psychologists have called 'role theory', which stresses the importance of role and role-taking—as, for example, child and parent,
husband and wife, employer and employee—in the organization
of social life.

Games like rounders, football and basketball imply a reciprocity of a more complicated kind. There are many people involved.
A child has to know approximately what each member of his team
and what each member of the opposing team will do in response
to any move he makes. There are also special techniques which
have to be learned and practised. This complex reciprocity and
these techniques provide organization, but not enough. It has to
be 'tightened' by the institution of rules.

Mead says that the child's taking alternate roles with himself

---

[1] In this discussion of children's role-taking and of the significance of rules
in the organization of children's games, we follow the writings of G. H. Mead (9).

---

or with an imaginary companion constitutes play proper. An activity which is organized and includes other people is different; it is a game. Games are one means by which the 'me's' are acquired and the 'organized other' is developed. For Mead, therefore, games are important in the growth of the child's self-concept in that through them a child asserts – submits, accepts – rejects, and assesses himself in relation to others (see pages 44–5). Here Mead invokes the same kind of distinction made at the beginning of this chapter, namely, that between the spontaneous play of very young children and the organized play of older children and adults.

Contemporary studies

These studies are to be found in the published work of psychologists whose investigations have been mentioned earlier in this book. In keeping with the theoretical trends outlined earlier, they have sought to explain play in terms of the basic needs which children feel to be active and adventurous, to explore and to solve problems. The reader will recall Groos's 'joy in being a cause' and how contemporary thinkers, like White, Stott and Harlow, have interpreted children's activities in a similar way (page 154).

Piaget has done a great deal of work on this subject. In his earlier writings he studied the rules of children's games and their relation to children's moral development (this will be considered in some detail in the next chapter). His later studies of play were bound up with his experimental studies of children's thinking.

Play, he says (13, 14), involves a process of *assimilation*, of fitting reality to suit one's immediate needs and purposes. Children use this process in their make-believe play ('Let's pretend'); so do adults when they indulge in wish-fulfilling fantasy. The scientist assimilates when, thinking hypothetically, he says, 'Let's forget reality for a moment and assume that such-and-such could be so. What would happen then?' Assimilation is to be contrasted with *accommodation*, a process by which needs and moods are modified to accord with reality. For a child there are objects which have qualities; they are hard or soft, hot or cold. He must sometimes stop pretending, and adapt his thinking and movements to their nature. Similarly for the scientist: there are objects which behave in certain ways and in accord with the laws his science has devised.

He has his assimilative, hypothetical flight. Then, in order to test his hypothesis, he too must stop pretending and accommodate his thinking to the world of actual objects and the laws they follow. For Piaget serious thought requires both assimilation and accommodation.

In stressing that play is assimilation, Piaget preserves in his idea of play the mood of fun and pleasure. Activity in which a child consciously strains to master or to learn involves accommodation. Such activity is not, in Piaget's opinion, play. Imaginative and symbolic play is play's ideal form.

In a tentative way, an analogy has been suggested between the child at play and the scientist at work. The historian Huizinga (7) has gone further by exploring the possibility that culture itself, man's economic, political and religious activities, bear the stamp of play. For Huizinga, the study of children's play may have implications beyond our understanding of children. Such a study, he suggests, may provide an insight into the motives of individuals, and an understanding of the whole way of life of a people. Huizinga says (7):[1]

'In the union of play and culture, play is primary, since the elements of play are present in animal life . . . It is doubly remarkable that birds, phylogenetically so far removed from human beings, should have so much in common with them. Wood-cocks perform dances, crows hold flying matches, bower-birds and others decorate their nests, song-birds chant their melodies. Thus competitions and exhibitions as amusements do not proceed from culture, they rather precede it.'

He goes on to elaborate mainly on play in the second sense in which we have defined it: as a contest and a challenge, with its tension and uncertainty. 'There is always the question "will it come off".' He regards spontaneous play as 'indicative of a culture only in a limited way'. He still sees an element of contest and uncertainty in solitary play—for example, when an individual solves mechanical puzzles or the problems in the 'problem corner' of magazines.

Synthesis and conclusion

The theories and studies of children's play which have been discussed may at first appear to contradict each other. Each tends to

[1] page 47.

single out one predominant aspect—surplus energy, or recreation, or emotional release, or mastery, and so on—and to treat it as the fundamental fact about play. What follows is not a new theory but a summary, one purpose of which is to show that the theories and studies outlined above complement rather than contradict each other.

Play is a means by which children have commerce with their environment; through play children explore and experiment, and so acquire skill in using their bodies and in manipulating objects; they also relate themselves both to their environment and to their own experiences. In order to achieve this commerce with the environment, certain conditions must be met. These include physical exercise, activity after relative confinement in home or school (surplus-energy theory), recuperation after close work (recreation theory), repeated practice of appropriate skills as the neuromuscular system matures (Groos's practice theory), the living out of emotional experiences (Freud), competence in coping with the social and physical environment (social and competence theories). In short, play furnishes an important means by which children develop, physically and psychologically.

In its essence play—unself-conscious, spontaneous, absorbing, the fun and pleasure—is the province of childhood. Adults will occasionally glimpse the mood of it—during a creative moment, when absorbed in a hobby, when watching children at play or when playing themselves. An analytical study of children's play has its particular danger: in attempting it, this mood may well elude us. Our theories suggest that play has its purposes; but children are blithely unconscious of them. If children become aware of them, or if we adults regard play as a form of training, the very essence of play is lost. There are a number of illuminating studies of children and of children at play which preserve this essence (e.g. 1, 17, 19, 21).

We adults may sometimes envy children their capacity to play. Children envy us out adult status. Reflecting on her own childhood, Monique Whittig (21) describes how little girls are aware of being children—of their commonplace status, their limited means for getting things done, the freedom they cannot enjoy. 'We cannot do that,' they will say, wide-eyed and breathless. 'We're children.' Play, after all, *is* only play. This explains children's fascination with the real, and the contrast they make between the 'real' and the 'pretend'. For them, it is much more exciting to use real pots and pans and real cups and saucers, and to do the job properly by using father's tools than it is to use their own tiny replicas.

A child will sometimes abandon play to do real work with real women or real men. Girls will sew or knit a garment, make a cake, or cook a dinner. Boys will help the farmer, shopkeeper or the milkman. Children will make real things, guided and urged by 'the organic laws of the tool world and their sense of industry', as Erikson has put it. His idea resembles what I have called the need to construct, and to construct something useful.

This 'sense of industry' applies to children's school work, as in the acquisition of reading, writing and computational skills. Delight in the 'real' is reflected in the way children will look forward to the time when they will be old enough to 'do' woodwork, metalwork or cookery. Then, like a brother or sister before them, a boy will take home a household article to be used day-by-day, a girl some delicacy to be eaten by the members of the family with relish and appropriate words of commendation.

REFERENCES

1   Cary, J. *The House of Children*. Carfax edition, Michael Joseph, London, 1951.

2   Erikson, E. 'Identity and the life cycle.' *Psychological Issues*, 1959, **1**, pp. 1–165.

3   Freud, S. (a) Volume 8: *Jokes and their Relation to the Unconscious*. (b) Volume 18: *Beyond the Pleasure Principle*. Standard edition of complete works of Freud (translated by Freud, A., Strachey, J.). Hogarth Press, London, 1953–64.

4   Gilmore, J. B. 'The role of anxiety and cognitive factors in children's play behaviour.' *Child Development*, 1966, **37**, pp. 397–415.

5   Groos, K. (a) *The Play of Animals*. (b) *The Play of Man*. Appleton, New York: (a) 1898, (b) 1901.

6   Hall, S. *Adolescence*. Appleton, New York, 1908.

7   Huizinga, J. *Homo Ludens*. Routledge, London, 1949.

8   Lehman, H. C., Witty, P. A. *The Psychology of Play Activities*. Barnes, New York, 1927.

9   Mead, G. H. *In* Strauss, A. (Ed.) *The Social Psychology of George Herbert Mead*. University of Chicago Press, Chicago, 1956.

10   Moore, T. 'Realism and fantasy in children's play.' *Journal of Child Psychology and Psychiatry*, 1954, **5**, pp. 15–56.

11 Nissen, H. W. 'Phylogenetic comparison.' *In* Stevens, S. S. (Ed.) *Handbook of Experimental Psychology*, New York, Wiley, 1956.

12 Patrick, G. T. W. *Psychology of Relaxation*. Houghton Mifflin, Boston, 1916.

13 Piaget, J. *Play, Dreams and Imitation in Childhood*. London, Routledge, 1952.

14 Piaget, J. 'A reply to Sutton Smith.' *Psychological Review*, 1966, **73**, pp. 111–12.

15 Roberts, J. M., Arth, M. J., Bush, R. R. 'Games in culture.' *American Anthropologist*, 1959, **61**, pp. 597–605.

16 Schiller, F. *On the Aesthetic Education of Man*. (A series of letters translated by Reginald Snell). Routledge, London, 1954.

17 Smith, R. P. *'Where did you go? Out. What did you do? Nothing.'* Norton, New York, 1957.

18 Spencer, H. *Principles of Psychology*. Williams and Norgate, London, Volume I, 1881.

19 Sutton Smith, B. *The Games of New Zealand Children*. University of California Press, Berkeley, 1959.

20 Sutton Smith, B. 'Piaget on play.' *Psychological Review*, 1966, **73**, pp. 104–10.

21 Wittig, M. *The Opoponaux* (translated by Helen Weaver). Owen, London 1965.

CHAPTER TWENTY

Children's Moral Development[1]

'MORAL action is action in accordance with values' (7).[2] This thought is implied in what has earlier been said about values (pp. 62–4); and although a person may behave in a way that is morally 'right' only from fear of punishment, it is generally agreed that true moral behaviour implies a special kind of disposition (dispositional tendency) which Freud called the 'super-ego'. It is the growth of this moral disposition that will now be considered.

By far the most influential empirical study of the children's moral development is that of Piaget (18). Many modern studies follow the procedures which Piaget adopted, and all owe much to his findings. These proceedings and these findings will now be described briefly.

Piaget: the rules of children's games

Piaget watched boys playing marbles and girls playing hop-scotch, and he asked them many questions about the rules of the games they played. As a result, he suggested that, following a very early stage (up to two or three years) of 'ruleless' sensori-motor activities in which the occurrence and significance of rules were absent, there were three quite distinct stages in the development of children's attitudes towards the rules.

Between the ages of about three and seven young children see

---

[1] This chapter mainly describes the ordinary child's moral growth, his moral triumphs, his moral lapses. It deals only very incidentally with the predominantly delinquent child for whom lapses are the rule rather than the exception.

[2] page 16.

the rules as immutably determined and sacrosanct. As Piaget puts
it:

'These same children harbour an almost mystical respect for rules:
rules are eternal, due to the authority of parents, of the Gentlemen of
the Commune, and even of an almighty God. It is forbidden to change
them, and even if the whole of general opinion supported such a
change general opinion would be wrong: the unanimous consent of
all the children would be powerless against the truth of
Tradition'(18).[1]

During the Primary School years, this attitude becomes more
relaxed. Children learn of possible variations in the rules. Yet an
element of the absolutism of younger children, and of the external
constraint by outside authority which this implies, still remains.

By the age of eleven, and progressively so in the years that
follow, children see the rules as convenient devices, mutually
agreed upon and designed to make their games go smoothly.

'The rule of the game appears to the child no longer as an external
law, sacred in so far as it has been laid down by adults; but as the outcome of a free decision and worthy of respect in the measure that it has
enlisted mutual consent' (18).[2]

Piaget: children's moral development

Piaget followed up this study with a second. He told children a
number of stories—about children who, for a good or evil purpose,
stole or cheated or deceived in some way, about others who
damaged property, deliberately or accidentally, or when in pursuit of some altruistic purpose. He asked the children numerous
questions about the moral issues involved in the stories. His
findings indicated that children's conception of justice, that is, of
moral laws and of the punishment to be inflicted on those who
disobey the laws, developed, as did their conception of the rules
of the games they played, in three distinct stages.

Children under seven take the same absolutist attitude towards
moral laws as they do to the rules of the games they play. For
them, moral laws are fixed, unchangeable things, determined by
an outside Authority. They have to be obeyed at all times; punishment for any infringement of the rules of moral behaviour must

---

[1] pages 52–3.   [2] page 57.

be severe, and an eye must be taken for an eye, a tooth for a tooth. The children also take an objective view of morality, that is, they evaluate an act in terms of its physical consequences, and a statement according to the degree to which it deviates from objective reality. They do not judge in terms of a person's intentions. If a lot of dishes are accidentally smashed, as when his mother's dress gets caught in the table cloth, and cloth and dishes are pulled off the table, a small child will open his eyes wide at the enormity of the offence. 'Mother is very, very naughty.' (Sometimes, on an occasion like this, we will stimulate this moral attitude and shake our heads in unison with the child and will repeat after him, 'Naughty, naughty'.) But the child thinks less of it if someone picks up only one cup and smashes it in a fit of spite or petty rage.

This objective view of morality is again illustrated in young children's responses to Piaget's story about a child who, when frightened by a dog, went home and told his mother a lie, saying that he had seen a dog as big as a cow: to the children this was particularly naughty because 'no one has ever seen a dog as big as a cow' (18).[1]

Piaget uses the term 'moral realism' to refer to the concept of justice implied in the attitudes and behaviour of young children as described above.

The Primary School stage, between seven and ten, is an intermediate one during which children retain some of the rigidity of this 'moral realism' but show, too, some of the characteristics of a third, and later, stage which Piaget calls 'moral relativism'. The significance of this second stage as an intermediate one can be illustrated from examples of the behaviour of Primary School children already given in the last chapter and in Chapter 14.

On the one hand, their 'moral realism' is seen in the way they will sometimes strive to attain the standards which adults impose, and even to go beyond them, as when a child demands perfect work and perfect behaviour of himself. It is seen in the perky righteousness with which they tell tales on the child who has infringed adult authority, and also in the severity of the 'treatment' they inflict on 'pupils' or 'children' when acting as 'teacher', 'mother', or 'father' in games of 'school' or 'house'. On the other hand, their 'moral relativism' is seen in the way they can be critical of adults; and, as Piaget has shown, Primary children can

[1] page 151.

often take account of the intentions of the person and judge in these terms when evaluating a moral act so that they do not always judge on the basis of morally extraneous factors, such as the amount of punishment which follows or the amount of damage which results. They are even able at times to make a moral generalization. Piaget illustrates this with a number of answers of children aged eight, nine and ten to the questions 'Why must we not tell a lie?' (18).[1] This exceptional answer was given by one eight-year-old child (a forward child as Piaget describes him), 'Because if everyone lied no one would know where they were.'

Gradually, then, children move towards the third stage, of 'moral relativism'. By about eleven, they are beginning to see the moral laws as means by which people can co-operate one with the other. The laws are not necessarily absolute and sacrosanct; their infringement may sometimes be justified as when someone tells a 'white' lie in order to save another from unnecessary pain. Since allowance must be made for circumstances, punishment for offenders need not always and necessarily be excessively punitive; in judging an act, a person's intentions must be taken into account. For these older children, it would be more immoral to smash one cup and saucer deliberately or for some spiteful purpose than to smash a table full of cups and saucers accidentally.

Probably the main criticism that most subsequent investigators would make of Piaget's work would be this: that he does not allow for individual differences in the rate of children's moral growth. Researches have shown that children may change from one stage to another before (or after) the age of seven or eleven as the case may be: that the more intelligent a child is, the more advanced his moral development (3, 16), that middle-class children tend to be more advanced than children living in slum areas (3, 6, 11), that girls are more advanced than boys (20).

Freud: children's moral development

According to Freud the 'super-ego' is formed during the first five years or so, and Freud's idea of this 'super-ego' is consistent with Piaget's description of the uncompromising 'moral realism' of young children.

[1] page 168.

At the Primary stage, this super-ego 'loosens', as Freud would put it (9). Children now begin to free themselves from the stern, forbidding demands they have previously made upon themselves. They begin to look more critically at adults, and, with the help and support of their companions, begin to evaluate the moral universe in which they live (see pp. 271–3). So, an individual child moves through a period of experiment and criticism to acquire, by eleven or thereabouts, a newly constituted and less stringent 'super-ego', which corresponds very much to Piaget's idea of 'moral relativism'.

But Freud goes further than Piaget by pointing out that later, during middle adolescence, many children again become absolutists. This is seen in the tendency of adolescents to be idealistic and perfectionist, to be impatient with the lack of either quality in the world as they see it. Sometimes, too, they are dogmatic in making ethical judgments, and they show a certain haughtiness, a tendency towards moral pride. Parents may find this quite irritating. It would seem that, like young children (though on a more mature level), adolescents must speak in absolutes and with a display of outward certitude, probably in order to ease their inner feelings of uncertainty.

As adolescents grow into adults the stringency of this newly expressed 'super-ego' is replaced by the more reasonable 'ego-ideal', as Freud's followers have maintained. It is manifest when children behave in a way that is a matured expression of Piaget's 'moral relativism'. Then the individual adolescent takes account of the intentions of others and of the circumstances surrounding an instance of moral or immoral behaviour. He is also easier towards himself, accepting his own weakness as well as his own strengths.

It may be well to digress from our main theme for a moment in order to consider the distinction between the terms 'super-ego' and 'ego-ideal', especially since an understanding of this distinction will be necessary for the discussion of the influence of parents on children's moral development which follows later in the chapter.

Freud's concept 'super-ego' signifies a severe form of conscience. It is expressed by the person who has set himself superhuman standards and who drives himself in an inexorable way to be perfect in everything he does; if he deviates even slightly from these standards, he experiences painful feelings of guilt and self-hatred.

It is understandable that Freud should concentrate on this severe form of conscience since he was concerned with mental illness, and a very severe super-ego may sometimes lead an individual to become neurotic. But the disadvantage of building a theory of personality on experiences with the mentally ill is the tendency to neglect more frequent, everyday manifestations of any psychological phenomenon. Some of his followers saw that Freud had done just this, since he made but little reference to a more benign form of conscience which they called the 'ego-ideal'.[1]

The 'ego-ideal' is expressed by the person who is concerned, and very much concerned, to maintain good standards of behaviour and achievement; but he is tolerant towards, and does not drive, himself to superhuman standards. When he fails to achieve the standards he has set for himself, he is more concerned to try again and to improve them than he is to punish himself with an excess of guilt and self-hatred. McDougall's self-regarding sentiment is closely related to the 'ego-ideal' of Freud's followers.[2]

Piaget's explanation of children's moral development

To return to the work of Piaget: he gives two reasons to explain why children's conception of the rules of the games they play and of justice changes in the way he describes. One reason is in terms of the important changes which take place in the way children perceive and think about the world as they grow older; another is in terms of children's co-operative activities with each other.

To take the first of these: from his studies of children's thinking, Piaget concluded that young children are 'ego-centric', meaning that a young child believes that everybody thinks, and sees things, as he does. He cannot realize or understand, for example, that his mother's view of a familiar object, such as a toy, is different

[1] In fact, Freud did use the term 'ego-ideal', but never meaning a benign conscience. He used it to indicate the way human beings sometimes compensate for their felt inadequacies by building up in their imagination an ideal self, or by hero-worshipping an actual person, living or dead. The ideal is not necessarily a moral one; it may be secular—a film or football star, Napoleon.

[2] The reader is referred to Flugel's book (7) for a more detailed study of the kinds of distinctions that have been made in this short digression.

from his own at any particular moment because she is looking at it from a completely different angle. Since he cannot comprehend differing viewpoints in such a case of simple perception, he certainly cannot comprehend the differing viewpoints, needs and circumstances of other people upon which a mature moral judgment must be based.

The second distinctive feature of young children's thinking is its 'realistic' nature. By this Piaget means that a young child cannot distinguish subjective phenomena, the images, impulses, feelings he experiences, from objective phenomena, what goes on outside, and independently of, these subjective experiences. An example of this confusion was given earlier (p. 232) with the small child who experienced an impulse to push and hurt his friend; and when subsequently his friend accidentally fell and hurt himself, the small child thought that it was he who was responsible. He could not distinguish between an impulse to do something, and his actually doing it. Similarly, when a young child knows that he must restrain such an impulse, he cannot realize that this is but his own moral command to himself, and not an outside authority (like the Eye of God) deterring him.

However, when children are beginning to develop the capacity to think 'non-egocentrically' at about the age of seven (and so able to see another's point of view), and when they are also beginning to distinguish what is subjective from what is objective (and so able to distinguish self-restraint from outward restraint), they are becoming cognitively prepared to develop a mature sense of reciprocal justice.

To take the second reason: for Piaget, children's co-operative activities together are a most important factor in furthering their moral development. As he puts it:

'The peculiar function of co-operation is to lead the child to the practice of reciprocity, hence of moral universality and generosity in his relations with his playmates' (18).[1]

Piaget also agrees with the point Isaacs has made (see pp. 271–3), that play with companions frees the child from too much parental constraint.

Summarizing briefly what has been said: for Piaget, cognitive defects in young children, their feelings that parents are omniscient

[1] page 63.

and omnipotent (see p. 364), and the constraint that parents impose on them combine to make these children 'moral realists'.
But their concept of reciprocal justice grows with new forms of
cognition and with the exercise of these in their play together. It
is understandable, therefore, that he should draw a parallel
between children's changing conceptions—of the rules of the
games they play and of justice.

Piaget's explanation: two critical comments

First, the sources of children's attitudes towards the rules of the
games they play and towards moral laws at varying stages in
their development may lie partly in their deeper feelings.[1]

A young child experiences many impulses—to hit, to steal, to
snatch, to shout angrily, to say a forbidden word (see pp. 252–3).
Since he has not acquired the ability to control these impulses, he
is somewhat at their mercy, and they are a source of great anxiety
to him. His idea of an immutable law existing there outside may
well serve an important purpose by providing psychological support to enable him to restrain these inner impulses. The anxiety
they cause him is then eased. However, as the child matures, he
acquires greater inner control over these impulses. The outer control provided by this idea of immutable and fixed laws is then no
longer necessary, and he can look at the moral laws with a degree
of objective equanimity.

The same kind of feelings may help to account for young
children's rigid attitude towards the rules of games. A young child
has not learned to co-operate with other children. His impulse is
to grab what he wants, to push the other fellow, and generally
to insist on having his own way. Co-operation seems incompre-
hensible to him except in terms of sacrosanct rules 'out there'
that restrain. But when the child does learn the art of co-operation,
he is no longer dependent upon these restraining rules; and he can
take a relatively relaxed attitude towards them.

The second comment is this: insofar as Piaget stresses the
parallel between learning the rules of games and learning the
moral laws, and insofar as he emphasized the importance of
children's groups in both kinds of learning ('co-operation among
equals', as he puts it), he tends to under-emphasize the role of

[1] see note 1, bottom of page 252.

parents in children's moral development. It is true that as children grow older and have a life of their own, they are no longer under the same amount of parental supervision and constraint as they were during their pre-school years. Yet, despite this, parents are still very much concerned about their children's moral development, even though, in general, they are content to allow the children themselves to decide the rules of the games they play.

Parental influences and children's moral development

Many research studies have been done during the last ten years on the relationship between the kinds of parents children have and the nature of their moral behaviour (e.g. 2, 13, 14, 16, 19). The results of these studies suggest these three generalizations:

When parents are warmly affectionate and impose reasonable control (warm democratic parents as described in Chapter 5), and when the child is motivated by a desire to continue to experience this warm affection, he develops the conception of morality akin to that described by Piaget as 'moral relativism' (2, 14, 19).

When parents are stern, cold and authoritarian (morally authoritarian parents as described in Chapter 5) and when the child is motivated by fear of losing their approval and support, he develops a conception of morality akin to that described by Piaget as 'moral realism'.

When parents are cold, hostile and punitive (punitively authoritarian parents as described in Chapter 5), and when the child is motivated only by fear of severe physical punishment, he does not develop a conscience of any kind. The only morality he acquires is that of restraint through fear of physical punishment (see also p. 78–9).

These generalizations illustrate, as did the summary statements given earlier (p. 82), the tendency for children's personalities to reflect, in some respects at least, the personalities of their parents. The 'moral relativism' of the first child reflects his parents' benign 'ego ideal', the 'moral realism' of the second his parents' forbidding and demanding 'super-ego'. The amorality of the third child reflects his parents' lack of either kind of conscience.

Yet each of the three relationships has its own unique origins in terms of the processes described earlier (pp. 362–6) whereby children tend to become like others.

Warm, affectionate parents encourage all the processes—empathy, suggestibility, identification and introjection. Since the parents do not threaten to withdraw their affection, the rapport between child and parents is relatively unconditional. Consequently, he feels personally free to explore and to question the moral universe.

In the case of the second parent, rapport is conditional and, from the child's point of view, precarious, since the parents may coldly withdraw their approval and support when he has done wrong. At such times, the child will often seek to re-establish rapport with his parents and to re-elicit their goodwill by confessing and seeking their forgiveness.

The third child stands aloof from his punitive parents. He adapts to life and to his companions in the same aggressive manner his father adapts to him. In this way the child wreaks his vengeance on a world that has shown him too little tenderness. It is as if he says, 'If I cannot get your love, then I'll get your admiration' (15). Anna Freud spoke of such a process as 'identification with the aggressor' (8).

Of course, children's moral development is complex, and the influences outside the family are many—companions, school, films, television. Yet research (16) is tending to suggest that parental influences are primary; primary in the sense that a child will come to these outside influences already dispositionally set to react in a particular way, a dispositional set determined by the influence of his parents.

Since he has developed few inner controls, the child of punitively authoritarian parents is highly vulnerable to outside influences, for example, to those of his 'gang'. Again, he has known little but brutality, and when he visits a cinema, he may well identify with the brutal in the film.

The rigid inner controls of children of morally authoritarian parents enable them to resist such outside influences as these. But because the children lack flexibility, they may find it difficult to assess unfamiliar situations, or, in chastising themselves, to distinguish a minor misdemeanour from a serious one. A child may give himself a painful sense of guilt for the slightest misdeed. Of course, an overstrict environment can impose a morality a child cannot sustain; he may break down under the stress of it with a bout of delinquency.[1]

---

[1] See the reference to a 'a dreadful freedom' in the account of his father given by the younger son (p. 55).

The warm affection of democratic parents is more likely to encourage in children a combination of inner control and flexibility. They are then able to assess outside influences, and to accept or discard them in the light of the standards they have acquired. When they evaluate their own behaviour, they are able to distinguish the serious misdemeanour from the not so serious.

The three generalizations provide pointers to the respective effects of affection, of moral and of punitive authoritarianism.[1] But since few parents would fit perfectly within any one of the three categories, one needs to be careful in applying the generalizations to individual families. Also, two siblings may react to their parents in quite different ways. This, too, has been illustrated at the beginning of Chapter 4 in the contrasting ways the two brothers react to a father who is (predominantly) morally authoritarian.

The reader is, therefore, referred back to the words of caution given earlier when the influence of parents' and teachers' attitudes on children's general behaviour was considered (pp. 80–2; p. 88).

The Character Education Inquiry: description

No consideration of children's moral development is complete without reference to the Character Education Inquiry (the C.E.I.) by Hartshorne and May, an extensive study of children's honesty, generosity, persistence and self-control (10). It consisted of three main parts and took five years to complete. In all nearly one thousand children, aged from ten to fifteen, participated. We are concerned here mainly with the first part (10, 1928) which is a study of three kinds of dishonest behaviour in children: cheating, lying, stealing.

The children were given a number of performance tasks such as the following:

They were asked:

To mark their own **test** papers in arithmetic.
To report the longest they had jumped in a series of standing jumps.

---

[1] Only three are mentioned here of the six types of parents described in Chapter 5. This is because the literature is not clear about the influence of all six on children's moral development. To date, it is parsimonious to confine oneself to these three generalizations.

To say whether or not they had finished a task specially devised so as to be impossible to complete in the allotted time.

To say, when all the tests were finished, whether or not they had cheated in one or more.

They were given the opportunity:

To peep at other children's answers after being told to keep their eyes closed.

To keep the excess change which was purposely given them when they went on an errand.

They were given homework specially designed to test their honesty; they were even observed at parties.

The findings showed that there were marked individual differences between children in the number of times they cheated, or lied, or stole. For example, in the ten tests of cheating, 7 per cent of the children did not cheat at all, 3 per cent of the children did so in all ten tests, just over 50 per cent cheated in three tests or less, just under 50 per cent in four tests or more.

Such individual differences as these were, in part, accounted for by differences between the children on those variables, intelligence, socio-economic status, sex, which, as already has been seen, influence the rate of children's moral development. More intelligent children cheated less, so did those of higher socio-economic status; and girls cheated less than boys.

There were considerable differences between children in the occasions when they were dishonest. Those who cheated or lied or stole in one situation were often scrupulously honest in another.[1,3] And children appeared to be inconsistent. Those who were dishonest were not always so in all three ways; for example, the ones who stole did not necessarily cheat or lie.[2,3] Children were most consistent on those tests which were similar in some fundamental way, irrespective of whether, according to the classifications Hartshorne and May had made, the tests were tests

[1] A trend shown by the low correlations between tests of the same type of dishonesty (cheating or lying or stealing).

[2] A trend shown by the low correlations between tests of one type of dishonesty and tests of another, e.g. the correlation between tests of lying and tests of stealing was ·132.

[3] None of the correlations under 1 and 2 were above ·5; and most of them were around ·2 or ·3.

of cheating or lying or stealing. It was found, for example, that some children responded similarly to tests which involved academic achievement and which were done in the classroom, others to tests done outside the classroom—on the sportsfield, at home, at a party.[1]

Because the correlations were small and because groups of children tended to respond similarly to similar kinds of tests, Hartshorne and May argued as follows. Since children behave honestly or dishonestly in any one particular situation to the extent that it is like other situations in which they have behaved honestly or dishonestly on previous occasions, one cannot speak of a trait (or disposition) of honesty but only of 'groups of specific habits'. This argument, with its conclusion, has led to many theoretical controversies (e.g. 1). We will return to it during the following discussion of these results.

The Character Education Inquiry: discussion

Since the qualities and the behaviour which we call moral are acquired during the process of growth, children's moral development, as has been seen is the case with their social and emotional development, is a gradual process in which children go from inept to more apt behaviour. Consequently, one can expect the kinds of lapses, which the C.E.I. study has demonstrated, even though the children are ten years old and more. Younger children cherish their moral certainty with dogmatism and righteousness (as when they tell tales). The difficult part comes later when children face new social situations with the inevitable conflicts—truth versus the goodwill of companions, honesty versus loyalty to a friend, candour versus courtesy, and so on. The older child begins to struggle between uncertainty about himself and the temptation to gain spurious certainty by a little conceit here, a little deception there, occasional exaggeration. We adults, in our own weakness, have also known, and sometimes succumbed, to the same temptation.

It is understandable, too, that children should differ from one another in the occasions when they are dishonest and in the types of dishonesty they show. For, in the process of development,

[1] Shown by the higher correlations between such tests—generally higher than ·4.

children are faced with a complicated world of people and of
institutions, all exerting pressures upon them, complementary or
conflicting. For each child, there will be the special situations in
which he is vulnerable and most easily tempted. What these situations are will depend upon the nature of the pressures, the skills
and personal qualities the child has, and those he lacks.

To take some examples: particular aspects of life in the society
in which they live will come to have special meaning and significance for particular children. For one, academic work is important.
He likes it: or, perhaps, his parents do, and are waiting at the end
of the day to know how well he has done in each class test. For
another child, it is athletic achievement, and his life revolves
around it; or, perhaps, here again, father may be eagerly waiting
to hear each day how many goals the boy has scored.

For the academic child, the arithmetic test is crucial; and he
may be tempted. For the athletic child, it is the test of standing
long jump. The child who is timid may be desperate to get some
money with which to bribe the bully; he keeps the excess change,
but does not cheat or lie. The child of the authoritarian parents,
who goes to the fair and other exciting places when he is told not
to, may lie; but he does not cheat or steal.

Of course, when children do respond in the same way to a
particular situation, such as altering the answers to their sums
to make them correct after a test in arithmetic, the reasons they do
so are likely to be many and varied. For one child, it is to avoid
a reprimand, for another to score over his neighbour. One boy
is so near the right answer that the temptation is too much;
another does not care about school work and just wants to get
by in the easiest way possible. By contrast, a child may alter his
answers because he cares very much indeed, and is fired by a
restless perfectionism. Then, the very conscientiousness we applaud
becomes the source of the child's wrong-doing, and his dishonesty
is but a mirror of his virtue. The motives for children's moral
behaviour are, indeed, most complex.

We can now return to the conclusion of Hartshorne and May
that there is no trait (or disposition) of honesty, only 'groups of
specific habits'. It will be recalled that, in their argument, they
emphasize the importance of the immediate, particular situation,
and how its similarity or lack of similarity to previous situations
will determine the way a child will respond to it. The particular

situation has also been stressed so far in this discussion, but with a rather different emphasis.

Hartshorne and May tend to speak of small, concrete similarities or dissimilarities, such as a situation involving pencil, paper, writing, classroom, marks as compared, for example, with one involving beans, ropes, running, sportsfield, points. Yet, what is important in determining similarity or difference in behaviour from one situation to another is not so much these more superficial similarities or differences; it is similarity or difference in the significance and import that each situation has for the child. While an arithmetic test and an English test are similar in that both entail pencil, paper, writing, classroom, marks, a more crucial similarity is that they both represent academic situations; and around academic situations a child would have developed certain dispositions, that is, a sentiment of love or hate, needs, goals and so on, as already described. Because this is so (and other things being equal, such as his ability in both subjects) a child's responses to both tests are likely to be the same. From the moral point of view, too, he is likely to respond in the same way, being equally tempted by both, or perhaps not tempted at all by either.

There is a sense in which emphasis on the immediate situation is justified in a study of children's behaviour. They have not yet developed full control, so that they are very likely to be impelled by the emotional significance that the immediate situation has for them. In fact, however, such an emphasis does not complete the picture of children's moral development. The idea of a general disposition towards honesty cannot be dismissed even on the evidence presented by the C.E.I.

From a technical point of view, Cattell has argued that the inter-test correlations obtained were not so small (as Hartshorne and May thought they were) that one can dismiss out of hand the possibility of a general factor, such as a disposition of honesty. Speaking of the results, he says, 'Substantial positive correlations of trait elements were found. The correlations are entirely consistent with a general factor being at work' (5).[1]

Secondly, with some exceptions (for example, children in lower socio-economic groups), the older the children in the C.E.I. study, the more honest they were as a group, and the more consistently honest they were as individuals. The dishonest

[1] page 118.

ones were the exception. It could be argued from this evidence that, as most children grow older, a disposition towards moral behaviour gains strength. Then, in determining behaviour, the particular situation is not as important as the disposition. In speaking of this trend towards more honest behaviour by the older children of the C.E.I. study, Allport has said, 'This result is just what one would expect in the course of normal socialization when emphasis in training is placed upon virtuous ideals, and only occasional lapses are allowed' (1).[1]

Allport implies here that learning moral ideas and moral behaviour takes time, that moral growth is not completed in childhood but proceeds over a long span of time, through adolescence and, for that matter, into adulthood. This idea of long years of growth conflicts with the impression that some people still have that there is an age, perhaps as young as five, when moral growth is complete. Even psychologists may unwittingly give this impression when they speak about identification, introjection and so on, as was done in the last chapter, and when they say that, by five, children have 'introjected parental standards'. This can often be said with an air of finality which, unwittingly again, reinforces the impression.

Incidentally, such a misconception can have its practical hazards. Because of it, a parent or teacher may expect perfect moral behaviour after a certain age. She then becomes so shocked by, or so intolerant of, the occasional lapse that she is unprepared to explore the possibility that it is an understandable one.

Modern studies agree with Allport in seeing the process of moral growth as a long one with no point in time when it is complete. Parents are important, and this has already been emphasized; but moral development is seen as more than just introjection of parental standards. It is intimately related to, and dependent upon, children's growing knowledge about the universe and the people in it, their activities in school and at play. It is also closely related to, and dependent upon, children's cognitive development, but in a broader sense than that implied by Piaget. For, as is the case with their grasp of the objective universe, so in their grasp of the moral universe, children move from the concrete to the abstract.

This movement is illustrated in a study by Havighurst (12). The study also illustrates the shift from home to outside influences

[1] page 253.

as the child gets older. Children, aged eight to eighteen, were asked to write a brief essay on, or tell about 'The person I would like to be like'. The results showed a definite tendency for children to progress, in their notion of an 'ego-ideal', from the concrete to the abstract. The youngest children, six to eight years old, chose their parents or some other members of their families; older children chose either attractive and successful young adults whom they knew and saw going about their daily work, or glamorous adults with romantic fame, such as film-stars and sportsmen. The adolescents who were about fifteen and more years of age, tended to depict their ego-ideal as a composite of desirable personal qualities not necessarily related to any known person.

This same tendency to progress from the concrete to the abstract has been shown by Kohlberg (17). When he told a group of four-year-olds about imaginary situations in which the good, conforming act was punished and the bad, disobedient act was rewarded,[1] the children judged the 'good' act 'bad' and the 'bad' act 'good'. That is, they judged the acts by the sanctions applied to them and not by moral standards. Older children of seven or so who were asked to judge found it difficult to unravel the confusion they felt. Even though most of them did eventually judge the 'good' act 'good' and the 'bad' act 'bad', some still continued to assert that an act can be bad because punishment is attached to it. Only those children in the group who were ten or eleven years old and more had acquired abstract notions of morality, so freeing them to cope with the confusing, concrete particulars with which Kohlberg presented them.

Such an experiment indicates that children's moral development is related to the growth of their ability to form concepts, that is, of their ability to abstract the essential ingredients of a moral situation and, if necessary, to deal with one separately from the rest. For example, children need to be able to separate such ingredients as praise, punishment, obedience, disobedience, consequence, intention; yet they also need to be able to judge the total situation and not to confuse one ingredient with the whole,

[1] For example, one story went much like this. A boy was told by his mother to look after the baby while she went shopping. The baby was lying on a couch. The boy went out to play leaving the baby alone. When the boy's mother came back, she gave him a packet of his favourite sweets.

for example, to equate praise with 'good' or punishment with 'bad'.

It is understandable from what has been said above that there should be individual differences in the rate of moral development according to children's intelligence, knowledge, socio-economic status and so on. Much research work needs yet to be done to relate the rate of moral growth in an exact way to such personal and social variables as these.

Concluding statement

Insofar as moral growth is a slow process, and insofar as the moral world is a complex one for children, the occasional lapses can be expected. These are sometimes group lapses, as when suddenly, at school, there occur many cases of cheating during examinations. There may even be a sudden outbreak of delinquency, such as pilfering from a local chain store. When such things happen parents and teachers become highly alarmed; and rightly so, of course. They must act decisively to stop this, so that the children are made aware of the moral structure of the world in which they live. Often, these lapses can be experiments aimed to test the moral universe. These experiments may be individually inspired, but are often made breathlessly more daring when done in a group. Cary (4) puts the matter neatly when he compares the sudden temptation which may seize a child with the inspiration that comes to the artist and with the loss of control which may overtake the brilliant speaker so that he is carried away to say rash and audacious things.

'The suddenness of temptation or, rather, inspiration, which (like many that come to an artist) is so quick that he doesn't even notice it, it leaves no moment of reflection. The imagination sees its opportunity, its prey, and instantly leaps upon it. You can watch this happen with any good talker, and you can see such inspired talkers carried suddenly away into brutalities. They drop bricks. That is to say, they are whirled into delinquency before they know it.

Such people, it is said, have given way to a sudden temptation. It has been too attractive for their self-control. For children, with their powerful imaginations and weak control, the wonder is not that they do some wrong, but that they don't do much more.'

In conclusion: the researches which have been quoted and the discussions which have followed in this chapter suggest that, from the point of view of a child's 'moral becoming', the main psychological ingredients would appear to be: affection (to give security and self-esteem as the child finds his way through the moral universe), control (to protect him from his own impulsiveness until he has acquired his own inner controls), freedom (to explore and to question the moral universe, to talk or not to talk about his moral problems and experiences).

REFERENCES

1   Allport, G. W. *Personality*. Constable, London, 1937.
2   Aronfreed, J. 'The nature, variety and social patterning of moral responses to transgression.' *Journal of Abnormal and Social Psychology*, 1961, **63**, pp. 223–41.
3   Boehm, L. 'The development of conscience: a comparison of American children of different mental and socio-economic levels.' *Child Development*, 1962, **33**, pp. 575–90.
4   Cary, J. *Charlie is My Darling*. Carfax edition, Michael Joseph, London, 1951. Prefatory essay.
5   Cattell, R. B. *Description and Measurement of Personality*. Harrap, London, 1945.
6   Dolger, L., Ginandes, J. 'Children's attitude towards discipline as related to socio-economic status.' *Journal of Experimental Psychology*, 1946, **15**, pp. 161–5.
7   Flugel, J. C. *Man, Morals, and Society*. Duckworth, London, 1945.
8   Freud, A. *The Ego and the Mechanism of Defence*. International Universities Press, New York, 1946.
9   Freud, S. *New Introductory Lectures in Psychoanalysis*. Allen and Unwin, London, 1945.
10 Hartshorne, H., May, M. A. I *Studies in Deceit*, 1928; II *Studies in Service and Self-Control*, 1929; III *Studies in the Organization of Character*, 1930. Macmillan, New York.
11 Harrower, M. 'Social status and the moral development of the child.' *British Journal of Educational Psychology*, 1934, **4**, pp. 75–95.
12 Havighurst, R. J., Robinson, M. Z., Door, M. 'The development of the ideal self in childhood and adolescence.' *Journal of Educational Research*, 1946, **40**, pp. 241–57.
13 Hoffman, M. L. 'Power assertion by the parent and its impact on the child.' *Child Development*, 1960, **31**, pp. 128–43.
14 Hoffman, M. L. 'Child rearing practices and moral development.' *Child Development*, 1963, **34**, pp. 295–318.

15 Horney, K. *The Neurotic Personality of Our Time.* Norton, New York, 1937.

16 Johnson, R. C. 'A study of children's moral judgments.' *Child Development*, 1962, **33**, pp. 327–54.

17 Kohlberg, L. 'Moral development and identification.' *In Child Psychology 62nd Yearbook of the National Society for the Study of Education.* University of Chicago Press, Chicago, 1964, Part I, pp. 227–332.

18 Piaget, J. *The Moral Judgment of the Child.* Routledge & Kegan Paul, London, 1932.

19 Sears, R. R., Maccoby, E. E., Levin, H. *Patterns of Child Rearing.* Row, Peterson, New York, 1957.

20 Terman, L. M., Tyler, L. E. 'Psychological sex differences.' *In* Carmichael L. (Ed.) *Manual of Child Psychology.* Wiley, New York, 1954, especially pp. 1098–1100.

PART SIX

The Observational Study of Children

CHAPTER TWENTY-ONE

Individual Personalities in School and Classroom

In the following extract a teacher recalls his first arrival and final departure from a school where he had taught for two years.

'I was standing at the exit of a swaying tram which was clanking its way through a city street towards a school. As the tram slowed down, I looked at the school building where I knew I would teach for a long time. To me at this moment, it was just a two-storeyed brick building, the same as most school buildings found in this part of the city. As yet, only a few children were about, some near the gates, some in the school playground and two peeping out of an upstairs classroom window.

'I walked up the steps into the school and entered a large central hall with a multitude of doors and corridors leading off it. No one appeared to be about until I saw a man of fifty or more years with a stooped gait walking towards me, carrying a bucket and mop in one hand. As I learned later, this was Mr. Harris, the caretaker. He greeted me as the "new one" and said that Mr. Jackes, the headmaster, would not be long.

'Two years later I left the school for the last time, and I watched it disappear as I stood on the same spot and in the same tram. But I did not see a dingy building. I saw classrooms, and especially the one in which I had taught. I looked up at the window and there was Edward, who had been my monitor, waving me goodbye. I waved back. I looked at the window of the adjacent classroom where I knew Mr. Eames would be cleaning up the debris of the day and preparing the blackboard work of tomorrow in his usual conscientious manner. In the little room on a wing of the building, Mr. Jackes, the headmaster, tired after the weighty responsibilities of the day, would be patiently interviewing a parent. On the other side of the building I knew that children would be rushing down the steps and out of the school, cautioned by Mr. Spray, who would be on duty, to "take it easy" and "not to run". Mr. Harris would be sprinkling wet sand over the floor of Room One in preparation for sweeping it. I saw some children gazing through the windows at the disappearing tram and knew that, of those I had taught, some would be saying, with regret or relief or indifference, "He's on that tram."

'When I looked at the fast-disappearing playground, I did not see just boys and girls. I saw John, Harry, Jean, Hazel and a whole group of particular children as they pressed their faces against the railings. I saw Thelma, so good at English, so poor at arithmetic; and Mary, so sensitive and introverted that one wondered what would happen to her in the tough environment in which she lived. There was Horace who had just rushed to the railings to see my tram off—Horace, the difficult boy of my class, product of a broken home and now a State ward. My attempts to "study" him had not always met with success. But as he waved and smiled from a distance, all was forgiven—my own as well as his mistakes.'

A teacher is likely to experience a number of such comings and going during the course of his career. He will enter a classroom of anonymous children who, as far as he can see at first, have few qualities that separate one child from another. Soon they will become for him a unique group whom he will judge 'a good class', 'a responsive group' (or perhaps the opposite), and to whom he will adapt and respond. For the children, the teacher is new and strange, but soon they will get to know him and he will become for them a unique person to whose idiosyncrasies they will respond and adapt, both individually and as a group.

How does this process of 'getting to know' take place? It is obvious that we *learn* about the institutions and people of a city in which we live, and about our colleagues and the children of a school in which we teach, but not always in the deliberate and conscious way in which we learn our multiplication tables or the factual details we 'swot up' for an examination. Without deliberately setting out to do so, we 'get to know' the dispositional tendencies of people, particularly of those who are important to us; we then use the knowledge we acquire to make judgments about them and to predict their behaviour. Probably we are not even aware of many of the cues which determine our judgments of an adult or a child, such as tone of voice, a movement of the head, a peculiar gait, and a host of other small details of behaviour. Yet our contact with people is an interplay of responses based often in this unconscious way, on the knowledge we have acquired. In other words, we adapt to and respond to other people in terms of our knowledge of their dispositional tendencies.

Consider the clever hostess. She weighs up the dispositional tendencies of her prospective guests and groups them in such a way that her dinner-party will be a success. Consider, too, the teacher who is aware of individual differences in his children. He is able to encourage, coax, stimulate or admonish as the need arises and as the personalities of individual children direct.

A baby comes into a world which contains objects having certain qualities, into a technologically advanced culture, and into a society of people whose personalities have already been formed. As the baby develops, he learns the nature of these objects—whether they are hot or cold, hard or soft, heavy or light—and he reacts accordingly. He learns not to touch one object because it will burn him, to touch another because it is smooth and soft, to lift this one but not to attempt to lift that. Similarly, he learns about people and what makes them happy or sad, affectionate and loving, or angry and hating, and, according to the way in which he has learned, so he adapts himself dynamically to people.

This dynamic adaptation to people is shown in children's reactions to their teachers. If a teacher terrifies them with undue severity, they may try individually or collectively to placate him. If he lacks the ability to guide them firmly they may tend to become cheeky or unruly. To his ability to be friendly yet firm, kind yet fair, they may respond with a spontaneity that is neither submission nor cheeky unruliness. If the teacher likes talking about his war experiences, the children will deftly divert him into recounting an anecdote, especially at the beginning of what would be a dull lesson in, say, English grammar. They may have heard the anecdote many times before, but that does not matter.

The adaptation is a two-way process in that teachers are observing children's responses to themselves and are also adapting their behaviour to accord with the children's age and ability, their social and emotional maturity. This can be a trial-and-error process (with many errors) when a teacher takes over a new class. Thus, the new teacher may at first make mistakes with individual children. He may, for example, over-estimate Mary's ability and expect more from her than she is capable of doing. He may chide John for untidy work and Albert for inattention. Later, he may discover that John has only recently recovered from a broken finger and that Albert gets up very early to do a paper round before coming to school. He will also be unaware at first of the temperamental differences between a William, a Peter and a Paul (see Chapter 6).

A new teacher may also make mistakes with the group as a whole. For example, he taxes a class of older children too hard at first and they respond by becoming passively resistant. He may then have to retreat very gently, diplomatically, unostentatiously. On the other hand, he may score some signal successes even within the first few weeks of taking a class. He hits it off with James, who has been a school problem for years, by discovering, appreciating, and capitalizing upon an extraordinary talent James has for drawing caricatures. He gains the full co-operation of a class by initiating an activity or project that appeals to all the children.

Although I have talked about 'getting to know' and about 'cues of which we are unconscious or unaware', this is not to imply that there is any mystery in learning about other people, although much research is still needed to extend our knowledge of such learning. The following simple techniques may be suggested as the main ways by which we acquire data from which the dispositional tendencies of individuals are inferred:

1   *Observation of overt behaviour:* observing a person behaving (talking and doing) in many situations.
2   *Conversation:* conversing with the person himself, and with other people about him.
3   *Study of productions:* studying the results of a person's constructive, creative, destructive efforts.

The techniques used by the psychologist in his study of personality, and described in the next chapter, are basically an extension and refinement of these.

During his work from day to day the teacher uses these three methods of getting to know others. First, he *observes* children in different situations in classroom and playground as they work, play, argue, fight, laugh and cry. Secondly, he *converses* with the children of his class about their likes and dislikes, their interests, needs and leisure-time pursuits. He talks casually with individual children about these things and about their past and present history and future aspirations. He listens to the remarks of other teachers and chats with them about school histories and family backgrounds. He converses with parents. Thirdly, he *studies the work children produce* and the attitudes they have towards classroom activities. From the constructive, academic work he judges individual children as bright or dull, persevering or easily discouraged, hardworking or lazy, co-operative or stubborn. He may go further and study his children's imaginative and creative work and give his class written work aimed to discover needs, interests, aspirations and leisure-time pursuits—such subjects, for example, as, 'When I grow up', 'What I like doing best', 'My mates and I'. He may also study children's free drawings and paintings, a more sophisticated mode of observation to which more detailed reference will be made in the chapter which follows.

It is not always easy to get children to write spontaneously on such topics as those suggested above. They will probably do so more readily if they have been used and encouraged to express themselves without too much stress on neatness and punctuation. It is certainly essential that written work designed to reveal personality should be done freely and without the restraint which stress on neatness and punctuation imposes on the creative originality of children.

Desultory observation of children in the classroom can lead to many errors, of course. It is so easy to acquire general impressions of individual children and, in doing so, to see one child as the paragon of all virtues and another as entirely bad without any redeeming qualities whatsoever. The negative general impression particularly may sometimes be carried on from class to class. Thus, Teacher A tells Teacher B, who is taking over his class, that he must keep a sharp eye on young Smith who is this, that and the other, and that if Smith starts anything, Teacher B must put him smartly in his place. Even though A says this in the privacy of the staff-room, Teacher B has been put on the defensive, and is expecting the kind of behaviour from Smith that A predicts. Smith guesses this or infers it from close observation of B's guarded behaviour towards him. Prediction and expectation are often fulfilled, and Smith proceeds to behave as A said and as B has been led to expect that he would.

It would be silly to attribute all bad behaviour in schools to negative predictions and expectations on the part of teachers, for bad behaviour has many facets and many causes. Nevertheless, negative predictions and expectations may sometimes encourage the expression of the stated and expected behaviour. Smith has been assigned a negative role and his concept of himself grows in relation to this role; he sees himself in terms of it and acts accordingly.

Because of the possibility of this and other errors some educationists would say that teachers should avoid studying children; that, as teachers, they should confine themselves to the three R's and such necessary extras as art and handwork, and not attempt to be amateur psychologists or psychotherapists. However, the position is not as simple as this for a number of reasons. First, teachers will in any case make judgments about children's personalities. Secondly, the mistakes a teacher makes when he takes over a new class, such mistakes as those described at the beginning of this chapter, arise not so much from faulty teaching as from a misunderstanding of the nature of the group and of the individual children within it. Thirdly, knowledge of children's needs and interests is valuable in teaching them even the three R's. Put in crude slogan form, 'We can teach bills to Bill better when we know Bill.' '$2\frac{3}{4}$ yards of cloth at 2/9 a yard' can be very abstract to a boy. But the teacher discovers that Bill is beginning to build a model railway, or is planning a camping expedition with a group of friends. Either of these provides an excellent means by which Bill can be taught about bills.

It is, therefore, not a case of avoiding judgments, but rather of making more careful observations upon which to base judgments. It follows from this that an important task for the teacher on taking over a new class is to study the cumulative record cards of his new pupils, and to get to know the psychological characteristics of children within the age-group he is to teach during the ensuing year.

CHAPTER TWENTY-TWO

Observing and Analysing Children's Behaviour

THIS chapter has three purposes. The first is to amplify the simple statements given in the last chapter about the way to get to know people. The second is to look at the way the trained observer gets to know about people. These two purposes serve yet a third in that much of the material to be presented will form useful background knowledge for the guide to a study of an individual child given in Chapter 24.[1]

Since, as already mentioned, the methods used by the trained observer are, in essence, an extension and refinement of the means used in everyday life, the three main methods of getting to know people—observation of children's overt behaviour, conversation with the children and with others about them, and study of children's creative work—will be followed through here in that order.

Observation of children's overt behaviour

Suppose a young teacher visits a friend who is also a teacher, and, in the course of casual conversation, asks his host, 'What do children here do with themselves in their leisure time?' His friend says, 'Oh! I've watched them often enough. They play in the park; some go to the pictures, or to the football match on a Saturday afternoon.' He may then add, 'We'll go for a walk after lunch and have a look.'

During their walk, the two young teachers see a group of girls

[1] In this chapter, the phrases 'the child study' or 'the study guide' refer always to the particular guide presented in Chapter 24.

playing hopscotch on the pavement, some boys with scooters and some with bicycles busily riding up and down a quiet road. One boy whom they see has a four-wheeled trolley steered by rope attached to its front wheels; on it he is hurtling down a sloping pavement at break-neck speed. In the park, children are playing —on the swings, see-saws and climbing frames, at hide-and-seek, cowboys and Indians, cricket, rounders, and at a host of other games. On their way back, the teachers call at a friend's house and find the children there variously employed—a boy is busy with a meccano set, a group of small girls is playing house, a little boy is dabbing away at a piece of dough 'helping' his mother to make a cake.

When they return home, the host says, 'Now you have a good idea of what children here do during their leisure time.' It would appear that a simple question has been simply answered.

However, the trained observer would point out that the question asked was not a simple one and that the answer so far obtained is somewhat superficial and possibly inaccurate—not that this matters at all within the context of what the teachers were doing. They had an enjoyable experience and learned a good deal about children. But, for our purposes, it is of value to consider why the trained observer would say this. The reasons he would give would be mainly these:

1 The teachers observed particular children—the ones who happened to be about at the time. They did not observe all the children in the town. Some were having a late lunch, some had gone away with the school football team, and so on. They saw both boys and girls, but did they see more boys than girls or vice versa? They saw children of many ages, but did they see more children of one age than another? Were there any age-groups missing? (This introduces the problem of selecting the children to be observed, or *population sampling*.)

2 They observed children only for an hour or so on a Saturday afternoon. But what do children do on a Saturday morning or during the hours after school each day? Again, they observed on a beautiful, sunny afternoon in summer. What do the children do on a rainy day in summer or a winter's afternoon? (This introduces the problem of selecting times for observation, or *time sampling*.)

3   They observed only in specific places—in the street, in the park, at home. But are there other places where children play? Do they play the same games in these places as they do in the places where they were observed? (This introduces the problem of selecting situations, or *situation sampling*.)

4   When they arrived home, the teachers talked about the games they had seen. But, have they good memories? There is the possibility that, according to their own interests or their own childhood experiences and preferences, they were prone to remember some games and to forget others. (This introduces the problem of *accurate recording*.)

5   As the two teachers recalled what they saw, to what extent did they agree as to the games that were played? (This introduces the problem of checking the observations of one person with those of another, or of obtaining a measure of the *reliability* of the findings.)

6   If the teachers were to repeat their observations on another beautiful, sunny Saturday afternoon in summer would they have had the same results? (This introduces the problem of the extent of agreement between an experiment and its repetition under circumstances as close as possible to the original. This gives a further measure of the *reliability* of the findings.)

7   Were the children aware that adults were watching them and, if so, did this cause them to modify their behaviour? (This introduces the problem of *interference* with the observed behaviour because of the technique used, namely observation.)

The practical import of some of these technical problems which the trained observer would raise will be clearly seen when suggestions are made for the child study.

Observation again: the 'ripples' of behaviour

In the study of children's games the events to be observed are clearly laid down and can be fairly easily identified. It is obvious that these boys are playing cricket not football, that these girls are skipping not playing hopscotch, that these children are playing tag not hide-and-seek. The number of games being played may have been very numerous and the students may have failed to detect all of them. Nevertheless, the selection of events to be observed is clearly laid down by the nature of the inquiry.

OBSERVING AND ANALYSING BEHAVIOUR 417

In any observational study some kind of selection has to be made because, if a person attempted to observe the activities of even a group of five children for only eight or so hours, and tried to record every event, small or large, that took place (the narrative description of behaviour), he would write a fair-sized book. While within the whole stream of children's behaviour there are fairly clearly observable 'rapids' (as the games of children may be called), there are also innumerable 'ripples' of behaviour—laughing, crying, co-operating, competing, quarrelling and so on. As one moves through the 'stream' to the 'rapids' and then to the 'ripples', observation and recording become more difficult. Because this is so, when a particular 'ripple' of behaviour is being observed, a classified list of the kinds of behaviour which indicate the 'ripple' is usually prepared beforehand. To take two examples: here, first, is Sears's classification of aggressive behaviour of children in nursery schools, classified into six categories (6).[1]

Injury to person (including hurting someone, getting someone punished, damaging another's property, derogating status).

Discomforting another (including threatening gestures and language).

Ensuring compliance with demands.

Destruction of inanimate objects or constructions (in the form of displaced aggression or non-directed aggression).

Having object in own possession (taking things away from another).

Removal of immediate or anticipated frustration (removing barriers, minimizing injuries from another person, maintaining status as in 'saving face', taking back an object that has been previously taken away by someone else, retaliation).

Secondly, here are four of the ten categories of sympathetic behaviour prepared by Murphy (3).[2]

Helps. Helps out of physical distress situation—picks child up after falling; helps with play—gives toy, plays with child, pushes swing, helps climb.

Comforts. Pets, pats, hugs, kisses; reassures, e.g. 'I won't hurt you'; expression of solicitude, e.g. 'That's too bad', 'That hurts, doesn't it?'

Questions. 'Why is he crying?' 'Did it hurt you?' (to child); 'What

[1] page 153. [2] pages 119–29.

are you going to do about it?' (to teacher); 'What's the matter?' (to animal or to a child).

Anxious, disorganized. Stares with anxious expression; evidence of worry, shakes head, frowns, lips pressed together, etc.; cries, whimpers.

By making a prepared list, the events the investigator is going to observe are clearly set out and by using categories he is able not only to count the number of times that aggressive or sympathetic behaviour occurs but also to study the qualitative forms that each takes.

For the child study the narrative method will be suggested and an actual example will be given. But it may be added that the study is not presented as a hard and fast set of procedures. There is no reason why a student should not prepare his own classified list of a 'ripple' of behaviours, if he feels able and wishes to do so.

Asking questions of the children

The doubts, questions and problems raised so far show that observing even such relatively obvious behaviour as children's play in a scientific way (as distinct from an impressionistic one) is difficult, time-consuming, and requires careful planning beforehand. A research worker could spend two years, indeed, a whole life-time, working on this task alone. One may ask, therefore, if there is some way to short-cut the long process of observation and still obtain the information one requires. A simple answer suggests itself, namely to ask the children what games they play.

There are three main ways by which this could be done: (*a*) by asking the children to keep a diary of their activities outside school and of the games they play in the school playground; (*b*) by talking with them; (*c*) by giving them a written questionnaire to answer.

The diary method would probably not be very successful. It would be difficult for children to be as precise and systematic in their recording as one would wish and, even if they were systematic and precise, the contents of the diary might be long, rambling and difficult to analyse. In talking with children one may be casually conversational or by contrast formal, following a standardized procedure with a prepared set of questions. Research findings with adults suggest that interviewing is more successful when the procedure adopted is a compromise between these two extremes—that is, a procedure which includes a prepared set of questions, but which is flexible enough to allow for questions and discussions outside this routine. Probably this applies also to children. It certainly accords with common sense, since most people would agree that a prepared set of questions asked in a formal way and within the formal setting of the classroom would restrict the spontaneity of a child's responses to questions about his personal, out-of-school activities. It would be better to approach the task in a friendly, apparently casual way within the informal environment of the playground or during the conversational setting of handwork, gardening or games lessons. At the same time, one can be quite definite regarding the information required and the types of questions to ask in order to obtain it.

A written questionnaire could be constructed as follows:

1   Think back carefully over the last seven days (since last Wednesday) and write a list of all the kinds of games you have played during the last week.
2   You probably play some of these games more often than others. Think back again and say how many times in the last seven days you have played each of the games you have mentioned. Do this by putting a tick (√) beside a game for each time you played it.
3   You probably like playing some games more than you do others. Put your games in a list so that you have the game you like playing most at the top of your list, the one you like next best second, and so on, with the one you like playing least of all right at the bottom.
4   Write a sentence (or a few sentences) telling why you like playing the game you have placed at the top of your list and a sentence (or a few sentences) telling why you don't like the game you have placed at the bottom. Here are two examples: I like cricket because I'm good at batting. I do not like playing cowboys and Indians because it is too rough.

The questionnaire method has advantages. Questionnaires are easy to distribute and the student can catch a very large number of children in his net. When he has decided on the structure of his sample, it is easier to distribute questionnaires according to these specific proportions (of boys and girls, of each age-group and so on) than it is to find these children and then observe them in streets and parks.

But there are serious disadvantages in the method too. Questionnaires can only be given to children who can read and write, and this will severely limit the age-range of the children who can take part. Some children may not include even a favoured game because they cannot spell it. Also, they are likely to include only games of which they know adults approve, and unlikely to include escapades and forbidden games. This last objection also applies, to a large extent, to interviews and to the use of unconcealed observers.

It is, of course, possible to combine questionnaires either with interviewing or with observing a small group of the children who have answered the questionnaire, or with both. In this way, information collected in the questionnaire can be checked.

In the child study guide questionnaires are not appropriate, but the student will be advised to talk with the child and, before doing so, to prepare a set of questions which will guide him in obtaining the information he wants in as informal a way as possible.

Asking other people

If a person finds himself in a strange city and wants to go to a particular street or shop he can, instead of getting a street map and laboriously working out the way he has to go, simply ask someone who knows the city well. And if he wants to know something about the personality of a child, again he can ask someone, a parent or a teacher, who knows the child well. Trained observers using the sorts of techniques described above have often obtained teachers' assessments of children to check (obtain the reliability of) their results. The agreement is usually very high. But parents and teachers are busy people and if one wants information from them, it is a good idea to prepare a simple way by which they can record their judgments. To do this, rating scales are often used.

When a teacher assesses a child for a particular ability (such as intellectual, mechanical, creative), or for a particular trait (such as dependence, predictability, conscientiousness), he may simply use the three categories High, Medium, Low.

This is a numerical rating scale and it is regarded as continuous in the same way as is the scale on a ruler or a thermometer; a child can be assessed anywhere along it and if necessary between the points on the scale where numbers fall (see below). 'High', 'medium' and so on are so vague that differences may arise between individual raters because of the different standards each will adopt. Graphic scales are therefore to be preferred because these provide a definition of the trait to be rated and a descriptive statement for each point of the scale, as in the two examples given in Fig. 12 (see page 422).

3	2	1
High	Medium	Low

This three-point scale could be extended to a five-point scale:

5	4	3	2	1
Very High	High	Medium	Low	Very low

Rating scales are not only a convenient way of asking other people's opinions; they are also used by observers themselves to sum up the results of their own observations. Baldwin, for example, used such scales in his investigations of the relationships between parents' behaviour and attitudes and the behaviour of their children, some of the results of which have been discussed in Chapter 5.

Errors and rating scales

With the prevalence of cumulative record cards in school today, teachers frequently use rating scales, and so it is worth looking for a moment at some of the errors that may possibly creep in when rating scales are used.

First, there is the error of 'central tendency'—that is, the tendency to say of the top of the scale, 'nobody can be as good as that', and of the bottom of the scale, 'nobody can be as bad as that'. The assessor then uses only the middle part of the scale.

Secondly, there are what could be called the 'hard' and the 'soft' constant errors—that is, the tendencies to mark or check hard and to use only the bottom half of the scale, or to mark leniently and use only the top half of the scale.

Thirdly, there is the error which can arise from what has been called the 'halo effect', or the tendency to look at the name of the person, make a general judgment such as, 'He's a nice fellow' (or

CREATIVITY: The ability to be imaginative and original in the handling of words. ideas, materials.

5	4	3	2	1
Shows ingenuity and intuition. Highly original.	Is resourceful in modifying, recombining words, ideas and materials of his own and others.	Is able sometimes to break away from a routine, and to recombine words, ideas and/or materials in an original form.	Seldom has a novel idea and is usually content to follow a routine.	Wholly imitative. Dependent on routine and will even resist change.

CURIOSITY: The desire to inquire, explore and actively to seek new knowledge.

5	4	3	2	1
Constantly enquiring and spontaneously seeking new knowledge.	More than ordinary 'thirst for knowledge'.	Shows interest in new objects and new ideas and sometimes will spontaneously seek to enlarge his knowledge.	Seems generally indifferent and new objects and ideas stimulate him only temporarily.	Indifferent; displays little or no interest in old or new ideas.

FIG. 12 Examples of scales to rate creativity and curiosity

the opposite), and mark every trait according to this over-all judgment.

As a safeguard against the first two errors a teacher, as he rates, should constantly remind himself that he is using a five-point, and not a three-point scale; also that in a class of forty or more children, for most traits there will be at least one or two children who are likely to be at one or other extreme. Further, if he is using scales that have been used extensively with many children under highly standardized conditions, he can compare the way his own total ratings for his class are distributed with the distributions obtained under these standardized conditions with many children (4, 5). It has been found, for example, that on some traits, such as suggestibility, cheerfulness, friendliness, ratings are high, with many more children rated 4 and 5 than are rated 1 and 2; on other traits, such as cruelty, jealousy, shyness, ratings are low, with many more children rated 1 and 2 than 4 and 5. On yet other traits, such as originality, physical fear, aggressiveness, the ratings are such that, when the children are classified into groups according to these ratings, the number of children in each group does approximately accord with what is known as a 'normal' distribution. This means that, when a five-point scale is used, a large group of ratings on these traits would be distributed approximately as follows:

Items of scale	1	2	3	4	5
Number of children	7%	24%	38%	24%	7%

The errors in rating may often be accounted for by the way scales are prepared, as when they are compiled using only vague terms, such as 'high', 'low', 'average'. If scales are specially compiled for a particular situation (for example, the school and classroom) and refer to specific kinds of behaviour common in this situation, then the scale itself constantly reminds the rater that the rating is a *behaviour* rating, and that he needs continually to reflect back to his own observations of a child's actual behaviour.

In the study guide, the method of rating will be combined with the narrative method—that is, the student observes the child for stated periods, records the child's actual behaviour and then rates him on the basis of the behaviour he observes. It will also be suggested that the student obtains some indication of the validity and the reliability[1] of his ratings.

The reader will notice in the graphic scales for the child study that descriptions of behaviour corresponding to each number on the rating scales are often quite extended ones. In this sense, it may be said that two methods of study have been combined, namely a classification of behaviour and the use of rating scales. Actually, this is not so. To illustrate, reproduced here for the convenience of the reader is an example of one of these descriptive statements which will be used to assess the trait of curiosity.

An extraordinary thirst for knowledge shown in, say, four or more of the following ways. He is stimulated by new ideas (given by his teacher, friend or parent) and will follow these through to a systematic

---

[1] These are technical terms used in test measurement. Validity concerns the extent to which a test or rating scale actually does measure the ability or trait it has been designed to measure. For example, a test of clerical ability would be said to be valid if all who scored high on the test turned out to be very good clerks and all who scored low turned out to be poor clerks.

Reliability refers to the accuracy of the score which the test or scale gives (irrespective of what the score itself stands for). For example, a test would be said to be reliable if individuals, when they take the test or an equivalent form of the test for the second time, get the same score as they did the first time.

conclusion (a completed work-book with notes and illustrations, a collection of some kind). He observes or attends carefully and makes interesting contributions in discussions. He asks questions (because he wants to find out, not to seek attention). He reads a lot (for information rather than just as a pleasurable escape). He explores and knows much about the environment in which he lives (fields, streets). He performs simple experiments (e.g. growing a plant from seed and making daily notes and drawings). He pursues such activities as these spontaneously, and stimulation from outside seems secondary to a primary desire to know. The above implies a *general* curiosity which includes two or three special interests (e.g. stamps, photography, nature study).

In this statement, as well as the others given in the child study guide, the lists of behaviour are not by any means intended as exhaustive ones, but rather as illustrations of the kinds of behaviour which typify the trait being assessed, and which are likely to be seen in the classroom.

Imaginative productions

It is the outer manifestations of children's dispositions that have so far been considered. Through observing these we not only find out about such things as the games children play but also infer dispositions such as 'sympathy', 'creativity', 'aggressiveness' and so on. The teacher infers from the way the child works and behaves in school that he is 'painstaking', 'enthusiastic', 'persevering' (or the opposite of these). He tries in the school report to summarize these inferences.

But a child has his own private world, his inner anxieties, aspirations, dreams and fantasies. He has his inner feelings about the universe in which he lives—that it is safe and friendly, or insecure and hostile. One may ask, 'How do children reveal these inner experiences?'

They do so, of course, in their outward behaviour. But, to infer these inner states from outward behaviour is difficult because this requires an interpretation beyond that required to infer that a child is sympathetic, withdrawn, aggressive and so on. In the midst of a boisterous game a boy becomes suddenly quiet; he moves silently away from the group and goes off by himself. He returns to the group after a little while and is soon even more boisterous than he was before he left. A little girl suddenly rushes to the kitchen and buries herself in her mother's skirts for no apparent reason. One may ask whether the boy and girl, each in his or her own way, experienced an acute and sudden feeling of anxiety. A child is playing with her doll; the doll is 'naughty', 'disobedient', and has to be smacked and disciplined; she is having a *'terrible'* morning with her. Does this mean that the child feels she would like to kick over the traces but, fearing to do so in actual life, does so vicariously through the doll? Or is she playing out an actual experience and identifying herself with her mother (who is good) and projecting her own unacceptable self on to the doll (who is bad)? Or is too much being read into the situation and is the child merely imitating or in high spirits, so that these interpretations are inappropriate?

Children reveal this inner world, too, in their creative productions—their diaries, the stories they write, their paintings and drawings, or their reaction when we show them a picture and ask them to write about it.

Sometimes adults have harmless fun amongst themselves attempting to infer their own inner experiences. For example, a party which has been an enjoyable and, at times, a boisterous one is coming to an end. Everybody is now rather quiet, sitting round the fire in meditative mood. But one member of the group, who is less tired than the others, suggests that each one, in turn, describes the pictures he 'sees' in the fire. One person sees a lonely man walking across a field to his little hut at the foot of the mountain. Another sees brightly dressed villagers dancing on a village green, and a third sees a large concert hall with the audience awaiting the arrival of the artist on the stage.

One of the assembled company asks what the stories mean and then all laughingly agree to try to interpret the pictures seen in the light of what they know about the person who 'saw' them. They decide that the response of the first person reflects his tendency sometimes to feel a little isolated and 'out of things'; that of the second reflects her gaiety, her love of life and colour, her hatred of the drab, industrial surroundings in which she lives. The third person plays the piano well, and the company decide that his response reflects his aspirations to be a concert pianist.

If children write assiduously and with great concentration, we say they are *persevering*; if they draw and paint, that they are *creative*; if they romp and play, that they are *active*; if they tell stories and use fantasy, that they are *imaginative*. But it is possible to go further than this and look not only at the children's behaviour but also at the products of their behaviour to try to discover what they tell us about the inner world of the child. These imaginative products are obtained when children are provided with opportunities to express themselves freely.

Although the psychologist, when he is assessing a child's fantasy life, uses methods which are derived from the simpler everyday methods described above, he would not be satisfied with the sporadic and perhaps haphazard ways they are carried out in everyday life because the control he seeks is lacking. The judgments made that the boy and girl had a sudden acute feeling of anxiety, the interpretations of the small girl's doll-play, are conjectural and may go unchecked. An open fire is unstable and temporary: it is not quite the same for each successive person because the fire is dying down as each speaks. It could be argued that the differences in the stories were due not only to imaginative differences between the people 'seeing', but also to the fact that for each person the fire was, strictly speaking, a different one. If, therefore, the psychologist wishes to compare the fantasies of two or more people, the material from which the fantasies is derived must remain objectively the same and not be subject to the process of continuous change as is the fire.

Yet, implicitly, the party-goers accepted a principle accepted also by the trained observer, namely that the products of our imagination are not just accidental. All are determined by a memory, an attitude or interest; by some joy, fear, hope of the past, present or future. The stimulus, the fire, is incidental, a kind of screen upon which these joys, fears and hopes are *projected* in story form. The stories, therefore, have meaning and are a clue to the inner aspects of the story-tellers' personality.

The psychologists have their own special methods of obtaining and studying imaginative productions. These include standard sets of pictures from which stories are made up and which are called thematic apperception tests, meaning tests in which stories or themes are imaginatively perceived; unstructured material[1] to which responses have to be made, for example, the Rorschach

---

[1] Unstructured material means material that is ambiguous and has no definite form so that it can be interpreted in a variety of different ways. An open fire is a good example of ambiguous material.

test which consists of a set of ten symmetrical ink-blots, three of which are coloured; miniature life situations in which a child is given a wide range of toys—dolls representing the family, farm and other mechanical toys such as tractors, boats, planes, cars and so on—and is allowed to build situations from these as he wishes. The reader who would like to study these techniques in more detail is referred to a book (2) which gives descriptive studies of most of the tests of this sort, collectively called projective tests.

For the purposes of the child study we need to be more modest than this, since to use the techniques briefly referred to here would demand many years of theoretical study and practical application of the tests themselves. Two simple suggestions only are made, namely study of the child's imaginative written work on chosen topics such as 'When I grow up' or 'My two greatest wishes', and a study of some of the child's drawings and paintings. Insofar as this second suggestion has been made, a word or two will now be said about the way the psychologist interprets children's paintings.

When a child draws or paints he may do so for a number of reasons—to relive past pleasurable experiences, to relieve inner tensions (of anger, fear, anxiety, doubt), to clarify his under-standing of an object or situation, or simply for the sheer joy of spontaneous expression.

That children reveal definite personality characteristics in their artistic productions has been shown by Alschuler and Hattwick (1), who used such features as colour to infer emotions, line and form to infer energy and control, and use of space to reveal ex-pansive or restrictive use of the environment.

These three main cues can be amplified as follows. Use of greens, yellows, light blues is said to denote a happy mood or general outlook on life; whereas use of blacks, purples and dark blues is said to denote a sombre mood or a sad or gloomy outlook on life. With regard to form and line, some children's drawings and paintings are neat and precise with all lines straight. They have form but little originality, as if the children's fears that they may 'go wrong' inhibit any spontaneity. Some productions, on the other hand, are overflowing with ideas, but chaotic and with-out form, suggesting a lack of discipline or control in the use of media and in the expression of ideas. Sometimes a child confines his drawings to a small space in one corner of the sheet, which is said to suggest a self-effacing diffidence in expressing himself and to be reflected in real life in excessive constriction—both of emotional expression and of the situations and places he is prepared to play in and to explore. By contrast, another child uses the whole space with an abandon that is said to suggest a far greater expansiveness in expressing himself and in exploring new situations and new places.

The above interpretations may sound somewhat facile, but it should be remembered that when children's pictures are interpreted, they are not interpreted *in vacuo* but in relation to all other available information about the child, and only after the child has been encouraged to talk about his pictures and, perhaps, to tell stories about them. It may be added here that formal criticisms of a child's pictures on the basis that they do not accurately represent the shape or relative size of an object miss the essential point, namely the significance of children's paintings for their personal lives. Thus, when a small child draws his house with Mummy and Daddy standing outside and makes both much bigger than the house, it is understandable because his mother and father are much more significant for him and loom larger in his personal life than does the house which he probably takes very much for granted.

The main difficulty with all methods which use imaginative productions is that of interpretation. Generally, in the case of overt behaviour, two observers will agree that Albert's behaviour shows that he is sad (because he cries), happy (because he laughs), aggressive (because he punches other children). However, sadness, happiness, aggressiveness cannot be as directly inferred from his painting, from the stories he tells, from his responses to miniature life situations or ambiguous material. Experts in these fields would say that, while they are prepared to suggest some guiding principles, interpretation is, in the last analysis, essentially individual, and they would not be prepared to accept rigidly fixed rules of interpretation to be applied universally like mathematical formulae. Indeed, those who use and advocate projective tests and imaginative productions see them more as helpful devices to be used in conjunction with other ways of observing, as a way of obtaining a broader understanding of the person—of his attitudes towards the world and his position in it, his feelings of success or failure, his contentment about the past and the present, his aspirations about the future.

The student is cautioned, therefore, not to be too facile in his interpretations because he must remember he is not experienced in the use of projective techniques. He should use imaginative material, not as a basis for an analysis of the child he is studying, but as tentative confirmation of what he has already learnt using the methods of observation previously described.

It is in this guarded sense that an imaginative piece of written work and a study of the child's drawings are suggested for the child study. Such a suggestion accords with the general theme of this book, namely that of 'creative becoming'.

REFERENCES

1   Alschuler, R. H., Hattwick, L. W. *Painting and Personality*. University of Chicago Press, Chicago, 1947.
2   Anderson, H. H., Anderson, G. L. *An Introduction to Projective Techniques*. Prentice-Hall, New York, 1952.
3   Murphy, L. B. *Social Behaviour and Child Personality*. Columbia University Press, New York, 1937.
4   Olson, W. C. *Problem Tendencies in Children*. University of Minnesota Press, Minneapolis, 1930.
5   Richards, T. W., Powell, P. S. 'Fels child behaviour rating scales.' *Genetic Psychology Monographs*, 1941, **24**, pp. 257–95.
6   Sears, R. R., Whiting, J. W. M., Nowlis, V., Sears, P. S. 'Some child-rearing antecedents of aggression and dependency in young children.' *Genetic Psychology Monographs*, 1953, **47**, pp. 133–234.

CHAPTER TWENTY-THREE

Children's Academic Abilities

THE next and final chapter in this book presents a guide to the student-teacher for the study of an individual child in the classroom. The guide will include reference to academic work, and some suggestions about the way a child's current academic achievement, and his progress over the years, may be presented. In this chapter, statistical procedures and the psychology of abilities will be discussed within the limits required for the child study. The child to be studied will be called Geoffrey.

To ask a student to present a summary statement of Geoffrey's academic achievement appears at first sight a fairly simple assignment which may be done quite easily by, for example, obtaining Geoffrey's marks in the various subjects, examining these and perhaps putting them in graphical form in order to see at a glance the way the marks lie relative to each other. It may appear equally simple to represent Geoffrey's progress over the years in the main subjects by means of a graph, again using the marks he obtained in each subject during each year.

But to depict a child's academic achievement and progress throughout the years is not as simple as this. The graphs may be quite misleading and the conclusions drawn from them quite erroneous. It is necessary to explain why this may be so. The reader will then be in a better position to understand why the procedures explained later have been adopted.

Suppose that Geoffrey says to a student-teacher, 'I got eighty-five out of a hundred in Arithmetic in the exams last term.' The student would almost certainly reply, 'That's very good.' He may then decide to investigate more precisely what this mark of 85 means. Accordingly, he studies the class results for this examination in Arithmetic, and finds that the average mark obtained was 84, that 5 children out of 40 obtained a mark of 90 or more, and that the lowest mark was 70. This causes him to question whether Geoffrey's mark of 85 was 'very good'. He makes further checks. First of all, he inquires whether the class is a bright, average or backward one. He asks the teachers; he examines the children's I.Q.s. As a result, he may find that it *is* a very bright class and that the average achievement in other subjects is also very high. He is, then, still happy to apply the phrase 'very good' to Geoffrey's mark of 85, since this achievement is slightly above average amongst a group of children whose achievement is remarkably high.

On the other hand, if he found that the class was just below average intelligence and achieved much lower marks in other subjects, he would be puzzled by these high marks in Arithmetic and would investigate to see whether the test was too easy for children of this age, or whether the standard of marking was too low. Either or both of these might be found to be so, in which case the student would conclude that perhaps a mark of 85 was not so good after all.

The point of this illustration is that a single mark (or raw score as the statistician would call it) has little absolute meaning and must be interpreted with reference to the following:

the kind of test it was: whether a rote memory test or one requiring application of the material learned to new situations;

the average class mark (or arithmetic mean);

the range of the class marks (from the highest to the lowest);

whether most of the marks are clustered close to the average mark, or widely dispersed;

the kind of class it is: bright, average or backward.

Similarly, to compare a mark (or raw score) in one subject with a mark in another subject has little meaning in itself. For example, Geoffrey may say to the student-teacher, 'I am better at Arithmetic than I am at English. I got eighty-five for Arithmetic and only sixty for English.' Yet, when he examines the class marks, the student finds this:

	Geoffrey's class position	Average or mean class mark	Range of marks
Arithmetic	13th	84	70 to 95
English	13th	57	31 to 80

The class mean is 27 marks higher in Arithmetic than in English and the range or variability of the marks in Arithmetic is only half that in English. The influence of these differences of mean and variability can be illustrated by considering two hypothetical cases which are as extreme as possible. Suppose that one child had the highest class mark in Arithmetic and the lowest in English, and that another child had the lowest mark in Arithmetic and the highest in English. In terms of average position in class they would be equal (as far as these two subjects are concerned). But their total marks for the two subjects are not equal; for the one the total mark is 150, for the other 126.

Enough has been said to indicate that marks in different subjects are not always comparable. To make them so, they generally have to be converted into a different kind of unit.

One simple way of doing this is to use Geoffrey's class positions in the various subjects and to draw graphs based on these. But positions in class in each subject are strictly comparable only when all the pupils in Geoffrey's class are taking all subjects. In Primary Schools this is usually the case but there may be exceptions, as when boys and girls divide for Crafts and Needlework. In Secondary Schools particularly, children divide into different class groups according to the subjects they take. It often happens then that, when marks only are taken as measures of the children's performance, one group is placed at an advantage in comparison with another, as when the marks obtained in one subject, say, Manual Crafts, which only the boys take, are much higher than those obtained in another subject, say, Domestic Science, which only the girls take. Further, if one wishes to compare Geoffrey's achievement in a particular subject over a period of three or four years, his position in class in this subject during each of these years may not be comparable because the size of the class may have varied considerably from year to year. For example, to be tenth in a class of thirty is not the same as being tenth in a class of forty.

When there are these complicating features, positions in class should not be used. Geoffrey's marks are best converted into yet a different kind of unit in order to make them comparable. There is a number of ways by which marks can be so converted. For the teacher the most important kinds of units are probably percentiles, standard scores, T-scores, age-equivalents.[1]

For the purpose of the child study it is proposed that, when positions in class are not comparable because of the sorts of complications indicated above, marks from subject to subject be made into comparable units by converting them into percentile ranks. Two ways by which this can be done will now be demonstrated, taking Geoffrey's mark of 85 in Arithmetic and 60 in English as examples.

Suppose that the distribution of class marks in Arithmetic and English were those given in the tables which follow (Fig. 13).

From the figures under *cf*, cumulative frequency curves (*cf* curves as they are called[2]) can be constructed as shown in Fig. 14.

The left vertical axis is constructed so as to include the highest cumulative frequency which equals the total number of children in the class; the horizontal axis is constructed to include the whole range of marks obtained. A vertical scale has been constructed on the right of the two *cf* curves, each of which divides the vertical axis into 100 equal units. By using this scale, percentile ranks corresponding to any given mark can be read off.

To illustrate how this may be done we will take Geoffrey's marks of 85 in Arithmetic and 60 in English. A perpendicular is erected from the base line at the points 85 (Arithmetic) and 60 (English) until they meet the *cf* curve; a horizontal line is drawn from this point until it meets the scale at the right. A mark of 85 in Arithmetic gives a percentile rank of 30, a mark of 60 in English also gives a percentile rank of 30. Therefore, despite the large difference in the marks themselves, there is no difference between them when they are expressed as percentile ranks. Indeed, the much lower mark in English gives a slightly higher percentile rank, so that Geoffrey was not justified in his belief, based on the

---

[1] It would go beyond our immediate purpose to explain the way all four kinds of derived scores are computed and to consider the assumptions, statistical merits and limitations of each one. The interested reader is referred to other sources (e.g. 4, 6, 13, 14, 16).

[2] *cf* denotes cumulative frequency, obtained by adding in successive frequencies from the bottom to the top of the *f* column.

Arithmetic			English					
Mark	f	cf	Mark	f	cf	Mark	f	cf
95	1	40	80	1	40	55	1	23
94	0	39	79	0	39	54	1	22
93	0	39	78	1	39	53	0	21
92	1	39	99	0	38	52	2	21
91	1	38	76	0	38	51	1	19
90	1	37	75	0	38	50	1	18
89	2	36	74	1	38	49	1	17
88	2	34	73	0	37	48	2	16
87	2	32	72	0	37	47	1	14
86	2	30	71	1	37	46	1	13
85	3	28	70	0	36	45	1	12
84	2	25	69	0	36	44	1	11
83	2	23	68	1	36	43	2	10
82	2	21	67	2	35	42	1	8
81	2	19	66	1	33	41	1	7
80	2	17	65	1	32	40	1	6
79	2	15	64	1	31	39	0	5
78	2	13	63	1	30	38	1	5
77	2	11	62	0	29	37	1	4
76	3	9	61	1	29	36	1	3
75	1	6	60	1	28	35	1	2
74	1	5	59	0	27	34	0	1
73	1	4	58	2	27	33	0	1
72	1	3	57	1	25	32	0	1
71	1	2	56	1	24	31	1	1
70	1	1						

FIG. 13 Tables showing distributions of class marks[1]

actual marks he obtained in the two subjects, that he was better at Arithmetic than English.

The cf curve and percentile rank scale form a ready reckoner which can be used in the way described to convert any mark into a percentile rank. But while the cf curve and the scale have the advantage of being a form of ready reckoner, marks can also be converted into percentile ranks arithmetically, and when only one child's mark need to be converted, this would certainly be quicker and more accurate than drawing a diagram.

[1] f denotes frequency, that is, the number of children who obtained each given mark.

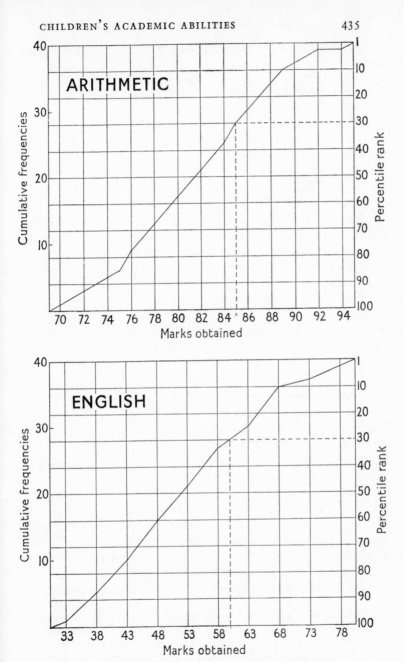

Fig. 14 Cumulative frequency curves based on the tables in Fig. 13

Arithmetical conversion can be done by using this simple formula:

$$\text{Percentile Rank (P.R.)} = \frac{\text{Rank number} - \frac{1}{2}}{N} \times 100$$

where N = the number of children in the class.

Geoffrey's class position (or rank), 13th in the class in English, may be taken as an example:

$$\text{P.R.} = \frac{13 - \frac{1}{2}}{40} \times 100 = \frac{12 \cdot 5}{40} \times 100 = 31 \cdot 25$$

You will notice that the *cf* curve gives a percentile rank of 30. *Cf* curves are not as accurate as arithmetical calculations, but accurate enough for everyday purposes. And, as has already been mentioned, once drawn, the *cf* curve does show the class position at a glance.

If there is a tie and more than one child has the same rank, the fraction of $\frac{1}{2}$ used in the formula for P.R. is replaced by $1 - \frac{1}{2}t$, where t = the number of tied children. Take, for example, Geoffrey's mark in Arithmetic, where two other children tied with him for 13th place, then:

$$\text{P.R.} = \frac{13 - [1 - \frac{1}{2}(3)]}{40} \times 100 = \frac{13 \cdot 5}{40} \times 100 = 33 \cdot 75$$

The reason for making the calculation in this way is that, in the illustration just given, the numerator $13 \cdot 5$ equals the number of children *above* the thirteenth rank plus one half of the number of children occupying the thirteenth rank, that is $12 + 1\frac{1}{2}$.[1]

It is important to realize that a percentile rank is not a score; it is, as its title indicates, a rank, and gives the rank order assuming the group consists of one hundred children. Geoffrey's percentile rank of 34 in Arithmetic and 31 in English (as calculated by the above formula) means that, had there been a similar group of 100 children in his class, he would have been superior to 66 and 69.

Percentile ranks can be easily computed and do not presuppose

---

[1] The above equation defines a 'percentile rank'. The word 'percentile' alone implies numbering in the reverse order; that is, an individual with the *highest* mark is allotted a percentile of 100, but a percentile *rank* of 1; an individual with the *lowest* mark is allotted a percentile of 0, but a percentile rank of 100. So, the percentiles corresponding to the above percentile ranks are $68 \cdot 75$ and $66 \cdot 25$.

a wide knowledge of statistical techniques. Further, they are much used at the present time, since raw scores from achievement tests and even tests of general ability are often expressed in terms of percentiles. Thus knowledge of them, of their meaning and the way they are calculated, is useful for the classroom teacher. It is with these thoughts in mind that they have been described here.

But notice that, while the distribution of class marks and Geoffrey's marks of 85 and 60 have been taken to demonstrate the way percentile scores are calculated, Geoffrey's position in class in each subject gives a similar result. Percentile ranks (34 and 31), percentiles (66 and 69) and position in class (13th in each subject) show that, in these terms, Geoffrey's performance in both subjects has nearly equal merit. This illustrates the point made earlier that, when the same group of children take all subjects, class positions can be taken, and there is no advantage in converting class ranks into percentile ranks and/or percentiles.

Further, to refer to an example given earlier, suppose the distribution of marks in Arithmetic was, instead, that of the marks obtained by boys in Manual Crafts, and suppose the distribution of marks in English was, instead, that of girls in Domestic Science. When, despite such differences, class marks only are taken, the disadvantage at which the girls are placed is clearly illustrated.

But it is necessary to caution the reader (since the impression may have been given that percentile scores overcome all the problems of representing marks which were discussed earlier) that the use of percentile ranks has at least these two disadvantages. First, it is possible for a class to be better at Arithmetic than at English. To explain further: occasionally one finds an individual child who is brilliant at computation and arithmetic reasoning, but who is quite unable to express himself in writing. One could conceivably have a whole class of such children. Sometimes, too, classes are organized according to ability in particular subjects so that, for example, Group A is good at English, average at Mathematics, Group B good at Mathematics, average at English. But, by converting the marks obtained by such classes into percentile ranks, these differences in basic ability are hidden, since conversion of marks obtained in each subject into percentile ranks assumes that the average class ability in all subjects is the same.

Secondly, equal differences in percentile ranks do not in general represent equal differences in marks. When the cf curve is more nearly horizontal (as at the top and bottom of the *cf* curve), a distance of a relatively large number of marks corresponds to a small difference in the number of percentile ranks. When the curve is more nearly vertical (as in the middle), the opposite is the case and relatively small distances in marks correspond to relatively large differences in percentile ranks. This will be made clearer by an inspection of the *cf* curves in Fig. 14.

Because intervals between units will almost certainly be unequal percentile ranks should not, strictly speaking, be treated arithmetically. If, for example, a child has percentile ranks of 47, 60, 67 and 72 in four different subjects, these should not be added to give a composite score from which an average score can be computed. As stated before, percentile ranks provide a basis for comparison and this is their major function.[1]

In conclusion, it is well to remind the student that when comparing percentile ranks obtained in the different subjects, Geoffrey's results are being compared with those of his class, and that his results must be interpreted in terms of the kind of class it is—bright, average, below average; with or without special abilities.

A reader may wonder why the use of standardized achievement tests has not been suggested for measuring and depicting Geoffrey's achievement in the various subjects. These tests will now be briefly explained and the reasons given why they have not been adopted here.

A standardized test is one for which the procedure for giving the test, the apparatus used in the test, the content and ways of scoring the test are rigidly laid down. The test will have been given to a large and representative sample of children of various ages (depending on the content and purpose of the test) and, from the scores obtained by all these children a table will have been compiled whereby any score obtained by a child can be converted into another unit, such as an age score, an achievement

---

[1] In fact, adding percentile ranks does produce a fair approximation to equal weighting within certain limits. When the ranks are between the 25th and 75th percentile, between which the slope of the curve is fairly uniform, they can be added with little error. But, as Garrett puts it, 'percentile ranks greater than 75 or less than 25 should be combined, if at all, with full knowledge of their limitations' (4, page 160). Vernon does not favour combining percentiles: 'It is advisable never to use percentiles for combining marks. The same is true of rank orders' (16, page 71).

quotient, or a percentile, making comparison possible between the scores of different children.

When class marks in English and Arithmetic were converted into percentile ranks, we were able to compare Geoffrey's achievement only with the achievements of each of the members of his own class. But because standardized achievement tests are initially given to many children in many schools, Geoffrey's result on these tests can be compared with the results obtained by this larger sample. Such a comparison may appear at first sight a more important one to obtain.

However, although they do permit this wider comparison, standardized achievement tests have two main disadvantages. First, for some subjects they presuppose a range of skills at various ages and therefore, by implication, a definite sequence in which skills are taught according to age. Yet all schools do not begin teaching the same skills at exactly the same ages. In one school, for example, decimals may be taught in Class 4, at an average age of ten; in another school they may not be taught until Class 5, when children are of an average age of eleven. (This first criticism of standardized achievement tests does not apply to Reading to the same degree that it applies to Arithmetic.) Secondly, schools may specialize in particular ways, according to the needs of the district or the qualifications and interests of the teachers. Because this is so, a child's scores on standardized achievement test must be carefully considered in the light of the general programme of work and the local and distinctive emphasis of his own school.

Further, we think here in terms of a study of a particular child in a particular school and class, and the aim of the study is to see how Geoffrey behaves and how he works in this environment and amongst his own companions. A comparison of Geoffrey's results with his own class group is, therefore, most appropriate for this purpose.

What has been said does not preclude a student from using standardized tests if he wishes to obtain a comparison of the achievement of the child he is studying with a wider sample of children. But if he does so, this word of caution needs to be given. Like class marks, the scores a child obtains on standardized tests of achievement in various subjects are not necessarily comparable. The tests may not have been standardized on the same children; the mean (or average) 'quotients', and also the indices showing the variability between quotients (usually expressed as the standard deviation), may not be the same respectively for all tests at each chronological age level. Comparison between the scores obtained is valid only when the means are approximately the same and also when the standard deviations are approximately the same for all tests. Comparison is also more valid when each of these tests has been standardized on the same group of children. If the same group has not been used, then each of the separate groups upon which each test was standardized should be similar on important variables, such as proportion of boys and girls, age-range, intelligence, and socio-economic status.

The student is therefore advised, even in the case of standardized achievement tests, not to rush into comparisons and draw psychographs[1] until he has checked on such matters as these.

So far, the procedures described have been concerned with comparing Geoffrey's achievement and his progress through the years with the achievement and progress of the other members of his class. We will now go on to consider Geoffrey's achievement in relation also to his own general ability.

Usually a teacher forms an opinion about how much a child *should* achieve academically. And so Geoffrey's teacher may say to the student, 'I have a feeling that Geoffrey is capable of better work.' Such a statement implies that Geoffrey's actual achievement does not meet the teacher's expectations of him, expectations based upon his estimate of Geoffrey's potential achievement. This latter estimate, in turn, will probably be based on one or more such things as his general impressions of Geoffrey's ability (more specifically, perhaps, on the fact that Geoffrey's work is inconsistent—very good at certain times, not so good at others), or on Geoffrey's intelligence quotient (I.Q.). But the teacher may not have made any precise study and his statement is a subjective one; as he himself may put it, 'I have a *feeling* . . .' He may ask the student to see if he can find out anything about this 'feeling' during the course of the study.

The way in which Geoffrey's actual achievement may be compared with an estimate of his expected achievement will now be presented.

[1] When the raw scores obtained by a child on a set of tests have been converted into units of the same kind, the result is called a score *profile*. When the results are expressed graphically, the term *psychogram* or *psychograph* is sometimes used.

Geoffrey will again be compared with members of his own class so that his expected achievement will be depicted in relation to their achievements. In giving details of the procedure suggested for this purpose, the more theoretical discussion of intelligence, intelligence testing, and I.Q., given in Chapter 15, will be considered within the more practical setting of this particular case study.

The generally accepted measure of a child's expected performance is derived from his score on a standardized test of intelligence, sometimes called a test of general ability. This score is expressed either as a mental age score or as an intelligence quotient (I.Q.). It is then compared with the child's achievement, which can also be expressed either as an achievement age or as an achievement quotient.

In making such comparisons, some educationists have in the past spoken in these terms: if the scores obtained on the achievement tests and the intelligence tests are approximately equal, the child is working 'up to his full capacity'; if the intelligence score is the higher of the two, he is working 'below his capacity'; if the reverse is the case and the achievement score is higher, he is working 'beyond his capacity'. Such judgments raise a number of difficulties. For example, a child cannot achieve 'beyond his capacity', so that this phrase should read 'beyond his expectation as estimated by so-and-so test'.

The point is that use of the term 'capacity', without the qualification that it is a measured capacity, implies that the score on an intelligence test measures something fixed, unchanging and inherited. However, it is doubtful whether tests do measure innate ability in this pure sense. Although intelligence may be defined as an *innate* capacity—'to see relations, to make generalizations about and to organize ideas', or whatever other definition one adopts—it can be measured only by using the knowledge and skills a child has already acquired. Because this is so, the relationships between a child's score on an intelligence test and his achievement in school subjects will depend to some extent on the type of test used. The relationship is likely to be higher when only items of a verbal and numerical kind are used than when only non-verbal items are used.

There is this further point: educational achievement is not accounted for wholly in terms of innate capacity. In summarizing the researches on this topic, Vernon (18) mentions three main components as being responsible for educational achievement, namely innate intellectual capacity (called the *g* factor); industriousness, interest and social background (called the *X* factor); and a general educational component (called the *v-ed* factor). The last component could be called a developed capacity to do school work. Research workers have accepted it as a component that is distinct from *g* and *X* since, when a representative group of children is tested, the correlation coefficients (statistical statements of the relationships existing between tests) obtained for the various school subjects, such as literature, word reading, spelling, and practical subjects like handwork, drawing and so on, are greater than can be accounted for by the part played by *g* and *X* together.

It is better, therefore, to think of a child's score on an intelligence test as 'a reasonable measure of his expected achievement' and not as an absolute one. This is further justified because a child's I.Q. may fluctuate from year to year, not only because its measurement depends, in part, on a child's achievement, but also because of the personal variables which may operate at the time of testing and which may influence the result, such as accidents, emotional upsets or moods of the moment.

An I.Q. is a measure of the *rate* of the child's mental growth. The classical method of computing I.Q. is:

$$\text{I.Q.} = \frac{\text{Mental Age (M.A.)}^1}{\text{Chronological Age (C.A.)}} \times 100$$

It can be seen from this formula[2] that when a child's mental age is equal to his chronological age his I.Q. is 100. We predict that this *rate* of growth will continue so that, if he was ten years old when he took the test which gave this result, we predict that when he is twelve his mental age will be twelve, and when he is four-

[1] The mental age of a child is given as the average chronological age of those children who score the same as he does on a standardized test. For example, if the average age of children who score the same as he does is 8, then the child has a mental age of 8.

[2] Most intelligence tests of today use what is called the deviation I.Q. and these I.Q.s are not calculated according to this classical formula. The method of obtaining mental ages and I.Q.s from these tests will be explained later in this chapter. But the deviation I.Q. is still a measure of the *rate* of mental growth and does not influence the above argument.

teen his mental age will be fourteen. Or again, if a child has an
I.Q. of 125 we predict that his mental age will be 25 per cent
above his chronological age—that is, at eight years he will have
a mental age of ten, at twelve a mental age of fifteen and so
on.[1]

But while researches show that for most children this rate
remains fairly constant throughout the years, it is understandable
that there should be individual exceptions and that with some
children the rate of growth may fluctuate from time to time.
Much the same applies to the rate of physical growth—for example, height increase. If a child is of a certain height at a certain
age, we can predict what his height will probably be, say, five
years later. We make this prediction on the basis of the many
studies that have been made of the proportional height increases
of children over a span of years. The prediction is on the average
true, but there will be individual deviations from it.

Research studies confirm in general the predictability of children's I.Q.s over a span of years, and show that the older the child
is when he is tested, the greater the predictability becomes. One
study (1) shows approximately the following degrees of predictability, expressed as correlations,[2] from a very early age to the age
of 18.

Age when tested	Predictability at 18 years of age
before two years	·00
two years	·20
five years	·60
ten years	·88
fifteen years	·92
seventeen years	·92

Even at seventeen, when only one year intervenes between the
two testings, the prediction of ·92 is not a perfect one.

Studies have also been carried out which show individual differences in rates of development over periods up to eighteen years.
The cases presented show variety in the types and in the extent

[1] There is a limit to such a use of mental ages, since researches show that *rate*
of mental growth in the way it is described here does not increase after the age of
about twenty. Consequently the use of mental ages is best confined to children of
school age.

[2] On a correlation scale ·00 indicates no predictability, 1·00 indicates perfect
predictability. (See note page 19).

of the changes that take place. The measured I.Q.s of some children rise consistently and of others fall equally consistently, while some remain relatively constant, fluctuating only within small limits. To take a few actual examples from one such investigation (12): one child rose steadily from I.Q. 120 at three years of age to 180 at twelve; the I.Q. of another declined from 130 to 100 over the same period; another fluctuated only slightly between I.Q. 100 and I.Q. 95. Sontag speaks of I.Q. changes that are of a 'highly idiosyncratic nature', meaning that they are changes which do not follow the general trends but are peculiar to the individual child. Similar types and degrees of variations were found by Bayley (1) and Honzik (5) over periods of eighteen years.[1]

Yet, despite these complications, it would be foolish to dismiss a child's score on an intelligence test and the mental age or I.Q. derived from this source as of no value. Used with care, they are valuable pieces of information. Given the usual circumstances in which a child has received a steady and uniformly good education over the years and has not been subject to extraordinary outside stress, the chances are that the relationship between intelligence test scores and achievement scores will be a close one. Further, a teacher sets work in terms of his expectations of individual children. He allows John to do a certain standard of work; he demands a higher standard from Jim. It is useful, therefore, to have some more objective guide than the teacher's intuitive judgments alone provide.

So much for the theoretical statement and for the reservation that the measure upon which the criterion of expected achievement is based, namely a score obtained on a test of general intelligence, is not an absolute one but a useful working guide.

The measure suggested here of the expected achievement of any particular child is the child's rank (or position) in class based on the children's mental ages. This expected rank may be compared with Geoffrey's actual class rank—that is, his final position in class based on the total marks he and his classmates obtained in all subjects. According to whether his final class ranking is above, at, or below his expected rank, so the student would judge that Geoffrey is working above, at, or below his expected achievement in relation to the other members of his class.

[1] See discussion of intelligence and I.Q. constancy on pages 299–305.

The procedures to be followed in order to obtain the children's mental ages differ according to whether the intelligence test was given: (*a*) at the time of the study, or only a short while before, or (*b*) a relatively long time (say, six months or more) before the study began.

The procedures are as follows:

In the case of (*a*): find out the *raw score* obtained by the child in the intelligence test taken by all members of the class; from the table of norms which the test provides, find the age for which this raw score gives an I.Q. of 100. This is the child's mental age.

In the case of (*b*): find the raw score corresponding to both the child's *present age* and his I.Q. as measured six months or more ago; convert this raw score into a mental age as under (*a*).

Although these procedures may appear difficult at first, in actual practice they are not, as the following example shows.

Fig. 15 presents a section from a table of norms provided for a non-verbal test of general intelligence.[1]

Procedure (*a*): Suppose Geoffrey was exactly ten years old when he took the test and scored 35 (giving him an I.Q. of 105). Reading horizontally along the line from 35, we find that an I.Q. of 100 for score 35 gives ages 10·8 and 10·9.[2] Geoffrey's mental age is taken as between 10·8 and 10·9.

Procedure (*b*): Suppose six months have elapsed since Geoffrey took the test. He is now aged 10·6. Looking vertically down the 10·6 column we come to I.Q. 105 (the I.Q. Geoffrey obtained when the test was given). Reading horizontally to the left of I.Q. 105, we come to a score of 38. Reading again along the 38 line as far as I.Q. 100, we find that this gives mental ages of 11·5 and 11·6.

Geoffrey's mental age six months after the test is therefore taken to be between 11·5 and 11·6. Such a calculation is based on the assumption that Geoffrey *would* score 38 on the test were he to take it again six months later. This assumption in turn assumes that he maintains the same *rate* of development during the inter-vening six months which his I.Q. of 105 indicates.

[1] *A.C.E.R. Junior Non-Verbal Test Manual*. Australian Council for Educational Research, Melbourne. Reproduced by kind permission of the Director, Dr. W. C. Radford.

[2] In the part of the table reproduced and in what follows, the figure before the point indicates years, the figure after the point indicates months. For example, 10·9 means 10 years 9 months.

It should be explained here why mental ages and not I.Q. scores have been used to rank the children in class. An I.Q. score, as already mentioned, is a measure of a child's rate of mental growth. A mental age is a measure of a child's status in terms of his general ability at a particular point in time. I.Q.s are the appro-

Test Score	AGE IN YEARS AND COMPLETED MONTHS AT DATE OF TEST																		
	10·0	10·1	10·2	10·3	10·4	10·5	10·6	10·7	10·8	10·9	10·10	10·11	11·0	11·1	11·2	11·3	11·4	11·5	11·6
35	105	104	104	103	102	102	101	101	100	100	99	99	98	98	98	97	97	96	96
36	106	105	105	104	104	103	102	102	101	101	100	100	99	99	99	98	98	98	97
37	107	107	106	105	105	104	103	103	102	102	102	101	101	100	100	100	99	99	98
38	109	108	107	107	106	105	105	104	104	103	103	103	102	102	101	101	101	100	100

FIG. 15 Table of norms showing I.Q.s according to the raw scores obtained in the test and the age of the child when tested

priate measures to use when we want to predict children's probable performance some years hence; but mental ages are a more appropriate basis for comparing children's general ability at any one time. If the chronological ages of the children in the class were all exactly the same, the ranking using I.Q.s would be the same as that when mental ages are used. But when, as almost certainly will be the case, there are differences in chronological age, the two rankings would not be the same. When rankings are based on I.Q.s, older children are ranked lower and younger children higher than when rankings are based on mental ages.

To take an example from the section of the table provided: Bill, whose chronological age is eleven, obtains a raw score of 35 on the intelligence test. When converted into an I.Q. according to his chronological age, this gives him an I.Q. of 98. As we have seen, Geoffrey, who is ten when he takes the test, obtains the same raw score of 35. But, because he is a year younger, this gives him an I.Q. of 105. But the age for which a raw score of 35 gives an I.Q. of 100 is 10·8 to 10·9 years. This, then, is the mental age of both children and it gives them the same class position.

We come now to the last phase in the appraisal of Geoffrey's ability and achievements, namely an investigation by the use of diagnostic tests of Geoffrey's individual strengths and weaknesses in the main school subjects. The procedures previously described provide important information about general strengths and weaknesses in the major subjects in relation to the strengths and weaknesses of the other children. But, as we are concerned with Geoffrey as an individual, it is of value to obtain a more detailed picture of his strengths and weaknesses in the main school subjects.

Diagnostic tests are planned to do this in a more systematic way than are the usual classroom tests or a test of general ability, since they involve the analysis of complex skills such as reading, long division of money, division of fractions, into their component skills. This analysis provides the basis for developing tests for each of the component skills. The scores in the component skills then enable us to see where Geoffrey's strengths and weaknesses lie. It may be found, for example, that he is good at mechanical computation but poor at reasoning out arithmetical problems; and that even though he is good at computation, he has certain basic weaknesses, such as in subtraction or in certain multiplication tables. In this way diagnostic tests detect the sources of Geoffrey's errors and provide information upon which special teaching can be based.

Of course, any test can be diagnostic if it provides two or more separate scores. A general test of intelligence may contain verbal, numerical and performance items, and give separate scores for each of these and separate norms to convert them into comparable scores. From such a test we may infer a child's relative ability in these three types of skills. Diagnosis is a matter of degree; the more detailed the analysis into sub-skills, the more thoroughly a test can fulfil a diagnostic function.

Diagnostic tests have been mainly prepared in the basic skills such as Reading, English usage, Spelling and Arithmetic. Because ability in these subjects is important for success in all subjects, it would be of value to give Geoffrey diagnostic tests in order to report on the kinds of strengths and weaknesses indicated above as a basis for any necessary remedial teaching and for the selection of remedial exercises.

REFERENCES AND BIBLIOGRAPHY

It is important for the reader to realize that this chapter is very limited in the scope of its discussion of children's achievement and abilities, and in the measurement of these. Consequently, where it is appropriate, specific reference is made below to the particular chapters which deal with the problems raised.

1   Bayley, N. 'Consistency and variability in growth from birth to eighteen years.' *Journal of Genetic Psychology*, 1949, **75**, pp. 165–96.
2   Duncan, J. *Backwardness in Reading: Remedies and Prevention*. George G. Harrap, London, 1953.
3   Dunn, S. S. *Testing in the Primary School*. Australian Council for Educational Research, Melbourne, 1962.
4   Garrett, H. E. *Statistics in Psychology and Education*. Longmans, Green, London, 1947.
5   Honzik, M. P., MacFarlane, J. W., Allen, L. 'The stability of mental test performance between two and eighteen years.' *Journal of Experimental Education*, 1948, **18**, pp. 309–24.
6   Lindquist, E. F. *A First Course in Statistics*. Houghton Mifflin, Boston, Mass., 1942. Especially Chapter 3, 'Percentiles'.
7   Oeser, O. A. (Ed.) *Teacher, Pupil and Task*. Tavistock Publications, London, 1955. Especially Chapter 7, Donbay, C. H., Dougals, G. 'Psychological tests and testing'; Chapter 9, Laffitte, P., Holt, N. F. 'The purpose and conduct of examinations'.
8   Schonell, F. J. *Diagnosis of Individual Difficulties in Arithmetic*. Oliver & Boyd, Edinburgh, revised edition, 1942.
9   Schonell, F. J. *Backwardness in the Basis Subjects*. Oliver & Boyd, Edinburgh, 1942.
10 Schonell, F. J., Schonell, F. E. *Diagnostic and Attainment Tests*. Oliver & Boyd, Edinburgh, third edition, 1956.
11 Schonell, F. J. *The Psychology and Teaching of Reading*. Oliver & Boyd, Edinburgh, 1951.
12 Sontag, L. W., Baker, C. T., Nelson, V. L. 'Mental growth and personality development.' *Monograph, Society for Research in Child Development*, 1958, **23**, No. 2.
13 Sumner, W. L. *Statistics in School*. Blackwell, Oxford, 1948. Especially Chapter 2, 'Distributions and dispersions of scores'.
14 Thorndike, R. L., Hagen, E. *Measurement and Evaluation in Psychology and Education*. Wiley, New York and London, 1961. Especially Chapter 6, 'Norms and units of measurement'.
15 Vernon, M. D. *Backwardness in Reading*. Cambridge University Press, London, 1958.
16 Vernon, P. E. *The Measurement of Abilities*. University of London Press,

London, second edition, 1956. Especially Chapter 4, 'Interpretation of school marks and test scores'.

17 Vernon, P. E. *Intelligence and Attainment Tests*. University of London Press London, 1960.

18 Vernon, P. E. *The Structure of Human Abilities*. Methuen, London, revised edition, 1961.

CHAPTER TWENTY-FOUR

An Individual Child in School and Classroom

EVEN though he has probably not received special training in the observation of children and in the application of tests like those mentioned in previous chapters, the student-teacher is not precluded from making studies of groups of children or of an individual child. He may, for example, observe and record the games children play, as did the young teachers mentioned in Chapter 22; or he may study children's spontaneous behaviour in such environments as streets, parks, stores, swimming-pools, or on the beach. This is valuable work and would give students information which they cannot always find in books on child psychology. Most of the investigations mentioned in this book were carried out in adult-created environments—in nursery and day schools, clubs, child development centres, clinics. To confine observations in this way has serious disadvantages. First, the kinds of behaviour that can be observed are restricted because, however permissive the institution may be, some restraint on children must inevitably be exercised. Furthermore, the kinds of activities a child chooses will be partly determined by the material which adults have provided and by the suggestions which they have made to him. Secondly, the children who are observed will be confined to those who attend nursery schools, child development centres, clinics, or clubs. Children who do not do so cannot be included in one's sample. Observations of children's natural behaviour in environments of their own choosing are valuable, therefore, in giving us a larger cross-section of children from whom to choose and a wider knowledge of their ways, even though scientific control is not a feature of this kind of observation. Actually, in this book, while reference has been made to many controlled studies of children within an adult-created environment, many of the descriptive illustrations have been obtained from the observation of children's behaviour in these wider environments.

Studies of children carried out by the student himself would give him first-hand acquaintance with many of the different spheres of a child's life—the way he co-operates with and maintains his own amongst his fellows, the way he responds to school and to the demands it makes upon him; in short, how the child attempts to satisfy his basic needs for security, recognition, adventure and personal achievement. In the course of his study, the student may notice some interesting causal connections between one event and another—that, for example, Geoffrey's apparently impulsive and 'senseless' behaviour in drawing a heavy pencilled scribble across Peter's neat exercise book was linked to an incident occurring during the previous recess when Peter had kicked the marbles out of the ring and spoilt the game that Geoffrey and his friend Dick were playing. Some observations may make the student more conscious of individual variations in the way different children will react to the same situation. He notices, for example, that Dick took Peter's rough interference philosophically and was not driven to seek retaliation as was Geoffrey.

If a student decides to study children in streets, parks, or swimming-pools, he may, under the guidance of a tutor, follow the suggestions made in the last chapter regarding sampling, reliability, preparation of classified lists of behaviour and so on. But the purpose of this chapter is to outline a plan which may be followed in a study of an individual child within the school and classroom. Three ways of obtaining information will be considered there, namely the study of cumulative school records, direct observation, and the study of creative and constructive productions. Suggestions for a synthesis of the total study will also be given, in order to draw together the information obtained.

A Information from cumulative school records

These records would give the student information such as the following.

PHYSICAL

Geoffrey's height, his weight, his health record, his attendance at school, his absences (and the reasons for these) would be recorded.

The student may add to this information a short general description of Geoffrey's physical appearance—whether he is predominantly round, muscular, or linear; the tempo of his movements—whether they are relaxed and slow, energetic and forceful, or tense and fast (see the first paragraph of each of the three descriptions given in Chapter 6, pages 102–5).

HOME BACKGROUND

The record would show the occupations of Geoffrey's father and mother; the number and the ages of his brothers and sisters; his position in the family; any singular features of his family life, such as the long illness or death of one parent, or if his father had been unemployed.

From their day-to-day life with him, parents can often make a good estimate of a child's abilities and can frequently contribute in a unique way to an evaluation of these abilities. They may notice, for example, that he is quick at calculations, that he reads a lot and has a good vocabulary. They have also a better opportunity than the teacher to see how the child applies what he learns at school to everyday situations: for example, in numerous play situations, in shopping, in reading the newspaper. The parents also have intimate knowledge of special interests and skills about which a teacher may not know, such as the child's interest in and skill with motor engines, radios, or a sewing machine.

From this conversation with the child's parents the student can find out about these things; he may also be able to assess the importance that they attach to Geoffrey's education, the degree to which they encourage him, and the amount of educational material, such as books, which the home provides.

It is difficult for all parents to comprehend the spirit and purpose of a child study; some might regard a visit from a student as an intrusion into their private life. In deciding whether or not to visit the home, the student should be guided by the advice of the head teacher and the staff.

If he does visit the home, the student needs to be informal and conversational as he seeks to assess the factors spoken of above. It is best that such a visit should take place when the study is nearly completed. To know that he is being singled out in this way, or to know that he is a special subject for study would almost certainly make any child self-conscious so that his behaviour would not be natural and spontaneous.

ACADEMIC ACHIEVEMENT

The cumulative record card will give the student information also about Geoffrey's present academic achievement and his achievement throughout the years. The suggestions which follow on how to depict these bring together the procedures described in the last chapter. These alternative procedures were discussed in order to allow for differing circumstances, such as a child moving from one class to another of higher or lower ability; a wide range of chronological ages in a class; a school, such as a secondary school, where children are taking differing groups of subjects. In most circumstances the greater amount of work required for the more complicated techniques, such as converting marks into percentile ranks instead of using positions in class, and the use of mental ages instead of I.Q.s, may not be warranted. These points will be discussed in the course of this phase of the child study.

Comparison of Geoffrey's present achievement with the present achievement of other members of his class

Geoffrey's marks in the main school subjects can be converted into percentile ranks, or, if all the children in the class have taken all subjects, then Geoffrey's class position in each subject can be obtained and a psychograph drawn. The psychograph given overleaf (Fig. 16) uses percentile ranks.

Comparison of Geoffrey's achievement through the years with the concurrent achievement of the other children in his class

Such a comparison can be obtained by converting the total marks Geoffrey obtained at the end of each school year into percentile ranks; or, if all subjects are taken by all pupils, his final class positions. Either of these gives a composite achievement rank for each year. It is easily seen that composite ranks, while giving an over-all statement of progress, hide the 'ups' that may characterize development in some school subjects and the 'downs' that may characterize lack of development in others. It is suggested, therefore, that the student also follows the same procedure,

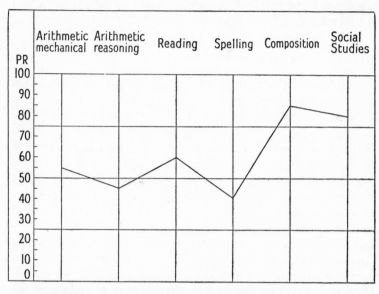

FIG. 16 Profile using percentile ranks and showing achievements in six subjects

obtaining percentile ranks (or class positions) over the years in at least two or three key subjects, such as Reading, Arithmetic, Spelling, or Composition. He can be guided in his choice of subjects by the teacher, who may be especially interested to know Geoffrey's history in certain subjects.

Profiles can then be drawn, one showing general achievement and others showing achievement in specific subjects, as in Fig. 17.

The procedures just described presuppose that Geoffrey has remained in the same class and that the children in the class have remained the same, or approximately the same, during these years. A difference of four or five in a class of forty is unlikely to make any appreciable difference, particularly if percentiles are used, since they are based on a group size of one hundred whatever the actual size of the group.

It is important to realize that class positions or percentile ranks would not be comparable in circumstances such as the following: if Geoffrey has changed classes and moved, for example, into a class of higher or lower ability, or from one in which the children have been specially chosen because they are good at Mathematics and poor at English to one in which the children have been specially chosen because they are poor at Mathematics and good

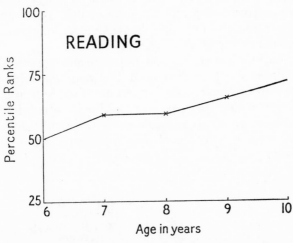

FIG. 17 Profile using percentile ranks showing achievement in one subject over a period of four years

at English; if the personnel of the class has markedly changed over the years as when, for some reason, a large number of children leaves to be replaced by others.

When one or more of such circumstances are the case the student would not draw a psychograph, but present the figures showing Geoffrey's percentile ranks from year to year, or his class positions, whichever have been used, and consider these in the light of the changed circumstances.

Achievement in relation to Geoffrey's general ability

The criterion of expected achievement suggested in the last chapter was Geoffrey's position in class according to the children's mental ages. A method of obtaining mental ages from scores on an intelligence test was explained, and, since most intelligence tests are now standardized so that the score for the average child of a given age is converted to an I.Q. of 100, this is usually possible. If it is not possible to do this from the way the table of norms has been compiled, then the student can rank children according to their I.Q.s. As was pointed out in the last chapter, there are theoretical objections to this procedure. But, as was also pointed out, in practise, when the range of the chronological ages of the children in the class is not great (say, no more than six months), the ranking according to I.Q.s and the ranking according to mental ages will not be appreciably different.

By using the chosen criterion, I.Q. or mental age according to the circumstances prevailing, and by using the criterion of achievement suggested in the last chapter, namely final position in class, the student can compare Geoffrey's expected achievement with his present achievement and also with his achievement over the years. A psychograph showing this comparison can be drawn as in Fig. 18.

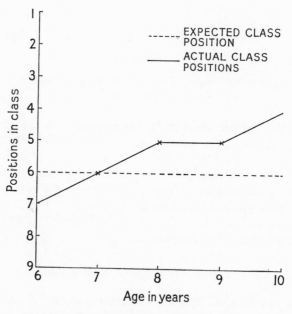

FIG. 18 Actual achievement compared with expected achievement, both expressed as positions in class

This developmental psychograph also presupposes that the class has consisted of the same children and that their mental ages relative to one another have remained constant throughout the years, so that the expected class position of each child in the class has also remained what it was at the time the test was given. Here again, if Geoffrey has changed classes, or if the personnel of the class has markedly changed, the student would have to discover Geoffrey's expected position for each of a number of years separately, since, given such circumstances as these, his expected position would not be the same from year to year. A simple psychograph, such as the one above, with one straight line to depict expected positions year by year, would not then be possible. The student would then best be advised to present the figures showing expected and actual positions from year to year, and to discuss these in the light of changing circumstances.

Discovering individual strengths and weaknesses: diagnostic tests

Here the student should decide in collaboration with the teacher the kinds of diagnostic tests he would use in the chosen subjects. He should prepare himself by a close study of the content of the tests, making himself well acquainted with the sub-skills that are included within them, and the way the tests are to be administered.

Concluding statement of academic status

It is not enough merely to depict Geoffrey's academic status. The study should conclude with a rounded statement which summarizes the findings and which makes definite suggestions. This cannot be done without prior study of the implications of the statistical results obtained, and of the academic strengths and weaknesses which the findings reveal. If there are weaknesses, then suggestions may be made for special practice in certain sub-skills, or, in cases of serious weakness, for more systematic remedial teaching; if there are newly discovered strengths, then suggestions may be made for their development.

Also, of course, such a concluding statement presupposes discussion with Geoffrey's teacher. On the one hand, the student can give the teacher useful detailed information about Geoffrey which he may not know, since, with a large class, a teacher cannot know every individual child to the extent that he would like. On the other hand, the teacher has a general knowledge derived from his observation of Geoffrey in the day-to-day life in the classroom. He has, too, a background of experience of children's abilities and achievements from which to study and interpret the matters described above, including such difficult problems as the relationship which the student has discovered between Geoffrey's actual and expected achievement.

The point stressed here is this: to depict formal results based on simple statistical analysis is not enough; these results require interpretation and evaluation. But these are possible only within the wider context of the knowledge of the child himself which the teacher and the parent possess.

B   Direct observation

Periods of observation are best planned in such a way that the student sees the child taking part in a variety of activities during various times of the school day and week. He should observe, for example, during early and late morning, early and late afternoon, at least once on each day of the week (time sampling). The occasions when he does observe will depend, of course, upon such things as the way activities are organized in the school, the age and sex of the child, and so on. But he should observe during the course of a number of different sorts of lessons (painting, social studies, physical education, a lesson that is mainly oral, one that is mainly writing) and also during a morning and an afternoon recess (situation sampling). This makes seven observation periods each lasting, say, fifteen minutes if it is a period involving much social or physical activity (group work in social studies, physical education), or longer, say, half an hour when social and physical activity is less (a handwriting or a composition lesson).

As the student observes he should write down what he sees. If the situation does not allow him to write in any detail, as when he is observing in the playground, he can jot down key words so that, when he comes to write a full account after the period of observation is over, he is reminded both of the events that occurred and of the sequence of their occurrence. It is important that the student should record actual behaviour only, and that he does not, at this stage, interpret by using words like 'co-operative', 'aggressive', 'sympathetic' and so on. Interpretation of the behaviour must come later.

By following this narrative method, the student can obtain a permanent record of what happened during each observation period. (This assumes, of course, that he has observed and recorded accurately.) In order to get some idea of how accurate he is as an observer and recorder, he may be able to get another student to observe with him during at least one observation period, and then compare his own narrative account with that of his colleague.

A still more difficult task is that of making the jump from a statement of actual behaviour to inferences about the dispositional tendencies which the behaviour reveals. The procedure to be followed through here is this: that the student uses graphic scales to rate Geoffrey on four or five selected traits. A small number of traits is suggested, and not a large number like twenty or thirty, on the grounds that it is better for a student to study in some detail the nuances of a few traits and to rate only after a great deal of thought about them, rather than to rate a large number of traits more superficially. For each period of observation, the student should rate the child on the traits he has chosen. Theoretically, this could give one rating on each trait for each period of observation. In practice, of course, a rating on a trait may not be possible after a particular period of observation because evidence of it does not occur. But by following time and situation sampling procedures and by observing seven or eight times, it is likely that each of the traits that the student has chosen will be rated a sufficient number of times. The separate ratings for a trait can then be averaged and the average accepted as the final rating on this trait.

What traits the student chooses will depend upon the child he is studying. He may himself become interested in qualities that immediately strike him about Geoffrey. He notices, for example, that he appears to be inquisitive, emotionally excitable, very gregarious, and decide to observe these qualities more closely. The teacher, too, may make suggestions from his own knowledge of Geoffrey, or because he is himself uncertain about qualities that interest him, such as how sociable Geoffrey is, whether he readily accepts and is accepted by other children, whether he has the self-confidence to enable him to be the leader of a group.

Here are four possible traits (with definitions) that may be chosen.

Concentration: the degree to which the child sustains attention or persists in a task even in the face of distraction.

Emotional stability—in response to frustrating or difficult situations: the degree of negative emotion (anger, irritability, dejection) the child expresses in response to the frustrations that inevitably arise during school life.

Curiosity: the degree to which the child spontaneously seeks new knowledge.

Self-confidence: the degree to which the child has a firmly based self-esteem and accepts his assets without conceit and his limitations without inferiority.

The graphic scales for rating these four traits are now presented.

CONCENTRATION

5   Is able to become completely absorbed in school tasks and will continue despite sources of distraction (such as a noisy class or the conversation of a few children near him). If directly interfered with (as by one of those incorrigible 'wanderers' who come round for a 'look' and a 'chat'), he will continue working immediately afterwards.

4   Usually absorbs himself in a task, but cannot always resist such things as the exciting chatter of other children, and will occasionally be distracted by them. But he goes back to his work immediately it is all over, and gives the impression that completing the task is more important to him than the chattering.

3   Concentrates well when there are few distractions and will, for example, follow the directions given by his teacher so that when told to start work, he does so without asking lots of questions. But he does not give the impression of being as *absorbed* in a task or as *detached* from outside events as 4.

2   Is easily distracted by outside events, and is often a source of distraction to others. He may be the incorrigible 'wanderer'. He seems to have one eye on possible ways of avoiding 'settling down'. Even when the teacher has given careful instructions and everyone else in the class has understood and started work, he may put up his hand and say, 'Please, Sir, what have we got to do?'

1   Easily distracted, his constant activity and chatter makes serious concentration on a task impossible for him. He may continually interfere with the work of others and consequently upset class routine and order frequently. On the other hand, he may just sit quietly doing nothing in particular, staring into space or doodling aimlessly.

EMOTIONAL STABILITY

5   Always calm and stable. Takes such things as the occasional rough spots during play in his stride (e.g. quarrels, disagreements), and accepts inevitable frustrations (a sum that does not come out, loss of a needed article). He is the kind of child of whom we often say, 'Nothing seems to upset him.'

4   In ordinary circumstances he is calm and controlled. He may 'let off steam' occasionally when he is provoked unduly. But his disturbance is short-lived and he quickly settles down again and carries on as if nothing had happened.

3   Like the average child, he is calm and stable under most ordinary circumstances. Under certain distressing situations (e.g. loss of friendship, being severely teased by companions, criticized by the teacher) he will become disturbed and it may take him some time (perhaps a morning or a day) to get over one of these situations.

2   Frequent emotional outbursts (e.g. of irritability, anger, stubbornness, crying) at slight provocation.

1   Extreme lack of emotional control. Without apparent provocation, he will run into a temper tantrum, negativism, or outbursts of weeping.

CURIOSITY

5   An extraordinary thirst for knowledge shown in, say, four or more of the following ways. He is stimulated by new ideas (given by his teacher, friend or parent) and will follow these through to a systematic conclusion (a completed work-book with notes and illustrations, a collection of some kind). He observes or attends carefully and makes interesting contributions in discussions. He asks questions (because he wants to find out, not to seek attention). He reads a lot (for information rather than just as a pleasurable escape). He explores and knows much about the environment in which he lives (fields, streets). He performs simple experiments (e.g. growing a plant from seed and making daily

notes and drawings). He pursues such activities as these spontaneously, and stimulation from outside seems secondary to a primary desire to know. The above implies a *general* curiosity which includes two or three special interests (e.g. stamps, photography, nature study).

4   More than ordinary thirst for knowledge shown by, say, three of the kinds of activities under 5 and also two special interests.

3   While at most times he tends to accept everyday phenomena (in nature and in the material world) and is not driven to study the reasons for them, when something interesting is pointed out to him (by teacher, friend or parent) he does show interest and will follow this interest, asking questions, reading, writing, illustrating. He also shares the interests of the majority of the group as the children's curiosity moves from one activity to another (stamps, aeroplanes and flying, space flights and astronauts). He will follow these with enthusiasm as long as the 'craze' lasts. He has a special interest which he pursues fairly consistently, and he will speak of his 'hobby'.

2   Seems generally indifferent. New objects and ideas stimulate him only temporarily and only sometimes does he get caught up in group 'crazes'. His history shows that he has had interests and hobbies, but that they have been short-lived. If he has a hobby at present, then he pursues it in a spasmodic way and on special occasions—a rainy day, when he is sick and at home for a day.

1   Indifferent. He shows none of the characteristics under 5 and displays little or no interest in new ideas or even in current 'crazes'.

SELF-CONFIDENCE

5   Very self-assured at all times. This is seen when he answers questions in class, contributes during an oral lesson, explains a problem on the blackboard, speaks to adults in authority (head teacher, class teacher, student-teacher). He accepts his assets without conceit and his limitations without inferiority. (Assets and limitations refer to such things as physique and general appearance, abilities, dispositions, past misdemeanours.)

4   Very self-assured at most times as in the situations under 5. But there will be one or two things, such as making a mistake in carrying a message, or a couple of situations when he is a little self-conscious (e.g. speaking to adults), or something about

himself (being shorter than average, not quite so good at one particular subject), that he finds hard to accept.

3   Has an average degree of self-assurance. Shows some areas in which he is uncertain, e.g. may falter a little when tackling a new skill, be self-conscious when made the centre of attention in class, or feel inferior about a physical defect, imagined or real, or about 'not-so-good' ability in one or two subjects.

2   Lacks confidence. Is diffident about tackling new skills, and may ask many questions, seeking help from others or constant assurances that what he is doing is right. There is the suggestion of a general inferiority rather than inferiority about one or two situations.

1   Extreme lack of self-confidence which seems to colour the child's whole life and impedes his efforts even to work on well-tried skills. When attempting a new skill he will give up very easily.

In order to gain a measure of the reliability of his ratings, the student may get another student to study his narratives and, on the information which they give, to rate Geoffrey on the four traits. The two students can then together compare their separate ratings. Using the same graphic scales, the class teacher could also be asked to rate the child from his own knowledge of him and before he has seen the ratings made by the student. Teacher and student can then compare and discuss their two sets of ratings.[1]

When the ratings on each trait have been made, a psychograph may be constructed as follows:

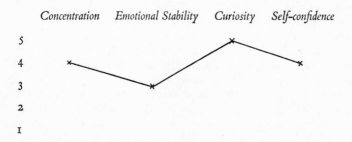

[1] If we accept that the teacher's wider knowledge of Geoffrey enables him to make true ratings, then the degree to which the respective ratings of class teacher and student agree may be taken as a measure of the validity of the student's ratings (see note, page 423).

A student may not, of course, want to confine himself to just four or five traits in this way, despite my suggestion, preferring instead to cover a wider range of the child's personality. If so, he could take a large number of prepared rating scales, such as the Fels Children's Behaviour Rating Scales (2) or those prepared by MacFarlane (1), and proceed in the same way as described above. The use of well-prepared scales is suggested because preparing one's own on twenty or thirty traits, as has been done here for four traits, would be a prodigious task.

Here is a narrative account of an actual observation period followed by suggested ratings.

Situation: Painting lesson with the boys of Classes 4 and 5. 2–3 p.m. *Period of observation:* 25 minutes followed by about 5 minutes' conversation. *Subject:* Geoffrey, aged 10 years.

Geoff came in with the other boys. He stopped, looked around and then walked slowly to his seat. He sat down and made some remark to the boy next to him. He gathered together the material on his desk—pencil, paper, paints, brushes. Then a boy came along and quickly snatched Geoff's pencil and tried to put his own, which was much smaller, on Geoff's desk. Geoff immediately resisted this, quickly snatched back his own pencil and gave the boy a hard push, saying, 'Oh, no, you don't.' The boy retrieved his own pencil and went away. The teacher introduced the lesson by telling the boys that they could make a painting about some personal experience. For those who were uncertain, he suggested such themes as 'At the fair', 'Saturday afternoon', 'At the swimming pool', 'A picnic'. He suggested, too, that they could do three or four small paintings to illustrate different experiences and then paint a bigger picture of their favourite one. Geoff put his hand up and asked, 'Please, Sir, can I do a painting about a book I have read?' The teacher said that he could do this, and so could any other boy who wanted to. Geoff immediately set to work and became absorbed in what he was doing. A boy came along and asked if he could borrow his rubber. Geoff just pointed and nodded his head. Another boy came along and looked over Geoff's shoulder as he painted. (I think the boy would have liked a chat.) Geoff continued painting but did not look at the boy or say anything. He was obviously having trouble with his brush because he was constantly drawing it through his fingers and between his teeth and lips and then trying it out on scraps of paper. He flung it on the desk and made a face. He picked it up and brought it out to show the teacher, saying, 'The bristles won't go right.' (Indeed, the bristles did look like a miniature of those on a chimney-sweep's brush.) The teacher gave

him a new one. Geoff smiled and said, 'Thank you.' On his way back
to his seat, he took a quick glance at some paintings. He spoke to one
boy for a moment and pointed at something in the boy's painting.
Both boys laughed. Geoff then returned to his seat and resumed
painting again. All this took only fifteen minutes. I waited ten more
minutes during which time Geoff painted continuously and without
interruption from outside. I then went around the class to look at the
boys' work and spent about five minutes talking with Geoff. He had
done three small paintings—two country scenes and one of a wide
river with an island in the middle. He told me he'd been reading
Tom Sawyer and showed me an abridged edition. He spoke quickly
and freely about it and said he was going to make a big painting of the
island on which Tom and his friends had spent a few days. He said.
'I like "mooching" around like Tom: I have a big collection of bugs
and butterflies.' He pulled a piece of paper out of his pocket, unfolded it
and showed me some rough maps, with crosses to mark the places
where there were birds' nests he had found. He said, 'I'd like to do
nature study when I grow up.'

This is a simple narrative with nothing dramatic about it and
thus is fairly representative of the types of narratives the student
would obtain.

An attempt will now be made to rate Geoffrey on the four
traits. But it must be remembered that a single period of observation gives very limited material because it is confined to one
particular situation. Further observations would confirm or not
confirm the ratings which, as they stand, are only tentative.

Geoffrey's concentation was high. He was not easily distracted
and he dallied only on one occasion when he glanced at some of
the other boys' paintings on the way back to his seat. But it was 'a
quick glance'. The high concentration could have been influenced
by the fact that he had chosen to illustrate a subject in which he was
most interested. One might rate concentration at 4 to $4\frac{1}{2}$.

The general impression was that Geoff was emotionally quite
stable. He was angry with the boy who tried to take his pencil.
This was justified enough. His pique and expression of annoyance
with his brush was somewhat exaggerated. A rating of $3\frac{1}{2}$ to 4
is suggested.

It is not easy to rate Geoffrey on curiosity. The scale aims to
measure *general* curiosity while the observation reveals a specific
interest in nature study. The enthusiastic way he pursues this

interest, with collections and maps, suggests the possibility of 5 (which may be too high) but the fact that it is a single interest suggests 3 (which is almost certainly too low). Yet there is not enough data to be certain about a rating of 4. It may be well to leave rating curiosity for the moment.

Geoffrey's general demeanour, and the easy and friendly way he chatted suggests a tentative rating of $4\frac{1}{2}$ on self-confidence.

Environment, interests, special skills

For some children, the environment they inhabit is a narrow one—home, street, park. Others move away from these to explore widely in the surrounding districts, whether alone, with companions, or on family trips. A few children are especially privileged and will have travelled widely in their own country or even perhaps abroad. The school is, of course, part of a child's environment, but here wider out-of-school experiences are emphasized, including the books he has read, radio and television programmes, motion pictures which have made a particular impression upon him. A child, too, will probably have his particular out-of-school interests and special skills.

Information about these can be obtained by conversation with the child which, as suggested in Chapter 22, needs to be spontaneous, friendly and initiated casually rather than deliberately. The student could take advantage of those occasions when Geoffrey approaches him for help. If these do not arise he could 'engineer' situations by proffering help or asking Geoffrey to help him—to show him where the sports gear is kept, to collect books, to run an errand. Further, as Geoffrey is old enough to write at some length, appropriate written work may be given (to the whole class, of course, and not only to Geoffrey). One of such topics as these may be suggested: 'When I grow up', 'My two most exciting experiences', 'When I was afraid', 'My two greatest wishes'.

But because this study is orientated towards the child's life at school, merely describing his wider experiences or listing his interests and special skills is not enough. The student must consider what their possible educational implications might be. In doing so, he could ask himself such questions as these: are Geoffrey's wider experiences such that he should be encouraged (provided he is willing and happy to do so) to speak about them in class or to illustrate them in drawing and painting, so making learning more meaningful for the child himself, and, at the same time, broadening and enriching classroom work in general? Secondly, has he a special interest which, although at first appearing to have no clear relation to school work, may yet be used to further his academic progress in general or to improve in a particular subject in which he is weak? (An example of this was given earlier (Chapter 2) in the case of a remedial reading programme based on a boy's interest in roof-tiling.) Thirdly, has the child some skill, knowledge or organizing ability of a special kind so that he can be called upon to contribute to some school or class project? For example, he may be particularly skilled, say, at drawing, or have some special knowledge—of birds, butterflies, local buildings or whatever it might be—so that he could be asked to draw illustrations or to write a special feature for the school or class magazine. The idea behind this, of course, is that the recognition accorded Geoffrey in this way, and the stimulation he receives from the work, may renew his interest in the rest of his class work and also make the school a more meaningful place for him. Later, when he is a qualified teacher and has a class of his own, these are the sorts of questions the student will ask himself in thinking about any child. But more especially he will ask himself such questions when a child is retarded or apathetic about his school work.

C *Study of creative and constructive productions*

In Chapter 8 a distinction was made between constructive and creative activities on this basis: whereas in constructive activities children are bound more closely to the facts of the outside world, in creative activities they are given opportunity to be imaginative. This distinction, although not absolute in practice, needs to be borne in mind here. Constructive activities would include work in the three R's, maps, plans, tables and sketches. From specimens of Geoffrey's writing and arithmetic, and his work in social studies, the student can comment on the degree of skill the child has acquired, the degree of control he has over his media, the perseverance he shows and so on.

It is possible, of course, to go further than a study of these activities as skills in themselves by asking to what extent Geoffrey is able to use them as means by which he can express himself imaginatively—the extent to which he is able to go beyond the copying stage, beyond the given, to something new and original. Evidence of this may be seen in his free writing of stories and of actual experiences; in his original drawings in the more formal subjects, such as social studies, and even the originality implied in his spontaneous application of arithmetical skills to an everyday problem. As mentioned earlier, parents can be very helpful in an evaluation of this kind.

When interpreting children's free drawings and paintings it is necessary to be extremely tentative. But certain of the more simple indicators (form and line, use of space and colours) discussed in Chapter 22 could be studied to find out whether the characteristics they suggest are, in fact, borne out by the information about Geoffrey which has been obtained by other means. It will be recalled that the suggested characteristics were these: over-control, lack of control, or a balanced combination of control and creativity (form and line); an expansive or restrictive environment (use of space); a gloomy or gay outlook (use of colours).

Synthesis

There is a danger when a study is confined to recording achievement and drawing psychographs, to observing behaviour and using rating scales, that the uniqueness of a child will be lost within the details. Therefore the information obtained needs to be supplemented by a general description, a personality sketch which puts the information obtained within the context of a 'real' child, laughing, striving, fighting, alone or with his companions. (The sketches of William, Peter and Paul are examples of such general descriptions.) In doing so, the student could use the idea of basic needs (Chapter 8), and consider the extent to which Geoffrey is able to satisfy these. If he feels that certain needs are not satisfied, he could then indicate what may be done, particularly in the school and classroom, to remedy this.

This completes the study guide. It is not presented in an absolute sense, but as a series of suggestions to be adapted according to circumstances—the kind of school, the amount of time a student has to give to a child study and so on. Although a full study of one child is recommended, it must be admitted that to follow through all the four main phases of this guide is a major project. A student may find, for example, that seven or eight periods of observation, with the narrative and rating work involved, is too demanding, and decide to do only three or four. A student who has busy lesson commitments may have to select one or two aspects: making a study, for example, only of the child's present achievement and progress over the years, or only doing the observations, narratives and ratings. If just one aspect is taken it would be best not to take constructive and creative productions because inferences from these can only be tentative and would require confirmation from the information obtained by following the other three methods of study.

It is appropriate to end a book on children's personalities by suggestions for a child study, since personality, although it can be defined in the abstract and described in a general way, is manifest only in a single individual. Moreover, the more we observe children in groups and the more carefully we study one child, the more we will realize that, with the development of personality, as defined and described in this book, go the whole gamut of emotions—on the one hand, positive feelings of love, elation, pride in accomplishment, security in being harmoniously at one with others; on the other hand, negative emotions of hatred, dejection, inferiority, anxiety because of failure or because of isolation from others. Growing up is, in part, a joyous process and, in part, a painful process, but nevertheless an inevitable one. Sometimes, as we ponder on the cares and worries of adult living, we envy the child his apparent lack of responsibility. But children have their problems; they have their delights, too. It is well, therefore, not to err on the side which would over-stress their difficulties nor on the side which would see the years of childhood as some idyllic heaven.

REFERENCES

1   MacFarlane, J. W. *Studies in Child Guidance*. Society for Research in Child Development, Washington, D.C., 1938.
2   Richards, T. W., Powell, P. S. 'Fels child behaviour rating scales.' *Genetic Psychology Monographs*, 1941, **24**, pp. 257–95.

Index

Page numbers in *italics* refer to works cited in bibliographies

470